Arctic Governance in a Changing World

Mary H. Durfee
Professor Emerita, Michigan Technological University

Rachael Lorna Johnstone
Professor, University of Akureyri and Ilisimatusarfik (University of Greenland)

ROWMAN & LITTLEFIELD
Lanham • Boulder • New York • London

Executive Editor: Traci Crowell
Assistant Editor: Mary Malley
Senior Marketing Manager: Amy Whitaker
Interior Designer: Rosanne Schloss

Credits and acknowledgments for material borrowed from other sources, and reproduced with permission, appear on the appropriate page within the text.

Published by Rowman & Littlefield
An imprint of The Rowman & Littlefield Publishing Group, Inc.
4501 Forbes Boulevard, Suite 200, Lanham, Maryland 20706
www.rowman.com

6 Tinworth Street, London SE11 5AL, United Kingdom

British Library Cataloguing in Publication Information Available

Library of Congress Cataloging-in-Publication Data
Names: Durfee, Mary, author. | Johnstone, Rachael Lorna, author.
Title: Arctic governance in a changing world / Mary H. Durfee and Rachael Lorna Johnstone.
Description: Lanham : Rowman & Littlefield, [2019] | Series: New millennium books in international studies | Includes bibliographical references and index.
Identifiers: LCCN 2018040483 (print) | LCCN 2018055543 (ebook) | ISBN 9781442235649 (ebook) | ISBN 9781442235625 (cloth : alk. paper) | ISBN 9781442235632 (pbk. : alk. paper)
Subjects: LCSH: Arctic regions—Politics and government. | Arctic regions—Foreign relations. | Arctic regions—Economic conditions.
Classification: LCC G615 (ebook) | LCC G615 .D87 2019 (print) | DDC 327.0911/3—dc23
LC record available at https://lccn.loc.gov/2018040483

♾™ The paper used in this publication meets the minimum requirements of American National Standard for Information Sciences—Permanence of Paper for Printed Library Materials, ANSI/NISO Z39.48-1992.

Printed in the United States of America

To Don: who hopes for a better future
To K and Lo: whose future it is

Contents

Acknowledgments

WHEN WE FIRST agreed to write this book, neither of us appreciated quite what we were taking on. Putting on paper all the things we thought we knew about the Arctic and that we talked about, taught about, and forgot about on a daily basis did not seem such a difficult task. How wrong we were. The more we studied the Arctic, the more we realized what we did not know. The more we tried to write concisely and precisely, the more caveats we had to offer and the longer the parentheses became. Further, as time marched on, the Arctic—and the world—underwent major political shifts. The governments of Canada and the United States changed significantly and brought new approaches to climate change and indigenous rights. Russia annexed Crimea, and Western countries responded with sanctions. The price of oil collapsed. Canada took the European Union to the World Trade Organization over a ban on seal products. Meanwhile, permafrost and sea ice continued to melt, and hunger for industrialization continued unabated. Our own lives changed, too: Mary retired and moved two thousand miles, and Rachael took up a new position at Ilisimatusarfik (University of Greenland).

Cross-disciplinary research is always challenging. One realizes how much one takes for granted. We each forced the other to reassess our assumptions and to justify and explain the very foundations of our approaches to Arctic cooperation and international cooperation more broadly. While neither of us can perhaps be said to have undergone a profound conversion during the research and writing process, we have certainly become much more aware of the assumptions of our respective disciplines and recognize that what might seem obvious in one is certainly not obvious in another. Both of us have had to learn new ways of approaching problems. Rachael has had to wrap her head around the more abstract approaches of IR (international relations) theory—what she still calls, but not disparagingly, "the woolly stuff." She might also—whisper it—have become a little less positivistic. Mary is now an expert on the subtleties of legal terminology and will never (again) conflate "sign," "accede," or "ratify."

Neither of us anticipated that this book would take such a long time to write. Neither of us expected leukemia and the consequent treatment that would suck the energy from Mary and make every sentence a struggle. The cancer is now blessedly in remission.

There are literally dozens of people to thank for their support in bringing this book to fruition. First of all, Margaret Karns, professor emerita, University of Dayton, is the one who proposed the book to Mary and then got Rowman & Littlefield to keep pressing her. However, Mary was not willing to work on this without a coauthor to cover the more technical legal aspects. Mary firmly believed that a sound analysis of Arctic governance had to integrate international law as well as international relations. "Thanks" does not exactly cover our sentiments toward Timo Koivurova for pointing Mary in Rachael's direction! Timo has long been an inspiration to us both, as well as a bottomless well of knowledge that he shares graciously.

The staff at Rowman & Littlefield have never wavered in their confidence, support, and patience. Traci Crowell and Mary Malley merit a particular mention for gently pushing us with proposed deadlines and always believing that we would deliver—eventually.

Along the way, we have had invaluable input from our wonderful colleagues in the Arctic studies and Polar law communities. Rasmus Gjedssø Bertelsen, Romain Chuffart, Erik Franckx, Janice Glime, Soffía Guðmundsdóttir, Hjalti Þór Hreinsson, Timo Koivurova, Suzanne Lalonde, Marc Lanteigne, Bjarni Már Magnússon, Tony Penikett, Birger Poppel, Lindsay Arthur Tamm, and a wonderful group of graduate students at Ilisimatusarfik all commented on drafts of our work and corrected our many errors. Errors remaining are entirely the authors' responsibility. Lindsay Arthur Tamm, Rachael's outstanding research assistant and MA in Polar law candidate, provided some very useful research on Alaska. Irina Zhilina, MA in Polar law, advised on Russian sources. Rasmus Gjedssø Bertelsen went well beyond the call of duty and straightened out a number of misunderstandings on Nordic history. We would also like to thank the four anonymous reviewers at Rowman & Littlefield for some very useful critiques of the first draft that encouraged us to revise a number of areas and clarify others.

Proofreaders Mum and Dad Johnstone (Freda and Ronnie) and husband Durfee (Don) picked up many of our errors and at least made a good impression of being interested as they went about it. We might pretend to be independent women, but neither of us would have written this book without the unwavering support of our respective life partners, Don and Giorgio. Rachael's spirited children, K and Lo, provided both motivation to keep going and a welcome distraction, reminding us of what really matters and whose future this is all about.

The institutions behind us have also made this book possible, providing us both with the necessary time and resources. Michigan Tech University, the University of Akureyri, in Iceland, and Ilisimatusarfik have all played their part. Rachael has been made most welcome as a guest researcher at Elgin College, University of the Highlands and Islands, Scotland, and at the University of Genova, Italy. Mary, meanwhile, spent many happy research weeks at the Arctic Centre of the University of Lapland, in Finland, the University of Ghent, in Belgium, the Asser Institute, in The Hague, and at Corvinus University, in Hungary (this latter on a Fulbright scholarship).

Lastly, the most important inspiration and some of the best feedback we received on our journey was from our students. Being asked to explain things to critical young minds, being forced to answer new questions (and they *always* have new questions!), and reviewing student papers that bring new insights to old topics force us to keep learning, never believe we have gotten to the bottom of an issue, and always be prepared for new approaches. This book was originally intended as a textbook, and we sincerely hope it will be used as such. But never believe that a textbook is simplified or superficial! In trying to give answers to some of the puzzles about Arctic governance in a changing world, answers that would satisfy the astute and discriminating students that we have met in our collective decades of academia, we hope that we have provided an analysis that will also appeal to academics working in the field as well as to a wider public that is showing an ever-increasing interest in Arctic governance.

1

What the Arctic Tells Us about World Affairs

MOST PEOPLE HAVE never traveled above the Arctic Circle and probably never will. Yet the Arctic inspires the imaginations of many of us.[1] For some it is a distant, forbidding, cold, and empty space, but for others it might be a place of adventure. For four million people, it is home. Today's Arctic is much more familiar, cooperative, and connected to the larger world than one might imagine. The story of the Arctic in world affairs has many dimensions and is best seen from different perspectives.

This introductory chapter outlines key issues facing the Arctic and some of the tools to understand and address them. It begins by noting the similarities and dissimilarities with other parts of the world. It then offers typical media accounts of the Arctic—for example, whether there might be a scramble for resources—and contrasts them to the more common practices of international cooperation between states and the transnational relations among Arctic indigenous peoples.

The Arctic region, while distinctive in many ways, shares characteristics and similar challenges with many other places in the world (see box 1.1). First, climate change and the associated impacts on the wider environment can be observed everywhere in the world. Measurements indicate the Arctic is warming at about twice the global average.[2] Second, the forces of globalization through markets, communications, travel, and investment touch our lives. What we buy and sell, wear, and think come from many places, and the Arctic is among them. Third, those global connections, including how Arctic governments interact with each other, are facilitated by international law. Finally, many peoples of the Arctic, as in other parts of the world, are still coping with a history of conquest and colonialism.

BOX 1.1	Arctic Similarities to Other Parts of the World

- Experiences climate and environmental change
- Participates in economic globalization, for example, through global supply chains, shipping, and natural resources
- Applies international legal rules to reduce conflict and promote cooperation, for example, on human rights, trade, and shipping
- Faces the continuing impact of conquest and colonization caused by European arrival in the New World

In some respects, however, the Arctic is not like other places. It is one of the coldest regions of the world alongside Antarctica in the south and the Himalayas in Asia. It has extended periods of daylight and of darkness. The Arctic is sparsely populated and, in some parts, is poorly connected to the world by transportation links and telecommunications, though efforts are being made to improve connectivity.[3] Its towns and people are often distant from national capitals and business centers.

If one defines "urbanization" by the population of cities, then almost no part of the Arctic is urban. Murmansk and Arkhangelsk in Russia are the largest cities in the Arctic, with about 300,000 and 350,000 inhabitants, respectively. If one defines "urban" in terms of the services that cities provide, then even quite small Arctic towns are urban centers. The large distances between settlements and to major cities mean that even quite small communities perform roles typical of urban areas: education, health, culture, and transportation. Nuuk, the capital of Greenland, has about 17,000 residents, yet this constitutes more than 20 percent of the Greenlandic population. More than half of the population of Iceland (country population 350,000) lives in the capital area in and around Reykjavík. Nearly 300,000 of Alaska's population of 742,000 live in Anchorage, a city six hundred miles south of the Arctic Circle. About 90 percent of the Russian Arctic's population live in the two aforementioned cities or in smaller towns. Considered from the viewpoint of the functions of urban areas, more than half the Arctic population lives in urban areas—similar to the urbanized proportion of the rest of the world.[4]

COOPERATION UNDER UNCERTAINTY

Compared to many parts of the world, the Arctic enjoys very stable political systems, high levels of regional cooperation, very high average levels of national wealth, and almost no territorial disputes. Eight sovereign states (the Arctic Eight) have territory within the Arctic Circle, defined as the part of the world above 66°33' latitude from the equator: Canada, the Kingdom of Denmark (including Greenland and the Faroe Islands), Finland, Iceland, Norway, Sweden, the Russian Federation, and the United States.

Arctic countries participate actively in world trade, and the Arctic has been connected to global trade for centuries. Some of the states, notably the United States and Russia, have large militaries with forces in the Arctic. The Arctic region, however, has not seen hot conflict since World War II. Instead, Arctic states resolve Arctic issues primarily through negotiation, and they cooperate on common concerns.

Cooperation in the Arctic is not new, though the scope has increased dramatically since the end of the Cold War. The use of the Svalbard Islands north of Norway by people from many countries was causing growing problems. In 1920, as part of the peace negotiations after World War I, states solved their differences with the Svalbard Treaty (see box 1.2).[5] In 1973, during the height of the Cold War, Canada, Denmark,

BOX 1.2 | The Svalbard Treaty, 1920

The Treaty Concerning the Archipelago of Spitsbergen[a] governs the Spitsbergen Islands, also known as the Svalbard Islands. For centuries, the archipelago was used for fishing and hunting by people from many different places. Commercialization of mining operations—in particular coal—required a settlement to be reached to ensure effective governance and environmental protection. Both Norway and Russia claimed the islands as part of their territories, but there were other states whose nationals had economic interests and did not want to lose access. The problem was solved by agreeing to Norway's absolute sovereignty over the islands, but with a twist. Norway regulates activity, but any state that becomes party to the treaty can send its nationals to the islands for peaceful purposes, such as to work, fish, or mine. Any taxes or fees collected must be spent in Svalbard. Visitors do not need a visa, but living there a long time does not constitute residence for the purposes of obtaining Norwegian citizenship. Today, around three-quarters of Svalbard's year-round residents are Norwegian.

[a]Treaty Concerning the Archipelago of Spitsbergen, 1920, *League of Nations Treaty Series* 2 (1920), 7.

Norway, the then Soviet Union, and the United States agreed to a treaty to curtail commercial polar bear hunting and encourage better wildlife management.[6] Both treaties remain in force today.

Governance

The Arctic lands are sovereign territory governed by sovereign states, just like almost all other lands on earth.[7] The sovereign states may contain subnational administrative units (see map 1.1 and chapter 3). The Arctic Ocean is governed in many respects by the international law of the sea (see chapters 8 and 9). Much international cooperation in the Arctic is

Map 1.1   Arctic Administrative Areas

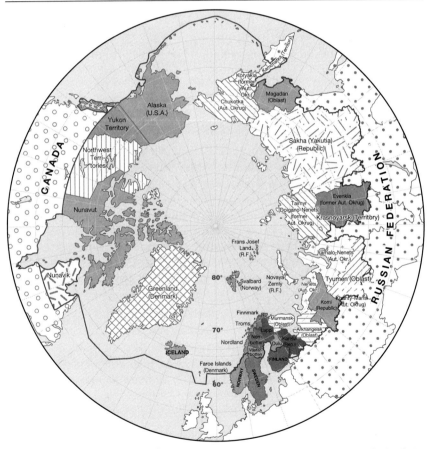

Source: Arctic Council, maps compiled by Winifred Dallmann, Norwegian Polar Institute, https://www.arctic-council.org/images/PDF_attachments/Maps/admin_areas_wNunavik .pdf.

conducted through the Arctic Council, an intergovernmental forum (see chapter 3). Through the Council's various working groups and projects, it has compiled studies of the biology, climate change, economy, public health, and much else in order to inform national policy making and planning and to further international cooperation. The Arctic Council has also developed innovative structures to include indigenous representatives, known as permanent participants. Meetings of the Council include as observers some non-Arctic states, international governmental organizations (IGOs), and nongovernmental organizations (NGOs).

The Arctic Council's mix of participants illustrates the concept of global governance. This type of governance looks beyond the state to other actors and processes in order to understand better how policies are made and implemented. These actors are linked through institutions like the Arctic Council working groups, which produce studies for the Council. These studies, along with policy interests of the Arctic Eight and the permanent participants, help shape the Council's agenda. Governance is not just about governments making regulations and laws. It is a process that involves negotiation, shared decision making, and policy development at multiple geographic and political levels.[8]

Cooperation

Where there is governance, there is usually also cooperation. The media tend to present the Arctic either as a place only of isolated raw nature (forgetting the people who live there) or as a place of looming conflicts over resources, including between great powers like the United States, Russia, and China. In 2008, Scott Borgerson published in *Foreign Affairs* an article anticipating dramatic showdowns between the states, as though an American Western movie were the script:

> The situation is especially dangerous because there are currently no overarching political or legal structures that can provide for the orderly development of the region or mediate political disagreements over Arctic resources or sea-lanes. The Arctic has always been frozen; as ice turns to water, it is not clear which rules should apply. The rapid melt is also rekindling numerous interstate rivalries and attracting energy-hungry newcomers, such as China, to the region. The Arctic powers are fast approaching diplomatic gridlock, and that could eventually lead to the sort of armed brinkmanship that plagues other territories, such as the desolate but resource-rich Spratly Islands, where multiple states claim sovereignty but no clear picture of ownership exists.[9]

BOX 1.3 | The Arctic Circle Assembly

In October 2017 hundreds of people converged in Reykjavík, Iceland, for the fifth annual Arctic Circle conference.[a] They came from the eight Arctic states as well as from many non-Arctic countries, such as China, India, Malaysia, New Zealand, Singapore, South Africa, and countries in the European Union, like Poland and France. Some of the attendees represented government agencies, including science, defense, and environment ministries. There were current and past prime ministers and ministers of foreign affairs. The prime minister of the Cook Islands, in the South Pacific, came to share the Cook Islands' approach to environmental change. The head of the Eastern Orthodox Church joined with other religious leaders to discuss the ethical responsibilities we all have in this time of climate change. The governor of Maine and one of the US senators from Alaska attended, as did representatives of local governments. Representatives of the many indigenous peoples of the Arctic were there. Arctic youth groups participated. Professors and students from universities from around the world presented papers and research results. Greenpeace and World Wildlife Fund sent delegates, as did IGOs. Corporations from oil and gas, shipping, green energy, investment, and new technology sectors took part.

Cooperation and information sharing dominated the meeting. Talk of military conflict or scrambles for resources was limited. Community responses to rapid environmental changes were discussed. Human security—food, health, economic, environmental, and cultural—occupied other speakers. Rules for using Arctic waters were explored, with lawyers and shippers noting points where the rules could be clarified or improved. Scientists and indigenous peoples shared ways they were blending old and new epistemologies. Most participants sought ways to minimize conflict between people and nature, states to people, people to people, and states to states.

[a]See Arctic Circle, accessed April 17, 2018, http://www.arcticcircle.org.

Compare the 2008 article to the people and topics taken up in the 2017 annual Arctic Circle Assembly, detailed in box 1.3.

What explains the disconnect between the commentary in the 2008 article and the Arctic cooperation indicated by the 2017 Arctic Circle conference? At the heart of the matter, the difference lies in making a too-easy assumption that states are the only players in world and Arctic affairs and that cooperation between them is always difficult due to states' ongoing pursuit of power as seen through self-interest. Once these assumptions are relaxed and attention is paid to other actors and processes in world affairs, the picture greatly changes. Through the Inuit Circumpolar Council, the Inuit have changed the political discourse within states by effectively arguing for their rights to participate without necessarily claiming statehood. Thus, a mix of international and domestic means has changed Arctic discourse. Jessica Shadian, for example, argued that the "Inuit have transcended their historical role as the outside 'other' throughout colonization and have become part of a larger ongoing re-construction of the inside."[10] Different explanations for what goes on in the Arctic and what decisions are made involving Arctic governance are therefore possible, and they will be pursued throughout this book.

Common versus More Complex Representations of Arctic Affairs

Let us begin by outlining reasons (also summarized in box 1.4) for the dissonance between the Arctic Circle meeting and the older *Foreign Affairs* article. First, the 2008 description largely excludes the indigenous peoples who live there. The Arctic is not an empty space. Land rights within the Arctic Eight are an important topic and a legal and governmental basis for indigenous peoples and other citizens to participate in domestic politics. Indigenous peoples have successfully connected cultural integrity with land rights throughout the Arctic and beyond. Nevertheless, crucial questions about whether, when, and how the people who live in the Arctic determine land use remain unanswered.

In contrast, the Arctic Eight almost never contest sovereignty over their Arctic lands among themselves. State boundaries are clear, with only one exception: tiny Hans Island, a half-mile square patch of land

---

BOX 1.4	**Why International Conflict Is Unlikely in the Arctic**

- People live in the region and participate in decisions *with* their governments.
- The region has layers of rules that shape action and negotiation.
- The so-called scramble for resources is not a free-for-all. International law governs states' rights over resources, and states in turn license and regulate resource activities.
- Complex problems encourage negotiation, and the different sets of rules (e.g., those governing trade versus marine pollution) encourage states to negotiate.

claimed by both Canada and Denmark/Greenland.[11] Most maritime boundaries have also been settled, and the disagreements that remain—for example, between the United States and Canada over the Beaufort Sea, as well as the international status of the Northwest Passage in the Canadian Arctic—are managed amicably. Indeed, maritime boundary delimitations in the Arctic are far ahead of the global average.[12]

Second, the description in *Foreign Affairs* neglected the layers upon layers of laws, domestic and international, in the region. At the global level, these laws guide behavior for states, firms, and individuals, including rules on maritime delimitations, shipping, human rights, and the economy (these are all explored in later chapters). Borgerson presented a revised view in a 2013 *Foreign Affairs* article: "A funny thing happened on the way to Arctic anarchy. Rather than harden positions, the possibility of increased tensions has spurred the countries concerned to work out their differences peacefully."[13]

These layers of rules produce complexity and space for negotiation.[14] Thus, complexity may encourage diplomatic strategic moves to discuss topics in one legal context rather than another, but complexity does not necessarily lead to any significant conflict between states. Other players and social systems aside from the sovereign state contribute their views and actions, which often leads to innovation. Complexity may prove a good context for more resilient systems of governance: systems that can recover or adapt to change.

A third reason for the differences between the article and the Arctic Circle conference is the image of energy-starved countries searching for new sources of fossil fuels and natural resources. The analogy to the South China Sea is far off the mark, because there are unique historic reasons for territorial and other maritime disputes there that do not apply to the Arctic. Undoubtedly there are disagreements regarding competing land and resource uses in the Arctic. However, these differences are primarily at the domestic level, between different economic and cultural interests—for example, between reindeer herders and mining companies.

Fourth, there are disagreements about how to characterize a problem or opportunity, who gets to decide an issue and at what level (community, subnational government, national, international, private authority or public), and who will pay. The meeting at the Arctic Circle illustrates how many groups with different goals and ethical systems have an interest in and might influence Arctic affairs. They might agree on an emerging issue like better Arctic infrastructure to support increased employment opportunities, access to services, resource development, and tourism, but disagree on who will pay. Sea level rise has begun to destroy villages, but there is little clarity on what governments, business, and citizens should do (see chapter 4).

Issues like these lend themselves to peaceful solutions through negotiation. States may also evaluate the best legal or diplomatic context to pursue their goals among sets of rules. For the Arctic Eight, the Arctic Council is commonly the best forum. For non-Arctic states like the United Kingdom, China, France, Germany, India, Japan, and South Korea, Arctic interests are managed through the UN, the law of the sea, the Svalbard Treaty, the Arctic Council, where many of them are observers, and other institutions.

THE ARCTIC AND ITS INDIGENOUS PEOPLES IN WORLD AFFAIRS

Only about 10 percent of the population of the Arctic is indigenous, but indigenous experience and success in living in the Arctic are unrivaled. Their role in what happens in the Arctic cannot be underestimated. They are key participants in the Arctic Council. In this book, when referring to distinct communities of indigenous persons, "indigenous people" is used in the singular to refer to a single group—for example, the Inuit are an indigenous people. "Indigenous peoples" in the plural refers to many groups of indigenous people—for example, the Sami in Fennoscandia, the Evenki in Russia, and the Inuit and Athabaskan in North America are all indigenous peoples (see table 3.1 in chapter 3). This is in accordance with the grammatical usage of "people" and "peoples" in international law.[15]

Danish anthropologist Frank Sejersen points out the one thing that indigenous peoples have in common: the colonial experience.[16] They have all been colonized by peoples who arrived centuries or even millennia after they did; who claimed their lands and resources; who undermined their traditions, often deliberately through assimilationist policies; and who ruled them without their consent. The consequences are ongoing: they have been subjected to paternalism and even today suffer from assumptions that they need protection and cannot be trusted to run their own affairs.[17] As a result, another feature shared by indigenous peoples in the Arctic today is a demand for greater control over their own affairs. This can be seen in the UN Declaration on the Rights of Indigenous Peoples that indigenous peoples patiently negotiated over more than two decades and to which states finally agreed in 2007.[18] The Declaration stretches from control over their children's education and indigenous culture to self-government. As we will see through a number of examples in this book, indigenous peoples are actors in the Arctic (and elsewhere); they are not objects in want of condescension or protection.

Colonialism replaced the names of places and features of the Arctic, though the ancient names are returning. Indigenous peoples generally named places for their physical characteristics. For example, *Ilulissat* in Greenlandic means "icebergs."[19] Nonnative place names are typically named after (European) people who "discovered" the places, or after places in the explorer's home country. For example, Greenland's capital of Nuuk used to be known by its Danish name, *Godthåb*, meaning "Good Hope." Barrow and Prudhoe Bay in Alaska are European American names; the places were originally named during a British expedition in 1826. In 2016, Barrow became known once more as *Utqiaġvik*, a "place to gather roots."

Popular discourses about indigenous peoples often portray them as victims—of climate change, pollution, ruthless market forces, and so forth.[20] This often emanates from well-intentioned but oversimplified imaginings of "untouched" indigenous cultures and a desire to preserve them untainted by modernity. Yet indigenous peoples are not passive recipients of change; they are not sitting around waiting for outside forces either to destroy or to save their ways of life.[21] It is true that a number of indigenous communities in the Arctic face immediate and difficult challenges from climate change, pollution, and globalization; but many are actively developing their own strategies for adaptation, in many cases working with national governments, international organizations, and multinational corporations.[22]

While their cultures have lost some of the resilience they had before colonialism, indigenous communities still solve problems with and without outside advice. The Iñupiat village of Kivalina in the Northwest Arctic Borough of Alaska is under existential threat: it is literally being washed off the map as a direct consequence of climate change. The villagers need assistance to move but plan to move together when the time comes.[23] Meanwhile, the neighboring Iñupiat-led North Slope Borough has built its strong economy by working with international oil companies.[24]

Indigenous communities around the Arctic have various value systems, economies, and traditions and face different consequences from climate change and international investment. Some see risks: from invasive species, permafrost collapse, disruption of food sources, marine oil spill dangers, mining waste, and damage to historic lands. Others see opportunities: from increased investment in infrastructure and search and rescue capabilities, job opportunities, income to strengthen their communities, and the promise of greater independence. Most see a mix of both.

THE ARCTIC REGION AND POLICY TOOLS USED TO MANAGE IT

Regions Are Created by People through Discourses

The Arctic offers many insights into the links between regions to nations to international relations. All regions are "imaginary" in the sense that they appear and disappear depending on what one emphasizes: environment, people, languages, geography, economics, or history. For example, in the political discourse of the Cold War it was common to speak about "Eastern" (communist) and "Western" (capitalist) Europe. These two kinds of polities were in opposition to each other, but the distinctions weakened when the Soviet Union collapsed in 1991. In the globalization context, many non-Arctic states are increasingly emphasizing their "Arctic" credentials—that is, their rights to take part in decision making and opportunities in the Arctic.[25]

Another kind of discourse about the Arctic can be seen through the lenses of science and mapping, which are discussed more in chapter 2. Mapping was a crucial activity as states asserted control over territories or expanded into the New World. Scientists and their equipment went along on early exploration trips.[26] Today, scientific research continues in a vast range of Arctic topics. Indigenous peoples now challenge the discourses of colonialism, even including the conduct of science. Indigenous knowledge, based on thousands of years of observation, is slowly making its way into partnerships with Western science.

Governing the Arctic: International Law

National governments have many instruments to manage their relationships with each other and within their national jurisdictions. Between states, they include international law, diplomacy, international organizations, defense and coast guard assets, science, and the soft power of culture. At home, laws, regulations, and broad decision processes for making public policy influence what happens in the Arctic. When states use these various tools, other actors like firms or environmental organizations will attempt to keep, expand, or change what the state does. In sum, private and public actors are humming with activity through their exchanges of goods, rules, and ideas within, and for, the Arctic.

To understand how the Arctic is governed, we must understand the basics of international law. The importance of public international law to Arctic governance cannot be overstated. In this chapter, its sources and basic logic are presented. How do we recognize international law in any given instance? Where does it come from, and why is it authoritative? Later chapters, including on security, indigenous and human rights, the law of the sea, shipping, and the environment will offer more detail on the application of international law in the Arctic.

It is easy to be cynical about international law: to see law as a sideshow compared to uses of military and economic power. It is easy to find examples of states ignoring international law: locking up their citizens without trials, polluting rivers that flow into neighboring states, and even invading other states. However, these examples of not observing international legal obligations stand out precisely because they are relatively unusual. We do not read reports about states using international law every day and abiding by it. It is not newsworthy when states allow foreign aircraft to land, admit foreign citizens and foreign imports, deliver international mail, prohibit corporations from dumping pollution into shared waterways, restrict their army exercises to their own territories, or refrain from killing civilians during armed conflicts. Yet all those mundane activities are grounded in international law. States do not come to blows over environmental disputes and they rarely litigate, but how they view their legal positions over a matter informs their expectations of behavior by others, their negotiations, and the settlements they reach.

Most people follow the law because they have no real interest in breaking it: we do not engage in violent acts, not because we fear punishment but because we have internalized a morality that such practices are wrong. States also generally accept that the use of force is not an acceptable method of dispute settlement. Even very powerful states rarely use force to control very small states. We might covet our neighbor's car, but we do not steal it; the United States does not drill for oil in Icelandic waters even if there is little Iceland could do to stop the activity. Then there are the laws we routinely break, but even here the law is still a constraining force. We might drive a little over the speed limit on a small neighborhood street, but only rarely do drivers drive down such a street at highway speeds. Not only would we face a ticket but we would also face social sanction (disapproval) from our peers for what would be viewed as reckless and irresponsible behavior.

Even when states commit what appear to be egregious breaches of international law, those states do not deny law's authority. The authors of this book could not find any examples of obvious violations of international law in the Arctic, but another example should be sufficient to illustrate the point: when Russia annexed Crimea (a part of Ukraine), it insisted that its actions were in conformity with international law. Most other states disagree with the Russian viewpoint, so the Russian action has not gained international legitimacy.

The Statute of the International Court of Justice (an annex to the UN Charter) identifies the sources of law: treaties, customary law, general principles, judicial decisions, and the writings of particularly esteemed scholars (see box 1.5).[27] It is the *states* that decide which laws apply to them; international law only becomes binding on a state with its consent, either explicit or by virtue of acquiescence.

BOX 1.5 | **Sources of International Law**

- Treaties: written agreements between states
- Custom: widespread practices that states deem legally binding
- General principles: practices commonly found in domestic systems
- Judicial decisions: decisions of international courts
- Writings of jurists: explanations of the law by highly qualified legal scholars

---

Treaties are the easiest to identify: we can find a written text that states' representatives have negotiated and agreed upon. These can be called agreements, conventions, covenants, pacts, charters, and the like. The key is that the states that agree on them intend to create binding obligations with regard to one another.

Customary international law emerges from state practice (what states do) and *opinio iuris* (legal opinion), which is best understood as how states describe what they do and how they respond to the behavior (practice) of other states. Examples of *opinio iuris* include Russia's purported justifications for the annexation of Crimea and the official statements of other states in response; Canada's assertions of historic sovereignty over the water of the Northwest Passage and the United States' assertions of the right of freedom of navigation (discussed in chapter 9); and statements made by state representatives on the adoption of the UN Declaration on the Rights of Indigenous Peoples at the UN General Assembly in 2007 (discussed in chapter 7).

In contemporary times, treaty law has codified much of customary law but has not replaced it. This is especially important if a state has not become a party to a treaty that most other states have ratified. So, while the United States has not acceded to the UN Convention on the Law of the Sea (UNCLOS), it has endorsed most of its content as customary law, considers itself bound to follow it, and objects vociferously to what it sees as breaches by other states (see chapters 8 and 9).[28]

General principles of law are less influential in modern practice, perhaps because customary law and treaty law have, over time, become more comprehensive and govern more areas of potential dispute. They are certain basic principles that are shared in legal systems around the world—for example, the principle that states must act in good faith in their international relations and the principle that if there is a wrong, there must be a remedy (reparation).

International court decisions bind only the parties to a given dispute and do not make law—that is, they do not create precedents in the common law sense of the term.[29] However, judicial decisions provide evidence of the law because they are authoritative interpretations of the treaties, customary international law, and (more seldom) general principles. Decisions of national supreme courts as well as those of international courts, like the International Court of Justice or the International Tribunal for the Law of the Sea, can be evidence of international law. Judgments of these latter two bodies are good predictors of how future litigation will go.

The writings of "highly qualified publicists" (legal scholars) are much less influential in contemporary times. Like court rulings, scholarship can provide insight into what the law is at any given time: the treaties, customs, and general principles that are applicable. As individual scholars have decreased in importance, institutions such as the International Law Association—an international nongovernmental organization for international legal scholars—have filled the gap by producing extensive academic reports on various topics of international law.[30]

WHAT THE ARCTIC TELLS US ABOUT INTERNATIONAL RELATIONS THEORY

The study of international relations includes the use of broad and abstract theories about how global politics works.[31] For much of the post-WWII period and continuing today, the aim in this kind of abstract theory is to understand and explain the behavior of, primarily, states. Often the theories have little connection to foreign policy, international law, or diplomacy, all of which are very real things to governments. There are other, medium-range theories—notably a family of them called regime theory—that work back and forth between rich evidence from world politics and the more abstract level of international relations theory.

There is no one abstract theory of international relations. Rather, there are many theories due to differences in assumptions about the nature of the international system, the actors of interest, methods, and, in some ways, the ultimate aim of the entire scholarly enterprise. Some are fundamentally materialist in nature, focusing on the physical assets of states and other actors. Others are ideational and emphasize how ideas affect what states and other players on the global scene do. Other flavors of theory have a sociological or institutional perspective. In this book, we consider primarily realism, liberalism, and critical theory, as the abstract theories, and regime theory for an approach long used to explain the Arctic.

Assumptions of Realism, Liberalism, and Critical Theories

All theories of international relations have to account for territorial states. Realist and liberal theories put the modern sovereign state at the center as the main actor of interest. Critical theories look at the other kinds of actors and do not always put the state at the center. "Decentering" from the state helps these scholars see where power is embedded into rules or behaviors and thus not otherwise readily visible. Decentering also allows the scholar (or activist) to imagine a greater range of actors with interests and potential authority. It is in this sense that critical theorists have a different aim than proponents of realism and liberalism: they want to make the world more just rather than only provide explanations. Table 1.1 summarizes these differences between the three systemic theories.

Table 1.1   Three Theories Compared

Theory	State Dominant	Power	Discourse	Nature of Cooperation	Causes of Instability
Realism	Yes	Material	Power-based diplomacy	Limited	Dissatisfied states
Liberalism	Yes	Material and ideational	Interest- and expectation-based diplomacy	Strengthens with institutions	Declining hegemon and weak institutions
Critical theory	Not necessarily	Diffused	Evaluate who sets the discourse	Involves struggle over who gets heard	Injustice

Increasingly, scholars doubt the wisdom of a focus on sovereign states, and some propose thinking in terms of international society, which has an extended heritage through a theoretical approach called the English School. The English School emphasizes some of the tools of states outlined above and assumes states are in a society. The approach has been further expanded to include global society—indigenous peoples, corporations, IGOs, and NGOs. The reason for moving attention away from states and to other players on the global scene is to capture more of global society and its effects.

Another reason for calls to move beyond the state is that societal actors internal to the state may, in fact, make the state. Theories of realism (classical, neo, offensive, and defensive) do not pay much attention to the internal politics of states at all. Liberal theories (classical, neo) do at times consider internal affairs in explaining how preferences become policy and how similar political cultures might be more inclined to cooperate than others. Critical theories also include the internal order, often through the study of different discourses on the public sphere by people possessing weaker and stronger access to power.[32]

International relations theories also vary in their views on the ease of cooperation. Realists do not believe cooperation is very stable, while liberal theorists, on the whole, consider that international institutions and organizations greatly facilitate cooperation and information sharing. Critical theorists look at different kinds of power and who can or cannot access decision-making power. They explain why so many people have so little say and explore ways in which change might be possible.

One reason for the great variation on the question of cooperation is that the theories disagree on how to include other actors besides states in world affairs. How much agency do they have? Do they possess authority, legitimacy, or accountability? Do domestic forces create what states do? Again, realist theories leave the other actors in the background. Even if the others do act on their own, states, if so inclined, can prevent their doing so. Liberals would, in contrast, give a much larger role to these players and to the preferences of domestic and other actors in making what appears to be a "decision" by the state.[33]

Critical theorists and liberals have taken a growing interest in identity. The interest goes beyond the realist distinction between great powers that structure the international system and middle and small powers that influence (at best) a region.[34] It now includes how states and other global actors imagine themselves. Identity affects what their interests might be and how that resonates with others. Identity is not just an internal state but is also created or partially built by others. Narratives about "Who am I?" or "Who is that over there?" come from history—especially critical moments—and aspirations. They also draw on narratives used by others.[35] What does the "West" mean to Russia, or "Russia" to the West? How do those experiences create expectations; how, for that matter, can we change identity in a meaningful way?

Liberalism and realism also assume the state is a rational actor. The state knows its interests and applies its power as well as it can to achieve its interests. Policy makers are rational when they make decisions regarding foreign policy. Liberals spend more time on domestic sources of interests to explain foreign policy preferences and behaviors, but they retain the assumption that states expect each other to behave rationally.

Critical theorists put great emphasis on tracing who has power; thus, they expand the range of possible players at home, in a region, or on an issue. In so doing, the approach opens prospects that politics can change, that the marginalized could increase their influence. Large corporations have ready access to governments and have little difficulty getting heard by governments. Being seen and heard matter for maintaining or expanding the scope of a nonstate actor's autonomy. The fact that indigenous peoples sit at the table with states on the Arctic Council illustrates how new ideas can inform international affairs. The indigenous peoples do not formally have the power to block decisions in the same way that the member states do. However, in practice, the Arctic Council does not adopt a policy when the permanent participants object.[36]

International relations theories differ on why instability arises in world affairs. For realists, dissatisfied states may build power and then use force to change the world. It is particularly problematic when one of the great powers goes into decline, thus opening a space for a dissatisfied power to try to change its status. Weak institutions are a cause of instability for liberal theorists. Institutions mediate power by improving the quality of information and, in doing so, encourage cooperation. Often a hegemon supports the rise of institutions to promote peace or improve welfare; thus, institutions may weaken when a major regional power or global hegemonic leader goes into decline. On one hand, institutions might moderate the impact of a declining hegemon and so may prove valuable to other states that continue to use the institutions. On the other hand, to the degree a given international institution is based on norms that were driven by the hegemon, that institution may decline in usefulness as the norms once supported by the hegemon decline and the rising power creates new norms or institutions. The new institutions may fail to continue to support an important activity between states.[37] Injustice for people is a bigger cause for instability for critical theorists. Revolution or significant civil unrest may destabilize regions and large swaths of the world unless real opportunities to get a say and a decent share of the economic pie are built in to decision making.

Regime Theory

Stephen Krasner, in a 1982 article, launched a new field of research called regime theory. He defines an international regime as a set of "principles, norms, rules, and decision-making procedures around which actor expectations converge in a given issue area."[38] Trade, investment, law of the sea, indigenous peoples' rights, the NATO alliance, and the Arctic are all examples of issue areas in which regimes have emerged and evolved to facilitate cooperation and governance. The approach yielded detailed studies of how the issue areas work, which has enriched understanding of global governance. One of the crucial studies was by Oran Young on how the Arctic Environmental Protection Strategy (AEPS) came into being in 1991 and its ensuing operation.[39]

Over time, Young's work on the Arctic has sharpened awareness of how to study regimes and the kinds of questions to ask about them. Ronald Mitchell summarized a key point of Young's findings: "Environmental governance emerges as institutions strive—in coincident or conflicting ways—to frame the issues, choose the arena for institutional development, and bargain over content."[40] Regimes do not exist in isolation from one another. Rather, according to Young, they can be embedded, nested, clustered, or overlapping. Complexity should be expected. A crucial point of regimes, however, is to set norms about what a problem is and how best to act. Ideally, any given regime has a mechanism to learn more about its core issues. Overlapping or nested regimes may help diffuse ideas. Arctic governance may provide good ideas to other places. It might take them from elsewhere, too. Whether the various issue areas reduce effectiveness is unclear. The 1973 Polar Bear Treaty, now nested in the larger Arctic regime, gave polar bears a chance to recover from excessive sport hunting. The Svalbard Treaty, now also part of governance of the Arctic, has worked well on land but is contested offshore in light of later changes in the law of the sea.

International relations theories need to be useful, whether abstract or more descriptive. In what way do ideas take center stage? When do military or economic forms of power structure the politics and governance of the Arctic? What processes account for most of the action, and do they come from within the Arctic or from other regimes and states?

Arctic Puzzles for International Relations Theorists
As you read the remainder of this book, reflect on the following puzzles and devise your own puzzles for theories of international relations and modern governance. Follow James N. Rosenau's advice on thinking theoretically. Ask of events: "Of what is this an instance?"

One Cannot Explain the Arctic without International Law
It is not plausible to understand the Arctic without international law. Realist theories discount the critical role international law plays in international affairs, but the Arctic states are diligently mapping and submitting data according to precise criteria set out in the UNCLOS to confirm their continental shelves. For liberals, the role of international law gets good exercise. It contributes to stability of expectations and facilitates communication. Regime theorists will ask for specifics in order to tease out whether norms or material power are at work. Critical theorists might argue that law explains why some voices are not heard. The legal concept of sovereignty silenced the voices of previously independent and organized peoples; it was a crucial tool of colonialism. Yet the interplay between domestic political rights and indigenous and human rights on the international plane has given a strong opening to individuals, indigenous peoples, and organizations to press for new structures, perhaps reshaping the very idea of sovereignty.

The Arctic Has Weak Institutions and Strong Cooperation
Realists would be surprised by the depth of cooperation in the Arctic but not by the weakness of the institutions. Realists might argue that each of the Arctic Eight has the greatest stake there is in the game: sovereign territory. No one would doubt each state would defend itself and its interests. At the same time states also seek more material power. Unilateral gains may be preferred, but cooperation can be rational if it extends capabilities at little or no risk. Liberal theorists would need to reconcile the weakness of the formal structures for cooperation with the high level of cooperation in practice. An answer to the liberal puzzle might be that strength comes through overlapping membership in IGOs and international forums, alongside state sovereignty. A branch of critical theory called constructivism emphasizes practices of states (and others) that create identities and social structures. If states regularly issue threats and build arms, then the world will look quite realist. If they meet and discuss common issues or, as in the Arctic, also actively cooperate with indigenous peoples, then world politics will look quite cooperative.[41]

The Arctic Illustrates Creative Uses of Sovereignty
These theories all include the idea and practice of territorial sovereignty, but they are strangely silent on the flexibility of sovereignty. Sovereignty can include unusual exceptions that solve other problems of higher salience. Sovereignty surprises are subtle but facilitate governance.

Human Security Rivals National Security
Realists begin with national security, thus sidelining human security issues (these issues are explored in chapter 4). On the other hand, the US Defense Department says climate change is the greatest threat facing the United States. It is not a threat from other states but is a threat embedded in global economic practices. Liberals would explain it through domestic politics of the Arctic Eight. In democratic societies, individuals and groups can influence politics without themselves being in government. Critical theorists would note that increasing activism by indigenous peoples is reshaping political choices at home and abroad. Practices and ideas, while painfully slow at times, are giving more emphasis to making people more secure. Regime theorists would ask which institutions open or close doors to improved human security.

Climate Change Matters in Governance Efforts
Barnett and Sikkink think that international relations theory needs a new narrative to replace the one about the "anarchy" of the international system emphasized by realists and by many liberals. They propose a narrative on governance.[42] How governance influences choices and values remains an open question even in stable times. Governance in the context of rapid climate change is a narrative in the making, filled with much uncertainty. Young has argued that "high levels of uncertainty alter normal utilitarian calculations."[43] This suggests that what might have been rational in the past may not work as well in the near future. In an age of great environmental uncertainty, people will need governance systems that allow multiple paths and mixes of actors. The Arctic may tell us a great deal about narratives of governance in an era of change.

ORGANIZATION OF THE BOOK

Chapter 2 provides a brief review of the natural and human history of the Arctic. It is divided into three main parts: natural history, the human settlement of the Arctic, and the rise of the modern state system.

Chapter 3, on players, explores who participates in Arctic decision making and how they do so. It considers the roles of indigenous peoples,

Arctic and non-Arctic states, international organizations and forums (including the Arctic Council), NGOs, business interests, and others.

Chapter 4 presents human and national security in the Arctic. Human security is a topic of considerable interest to the Arctic Council and is arguably the most important security topic for the region. National security is explored relative to security dilemmas and arms racing.

Chapter 5 explains the pillars of Arctic economies and the key challenges of ensuring sustainability. It discusses the management of different kinds of resources and the different priorities of the states that govern them.

Chapter 6 explores regional participation in global trade, investment, and money from an international political economy perspective.

Chapter 7 examines the rights of indigenous peoples and human rights in the Arctic. How do indigenous and human rights instruments influence state and corporate behavior? The chapter looks at both UN and regional systems and explores some of the main rights issues at stake in the contemporary Arctic.

Chapter 8 explains the international principles for governance of the world's oceans as relevant in the Arctic. It considers in turn the rules and processes to establish the boundaries of maritime zones and the rules for allocating resource rights.

Chapter 9 provides an in-depth review of Arctic navigation in light of increasing traffic, economics and trade, international law, and forums for regulation to protect the vulnerable Arctic marine environment and the safety of seafarers. It analyzes the legal controversies surrounding the straits in the Northwest Passage and the Northern Sea Route.

Chapter 10 explains the key principles of international environmental law and how they are applied to address crucial challenges in the Arctic, such as climate change, long-range contaminants, and protection of the marine environment.

The book concludes with chapter 11, on resilient governance. Resiliency in the face of change is an important goal, and the Arctic Council has been seized with that topic. Resilience is deeper than adapting to change. The notion of adaptation too often assumes that those taking the brunt of change are the ones who must adjust, rather than involving more equitable solutions where those who caused the change take on a greater share of responsibility to adapt and to assist. It is more than a technical question, especially in light of the fast rate of change in the Arctic. It may be best to see things in terms of relationships between actors and scales: Who and at what scale can moderate the impact of rapid change on society? Resilient governance is fundamentally about governance under uncertainty.

Arctic governance is unique, but the same could be said for any regional or national systems: each is of its own kind, with a patchwork of features that are not replicated elsewhere. However, they are all intertwined. This book aims to explain the principles and processes for Arctic governance and their evolution in light of their inseverable connections to world affairs.

FURTHER READING

Hønneland, Geir. *Arktiske utfordringer* [Arctic challenges]. Norway: Cappelen Damm, 2012.

Klabbers, Jan. *International Law*. Cambridge: Cambridge University Press, 2013.

Krasner, Stephen. "Structural Causes and Regime Consequences: Regimes as Intervening Variable." *International Organization* 36, no. 1 (1982): 185–205.

Lake, David. *Hierarchy in International Relations*. Ithaca, NY: Cornell University Press, 2011.

Moravcsik, Andrew. "Taking Preferences Seriously: A Liberal Theory of International Politics." *International Organization* 51, no. 4 (1997): 513–53.

The Spitsbergen Treaty: Multilateral Governance in the Arctic. Arctic Papers, Volume 1. Edited by Diane Wallis and Stewart Arnold. https://dianawallis.org.uk/en/document/spitsbergen-treaty-booklet.pdf.

Steinberg, Philip E., Jeremy Tasch, and Hannes Gerhardt. *Contesting the Arctic: Politics and Imaginaries in the Circumpolar North*. London: I. B. Tauris, 2015.

Stepien, Adam, Timo Koivurova, Anna Gremsperger, and Henna Niemi. "Arctic Indigenous Peoples and the Challenge of Climate Change." In *Arctic Marine Governance: Opportunities for Transatlantic Cooperation*, edited by Elizabeth Tedsen, Sandra Cavalieri, and R. Andreas Kraemer. Heidelberg: Springer, 2014.

Stokke, Olav Schram. "Institutional Complexity in Arctic Governance: Curse or Blessing?" In *Handbook of Politics in the Arctic*, edited by Leif Christian Jensen and Geir Hønneland. Cheltenham, UK: Edward Elgar, 2015.

Young, Oran. *Arctic Politics: Conflict and Cooperation in the Circumpolar North*. Hanover, NH: University Press of New England, 1992.

2

A Natural and Human History of the Arctic

HISTORIES—NATURAL, LEGAL, scientific, and cultural—are all around us. They come from evidence from the field, genetics, rocks, human artifacts, and from the oral or written word. For this book, histories provide a crucial basis for understanding the Arctic in world affairs now and in the future. This chapter has three parts: natural history, the settlement of the Arctic, and the formation of the modern state system.

History is selectively recorded, so one must always ask: *Whose* story? Then one must think about the story that was not told: the other points of view or events that are left out. What might a story from an Inuit community include about going to a new place in the Arctic or an early encounter with Europeans? Colonization has left lasting scars on indigenous communities and lives. To understand the rise of the modern state system, we need to see how states grew into the dominant territorial entities they are today and how they create and resolve problems. We can see today that different cultural and political histories affect policy pursuits in security, economy, human rights, and the environment.

THE NATURAL HISTORY OF THE ARCTIC

The Physical Geography of the Arctic

There is no single definition of the Arctic; rather, the boundaries depend on what is being studied. Map 2.1 shows five boundaries based on different definitions. Physical maps show an Arctic Circle at 66° N (north latitude). That latitude is the farthest south in the Northern Hemisphere where the sun never rises in midwinter and never sets in midsummer. Other lines on

Map 2.1   Biophysical Definitions of the Arctic

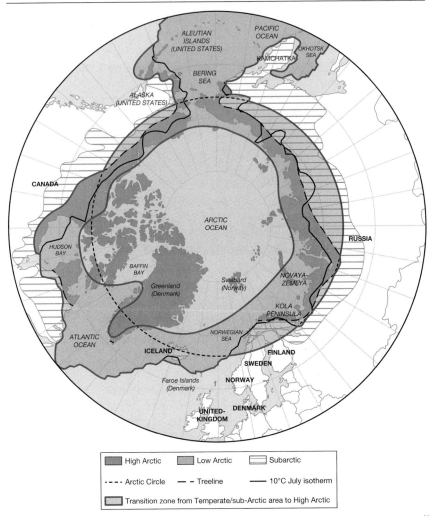

Legend:

- ■ High Arctic
- ■ Low Arctic
- ☐ Subarctic
- ---- Arctic Circle
- — - Treeline
- —— 10°C July isotherm
- ▨ Transition zone from Temperate/sub-Arctic area to High Arctic

Source: "Definition of the Arctic Region," Arctic Center, University of Lapland, https://www.arcticcentre.org/EN/communications/arcticregion/Maps/definitions.

the map show the complex ways cold temperatures define the Arctic. One line is the northerly extent of the tree line, which is the point beyond which trees will not grow. Another line traces the July 10°C isotherm, marking the boundary above which the average July temperature is below 10°C. The map also offers, based on a variety of measures, distinctions between the high and low Arctic, the Subarctic, and a variably sized transition zone between the high and low Arctics. The Arctic can also be defined according to sociological criteria, looking at shared human factors. For example, the boundary for the Arctic Human Development Reports follows the 60° parallel across most of North America and loops down to include all of the Aleutian Islands (51°–55° N).[1]

No geography of the Arctic would be complete without looking at what is underneath the Arctic Ocean on a bathymetric map (see map 2.2). Jurisdiction in and under the seas of the North Atlantic and the Arctic Ocean depends both on international law and the shape and

Map 2.2   Bathymetric Map of the Arctic

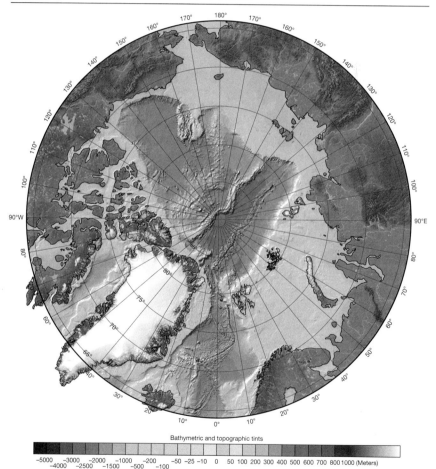

Source: Martin Jakobsson et al., "The International Bathymetric Chart of the Arctic Ocean (IBCAO) Version 3.0," *Geophysical Research Letters* 30, no. 12 (2012), https://doi.org/10.1029/2012GL052219.

consistency of the seafloor. The bathymetric map shows the underwater landscape including the continental shelves and the deep basins in the Arctic Ocean. It also shows underwater ridges, possibly connected to the landmasses of Canada, Greenland, and Russia. As we will see in chapter 8, the shelves, ridges, and islands are important in the management and politics of the Arctic due to rules of the law of the sea.

Cooling and Warming in the Arctic

Ice began to appear in the Arctic about 42 million years ago as the movement of the continents started to create what are now the Atlantic and Arctic Oceans and thus changed global ocean currents (see figure 2.1).[2] There were a number of ice ages and warm periods over the eons. Ancient remains of mosses from Canada's Baffin Island point to periods of relative warmth and cold over time.[3] Parts of the Arctic may be as warm now as 40,000 years ago, or even as warm as 120,000 years ago.

Evidence from ice cores, lake sediments, radiocarbon dating, remains of plants and animals, written and oral history, and genetic and archaeological evidence show uneven warming and cooling among different parts of the Arctic in the past.[4] Today, scientists are interested in the

Figure 2.1   The Mid-Atlantic Rift at Þingvellir, Iceland

recent (and more distant) history of the ice and climate in order to under-stand better what the Arctic and the earth might experience with current and future warming. The current warming trend very clearly appears in charts showing temperatures in different years and at different times of year.[5] The average temperature in the Arctic is 3°C above its reference point, and some places have risen above the 5°C mark.[6] The Paris Agree-ment that went into effect in 2016 aims to keep global averages below a 2°C level and urges a goal of 1.5°C.[7]

The formation of Arctic ice and the new configuration of the con-tinents produced the polar jet stream (there are also subtropical ones, a zone of convergence, and an Antarctic polar stream). The polar jet stream tends to keep cooler air in the north, and it interacts with the oceans. It is quite possible that the colder-than-normal winter in 2017–2018 in lower latitudes of North America and parts of Europe was due to weakening of the polar jet stream.[8] Arctic warming seems now to be affecting windiness in lower northern latitudes. Instead of major storms blowing away fairly quickly in the United States, Canada, and Europe, storms stay over one spot for longer periods, often dumping vast amounts of rain or snow.[9] In the Atlantic, the warm waters of the Gulf Stream keep places that would otherwise be frigid, like Iceland and the UK, warmer and moister.

After a warm period forty thousand years ago, the region cooled and warmed a number of times, most recently in the middle Holocene, between two thousand and ten thousand years ago. This was the Holo-cene Thermal Maximum (HTM). The HTM was very likely to have been produced by the earth's movement around the sun. It is called the preces-sion of the axes of the earth around the sun (imagine what happens to the axes of a gyroscope), and it brings more sunshine to the Arctic region when the northern axis points toward the sun. The full cycle takes twen-ty-six thousand years. Insolation (the amount of sun in the region) was about 10 percent higher than today. The warming effects in the HTM were slowed partly by an ice sheet called the Laurentide. Today's current temperatures are now widely at that higher HTM level in the Arctic again, but precession is not a cause of this warming.[10]

Changing Atmospheric Chemistry
Contemporary global warming is caused by anthropogenic (i.e., human-caused) releases of greenhouse gases (GHGs) and other human activi-ties.[11] In 2014 the World Meteorological Organization announced that its measurements of CO_2 and other GHGs for the planet rose at the highest rates recorded since 1984.[12] Today, the earth has far higher levels

of GHGs than before the Industrial Revolution. "In 2013, concentration of CO_2 in the atmosphere was 142% of the pre-industrial era (1750), and of methane and nitrous oxide, 253% and 121% respectively."[13] The earth has processes such as rock weathering, ocean absorption, and vegetation to reduce CO_2, but it remains unclear how rising temperatures will affect these processes and how long the processes would take to reduce the CO_2 in the atmosphere.[14]

Oceans are reservoirs (sinks) for CO_2. The Arctic Ocean is no exception, though its role as a sink may be changing. Recent measurements now show the Canadian Arctic and the Chukchi Sea are releasing carbon, thus making parts of the Arctic Ocean a source of CO_2. The reason may be that CO_2 is more readily lost from warmer water.[15] Increased levels of carbon in the ocean lead to ocean acidification, because oxygen mixes with water to make carbonic acid. To put it in perspective, "in the past 200 years alone, ocean water has become 30 percent more acidic—faster than any known change in ocean chemistry in the last 50 million years."[16] Some ocean animals in the Pacific Ocean are already having trouble forming shells because of the acidity.

Greenhouse Gases and Permafrost

The cold in the Arctic can reach into the top three hundred feet (approximately) of the ground, creating permafrost. Only the active layer (the top few inches/centimeters) freezes and thaws each year. Below the active layer, the ground stays frozen as permafrost. Permafrost contains ancient organic matter that is now frozen, and each year a bit more plant material is added, frozen, and unfrozen. Some plant remains have been frozen in permafrost for thousands of years, as the example of Baffin Island mosses showed. The permafrost stores carbon from the decayed plants and animals, and thus the lands surrounding the Arctic Ocean have been a carbon sink. The permafrost soil holds CO_2 and the even more powerful GHG, methane (CH_4). Widespread permafrost melt as a consequence of global warming threatens a catastrophic release of carbon.[17]

How much carbon does Arctic permafrost hold? According to the US National Snow and Ice Data Center (NSIDC),

> there is a huge amount of carbon stored in permafrost. Right now, the Earth's atmosphere contains about 850 gigatons of carbon. (A gigaton is one billion tons—about the weight of one hundred thousand school buses). We estimate that there are about 1,400 gigatons of carbon frozen in permafrost. So the carbon frozen in permafrost is greater than

the amount of carbon that is already in the atmosphere today. That doesn't mean that all of the carbon will decay and end up in the atmosphere. The trick is to find out how much of the frozen carbon is going to decay, how fast, and where.[18]

Sea Ice

The Arctic is an ocean surrounded by land, with passages to the Pacific and the Atlantic. The water of the Arctic Ocean is fresher than the waters of the Atlantic and Pacific. The Arctic Ocean has its own currents, and these have significant effects on the ice and the sea-ice-land interactions. The European Arctic has much less ice than Canada; there is less ice in the winter along the long Russian coast than around and within the Canadian archipelago, where the ice tends to stay and build up over the years. However, with global warming, even Canada has far less multiyear ice than in the past. There are other types of sea ice as well, with different characteristics. As will be discussed in chapter 9, ice will present hazards to shipping for some time to come. Box 2.1 provides a summary of the main kinds of sea ice.

Sea ice varies by season. Drift ice moves considerably with prevailing winds. The Beaufort Gyre in the Beaufort Sea travels clockwise and stays in the Arctic for a number of years; it carries mostly multiyear ice rather than new or first-year ice. The Transpolar Drift starts off the Arctic coast of Russia, flows north, and reaches the Atlantic by going along the

BOX 2.1	Types of Sea Ice

- Fast ice: ice that is attached to land
- Drift ice: offshore ice that moves around in response to currents and winds
- Multiyear ice (or old ice): sea ice that has been frozen for more than one year (up to five meters thick)
- First-year ice: ice that has frozen within the past year (usually one meter thick but can grow up to two meters, and not as dense as multiyear ice)
- New ice: seawater that has frozen but has not yet formed a solid pack of ice
- Pancake ice: small pieces of thin ice that float fairly close together on the sea surface
- Icebergs: lumps of freshwater ice that have broken off glaciers or ice shelves
- Polynyas: enclaves of open water locked within sea ice

eastern edge of Greenland. Transpolar Drift ice leaves the Arctic more rapidly than that of the Gyre, taking between one and two years. It is possible that in Greenland, warming will increase the number of icebergs that break off from glaciers and ice shelves, which would then flow into shipping lanes via the Transpolar Drift.

Ship captains and scientists have been recording the character and extent of sea ice for many years. Indigenous peoples of the Arctic have an even longer memory of the ice, and scientists are paying attention to that knowledge.[19] Old logs of ships that sailed in the region, measurements from scientific instruments, and now satellites and other kinds of remote sensing technologies provide very good information about the past and present ice. Ice-cover extent has been following a downward trajectory for the last four decades. The NSIDC reports results of the maximum extent of Arctic ice during the winter as estimated from satellite images. The year 2018 was the second lowest on record, with 2017 being the lowest maximum so far on record. The maximum extent came five days earlier (March 17, 2018) than the 1981–2010 median date of March 12, 2018.[20]

As well as covering a smaller area, the Arctic Ocean's ice cover is thinner. There are increasing leads (narrow cracks in the ice) and polynyas (larger and more permanent openings in the ice) that absorb more sunlight.[21] One Norwegian Polar Institute study reported algae blooms underneath snow-covered ice that might indicate an important ecological change due to warming. The algae consumed most of the available carbon. The blooms could alter the flow of biological carbon in the Arctic.[22] This means less carbon available to other plants, but blooms also absorb carbon dioxide from the ocean.

Glaciers and Ice Sheets

Ice sheets, ice caps, and glaciers are land-based forms of ice. Ice sheets cover a very large area of land: a minimum of fifty thousand square miles. They exist today only in Greenland and Antarctica. Ice caps are much smaller. Both produce glaciers that carve their way through the landscape until they melt, feeding rivers or flowing directly into the sea. Glaciers nearly everywhere in the world are in retreat due to warming.

Greenland's ice sheet covers 656,000 square miles. The ice sheet flows from the center outward through glaciers. Until recently, scientists monitored calving of ice from the glaciers, and evidence suggested the loss of ice through the glaciers was roughly equal to loss due to variations in snowfall and surface melt.

But the balance tipped dramatically between 2011 and 2014, when satellite data and modeling suggested that 70% of the annual 269 billion tons of snow and ice shed by Greenland was lost through surface melt, not calving. The accelerating surface melt has doubled Greenland's contribution to global sea level rise since 1992–2011, to 0.74 mm per year.[23]

Iceland has ice caps, which are much smaller versions of an ice sheet. Ice caps cover about 11 percent of its surface and include Vatnajökull, the largest ice cap in Europe. Vatnajökull is melting but will likely be around for at least another five hundred years, though smaller glaciers are at imminent risk.[24] All of Canada's ice caps are receding, as are those in Russia and Norway's Svalbard Islands. Melting of the ice sheets and ice caps will contribute substantially to sea-level rise. Were the Greenland ice sheet to melt entirely, global sea levels would rise twenty-four feet (seven meters).[25]

The speed and mechanics of ice melt are major topics of scientific research. White snow and ice reflect the sun's heat much more effectively than darker surfaces (the albedo effect). At present three different processes are reducing the albedo effect by causing the ice sheet to absorb more heat. First, there are supraglacial lakes that form on top of the ice as it melts. Supraglacial lakes, being darker, absorb the sun's heat more than white ice, increasing the rate of melting.[26] The second is "black" pollution, caused by incomplete combustion of fuels that darkens the surface, reducing the albedo effect.[27] In chapter 10, we will see how the Arctic Council is attempting to address this problem. The third process is bloom of algae and bacteria that grow in crevices and holes in the ice and, by being darker, permit more ice melt and hence widen the cracks, creating a feedback loop.

Arctic Warming and Ocean Currents

One of the big uncertainties for climate science is what will happen to ocean currents as the Arctic changes. As noted earlier, one possibility is a change in the polar jet stream affecting the Gulf Stream. Another and much better understood relationship comes from the interaction of the various ocean waters. One of the ways currents form is through changes in density. Heat and salinity affect density, and thus there is a thermohaline conveyor in the ocean ("thermo-," heat; "haline," salty).[28] As they meet waters in the Atlantic, the sinking Arctic waters push up the warmer, saltier waters, creating currents. This is how the Gulf Stream forms. If larger quantities of Arctic Ocean waters flow into the Atlantic, it is possible the thermohaline conveyor will slow or weaken. In that case, there might be a drop in temperatures in parts of Europe. How that would balance with increasingly warm Atlantic waters to the south of the Arctic Ocean remains unclear.

Biodiversity in the Arctic

The Arctic has relatively low biodiversity, meaning fewer types of animals and plants than in warmer regions.[29] The Arctic Council's Conservation of Arctic Flora and Fauna Working Group (CAFF) reports that there are more than twenty-one thousand species of plants, animals, and fungi.[30] Due to the environment, many of the species have a very limited geographical scope.[31] The Arctic and Subarctic contain 50 percent of the world's wetlands, a crucial habitat for animals and plants as well as for moderating the effects of flooding.[32]

The Barents, Norwegian, and Bering Seas are important habitats for some species of fish. Fish are believed to be uncommon under the Arctic Ocean ice. A 2012 study, however, discovered billions of juvenile Arctic cod under the ice of the central Arctic Ocean.[33] Fish are also moving northward from their habitats in the south, presumably to find cooler water and food. Warming may increase phytoplankton availability, the resource at the bottom of the food web. There have been booms of them off Greenland, apparently due to the release of iron from the melt of glaciers.[34]

As the ice changes, the Arctic becomes a different place for the creatures, plants, and humans that call it home. Increasingly, polar bears have to swim longer distances to find food, as they need sea ice and land-based ice shelves from which to hunt seal. In recent years near Svalbard, the bears have taken to eating bird eggs. These do not provide the fat calories of the seals, so while the bears might survive, they might not thrive. Polar bears turn to alternative sources if seal is in short supply, so one consequence might be reduced bird populations.[35]

Perhaps some Arctic species will not survive the changes, but many will. Some species will move further north or adapt to changed circumstances. There are already new species in the Arctic, and more species may arrive, with mixed effects on native species. Some species may have genes that will activate or change to help them cope with the new environment. For example, the Turkic-speaking Yakuts of Russia's Siberian Arctic came from central Asia. They and their horses moved north to escape the Mongols. In just eight hundred years, through Yakutsian breeding and living in the Arctic, the horses got smaller and hairier and their blood developed a substance that acts like a kind of antifreeze.[36]

Climate change in the Arctic has in the past been driven by movements of continents and long cycles of the earth's continuous journey around the sun. This time, however, climate change has a strong human cause: it is not a purely natural oscillation. This creates the uncertainty that comes from living in the midst of a global event where one cannot calculate precise impacts based on historic records. There is no uncertainty, however, that the climate is changing and generating wide environmental consequences and that human activity is a significant source of these changes.[37]

SETTLEMENT OF THE ARCTIC

Eurasia

Most people, if they think of the history of the Arctic at all, think of the "great age of Arctic exploration" from roughly the mid-1500s into the twentieth century. The greatest explorers of the Arctic, however, came tens of thousands of years before the flurry of North American activity by Europeans in the Age of Discovery. In Asiatic Siberia, tools embedded in wooly mammoths that date back forty-five thousand years have been found at 72° N.[38] Extended tool sets at Marmontova Kurta in European Siberia date to 40,000 BCE.[39]

The ice started to recede about 23,000 years ago, and clear evidence of human occupation comes in at 11,700 years ago. The earliest discovered stone tools in Scandinavia are different from those of the Sami, but more genetic research is needed to clarify the relationship between the earliest arrival and the somewhat later arrival of the Sami.[40] Some scholars say the ancestors of today's Sami people migrated northwest from the Ural Mountains and southern Russia about 11,000 years ago and moved to new areas as they became available, while others put it at 5,000 to 8,000 years ago.[41]

Today, the Sami homelands stretch from the Kola Peninsula of Russia through Finland, Sweden, and Norway. The Sami originally settled across a much larger area but were squeezed further north by later groups of settlers.[42] Linguistic and archeological evidence indicates the Sami lived from the northern end of the Baltic Sea's Gulf of Bothnia to the Far North. Depending on whether the climate was cooling or warming, they moved around and engaged in seal hunting, fishing, periods of agriculture, and reindeer herding. The Sami became expert at transportation technologies in snow and ice conditions and were early metalworkers.[43] Finns, who are not genetically related to the Sami, arrived in the Baltic from the Volga River about three thousand years ago and settled the coasts of the Gulf of Finland and Gulf of Bothnia.

Germanic tribes migrating north and east, perhaps from lands under what is now the North Sea, were ancestors of Scandinavians. In Sweden, "the mtDNA of everything from voles to bears shows these two groups [Sami and Germanic tribes] met up about halfway down in Sweden, or at about latitude 66°N."[44] Thus there was an extended period when the Sami and early Scandinavians lived near each other without either destroying or assimilating the other. They traded and shared ideas. Like Sweden, eastern and southern Norway were settled by people from southwest Europe, primarily from Germanic tribes, while the northern and Atlantic borders of today's Norway were populated by people from eastern Europe.[45] Map 2.3 below provides a graphic of language groups

Map 2.3   Language Groups in the Arctic

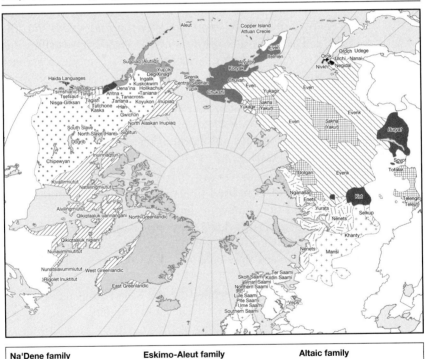

Na'Dene family
- Athabaskan branch
- Eyak branch
- Tlingit branch
- Haida branch

Indo-European family
- Germanic branch

Eskimo-Aleut family
- Inuit group of Eskimo branch
- Yupik group of Eskimo branch
- Aleut group

Uralic-Yukagiran family
- Finno-Ugric branch
- Samodic branch
- Yukagiran branch

Altaic family
- Turkic branch
- Mongolic branch
- Tunguso-Manchurian branch
- Chukotko-Kamchatkan family
- Ket (isolated language)
- Nivkh (isolated language)
- Tsimshianic (isolated language)

Source: CAFF, *Arctic Biodiversity Assessment* (Akureyri, Iceland: Arctic Council, 2013), 658, figure 20.5.

of today's indigenous peoples of the Arctic.[46] As the languages suggest, they came from many places in Eurasia.

Migrations to North America

From Siberia, some braved the Bering land bridge, now known as Beringia, and ultimately colonized all of the Americas from the shores of the Arctic Ocean to Tierra del Fuego at the tip of South America. They sailed the frigid waters and hunted Arctic lands for millennia, living and thriving in the region.[47] Artistic and religious traditions still exude the depth and power of the people and their lands.

Based on DNA evidence, it is now believed that there were perhaps three pulses of migration across the Bering land bridge between Siberia and Alaska.[48] Recent DNA work on an Alaskan archeological site revealed that a distinct group of people arrived about twenty-five thousand years ago.[49] These first arrivals differ from the much later migration of the Paleo-Eskimo culture.[50] The Paleo-Eskimo (sometimes called pre-Dorset) arrived in Alaska about 4,000 BCE and made their way to Greenland about five hundred years later. These people hunted on land and on water. They also lived farther south, in the transition zone between tundra and boreal forest in the Hudson Bay.[51] The Paleo-Eskimo are distinguishable from the later Dorset people and even later Thule people. Genetic evidence shows the Dorset were related to the Paleo-Eskimo pulse of migration and not to the Thule. The Dorset had a tool set mostly suitable for shore fishing and hunting marine animals like seal from the ice. Earlier Paleo-Eskimo cultures used bows and arrows, but the Dorset either did not use these or gave them up. Their art is exquisite and, according to Inuit oral tradition, they were known for their exceptional skill in spiritual matters.[52]

Around 1,000–900 CE the Thule culture arrived from Siberia. The Thule brought sophisticated technology and could hunt whale from boats. They had compound bows and other innovations that distinguished them from the Dorset. The Dorset disappeared from the Arctic about 1,000 CE, probably due to a warming Arctic that changed their capacity to find food. The Thule are the ancestors of today's Inuit.[53]

Linguistic analysis suggests clear ties between Siberian peoples and North America as well as the link Beringia provided between the two. One study looked at the similarity of words between the Na-Dene family of languages (Athabaskan) and the Ket indigenous people of the Russian Arctic. It showed a tie to the Yeneseian language family found outside of the Arctic in central Siberia.[54]

Migrations within what is now Russia were every bit as complex and puzzling as the move to North America but were less well studied.[55]

As with Beringia, Russian Arctic lands were once more expansive when ice sheets caused ocean levels to drop; thus, some archeological evidence is underwater. Genetic analyses show considerable movement—for example, the Khanty and the Mansi moved from west of the Urals eastward to the Ob.[56]

Economic Life

For roughly 98 percent of human history, subsistence economies have been the human way of life. People moved around in small groups in connection with the seasons and the animals. Arctic economies were self-sustaining: each community saw to its own needs. Great hunters who could provide for a community and for extended kin had great prestige, and giving gifts was full of social significance. Social and material technologies then, as now, allowed peoples to thrive in the challenging climates and provided aesthetic and spiritual satisfaction.

There were trade fairs where different communities could meet, exchange goods and information, and renew or create new ties that facilitated the well-being of families and villages. Coastal Inuit would trade with inland Inuit for ivory, skins, and wood. Trade routes were quite extensive, from Greenland to Alaska, and there were regular Inuit markets that drew participation from large areas.[57]

People obtained food and supplies according to the local landscape and available resources. They understood plant life cycles, when the different parts could be used and how the plants were related to others growing nearby. Fauna was big (muskox, caribou, seals, walrus, and whales), so the hunters and their kin could get a lot of food in relatively short order. The animals tended to move in herds according to regular migration patterns; thus, people planned (and still plan) hunting trips around established animal behavior and breeding patterns to ensure the sustainability of the take.

The Yamal-Nenets people of Siberia are an Arctic indigenous people who herd reindeer. They still take advantage of the different kinds of landscapes. A slight rise of even a few yards (meters) or less helps them see where to move the reindeer, and they respond to the availability of good grazing, as they have for millennia. Water appears in different forms and this, too, shapes how people live(d) on the land. Today, Arctic landscapes are increasingly fractured by industry, green energy installations like windmills, or environmental change, which can pose challenges to herders and other traditional users.[58] However, industrial developments also bring new opportunities: access to new markets for traditional goods, new vocational opportunities, and new resources (see chapter 5).

Viking Exploration

Viking expansion began around 800 CE. The Vikings came from what are now Norway, Sweden, and Denmark. They had settled agriculture and traded extensively with the Sami. Indeed, trade with the Vikings in Sami cold weather clothing and sailing technologies aided Viking navigation when they raided down Russian rivers.[59] The Vikings expanded in all directions. They went as far as the Mediterranean, the Black Sea, and the Caspian Sea. They established more enduring trade relations along the way and rented themselves out as professional fighters. The hird, the personal bodyguard for the Byzantine emperor, was composed of Vikings.

The beginnings of Denmark and Norway occurred during the Viking period, specifically during the Jelling dynasty in the late ninth and early tenth centuries CE.[60] Vikings also sailed west from the emerging Norwegian state forming around Harald Fairhair (850–932 CE). The Vikings who left and ultimately settled Iceland were likely disgruntled about Fairhair's taxation policies. There is evidence of Irish monks in Iceland before the arrival of the Vikings, but they did not persist after Viking settlement.[61] From Iceland, the Vikings continued westward to Greenland and established villages in the south and west, but these colonies disappeared in the fifteenth century. At about the same time, perhaps slightly later, Inuit explorer-colonizers arrived and settled the west coast of Greenland, where they continue to live today. The Vikings also landed on the shores of subarctic Labrador in what they called Vinland, where they caught fish, made some metal objects, and traded goods with indigenous peoples. The settlement was used for, at most, a few years.[62] At times, Vikings, Inuit, and likely other European and North American peoples traded with each other.[63]

The Pomors of Russia were nearly as adventurous as the Vikings at sea. They traded with people far to the north and probably discovered Novaya Zemlya and Svalbard. They lived on the White Sea, around the Arkhangelsk area. They originally came from Novgorod, one of the leading principalities in Russia. Rather than fight, the Pomors traded with indigenous peoples and took their sturdy ships into the Baltic Sea, Scandinavia, and along the coast of Siberia from at least 1200 CE. Pomor explorations encouraged Novgorod to press its rule into Sami lands, where the city came into contact with Scandinavians from Norway and Sweden. Conflict between Novgorod, Sweden, and Norway eventually led to the Treaty of Nöteborg (1323), between Novgorod and Sweden, and the Treaty of Novgorod (1326) with Norway. These agreements created a buffer zone where both respective entities could operate in Sami lands. The results for the Sami were double and even triple taxation from the political entities to the south.[64]

THE RISE OF THE SOVEREIGN EUROPEAN ARCTIC STATES AND COLONIZATION OF THE ARCTIC

Early Formation of the Arctic States of Europe

We have already discussed the Viking origins of Iceland. Denmark, Norway, and Sweden emerged in 900–1200 CE, with Denmark the most powerful at first. When they were Christianized between 965 CE and the early eleventh century, they kept their own laws and did not follow canon law. This cultural-legal fact allowed them to keep older institutions of shared decision making between the classes, and it reduced the influence of the Church. At the same time, Scandinavian townsfolk and landed aristocrats could participate in the larger European culture, including the Renaissance.

Known today for its peacekeeping efforts, Nobel Prize, and policies of neutrality, the early history of Scandinavia involved much warfare. In search of peace, Queen Margaret I of Denmark proposed and set up the Kalmar Union between Denmark, Sweden, and Norway—including Norway's dependencies of Iceland and Greenland. The union of the three lasted, mostly peacefully, from 1397 to 1523. This early effort at union prompted discussion of making a single Scandinavian state, a topic that surfaces periodically in Scandinavia. Sweden left the Union in 1523. Denmark and Norway stayed united at that point, but Iceland was transferred to Danish control. From the 1200s to the 1700s, Sweden governed much of coastal Finland, which also received strong German influences from the Hanseatic League during the medieval period.

Two hundred years of war followed the end of the Kalmar Union. The violence that ensued between Norway, Denmark, and Sweden was so extreme that peasants at the borders between Sweden and Denmark made their own peace agreements to limit the warfare.[65] They were not wealthy kingdoms, and the kings had to make deals with the nobility or turn to their old social institutions to raise taxes and conscripts. Rather like King John of England, the king of Denmark signed the *Handbinding* (a document similar to England's Magna Carta), agreeing with his nobles to limit his own authority. After the nobility in Denmark/Norway were soundly defeated by Sweden in 1660, the merchants of Copenhagen and the king consolidated the king's power in the Scandinavian version of absolutism. Thus, the landed elite lost power to the trading cities and the king.

Russia was largely on the distant periphery of western Europe; it was not quite European in culture, due to its adoption of Orthodox Christianity in 987.[66] Thus, Russian city-states were oriented to Constantinople, capital of the Eastern Roman Empire and later Byzantine Empire. The Orthodox Church used Greek rather than the Latin of the Catholic Church in Rome and developed the Cyrillic scripts used in Russia and some southern Slavic states today. The church in Constantinople was conservative in the sense that it was not as open to new ideas as in the West and it was very closely tied to the emperor.

Its political history also set Russia apart from the rest of Europe, due to its experience as a longtime tributary state to the Mongol Empire. The Mongols arrived in Russia in a series of invasions starting in 1223. Influenced by Imperial China, they built a system of suzerainty, where conquered polities paid tribute to the Mongols and did not have control over foreign policy but did have some internal autonomy. The Mongols set up systems for a census and taxed the lands based on the census, using local elites. Novgorod and Moscow executed these tasks, with Moscow proving so reliable that eventually it was paid to handle the tasks for all of the Russian lands of the Mongolian Empire, which led to Moscow dominating the other Russian cities. The Mongols supported and protected the Russian Orthodox Church as well.

When Russia did begin to interact more with European polities to the west, different diplomatic cultures made contact difficult. In this way Russia was oriented in faith (and trade) toward Constantinople but in politics and diplomacy toward the Mongolian capital in Saray to the east. It had diplomatic practices more akin to those to the east than to European powers like France or Austria. For example, only in the 1660s could foreign ambassadors "walk the streets of Moscow alone."[67] Russia did not have much contact with western Europe except Scandinavia and the Baltic Sea. There was nearly constant warfare from the twelfth century to the early nineteenth century between Sweden and Russia for control of the Baltic.

Constantinople fell to the Ottoman Turks in 1453. Over the next two centuries the Ottoman Empire expanded from Asia to Europe and to North Africa. Turks ruled the Crimea, Georgia, and the Balkans. Warfare between Russia and the Turks was common. At roughly the same time as the rise of the Ottomans, the Mongol Empire was weakening, and Russia pushed its authority eastward into central Asia as Mongolian authority collapsed.[68] Between 1670 and 1878 Russia turned to the south, fought the Ottoman Turks, and expanded its empire, gaining the Crimea and eventually the right to have its navy on the Black Sea.

The cultural differences deriving from Russia's orientation to Byzantium kept the country from full participation in European culture, economics, and technology. The Orthodox Church did not generally encourage science.[69] Elites were more likely to read and write Greek or their own Cyrillic script. There was almost no instruction available in Latin, so it was difficult for educated Russians to participate in the intellectual life of Western Europe. No science was taught in Russia until the seventeenth century. The first university, in Peter the Great's new city of St. Petersburg, was founded in 1724. Russian culture, therefore, received relatively limited influences from ideas in Western Europe.

The economies of medieval Norway and Sweden included mines, forestry, agriculture, and fishing. There were small private manufactures and some peasant-led trade. Denmark had fishing and excellent pastures for dairy production. The kings, allied with merchants rather than the aristocracy, creating a diversified economy with a sphere for civil society. The tsar of Russia, in contrast, centralized authority over all of society. There was only a tiny merchant class, little industry, and a mass of poor peasants. Russian manufactures were owned or directed by the state, as was trade. In stark contrast to Scandinavia, there were few signs of a civil society independent of the state.[70]

Rise of the Modern System of States

The Wars of Religion between Catholicism and Protestantism, especially the Thirty Years' War (1618–1648) killed millions and were a great drain on finances of the participants. One of the treaties that ended the Wars of Religion, the Treaty of Westphalia (1648), established the principle that the religion of the ruler was the official religion of the state and that foreign rulers and religious institutions must not interfere with such internal affairs. It gave little protection to citizens who followed a religion that differed from their rulers. By tradition, though not necessarily in reality, the Treaty is seen as the basis of state sovereignty over territory, hence the common name for the modern state system as the Westphalian model.

The demands of the war encouraged some leaders to reform their states. Gustav II (Gustavus Adolphus) of Sweden (king from 1611 to 1632) incurred a large debt to other heads of states. He chose to modernize Sweden to save money to pay the debts while continuing to fight. He reformed government and economic systems in order to improve efficiency and tax collection. He also modernized and reformed Sweden's military so effectively that Sweden became a Great Power of its time, dealing military defeats to many other European powers. Sweden's government structure hinted at what the state could become. The state became more capable at home at raising taxes and more interested in using technology and science to build power and influence.[71]

The explosion of European influence in the New World and on Arctic peoples distant from national capitals developed from the intersection of ideas on destiny and progress and the constant warfare between the Europeans that changed technology and economies. States' and individuals' new social and technological inventions based on the control of nature generated an energy and capacity for action. Europe became modern. At the same time, the states of Europe slowly built a more extensive framework of international law in order to create peace, enhance trade—and justify their own territorial expansion.

Mapping the Arctic, Gaining Control

One aim in colonialism is to arrange relations with the local people so that rules flow to the local people and resources to the governors. Science, mapping, education, and economic rules all operated as a "culture of control."[72] The indigenous peoples of the Arctic, who were quite diverse in culture, art, religion, and technology, thus share a "common experience of colonialism," the consequences of which are still playing out.[73]

Science, often supported with government money, serves the quest for knowledge and for control. In the Arctic, science was used to consolidate imperial and colonial claims. The close connection between science, the state, and territorial acquisition can be seen partly through efforts to map the High North. After the fall of Constantinople, land-based European access to India and China was cut off. Ancient Greek commentary suggested the Arctic had an island at the North Pole that was surrounded by ocean. The allure of a quick sailing route to China via the Arctic grew and spurred expeditions for the Northwest Passage.

The science was driven by a number of concerns, just as it is today. States were in search of the Northwest or Northeast Passage, resources, revenues, and prestige. The scientists (and some of the leaders of the states) were seized to learn more about the world in all its variety. All the European expeditions included cutting-edge scientific instruments of the time on the ships and included scientists on the crews. Peter the Great sponsored the Great Northern Expedition of 1733–1742, led by Vitus Bering (the strait is named after him), a Dane. This expedition included explorers born in the Russian Empire whose names now dot the Arctic Map: Laptev Sea, Lomonosov Ridge, and so forth.

Colonization

The arrival of Europeans in the New World began a process of conquest and colonialization. European doctrines of international law treated these new lands as terra nullius (land belonging to no one, which could be claimed) and refused to recognize the existing communities and their own legal systems.[74] Colonial practices in the New World were driven by the need to justify and mark European control and rights to exploit specific territory.

Indigenous peoples around the Arctic had traditional territories with their own concepts of property rights. Property rights were often very complex. For example, different groups might be in the same area but have varying rights to water, fish, vegetation, and the like. Explorers from Europe arrived in areas long occupied by other peoples and planted flags and fence posts to signal "ownership." French explorer de La Pérouse visited Alaska in July 1786. He considered it "theft" when Tlingit (a subarctic people of Alaska) took some of the expedition's pots and clothes. The French, however, did not consider it theft when they freely used water and hunted and fished wherever they liked.[75]

Even earlier, in 1340s Sweden, Sami lands were listed as terra nullius because only a few people were there. The Swedish king opened the land to Scandinavians to own, though the Sami retained some rights to graze reindeer.[76] Smaller self-governing communities were overwhelmed by the military might of the modern states, and the control was then justified according to imported legal principles.

Encounters between indigenous peoples and European explorers sometimes ended in tragedy. For example, when Englishman Martin Frobisher went on the first of his three trips to discover the Northwest Passage in the sixteenth century, he traded with some Inuit in Baffin Island. Frobisher hoped some of the Inuit men could help him find the passage. He sent five of his men on an expedition with some Inuit men, but they did not return. Frobisher took an Inuk hostage, perhaps originally with a view to trading him for the return of his own men. Inuit oral history recounts taking care of the five men until they sailed away on a vessel they had constructed themselves. Meanwhile, Frobisher took the Inuk to England as an "exhibit," where the captive died shortly after arrival.[77] On Frobisher's second voyage, he attempted to recover the missing sailors but, having failed to do that, captured an Inuk man, woman, and baby and took them back to England. They also died soon after arrival.[78]

In what is now Canada, the Hudson Bay Company was chartered in 1670 in London and opened trading posts on the shores of James Bay and Hudson Bay to trade European goods for furs with the indigenous peoples.[79] The firm acquired other firms and also moved up rivers and expanded trade. Increasingly the large firms applied English law wherever they set up operations. Indigenous peoples had no part in deciding those laws. The Europeans brought rules about land ownership and uses that were in sharp contrast to traditional uses. Indigenous conceptions recognized rights to use a resource for a period of time rather than the European ideal of exclusive, monopoly-style ownership. Governments sent police and soldiers to enforce these newly declared rights. Efforts to Christianize indigenous peoples weakened their cultures.

Russia began to govern coastal Alaska in 1784 and even had a settlement north of San Francisco (Fort Ross) in what is now Northern California.[80] Furs were Russia's main interest in both places. In 1867 the United States bought Alaska from Russia.[81] The inhabitants, primarily indigenous, were not consulted about the sale.

Different ideas of risk led to European North American sentiments that the indigenous peoples were superstitious and backward. Indigenous observations and stories help people survive in and make sense of a risky world. Empirical experience helps to avoid significant risks based on living with natural hazards in the environment. European North Americans did not share the same risk calculus, due to lack of experience. On Commander Peary's first expedition to Greenland, he decided to camp on an island. His wife wrote in her diary, "Here, in the angle of the island and huge glacier . . . we pitched the tent, though not without protest from the natives, who said that the waves from an iceberg breaking off the glacier might smash the boat and swamp the camp."[82] Nothing happened that night, but anyone watching a calving event's effect on a powered and modern ship can easily see why people who traveled regularly in smaller, paddled craft were cautious.

In northern Europe, colonization had a different emphasis. In Scandinavia, colonization/marginalization of the Sami was about building Scandinavian identity.[83] The centuries of sharing ideas and technologies gave way to a more restrictive approach. The Scandinavians emphasized how they controlled nature through, for example, agriculture, and built complex states through law and war. The Sami became people who needed to be "civilized" and whose way of life was less important.[84]

In the 1500s, the tsars of Russia started demanding a tax, paid in furs and ivory, from many indigenous communities. (Novgorod had done this as well, earlier.) In the 1550s, as Russia engaged in taking lands to the east, Tsar Ivan IV sent Yermak (Ermak), a Cossack, to subdue Siberia militarily for both security reasons and to build empire. Moscow also sent priests, supported by law from Moscow, to convert peoples of the Arctic to Christianity. The priests destroyed local religious sites and built orthodox churches on traditional religious sites. Other officials imprisoned local shamans.[85]

For a brief time in the 1920s and very early 1930s, the new Soviet government celebrated diversity. It assigned specific territories to indigenous people, developed written languages for them if there were none, and published books in their languages. There was some self-government. However, like colonizers elsewhere, the Soviets categorized people by how "civilized" they were and tried to help the very poorest communities develop according to Soviet conceptions of development. At the same time, Russian-speakers were encouraged to go east, and they did so, thus further spreading Russian even as the government supported the local languages.

Having been exiled repeatedly as a young revolutionary, Stalin perfected the gulag system in the Russian North to keep criminals, political opponents, and other undesirables far from the centers of power. However, to Stalin, the North was not just a convenient prison camp far removed from political influence; it was also a source of vast natural resources that could be exploited using the gulag labor.[86]

As Stalin consolidated his hold on power after the death of Lenin, he made vast changes for Russia's many indigenous peoples. Indigenous children were sent away to school. Rapid inward migration of workers (not just prisoners) from other parts of Russia reduced most indigenous communities to minorities in their traditional lands.[87] The Arctic became more urban.[88] The collectivization of their traditional industries (fishing and herding) transformed indigenous peoples into employees. The collapse of the Soviet model in the 1990s and withdrawal of state subsidies and sale of state enterprises then brought joblessness and depopulation.[89]

All of the Arctic states with indigenous populations separated indigenous children from their families in efforts to assimilate them to the culture and language of the colonizer. There remain survivors who recall forced separation from their families and transfer to residential schools or foster families. The trauma is intergenerational because such people, having been removed from their own families at an early age, do not naturally absorb the experiences or skills to raise their own children in turn and must "learn" to parent.[90] Sometimes, whole communities were moved. In 1953, concerned that Canada needed proof of "effective occupation" of distant and largely unpopulated Arctic lands to preempt any potential claims from its giant southern neighbor, the Canadian government forcibly moved an entire community to a place they had never been and for which they were utterly unprepared to live. Canadian government scientists had discovered Inuit habitation from centuries past in a spot 1,500 miles away from the location of the existing community. Illogically, government officials assumed that the people would "know" how to survive there. The Inuit transported were hunters of forests of the Subarctic. They did not have the traditions, knowledge, or resources to live in the High Arctic. The new arrivals called the place *Qausuittuq*, "the place with no dawn." Many perished.[91]

Changing State Borders through War

The current Scandinavian/Russian state borders owe much to three major wars: the Napoleonic Wars and the two world wars of the twentieth century.[92] Soviet/Russian borders changed again dramatically at the end of the Cold War, when various republics of the Soviet Union became independent.

The Napoleonic Wars, 1803–1815

In the nineteenth century, Denmark/Norway was allied with Napoleon, while Sweden was on the winning side. Napoleon demanded Denmark join his empire and sent troops to the border, but the British demanded the Danish fleet. Eventually, the British attacked the fleet and Copenhagen. After that, the Danes had no choice but to join Napoleon. Under the Treaty of Kiel peace agreement (1814), Denmark lost territory to Prussia, and Sweden took Norway. Norway established its own constitution and enjoyed a high degree of self-government, including its own parliament. However, it would not be until 1905 that Norway would become fully independent, following a Norwegian plebiscite that voted strongly in favor of independence.[93]

During the Napoleonic period, Russia started a war with Sweden (1808–1809) and invaded Finland; Sweden was unable to hold the Russians off and Russia took Finland. At the peace negotiations for ending the Napoleonic War, Russia supported Sweden on Norway, and Sweden gave up any claims to Finland.[94] The tsar made it a self-governing grand duchy with the tsar as its grand duke. Within that relationship, Finland created some of its own political organs, including a parliament, elected on the basis of universal adult suffrage.[95]

World War I, 1914–1918

All of the Scandinavian countries except Finland were neutral in WWI, and this neutrality was respected. Russia was one of the Allies (or Entente Powers) fighting against the Central Powers. Finland's grand duchy status protected its men from conscription, but Finland was nevertheless deeply affected by events in Russia. The Russian Revolution of October 1917 ended the monarchy and brought Lenin to power.

In the chaos of the Russian Revolution, Finland declared its independence on November 15, 1917. Finland was deeply divided between the wealthy and a growing working class. Moreover, food, coal, and many other supplies came from Russia and were no longer flowing freely. Economic pressures were high. A bloody civil war broke out. On April 13, 1918, just over a month after Lenin's separate peace agreement with Germany, German forces occupied Helsinki. The invasion and wider control of the Baltic saved the city from an even worse level of violence than had befallen the Finnish cities of Turku and Tampere.[96] The civil war ended in 1920 with agreements to protect worker rights.

World War II, 1939–1945

The Nordic countries again sought to stay neutral in WWII, but only Sweden succeeded, through a degree of cooperation with Germany. German industry was deeply dependent on northern Swedish iron ore exported via the northern Norwegian port of Narvik. The Allies sought to intercept shipping along the Norwegian coast, leading to German invasion and occupation of Denmark (as a stepping-stone) and Norway. The Danish government chose to cooperate with German occupation to protect Danish society and democracy to the greatest possible extent. Norway, assisted by Britain, France, and free Poland, fought on but was defeated. The Norwegian king and government were forced into exile and replaced by a Norwegian Nazi puppet regime led by Vidkun Quisling.

The Faroe Islands and Iceland were quickly occupied by Britain for their key strategic importance in the North Atlantic (and the Danish ambassador in Iceland supported this action rather than comply with instructions from Copenhagen). The United States became the protector of Greenland and Iceland from 1941. Iceland (which had negotiated self-rule in 1904 and in 1918 obtained its sovereignty in a union with the Kingdom of Denmark under a shared monarch) declared its complete independence from the Kingdom of Denmark in 1944 in accordance with the 1918 union treaty. (Denmark, under occupation, was in no position to argue.) Denmark and Norway were liberated at the defeat of Germany.

The Nazi-Soviet mutual nonaggression pact of 1935 put Finland in the Soviet sphere of influence. The Soviets took advantage of this understanding and launched the Winter War (1939–1940) on November 30, 1939, against Finland. The Finns put up a vigorous defense but conceded to Soviet territorial demands on March 13, 1940. The democracies of Europe, the United States, and Canada did next to nothing to stop the aggression.

With the German invasion of the USSR in June 1941, the situation changed for Finland. Finland entered WWII as a cobelligerent with Germany (it never made a formal alliance with Germany) in what is known as the Continuation War (1941–1945). Finland hoped to regain some of the lands it lost to the USSR by way of the alliance but was soon occupied by the Germans. The Germans, in addition to the broad front they opened on the USSR's western borders, also attacked much farther north to take the Kola Peninsula. Germany launched the attack from two fronts: Norway's Finnmark region and Finnish Lapland. Later in the war, in anticipation of German defeat, Finland signed an armistice agreement with the USSR (September 19, 1944) and a peace treaty with the Allies (1947).[97] The agreement with the USSR included the expulsion of German forces from Lapland, and Soviet forces helped liberate Finland. Retreating German forces burned down homes and infrastructure in Lapland. The Finnish-Soviet peace imposed costly reparations on Finland, the loss of access to the Arctic Ocean, and a Soviet military base near Helsinki. Finland's complex relationship and vulnerable border with the USSR led to foreign policy that avoided aggravating the Soviets, even as it created a strong democracy based on a free and open civil society and built a military disproportionately large for a country of its size.

Hot War to Cold War

In 1949, Denmark, Iceland, and Norway became founding members of the North Atlantic Treaty Organization (NATO). Denmark joined the European Union in 1973, followed by Sweden and Finland in 1995. Norway and Iceland remain outside the EU but are members of the European Economic Area within the European Free Trade Association. All the aforementioned Nordic countries except Finland participated in the US Marshall Plan in order to rebuild themselves and resist the spread of communism after WWII. The Plan was executed through the Organization for European Economic Cooperation, established in 1948. This organization was expanded in 1960 with the inclusion of Canada and the United States and became today's Organization of Economic Cooperation and Development (OECD).

International Cooperation

During the Cold War, the Arctic was a frontier with nuclear weapons lined up and pointed across the Arctic Ocean between the Soviet Union and North America. The Distant Early Warning (DEW) line of radar stations ran from the American Aleutian Islands, through Alaska and northern Canada, with additional radar stations in Greenland and Iceland as a first defense against a trans-Arctic Soviet attack (see chapter 4).

It was the indigenous leaders in the Arctic who led cooperation across the Cold War divide, while the Arctic states pointed bombers and missiles at each other. The Nordic Sami Council had been established in 1956 to promote the rights of Sami living in their three Nordic states. Inuit activism became internationalized in the 1970s with increasing recognition of the Inuit as a single people living in four states. In 1973 Inuit and Sami representatives met in Copenhagen, though without representatives from the Soviet Union. The Inuit Circumpolar Conference (later Council) (ICC) was formed in 1977 in Barrow, and at its first meeting, Alaskan, Canadian, and Greenlandic representatives attended. Their relatives from the Soviet Union could not.[98]

The first sign of state-to-state cooperation across the Iron Curtain was the Polar Bear Treaty in 1973, which has been amended over the decades and includes management agreements between US and Canadian indigenous governments.[99] A major policy window between the United States and the USSR opened with the 1986 meeting between US president Ronald Reagan and Soviet president Mikhail Gorbachev in Reykjavík. The summit was aimed at arms reduction, including nuclear disarmament. Although no agreement was reached, the talks promoted a greater understanding of each other's positions and pointed to areas of future cooperation and compromise.

A year later Gorbachev channeled cooperative momentum toward the Arctic in his famous speech at Murmansk in 1987. Gorbachev expressed concern about the "immense potential of nuclear destruction" in the Arctic and called for the Arctic to "become a zone of peace." He proposed six areas for cooperation to increase security in the Arctic—and, as important, trust between the superpowers. They were (1) a nuclear-free zone in northern Europe; (2) the reduction or elimination of naval and air-force activity in the European Arctic waters; (3) resource development in the Arctic—in particular, oil and gas; (4) scientific and social science research; (5) environmental protection; and (6) the development of the Northern Sea Route.[100]

Finland seized on Gorbachev's political opening and in 1989 invited representatives from each Arctic state and from three organizations representing indigenous people to Rovaniemi, the capital of Finnish Lapland, as part of what would become known as the Rovaniemi Process.[101] Of the six areas Gorbachev had nominated, the most promising and least contentious—but undoubtedly urgent—was environmental protection. Environment was the focus of the first Rovaniemi meeting.

In 1988 Mary Simon, a Canadian Inuk, led a delegation of North American Inuit through Siberia and Chukotka, where Inuit families, separated by the Cold War, were reunited. Reaching Moscow, Simon met with Gorbachev, who followed up his Murmansk words with action by permitting the Soviet/Russian Inuit to take part in cross-border cooperation. At the 1989 Sisimiut meeting of the ICC, Soviet indigenous representatives took part for the first time.[102]

CONCLUSIONS

It is fitting to end this chapter with the success of Inuit activists to reunite families across the Cold War divide. States rose to their preeminent place in world affairs through competition in war, technology, economic innovation, and the power of ideas. In the process, the modern state marginalized indigenous people. Warming and pollution caused by economic activity is changing life in the Arctic. The long history of indigenous peoples continues in the North, intertwined with the histories of states and international forums, creating a distinct approach to governance that will be explored in depth in the following chapter.

FURTHER READING

"Arctic Climate Impact Assessment." Accessed April 14, 2017. http://www.acia
.uaf.edu.

Asch, Michael. *Aboriginal and Treaty Rights in Canada: Essays on Law, Equality and Respect for Difference.* Vancouver: University of Øbia Press, 1997.

BBC One. *Frozen Planet* [documentary television series]. London: BBC, 2011.

Broadbent, Noel, and Jan Storå. *Lapps and Labyrinths: Saami Prehistory, Colonization and Cultural Resilience.* Washington, DC: National Museum of Natural History, 2010.

Cortzen, Jan. *Den grønlandske drøm: Polar-Paradiset—et folk på kant med fremtiden* [The Greenland dream: Polar paradise—a people on the verge of the future]. Nuuk, Greenland: Mediehuset Sermitsiaq AG, 2010.

Friedberg, Louise, dir. *Eksperimentet* [The Experiment]. 2010.

Gérin-Lajoie, José, Alain Cuerrier, and Laura Siegwart Collier. *"The Caribou Taste Different Now": Inuit Elders Observe Climate Change.* Iqaluit, Canada: Nunavut Arctic College, 2016.

Grant, Shelagh D. "Arctic Governance and the Relevance of History." In *Governing the North American Arctic: Sovereignty, Security and Institutions,* edited by Dawn Alexandrea Berry, Nigel Bowles, and Halbert Jones, 29–50. Basingstoke, UK: Palgrave Macmillan, 2016.

Harper, Kenn. *Minik: The New York Eskimo: An Arctic Explorer, a Museum, and the Betrayal of the Inuit People.* Hanover, NH: Steerforth Press, 2017.

Haycox, Stephen. *Frigid Embrace: Politics, Economics, and Environment in Alaska.* Corvallis: Oregon State University Press, 2002.

Hønneland, Geir. "Russian Identity between North and West." In *Russia and the Arctic: Environment, Identity and Foreign Policy.* London: I. B. Taurus, 2016.

Kotlyakov, V. M., A. A. Velichko, and S. A. Vasil'ev, eds. *Human Colonization of the Arctic: The Interaction between Early Migration and the Paleoenvironment.* London: Academic Press, 2017.

Krupnik, Igor, and Dyanna Jolly, eds. *The Earth Is Faster Now: Indigenous Observations of Arctic Environmental Change.* Fairbanks, AK: Arctic Research Consortium of the United States, 2002.

Palosaari, Teemu, and Nina Tynkkynen. "Arctic Securitization and Climate Change." In *Handbook of Politics in the Arctic*, edited by Leif Christian Jensen and Geir Hønneland. Cheltenham, UK: Edward Elgar, 2015.

Rasmussen, Knud. *Myter og Sagn fra Grønland* [Myths and Stories from Greenland]. Copenhagen: Sesam, 1998.

Rothwell, Donald. *The Polar Regions and the Development of International Law.* Cambridge: Cambridge University Press, 1996.

The Sea Ice Is Our Highway. Ottawa: Inuit Circumpolar Council–Canada, 2008.

Sejersen, Frank. *Rethinking Greenland and the Arctic in the Era of Climate Change.* Abingdon: Earthscan, 2015.

Working Group II. "Polar Regions." Chapter 28 of *Climate Change 2014: Impacts, Adaptation, and Vulnerability.* IPCC 5th Assessment Report. http://www.ipcc.ch/report/ar5/wg2/.

Young, T. Kue et al., eds. *Circumpolar Health Atlas.* Toronto: University of Toronto Press, 2012.

ZumBrunnen, Craig. "Climate Change in the Russian North: Threats Real and Potential." In *Russia and the North*, edited by Elana Wilson Rowe. Ottawa: University of Ottawa Press, 2009.

3

Arctic Players

THIS CHAPTER EXAMINES the institutional structures in which people make choices about how the Arctic should be governed. "Players" or "actors" in Arctic affairs come in many varieties and operate at different scales, and not all have the Arctic as their principal focus. As we saw in chapter 1, states are central actors, but an exclusive focus on states' behavior is insufficient to give a full picture of contemporary governance in the Arctic or anywhere else. Liberal emphasis on institutional cooperation is informative for understanding how the Arctic states mutually support each other, especially through the Arctic Council. The design of the Arctic Council allows the eight Arctic states (as full members of the Council) to constrain in some respects non-Arctic states. At the same time, it creates a unique space for indigenous peoples' organizations.[1] Indigenous peoples—nations in their own right but without statehood—have achieved varying degrees of self-government in the Arctic within their states and have a voice at the Arctic Council at a level unprecedented in any other international forum.

Both indigenous and nonindigenous persons vote for governments and make personal decisions that lead, collectively, to change—for example, out- or in-migration, urbanization, education, and employment. Nongovernmental organizations (NGOs) have a strong Arctic presence, including major international environmental NGOs with eye-catching (and lucrative) Arctic campaigns (see section below on nongovernmental organizations). These operate in different ways: some work primarily to influence national governments, while others build transnational networks to advance their aims, and still others go for direct, highly visual challenges to the power of states. Indigenous peoples have also created organizations (technically NGOs) to represent their interests. Industries influence national and international affairs, for example, by seconding their experts to serve on international standards committees and monitoring compliance with international trade agreements.[2] Researchers contribute to the shaping of Arctic affairs through their decisions about what to research, their findings, and their policy recommendations.

THE INDIGENOUS IN THE ARCTIC

Around four million people live in the Arctic according to the most common definitions.[3] The proportion of indigenous peoples varies between states, and precise numbers are elusive as not all groups and individuals who self-identify as indigenous are recognized as such (see table 3.1). The indigenous peoples live within the borders of eight Arctic states, but their homelands do not neatly correspond with the boundaries of these modern states. Russia recognizes forty small-numbered indigenous peoples in the Arctic region (the Russian North, Siberia, and the Far East) as well as another seven in other parts of Russia.[4] Under Russian law, the "small numbers" criterion means that indigenous peoples with more than fifty thousand members are not recognized.[5]

ARCTIC STATES

The Arctic states range from the very small Iceland to the Great Powers of the United States and Russia (see table 3.2). Both of the latter hold enormous political, economic, military, and cultural influence regionally and globally. Russia and the United States are two of the veto-wielding, permanent members of the UN Security Council. Canada is a middle-sized power, and the five Nordic states are usually classed as small states although they vary from populations of 350,000 (Iceland) to nearly ten million (Sweden). No state has its capital city above the Arctic Circle; Reykjavík is the closest but is still 168 miles away. Even Nuuk, the capital of Greenland, is located below 66° N, 165 miles from the Arctic Circle. While the state always has a crucial role in governing its Arctic regions, the Arctic region may be rather low in the state's priorities. In Russia, the Arctic is central to economy, hard security, and identity. In contrast, the Arctic is of relatively low priority in Sweden and the United States.

Table 3.1   Indigenous Peoples in the Arctic

People(s)	Approximate Population	Representation at Arctic Council	Principal Homelands
Inuit (Eskimo)	150,000	Inuit Circumpolar Council	Chukchi Peninsula (Russia), Northern Alaska, Northern Canada, and Greenland (Denmark)
Sami (Lapp)	80,000–100,000	Sami Council	Lapland (Northern Norway, Sweden, Finland, and the Kola Peninsula, Russia)
Athabaskan (Dene)	32,000	Arctic Athabaskan Council	Interior and Southern Alaska, Oregon, California, and the Southwest (United States); and Yukon, Alberta, British Columbia, Manitoba, and Saskatchewan (Canada)
Gwich'in (subgroup of Athabaskan)	9,000	Gwich'in Council International	Interior Northern Alaska (United States), Yukon and Northwest Territories (Canada)
Aleutian Islanders	7,000	Aleut International Association	Aleutian Islands (Russia and United States)
Forty small-numbered peoples, including the Aleutian, Evenki, Inuit, Kerek, Nenet, and Sami	270,000	Russian Association of Indigenous Peoples of the North (RAIPON)	Throughout the Russian North
Yakuts*	500,000	N/A	Sakha Republic (Russia)
Komi*	550,000	N/A	Komi Republic, Perm Krai, Nenets Autonomous Okrug, Arkhangelsk Oblast, and Murmansk Oblast (Russia)
Karelian**	70,000	N/A	Karelian Republic (Russia) and Eastern Finland

*Not recognized as indigenous by Russia
**Not recognized as indigenous by Russia or Finland

Table 3.2 Arctic States

	Population	Arctic Population	Arctic Indigenous Peoples	Total Territory (km²/mi²)	Total Arctic Territory (km²/mi²)	Arctic Regions	National GDP (raw, USD, 2016)	Arctic GRP (PPP, USD, 2010)*
United States	323.0m	740,000	Inuit, Athabaskan, Aleutian	9,857,306/3,805,927	1,717,856/663,268	Alaska	18.562bn	47.713bn
Canada	36.0m	110,000	Inuit, Athabaskan	9,984,670/3,855,103	3,921,739/1,514,192	Yukon, Northwest Territories, Nunavut, Nunavik, Nunatsiavut	1.532bn	07.269bn
Kingdom of Denmark	5.6m	57,000	Inuit	2,210,411/853,444	2,166,086/836,330	Greenland	303bn	03.227bn
Iceland	350,000	350,000	None	103,000/39,769	103,000/39,769	Whole	20bn	11.000bn
Norway	5.2m	478,000	Sami	385,178/148,718	113,000/43,630	Finnmark, Troms, and Nordland	376bn	18.451bn
Sweden	10.0m	510,000	Sami	450,295/173,860	153,430/59,240	Norrbotten, Västerbotten	498bn	20.345bn
Finland	5.5m	590,000	Sami	338,424/130,666	136,133/52,561	Lapland, Northern Ostrobothnia, Kainuu	239bn	19.961bn
Russia	144.0m	2.0m	40 recognized groups	17,098,242/6,601,668	10,500,000/4,054,073	Murmansk Oblast, Nenets Autonomous Okrug, Chukchi Autonomous Okrug, Yamalo-Nenets Autonomous Okrug, Vorkuta, Norilsk, Arkhangelsk region, Yakutia	1.268bn	314.773bn

*Most recent available figures from Lee Huskey, Ilmo Mäenpää, and Alexander Pelyasov, "Economic Systems," in *Arctic Human Development Report: Regional Processes and Global Linkages*, ed. Joan Nymand Larsen and Gail Fondahl (Akureyri, Iceland: Norden, 2014), 168, table 4.3. USD equivalents based on purchasing power parity.

We will now expand on the introduction provided in chapter 1 to explain the areas of each state that are considered Arctic, their inhabitants, the forms of self-government that exist there, and the main Arctic-related priorities. We begin with Alaska and move eastward.

The United States
The United States became Arctic with the purchase of Alaska from Russia in 1867—stimulated by a heavy Russian debt following the Crimean War.[6] Widely considered at the time to be an extravagance, the treaty was nevertheless approved by 37 of the 39 US senators, and the House, in which all tax bills must originate, voted by 113 to 43 to allocate the necessary federal funds to pay the asking price of $7.2 million USD (about $123 million USD in 2017).[7] Alaska's native population, being considered uncivilized, was not consulted about the sale and was transferred to US federal jurisdiction, together with their homelands.[8] Alaska became the forty-ninth state of the United States in 1959, only two years after significant oil reserves had been discovered and the federal government recognized that Alaska had a sufficient resource base to support itself.[9] Most of Alaska is located below the Arctic Circle, with its capital city, Juneau, located around 58° N (farther south than the northern coast of mainland Scotland) and its largest city, Anchorage, at 61° N. Although the biggest of the American states in terms of land mass, it is sparsely populated. Most Americans in the so-called lower forty-eight do not consider themselves citizens of an "Arctic state," and the noncontiguous state of Alaska is easily overlooked in domestic affairs.

On the opposite coast of the United States, the state of Maine is increasingly positioning itself as a relevant Arctic actor, with representatives holding sessions at major international forums such as the Arctic Circle and Arctic Frontiers to promote, inter alia, business links.[10] Portland hosted one of the Arctic Council meetings of the Senior Arctic Officials (SAOs).[11] Maine senator Angus King cofounded the Arctic Caucus of the US Senate alongside Alaska senator Lisa Murkowski. Nevertheless, in keeping with most contemporary accounts of Arctic relations, for the purposes of this book, the American Arctic will refer generally to the state of Alaska.

Of the three-quarters of a million Alaskan inhabitants, around 15 percent are indigenous, including Inuit, Athabaskan, Pacific North Coast Indians, and Aleut peoples.[12] The nonindigenous population is highly transient—with large numbers of people moving in and out for work or within the armed forces.[13]

Within Alaska, indigenous people have distinct rights that emanate from their position as original inhabitants of the state. On achieving statehood in 1959 (after the indigenous had been rendered a minority in their homeland), the government of Alaska was invited to select federal lands for transfer but was not permitted to take native lands. Nevertheless, Alaska began to appropriate areas that were long used by native Alaskans for their subsistence activities.[14] The federal land transfer program was suspended in 1966 in order to give time to settle the claims with Alaskan native tribes. Yet once more, it was a discovery of oil that spurred settlement: in 1967, the biggest oil reserve in North America was found at Prudhoe Bay.[15] In order to get the oil to market, a pipeline was required, and that could not be built until the status of the land was settled.[16]

In 1971 the Alaska Native Claims Settlement Act (ANCSA) was agreed between the US government and representatives of Alaskan indigenous communities.[17] It is a piece of federal legislation—a top-down law—rather than a treaty agreement between equal interested parties. The Act imposed a corporate structure with the effect of severing tribal land ownership and tribal governance systems. Alaska was divided into twelve regions, each of which had its own native regional corporation, and more than two hundred native villages were transformed into corporations. A further regional corporation was established in 1975 to represent Alaskan natives who no longer live in Alaska. The corporations were granted title to one-ninth of the land territory of Alaska, with the Act ostensibly extinguishing any other claim the natives might have on the other eight-ninths in exchange for a one-off payment of $962.5 million to Alaskan natives alive in 1971.[18] The corporations are for-profit entities in which the Alaskan natives (and now their descendants) are shareholders. (This is significantly different from the reservations established by treaties in the lower forty-eight.) The village corporations have surface rights, but the regional corporations enjoy subsurface rights (i.e., minerals and hydrocarbons).

When ANCSA was passed in 1971, there was a twenty-year moratorium on the transfer of the shares outside of native communities, but as 1991 approached, a movement emerged seeking to extend the limitation on transfer to nonnatives for fear that sales and other transfers of shares would mean that, over time, nonnatives would become the majority owners and hence exercise control over native lands. The 1991 amendments created a compromise solution whereby the corporations could decide (based on a shareholder vote) if and when to open up to nonnatives.

The ANCSA was an effort to privatize and corporatize native title; it is not in any way about indigenous self-governance or sovereignty, coming some years before the devolution agreements next door in Canada and further east in Greenland.[19] It extinguished traditional hunting and fishing rights, meaning that native Alaskans have (only) the same rights as nonnative Alaskans. It was an attempt to "modernize" the native Alaskans and, through corporatization of their "property," transform them into entrepreneurs.[20] Huhndorf and Huhndorf describe the process thus: "In short, the settlement aimed to integrate largely rural, subsistence-based communities into the mainstream capitalist system."[21]

The tribal structure remains, and there are still tribal councils with authority over their members. There are 211 native villages and 229 federally recognized tribes.[22] Besides these, Alaska contains cities (small by the standards of the lower forty-eight) and geographically enormous but sparsely populated boroughs (larger than some European countries) with a high degree of autonomy.[23] Alaskan governance is therefore a complicated web of international law, federal law, state law, municipal law, and tribal government.[24]

At the federal level, coordination of US Arctic policy is governed by the US Arctic Research Policy Act 1984. The act creates the eight-member US Arctic Research Commission (US ARC), consisting of four researchers, two representatives of commerce, one Alaskan indigenous representative, and a representative of the National Science Foundation. The Commission is staffed by the executive director (in Washington, DC) and the deputy executive director (Anchorage). US ARC's current priorities include environmental protection, Arctic human health, renewable energy, shipping, food security, and international scientific cooperation. The 1984 Act also created the Interagency Arctic Research Policy Committee, which coordinates between federal and state agencies on Arctic issues. It now operates as a working group of the National Science Foundation.

In the last few years of the Obama administration, the Arctic received increasing attention, with issues of Alaskan development and environmental protection occupying the forefront. Hillary Clinton was the first US secretary of state to attend the ministerial meeting of the Arctic Council in 2011. Nevertheless, the Arctic struggles to compete for priority against American interests in the lower forty-eight or in other, more troubled regions of the world. The US *National Strategy for the Arctic Region* pivots on three themes: national security, environmental stewardship, and cooperation. These themes are to be promoted in line with four principles: peace and stability, knowledge-based decision making (both scientific and indigenous), innovative cooperative arrangements, and cooperation with Alaska natives.[25] The strategy is at a relatively high level of abstraction with few concrete proposals or targets, but it does support the UN Convention on the Law of the Sea (UNCLOS),[26] indicating both a commitment to international customary law "reflected in the Convention" and a proposal to accede to it.[27] Accession must nevertheless overcome resistance in the Senate, where a two-thirds vote is required to become a party.

The Trump administration had not, at the time of writing, released any Arctic-specific policies but has indicated a willingness to overturn federal legislation on environmental protection, to reopen the offshore Arctic to hydrocarbon activities, and to permit exploration in the Arctic National Wildlife Refuge.[28] Trump has triggered the withdrawal process from the Paris Agreement on climate change, but this cannot be completed before the presidential elections in 2020 (see also chapter 10).[29] On the other hand, the United States continues to engage as before through the Arctic Council, and erstwhile secretary of state Rex Tillerson attended the 2017 Arctic Council ministerial meeting in Fairbanks.[30]

The state of Alaska has also developed its own Arctic policy, which is directed toward other Alaskan citizens and interest groups, other international Arctic actors, and, not least, the federal government, to argue that the views and interests of Alaskans should drive US Arctic policy.[31] The Alaskan approach prioritizes the well-being, traditional economies, and values of indigenous Alaskans, subsistence activities, economic development and sharing of its benefits, climate change and its impacts, and participation of Alaskans in decision making for the Arctic.

Canada

Canada's Arctic is usually defined as the territories of Yukon, the Northwest Territories, and Nunavut.[32] Nunavik (the northern region of Quebec) and Nunatsiavut (the northern tip of Labrador) are sometimes included based on geographic, climatic, social, and demographic similarities. It is interesting to note that the three Arctic territories of Canada remain under federal control and do not have full provincial status, unlike, for example, Ontario, Quebec, or even the tiny Prince Edward Island. Their status and powers are determined under a complex mix of treaties and federal law.[33]

Despite their vast sizes, the populations of Canada's Arctic territories are much smaller than any of the provinces. Yukon's nearly half a million square kilometers contains around thirty-four thousand people, 25 percent of whom are indigenous, mostly First Nations. The Northwest Territories consist of 1.3 million square kilometers but only homes around forty-two thousand people, around 36 percent being First Nations and 11 percent Inuit. The massive Nunavut—more than two million square kilometers, or around 20 percent of Canada—contains around thirty-two thousand people, over 80 percent of whom are Inuit.

While the Alaska Native Claims Settlement Act was about land and ownership, the agreements with the indigenous in Arctic Canada have gone further, promoting indigenous governance. Yukon and the Northwest Territories have the most extensive powers, especially with regard to natural resource management.[34] Nunavut has much further to go, and the federal government believes that the people are not ready for greater control over their own affairs.[35] Given that the territory has been under federal control for decades, Tony Penikett asks why they are not ready. Why is educational achievement still far below that of other parts of Canada? Why, for example, does Arctic Canada (Nunavut, Northwest Territories, and the Yukon) still have no university? Why, when the federal government had "absolute authority" over the three territories in the north, did it not ensure the training of professionals to take on leadership roles?[36]

All three territories still depend on a federal transfer for their budgets, though the Northwest Territories' hydrocarbon and mineral resources make it the least dependent of the three.[37] However, the federal government still holds enormous land and resource rights in the North, including vast territory in Nunavut that it secured through the Nunavut Land Claims Agreement in 1993.[38] In exchange for waiving any further claims of aboriginal title, the federal government awarded ownership of 135,000 square miles of land to Nunavut Tunngavik Inc. (NTI, then Tunngavik Federation of Nunavut) and over the course of fifteen years transferred $1.178 billion CAD, which are held in trust for NTI and regional Inuit associations.[39] The area of land in Nunavut held by NTI is enormous—bigger than Greece or New Mexico. However, it amounts to only 18 percent of the land in Nunavut, the rest being held by the federal government. Furthermore, the federal government transferred only 2 percent of the subsurface rights, retaining 98 percent of any mineral and hydrocarbon resources under federal authority.[40] The indigenous citizens of Nunavik in northern Quebec and Nunatsiavut in Labrador have also negotiated land claims and enjoy some devolved government though they are still part of their respective provinces.[41]

Under Prime Minister Harper's government (2006–2015), attention in Canada moved further north, with the sovereignty discourse playing well to domestic audiences. Sovereignty was the key to the Canadian's Arctic strategy, which is pointedly titled "Our North, Our Heritage, Our Future." "Use it or lose it" was the refrain of Prime

Minister Harper.[42] Ironically, Canada's sovereignty claim to all of its remote Arctic is based on the historic occupation by the Inuit—who are now Canadian citizens. However, those Inuit were only granted the vote in 1950, and their settlement of the most distant and inhospitable regions of Arctic Canada was the result of a forced deportation by the Canadian authorities as part of an "experiment" to test the outer limits of human survival in the North.[43] No one contests Canadian sovereignty over its land territory today, and the legal principles for allocating maritime zones, as we shall see in chapter 8, do not depend on being occupied or used in any manner.[44] In practice, this emphasis on "using it" is a green light for extraction of the natural resources scattered throughout this vast landmass.

The election of Trudeau's Liberal government in fall 2015 indicated a change of direction in Canada, with much more emphasis on reconciliation with the First Nations and Inuit peoples on a nation-to-nation basis and greater deference to their rights to self-government and decision making with regard to resources in their lands.[45] How far Trudeau's expressed intentions will be realized remains to be seen.

The three territories of northern Canada prepared a joint Arctic policy in 2007, three years before federal Canada released its strategy.[46] The territories published a revised version in 2014.[47] The key areas of concern are human development (with an emphasis on health, education, and employment); energy (including supply, especially of renewables, and demands for affordable energy); infrastructure (addressing the need for affordable housing, transport, and communications); and governance (in particular, increasing self-governance and settling land claims). Quebec has its own *Plan Nord* to promote economic development in the upper 72 percent of the province—an area of 463,000 square miles (including Nunavik) with a population of only 120,000, about one-third of whom are indigenous.[48]

The Kingdom of Denmark

The Kingdom of Denmark consists of Denmark, the Faroe Islands, and Greenland. It is a small state, negotiating its place and seeking peaceful cooperation in the European Union (EU), the Nordics, the Baltics, and the North Atlantic Treaty Organization (NATO), as well as the Arctic. Three centuries after the collapse of the Viking settlements, Denmark (re)colonized Greenland in the eighteenth century. Greenland possessed recognized colonial status until 1953, when it was controversially integrated into the Danish state as a "county" of Denmark.[49] Greenland recovered its status as a nation with the Home Rule Act in 1979, which was followed by the much more extensive Self-Government Act in 2009.[50] Of the three countries, only Denmark is a member of the EU (though Greenland was a member of the European Economic Community from 1973 to 1985). Only Greenland is geographically Arctic, but the Faroe Islands are highly engaged in Arctic cooperation, particularly within the West Nordic region.

The vast majority of the fifty-six thousand Greenlanders (around 88 percent) are of Inuit origin, and most of them speak Kalaallisut (West Greenlandic) as their first language. This is Greenland's official language, although there are two minority dialects: Inuktun (North Greenlandic), with around one thousand speakers, and Tunumiit oraasiat (East Greenlandic), with around three thousand speakers.[51] North and East Greenland were colonized much later than West Greenland and are culturally quite distinct.

Greenland enjoys a very high degree of autonomy within the Kingdom of Denmark under the Self-Government Act of 2009. Under both international law and Danish constitutional law, the Greenlanders' right to become independent at a time of their choosing is widely accepted. However, the Greenland economy remains heavily subsidized by a block grant from Denmark, and Greenland is not yet in a position to relinquish this. The grant currently constitutes more than half of government revenue in Greenland—but less than 1 percent of the Kingdom of Denmark's budget. Development of onshore mining or offshore hydrocarbons is seen as an essential economic condition for full independence, but Greenlanders and some environmental activists from outside have concerns about potential pollution. Oil exploration poses risks to the sustainability of the economically pivotal fishing industry as well as subsistence whaling and sealing. Meanwhile, mining developments raise concerns about environmental and social impacts, especially when uranium is involved. Greenland is also reliant on Danish workers to fill essential roles in the civil service, medical, teaching, welfare, and other professions. The University of Greenland, established in 1987, and other educational institutions are tailoring education programs to prepare a new generation of Greenlanders to take on more of these roles in preparation for ever-increasing autonomy. However, the university, befitting its size, only offers a limited number of degree programs, and many young people continue to travel to Denmark and elsewhere to obtain higher education.

The Faroe Islands likewise enjoy a high degree of autonomy. The population of around fifty thousand is only a little less than that of Greenland. Their independence movement ebbs and flows and, although the Faroe Islands receive a subsidy from Denmark, this is relatively small, at about 6 percent of the Faroese GDP.[52] Although they are subarctic, the Arctic region is of economic, political, and cultural importance in the Faroe Islands.

At the Arctic Council, Denmark, the Faroe Islands, and Greenland share a single seat, a matter of some contention when the Greenland government refused to participate in the Kiruna ministerial meeting of 2013 in protest at the lack of independent representation. The joint strategy for the three countries aims "to strengthen the Kingdom's status as global player in the Arctic."[53] Its core themes are peaceful cooperation and maritime safety; sustainable development of renewable and nonrenewable resources; respect for the vulnerable environment, in light of climate change and other factors; and international cooperation. The Faroe Islands have developed their own Arctic strategy, which sits alongside the joint strategy of the Kingdom of Denmark's three constituent nations. It is rather pointedly called *The Faroe Islands—A Nation in the Arctic*, demonstrating that geography is no obstacle to Arctic identity-building.[54]

Iceland

Notwithstanding the Faroese bold claim, it is Iceland that claims to be the only Arctic state entirely located within the Arctic region, even if only a tiny corner of the island of Grímsey is located above the Arctic Circle.[55] As for the Faroe Islands, this is based on a sociological rather than a geographical definition of the Arctic. Like Greenland, it is in a strategically important position in the North Atlantic from a security perspective and is a potential hub for Arctic transit shipping.

Iceland is the only Arctic state that has no indigenous population, having been settled by the Vikings from the late ninth century onward. Iceland is a unitary state where all legislative power is centralized, though there are municipalities to administer local services that serve populations ranging from a few dozen to around 120,000 in Reykjavík.

Iceland's international relations were, in the latter part of the twentieth and the beginning of the twenty-first century, directed principally toward the other four Nordic states, the EU (with some ambivalence), and North America. It is only in the last few years that increased attention has been directed northward, and Iceland now proudly positions itself internationally as an Arctic state (both an inspiration for and a consequence of the Arctic Circle Assembly discussed in chapter 1) with major interests to defend and to develop in the North. Iceland, although the smallest Arctic state, is quick to defend its rights to be involved in

Arctic affairs and is a strong supporter of the Arctic Council as the appropriate forum for decision making.[56]

Iceland was the first of the Arctic states to ratify the UNCLOS and the only Arctic state to have ratified by the time the first pan-Arctic cooperation, the Arctic Environmental Protection Strategy (AEPS), was agreed upon. International ocean governance remains today a crucial issue for domestic politics and economics, and it drives much of Iceland's international relations as an island state that is heavily dependent on fisheries.

Following a severe economic crisis in 2008, Iceland began negotiations to join the EU. It transpired that the EU was more keen for this union than Iceland itself was, and the latter suspended talks in September 2013 before unilaterally withdrawing the application altogether in March 2015. Iceland remains a member of the European Economic Area, which allows it most of the benefits of free movement and trade while allowing it to remain outside the EU's common fisheries and agricultural policies.

Norway

Finnmark, Troms, and Nordland counties are considered to be part of northern Norway, and Tromsø, capital of Troms county, is a major center for Arctic research and political cooperation, being the home of the Arctic Council secretariat. Norway also possesses sovereignty over the Svalbard (Spitsbergen) Islands, though it is a constrained sovereignty by virtue of the 1920 Spitsbergen Treaty (see box 1.2 in chapter 1, and chapter 8).

Norway has the largest Sami population of any Arctic state, with an estimated forty thousand to fifty thousand.[57] Norway's Sami parliament, although located in Finnmark, contains Sami representatives from all over Norway. Its responsibilities include promotion of Sami interests, culture, language, education, and development. In 2005 Norway devolved the Finnmark Estate (around forty-five thousand square kilometers constituting 95 percent of Finnmark county, population seventy-five thousand, of whom a majority are Sami) to management by a board of directors. The Norwegian Sami Parliament nominates three members to the board, and the Finnmark County Municipality the other three, hence a minimum of half of the board of directors will be Sami; in practice, the Sami are usually a majority on the board.[58]

Norway's small population of just over five million belies its financial clout, built on fisheries, hydrocarbons, and its technological expertise. Its quiet diplomacy, especially its careful management of European-Russian relations since the end of the Cold War, makes it the leader among the Nordic countries in Arctic relations. As a small Nordic state neighboring a military giant, Norway's Arctic policy is directed toward cooperation with Russia. Norway led the establishment of the Barents Euro-Arctic Council to enhance cross-border cooperation with its neighbor during a period of rapid change.[59] In Norway's current Arctic strategy, Russia is the only other state that is named, and cooperation with Russia is emphasized throughout, especially vis-à-vis the environment and marine resources.[60] The Arctic is crucial to Norway's self-identity and the image it presents internationally, with the High North (as the Norwegians have taken to calling it) described as "Norway's most important strategic priority area in the years ahead."[61]

Sweden

There is no designated Arctic region of Sweden. The county of Norrbotten (including most of the old province of Swedish Lapland) is situated mostly above the Arctic Circle, but the region of Västerbotten (which contains the rest of Swedish Lapland) is also included in the Arctic Council's unofficial compilation of Arctic administrative regions. The Arctic Human Development Report also includes both Norrbotten and Västerbotten in its remit.[62]

The Sami in Sweden, who number seventeen thousand to twenty thousand,[63] do not have a designated administrative region. Sami traditional practices (especially herding) in what was once the province of Laponia are the basis of the area's accreditation as a UNESCO World Heritage site (see box 3.1). The Sami Parliament of Sweden promotes

---

BOX 3.1 | **Laponia**

The Laponian Area is a designated World Heritage site,[a] by virtue of traditional Sami practices as well as its outstanding natural beauty. It contains four national parks. When it came time to set up the management board, the local Sami demanded the majority of seats, but the Swedish national and regional governments refused. Sami representatives campaigned on the basis of the UNESCO goals for the area for a decade. Today, they have the majority of seats and shape the management of the parks.[b]

[a]"Laponian Area," UNESCO World Heritage List, accessed May 2, 2018, https://whc.unesco.org/en/list/774.
[b]See Carina Green, *Managing Laponia: A World Heritage Site as Arena for Sami Ethno-Politics in Sweden*, Uppsala Studies in Cultural Anthropology 47 (Uppsala: Acta Universitatis Upsaliensis, 2009); and Carina Green and Jan Turtinen, "World Heritage Bureaucracy—How It Works and How It Affects Indigenous Peoples," in *Indigenous Rights in Modern Landscapes*, ed. Lars Elenius, Christina Allard, and Camilla Sandström (Didcot, UK: Taylor and Francis, 2016), 192–93.

increased internal self-determination (i.e., increased powers within the state of Sweden without any rights to secession) and promotes Sami culture, including traditional economic activities, education, and language.

Sweden, lacking an Arctic coastline, is not self-consciously an Arctic state but nevertheless released its own strategy in 2011.[64] It includes a lengthy chapter on Sweden's Arctic credentials, something that the Arctic coastal states take for granted.[65] Climate and environment feature strongly in Sweden's approach to the Arctic, alongside economic development and respect for the rights of indigenous peoples.

Finland

Although most of Finland is situated south of the Arctic Circle, it takes its position as an Arctic state very seriously, similar to Iceland, and points in its strategy to "a growing perception of the whole of Finland as an Arctic country."[66] The Arctic Circle runs through Finland's northernmost region, Lapland, although sociological and political definitions of the Finnish Arctic usually include all of Lapland and often the regions of Northern Ostrobothnia and Kainuu as well.

Finland has a relatively small Sami population of around seven thousand to eight thousand, although many people who self-identify as Sami are not recognized as such under Finnish law.[67] At the northernmost tip of Finnish Lapland is the Sami domicile region in which Sami are a majority and enjoy a degree of self-governance. The Sami in this area have voting rights to the Finnish Sami Parliament, which promotes and protects Sami language and culture and advocates for Sami rights as an indigenous people.

Finland was an early cheerleader for Arctic cooperation, especially in the creation of AEPS and the Arctic Council. With its careful and studied neutrality, especially during the Cold War, Finland is sufficiently unthreatening to be able to take a lead on Arctic cooperation (see chapter 2). For its own part, Finland, as a small state on the fringe of the EU (which it joined in 1995, alongside Sweden, *after* the collapse of the Soviet Union), can better protect its interests through multilateral cooperation than it could do acting alone. Finland is a great champion of the Arctic Council and supports its transformation into a treaty-based international organization.[68]

Finland promotes broad international cooperation in the Arctic beyond the Arctic Eight, often acting as a bridge between the EU and the Arctic states.[69] Finland also has a sensitivity to Russia that is unique, given its difficult history with its giant neighbor (see chapter 2).

Finland is the only state in the world whose harbors are *all* ice-covered in midwinter, and it has responded to this challenge by becoming the world's foremost icebreaker manufacturer. Finnish dockworkers built around 60 percent of all the icebreakers currently in operation; after Russia, Finland and Sweden have the most icebreakers.[70]

Russia

Russia is a former superpower seeking to maintain its global and regional influences. The Arctic is a strategic priority but has to compete with other regions that Russia considers its backyard—such as the former satellite states of the Soviet Union in Eastern Europe and the Caucasus. Russia has opposed Western policies in the Balkans and the Middle East, but nothing since the Cold War has caused as much alarm to the West or threatened Arctic cooperation as much as Russia's intervention in civil unrest in Ukraine, culminating in the annexation of Crimea in 2014.

Russia is geographically the largest state in the world, with more than seventeen million square kilometers (11.5 percent of the land surface of the earth and three million square kilometers larger than the continent of Antarctica). Half of the Arctic coastline and 40 percent of land territory above the Arctic Circle is Russian.[71] So which parts of Russia are "Arctic"? Russia's internal administrative system is complex, befitting its long and multiethnic history, diversity in population structures and environment, and political needs. It is administratively divided into eighty-three regions (federal subjects) plus two that most of the rest of the world considers to be part of Ukraine.[72] These federal subjects take different forms depending on their size, demographics, and political histories: there are twenty-one republics, nine krais, forty-six oblasts, four autonomous okrugs, one autonomous oblast, and two federal cities. A 2014 law of the Russian Federation designated a number of territories as part of the "Arctic Zone": Murmansk Oblast, Nenets Autonomous Okrug, Chukchi Autonomous Okrug, Yamalo-Nenets Autonomous Okrug, cities of Vorkuta and Norilsk, selected areas of the Arkhangelsk region, and Yakutia (Sakha Republic).[73] However, the Arctic character of Russia is as much about identity and imagination as it is about territory.[74]

Almost half of the Arctic's four million residents live in Russia, and together they produce more than 70 percent of all Arctic production.[75] However, the standard of living of the Russian Arctic residents does not reflect this.[76] Russia contains the biggest cities above the Arctic Circle, the largest being Arkhangelsk,[77] whose population of three hundred fifty thousand is certainly not large by international standards but is relatively an Arctic giant. Northern Russia's population has declined markedly since the 1990s, and this has been the major factor in the overall fall of the Arctic population by around 1.4 percent between 2000 and 2014.[78]

Fewer than 5 percent of Russian Arctic residents are recognized as indigenous,[79] and Russia's relations with its indigenous peoples are more strained than those in the other Arctic states.[80] Russia's recognized indigenous (or "small-numbered") peoples in the North, Siberia, and the Far East have greater protections than their seven counterparts elsewhere in Russia but fewer than those in other Arctic states.[81] To qualify, a group must demonstrate historical continuity through a territorial connection to the land of their ancestors and traditional ways of life, consider themselves a distinct ethnic group, and number no more than fifty thousand souls.[82] The 2010 Russian census counted around a quarter of a million.[83] This last criterion means that larger indigenous groups, such as the Yakuts in the Sakha Republic, the Karelians, and the Komi, are excluded from the protections that such status brings.[84]

Each indigenous people can establish its own representative organization, which is entitled in turn to be a member of the umbrella Russian Association of Indigenous Peoples of the North (RAIPON).[85] RAIPON has the legal status of an NGO. Under strict Russian laws regarding administration and registration of NGOs (and possibly as a response to RAIPON's criticism of government and defense of indigenous land rights in the Russian North),[86] it was suspended in 2012 and was unable to participate at the Arctic Council meeting of Senior Arctic Officials in November of that year, causing consternation among the other permanent participants and Arctic states. The Arctic Council meetings went on regardless.[87] RAIPON's status was reinstated a few months later, and it elected a new president who was less critical, based in Moscow, and closer to the federal government.[88] Although Sami constitute one of the legally recognized indigenous peoples of the North, Siberia, and the Far East, Russia does not recognize a Sami parliament. Russia's two thousand Sami established a Kola Sami Assembly in 2010, which is supported by the three Nordic Sami parliaments.[89]

Russia's strategic priorities for its Arctic principally relate to economic development (in particular, extractive industries), military security, and environmental security, and it seeks international cooperation to achieve these.[90] It often paints itself as a vulnerable outsider, fighting steadfastly to uphold international law and its own rights against political maneuvering by the other Arctic states, especially through NATO cooperation.[91] Russia is strongly committed to the UNCLOS as it has the most to gain from following UNCLOS principles on the allocation of marine resources.[92]

NON-ARCTIC STATES

The list of observers to the Arctic Council at any given time is a good indicator of states with foreign policy objectives in the region. Six European states are long-standing observers: France, Germany, the Netherlands, Poland, Spain, and the United Kingdom. Italy was admitted as an observer at the Kiruna meeting alongside five Asian states: China, India, Japan, Singapore, and South Korea in 2013. Switzerland was admitted in 2017. Of the new observers, China has received the most attention by far, stoking fears that its demand for energy and minerals was behind its desire to increase its influence in the High North and concerns that its investment in scientific research is a sideshow.

China's application for observer status in the Arctic Council was encouraged by the Icelandic chairmanship (2002–2004) and formally submitted in 2004. Iceland has courted Chinese investment and was the first European state to agree to a free trade deal with China in 2013.[93] China was probably the world's most rapidly changing state in the early twenty-first century, pulling hundreds of millions of people out of deep poverty and embracing its unique form of capitalism. This creates insatiable demand for natural resources in order to maintain rapid growth. However, China's political structure also enables it to play a long game. Unbelabored by democracy, the single-party system means that its leaders do not have to manage political successes around an electoral cycle, and they are quite willing to make investments that may take decades to provide a return. As tensions have risen between Russia and the West over its annexation of Crimea, sanctions have inhibited cooperation and investment by European firms in the Russian Arctic. Russia has therefore turned increasingly to China to develop its resources.[94] China published an official Arctic policy in January 2018.[95] It emphasizes China's position as a "near-Arctic state" whose environment is inseparably linked to the Arctic and which anticipates significant negative impacts from climate change. In a slight to the United States, it reiterates China's commitment to the Paris climate change agreement (see chapter 10). The policy champions Arctic governance according to international law—something that does not at first glance fit with realist expectations for such an economically and militarily powerful state. However, as the policy explains, international law guarantees China's rights to navigation, high seas fisheries, and research. The Arctic is an international region, and while China respects the legal rights of Arctic states (especially to resources), it will not accept an expansive interpretation or an extension of those rights. China refers to the UN Charter five times and explicitly reminds the reader that it is a permanent member of the Security Council. It promotes sustainable development, in particular the "Belt and Road Initiative" (see chapter 6). One surprising—but timely and pertinent—section refers to Chinese involvement in tourism. The policy is weak on indigenous peoples, promising to respect their "tradition and culture" and their "interests and concerns" but at no point their rights.

The focus on China has overshadowed the interests of the other Asian observer states. Japan released an official Arctic policy at the third Arctic Circle Assembly in Reykjavík in October 2015.[96] It emphasizes respect for the rule of law—in particular, the law of the sea, the rights of indigenous peoples, and environmental governance. Like China, both Japan and South Korea are major exporting economies—which need raw materials and efficient shipping routes. South Korea is an important shipbuilding nation, and Singapore is focused on shipping—including concerns that development of the Northern Sea Route will reduce demand for its own services as an important point of call for the Strait of Malacca route. India, a democratic, multiethnic, and federal state, is also a state with a rapidly growing economy, a population in excess of 1.2 billion souls (and growing fast) packed into a territory around one-third the size of China. All are experiencing the impacts of climate change, and cooperation on Arctic climate change research can give them crucial information about changes at home.[97]

INTERNATIONAL ORGANIZATIONS AND FORUMS

This section will explore the main regional and global bodies for cross-border cooperation in the Arctic (see table 3.3).

The European Union (EU)

The EU is not a state, let alone a federal state, because its authority is not inherent but derives from the consent of each of its twenty-eight member states by virtue of their accession through treaty.[98] It is, therefore, a treaty-based international organization with limited competences—those defined in its governing treaties. Nevertheless, its various treaties give it extensive powers over its member states and their five hundred million inhabitants and over a GDP of more than $16 trillion USD, making it the most powerful international organization in the world.

Three of the Arctic states are members of the EU: Denmark, Finland, and Sweden. However, the Arctic part of the Kingdom of Denmark (Greenland) left the European Economic Communities (as the entity was then) in 1985.[99] This means that up until 1973 and from 1985 to 1995,

Table 3.3 Regional International Organizations and Forums

Body	Arctic States	Non-Arctic Entities	Nonstate Actors	Priorities	Status
European Union (EU)	Denmark, Finland, Sweden	Austria, Belgium, Bulgaria, Croatia, Cyprus, Czech Republic, Estonia, France, Germany, Greece, Hungary, Ireland, Italy, Latvia, Lithuania, Malta, Netherlands, Poland, Portugal, Romania, Slovakia, Slovenia, Spain, United Kingdom*		Common trade area (free movement of persons, goods, capital, and services); fisheries and agriculture; democracy; science; environmental protection; regional development; legal harmonization; security	International organization
Arctic Council	Canada, Kingdom of Denmark, Finland, Iceland, Norway, Russia, Sweden, United States	As *observers*: China, France, Germany, India, Italy, Japan, Netherlands, Poland, Singapore, South Korea, Spain, Switzerland, United Kingdom	6 indigenous organizations (permanent participants); 13 intergovernmental organizations plus the EU ad hoc; 13 nongovernmental organizations	Environment; sustainable development	High-level intergovernmental forum
Arctic Five	Canada, Kingdom of Denmark, Norway, Russia, United States			Law of the sea; sovereignty	Informal

Organization	Members			Purpose	Type
Barents Euro-Arctic Council (BEAC)	Kingdom of Denmark, Finland, Iceland, Norway, Russia, Sweden *As observers:* Canada, United States	EU Commission *As observers:* France, Germany, Italy, Japan, Netherlands, Poland, United Kingdom		Economic cooperation; environment; sustainable development; transport; emergency response preparation; culture; education; energy; health; tourism; youth	Intergovernmental forum
Barents Regional Council (BRC)	4 Finnish regions; 3 Norwegian regions; 5 Russian regions; 2 Swedish regions		3 indigenous organizations	Environment; economic cooperation; transport; culture; education; energy; health; tourism; youth	Regional intergovernmental forum
Conference of Arctic Parliamentarians	Canada, Kingdom of Denmark, Finland, Iceland, Norway, Russia, Sweden, United States	EU Parliament		Support Arctic Council; human development; shipping; education; environment	Interparliamentary forum
Council for Baltic Sea States (CBSS)	Kingdom of Denmark, Finland, Iceland, Norway, Russia, Sweden *As observers:* United States	Estonia, European Union, Germany, Latvia, Lithuania, Poland *As observers:* Belarus, France, Hungary, Italy, Netherlands, Romania, Slovakia, Spain, Ukraine, United Kingdom	Belarus, France, Hungary, Italy, Netherlands, Romania, Slovakia, Spain, Ukraine, United States	Nuclear safety; maritime policy; sustainable development	Intergovernmental forum

(continued)

Table 3.3 *Continued*

Body	Arctic States	Non-Arctic Entities	Nonstate Actors	Priorities	Status
Nordic Council	Kingdom of Denmark, Finland, Iceland, Norway, Sweden			Education and language; research; gender equality; human development; environment	Interparliamentary forum
Nordic Council of Ministers	Kingdom of Denmark, Finland, Iceland, Norway, Sweden			Education and language; research; gender equality; human development; environment	Intergovernmental forum
North Atlantic Treaty Organization (NATO)	Canada, Kingdom of Denmark, Iceland, Norway, United States	Belgium, Bulgaria, Czech Republic, Estonia, France, Germany, Greece, Hungary, Italy, Latvia, Lithuania, Luxembourg, Netherlands, Poland, Portugal, Romania, Slovakia, Slovenia, Spain, Turkey, United Kingdom		Military security	International organization
Northern Forum	1 Finnish region; 1 Icelandic region; 1 US region; 9 Russian regions	1 South Korean region		Sustainable development; environment; culture	Regional intergovernmental forum

*The United Kingdom is due to leave the European Union in 2019.

the EU had no Arctic territory. It still has no Arctic coastline. Iceland and Norway are both members of the European Economic Area (EEA), meaning that they are subject to European laws in a number of areas, including environmental law. Norwegians, Icelanders, and Greenlanders also enjoy the basic principles of free movement of capital, labor, and goods and services within the EEA, and the EU has a generous bilateral agreement with Greenland primarily to promote and enhance education.[100] Although the EU has contained Arctic states Sweden and Finland for more than two decades, the EU has so many regional and international interests that the Arctic remains fairly peripheral, and on the whole, Arctic matters are viewed as foreign rather than internal affairs.[101]

Nevertheless, the EU views the Arctic as a region where it has many interests and should exert influence.[102] It is a major source of research funding and regional development cooperation in the Arctic.[103] The EU's application for observer status at the Arctic Council remains in limbo, but in practice, the EU is treated as all the other observers. The EU has to tread carefully and not appear to infringe on the sovereignty of the Arctic states in order to maintain its good relations with the Arctic states and its ad hoc observer status. With this in mind, the EU emphasizes the unique role of the Arctic Council and explicitly recognized state sovereignty and the UNCLOS as the basis for Arctic governance.[104] At the ministerial and SAO meetings of the Arctic Council, the EU has greater potential through its members, Denmark, Finland, and Sweden, to influence the shape of debate at the Arctic Council than it does directly as an observer, where its contribution is limited by the structure of the Arctic Council itself.[105] One area in which the EU acts as a single unit is in fisheries, so it is the EU Commission rather than individual member states (such as Spain and Ireland) that signed the central Arctic Ocean fisheries agreement (see chapter 8).[106] It also has sole competence for international trade (see chapter 6). The EU also has "shared competences" with the member states (meaning that the member states and the EU institutions both have regulatory powers) in areas of transport (including shipping), environment, energy, and animal welfare.[107]

The EU's relations with the Arctic did not get off to an auspicious start when the European Parliament in 2008 called for an environmental protection treaty for the Arctic comparable to the Madrid Protocol for Antarctica that severely restricts industrial activities, including a complete ban on natural resource exploitation. Although the resolution recognized that the Arctic territory was populated, it called for "as a minimum starting-point" a comparable natural reserve in the central Arctic Ocean, running roughshod over the established law of the sea.[108]

In 2009, the decision by the EU to ban the imports of seal products from Canada led to a full-scale dispute before the World Trade Organization and stalled the EU's efforts to be accepted as a standing observer at the Arctic Council.[109] Both of these EU policies can be attributed to an inadequate understanding of the Arctic and the peoples who live there. The first indicated a rejection of the sovereignty of Arctic states and their peoples' rights to make their own decisions regarding their natural resources; the second reflected ignorance regarding the traditions and diets of the Inuit and the limited alternatives, alongside their need for cash income from the sale of sealskin.

The EU has most recently identified three main priority areas in the Arctic: climate change and environmental protection; economic development; and international cooperation.[110] The EU's Northern Dimension predates the drive for a distinct Arctic strategy and is focused on the European North, including the Subarctic: the EU's northern states alongside Iceland, Norway, and Russia. It also embraces various regional bodies, including the Arctic Council, the Barents Euro-Arctic Council, the Council of the Baltic Sea States, and the Nordic Council of Ministers (discussed below).

The Arctic Council

The Arctic Council is the principal forum for cooperation on Arctic issues (see figure 3.1). At the top is the biennial ministerial meeting, the location of which coincides with the chairmanship (which changes every two years on a rotating basis). In alternate years, the deputy ministers hold a meeting. The SAOs are ambassadors or senior diplomats from each Arctic state with competence for Arctic affairs. They meet with the permanent participants (indigenous organizations) twice yearly. Observers (currently thirteen non-Arctic states, thirteen intergovernmental or inter-parliamentary organizations, and thirteen NGOs) may attend these meetings but not participate actively.

A number of subsidiary bodies exist, principally six working groups, which are essentially scientific bodies. They present findings to the SAOs and ministerial meeting but they can only make policy recommendations with the approval of all the member states (and, in practice, the permanent participants). The six working groups are the Arctic Contaminants Action Program (ACAP); the Arctic Monitoring and Assessment Programme (AMAP); Conservation of Arctic Flora and Fauna (CAFF); Emergency Prevention, Preparedness and Response (EPPR); Protection of the Arctic Marine Environment (PAME); and the Sustainable Development Working Group (SDWG). As the titles suggest, their mandates

Figure 3.1   The Arctic Council

Note: The Arctic Council diagram depicts eight Arctic states, the six permanent participants, and the six working groups as equal partners in a circle of cooperation. The observers, by contrast, are on an outer ring and are not even counted individually. No distinction is made between state observers and other observers (NGOs and IGOs).
Source: Reproduced with permission from Arctic Council Secretariat.

often overlap. The working groups are standing bodies, but there are also time-limited task forces that address specific issues (e.g., on scientific cooperation, Arctic maritime cooperation, and telecommunications), and now an "expert group" on black carbon. Gracyzk and Koivurova identify four main types of projects: Arctic environmental studies, assessments of human activities and their impacts, conservation of indigenous and other cultures in the Arctic, and overarching assessments.[111]

The reports of the working groups are highly regarded as authoritative and impartial assessments of the state of the Arctic. The Arctic

Council, by directing the plans of the working groups, shapes the discourse in and about the Arctic by directing attention to some things and not others. Further, as the working groups each must define the Arctic to set the limits on their work, this is another manner in which boundaries are created and the Arctic as a region is defined.[112]

The Sami Council and the Inuit Circumpolar Council had been involved from the early stages of the negotiations that created the Arctic Council and were at the table from the beginning. They were soon joined by RAIPON. The Aleut International Association first participated at the second ministerial meeting in 1998 and, under the US chairmanship, in 2000 the Gwich'in Council International and the Arctic Athabaskan Council were also welcomed into the fold.[113] The Arctic states are the members of the Arctic Council, and the indigenous associations are permanent participants. Although every international forum or international organization is unique (in that no two are the same), the Arctic Council stands apart in terms of the degree of integration of indigenous representation. The Arctic states and permanent participants sit together at the Arctic Council ministerial meetings and have equal rights to contribute to the agenda and debate.[114] Decisions are made by consensus between the member states and can in theory be reached notwithstanding opposition from the permanent participants.[115] Nevertheless, the involvement of the permanent participants in all of the discussions gives them a very strong influence. Michael Byers and Douglas Nord have suggested that the permanent participants effectively enjoy a veto and, while this might be too strong a claim, there is no doubt that the contributions from permanent participants help *shape* the consensus within the Arctic Council.[116]

At the 2011 Nuuk ministerial meeting, the criteria for admission of observers were clarified.[117] Observer status needs not only to be earned but also maintained. Observers must bow to Arctic states' sovereignty; recognize international law, in particular the law of the sea in the Arctic; respect the rights of indigenous peoples; demonstrate commitment, including financial commitment, to the work of the permanent participants; and show their capacity to contribute to Arctic interests, including scientific research.[118] The returns from this investment are uncertain; it is likely that the opportunity for informal contact at Arctic Council meetings is at least as important as the opportunity to sit (silently) and listen to the debates between the ministers or SAOs and the permanent participants.

Observers are expected to contribute principally through the working groups.[119] Unlike the member states and the permanent participants, observers may not propose items for the agenda or raise points during

Arctic Council meetings (ministerial or SAO meetings), although they are permitted to submit written statements.[120] Even at the subsidiary bodies, such as working groups, the observers sit apart at the "children's table" behind the main table, and they may speak only after the states and permanent participants have had their say, and even then at the discretion of the chair.[121] (Consider figure 3.1.) Observers are reviewed every four years but can be excluded at any time, as their observer status only exists as long as consensus exists among the ministers; in other words, it would require only one member state to exclude an observer.[122]

When the member and observer states' populations are counted together, more than half of the world's population is now represented in some manner.[123] The recent additions caused some alarm, with fears that they were muscling in to secure Arctic influence and concerns that an increase in observers would reduce the influence of the permanent participants,[124] but it seems that the permanent participants' special role has been carefully preserved.[125]

Prior to 2013 the Arctic Council's membership and observers reflected old powers and old politics: Western European nations and Russia. They had to decide how to respond to the rise of China (and other Asian states): Include and cooperate or exclude and limit? The decision in the end to include—but the conditions upon which that inclusion is granted and constrained—show the old powers including *and* limiting the rising Asian powers. This mirrors the US approach to the admission of China to the World Trade Organization at the turn of the twenty-first century based on Clinton advisor Joseph Nye's counsel to "integrate but hedge."[126] Nye in turn was following Reagan's "trust but verify" approach to improving US-Soviet relations.[127] The expression "trust but verify" comes originally from a Russian proverb.

The Arctic Council is disproportionately influential for what is structurally no more than a roundtable for discussion with no lawmaking powers or compliance mechanisms. It was established by the Ottawa Declaration rather than by a treaty and is not a full-fledged international organization. Views among the Arctic states differ, with Finland supporting the evolution of the Arctic Council into a treaty-based international organization and the United States opposing such a move.[128] Nevertheless, the establishment of the secretariat certainly gives the Arctic Council greater visibility on the international scene, and the Arctic Council secretariat staff enjoy the benefits of a diplomatic agreement with the host state, Norway. The Arctic Council cannot make treaties or other binding regulations on its members, but it is the venue for the negotiation of three treaties: on search and rescue (2011), emergency preparedness and response (2013), and cooperation in Arctic science (2017).[129] These treaties are nevertheless not Arctic Council treaties per se but rather multilateral treaties of the eight member states. Some see these treaties as a development from the Arctic Council as a "decision shaping" body toward a "decision making" body.[130] It may be useful to think of an "Arctic Council system" rather than a single body, to take into account the different layers.[131]

According to the Ottawa Declaration, the Arctic Council is established to "provide a means for promoting cooperation, coordination and interaction among the Arctic states, with the involvement of Arctic indigenous communities and other Arctic inhabitants on common Arctic issues, in particular issues of sustainable development and environmental protection in the Arctic."[132] A footnote to this paragraph excludes "matters related to military security" at the behest of a nervous United States. Since this is only a declaration and not a treaty that defines and limits the reach of the Arctic Council, there is nothing formally to stop the Arctic Council from considering any matter it wishes.[133] Nevertheless, it is unlikely that there would be consensus to include any hard security issues on the agenda.[134] Issues of human security, on the other hand, are very often subjects for Arctic Council working groups and programs.[135] Many security issues that pertain to the Arctic—such as nuclear weapons—are not actually *about* the Arctic but affect the Arctic only through coincidence of geography, so the Arctic Council would not be a natural home for negotiations. The Arctic Council has not gotten involved in negotiations over Arctic fisheries, including the latest agreement on the central Arctic Ocean (see chapter 8). Whaling is another contentious matter that is left off the table. In practice, the Arctic Council has so many potential issues of interest and so small a budget and staffing that there are plenty of easier areas for cooperation to keep it busy without wading into areas of dispute.[136] On the other hand, recent moves under the Arctic Council, including the negotiation of a treaty on search and rescue and the establishment of the Arctic Coast Guard Forum, involve direct cooperation between military organs, indicating that the two Arctic military giants are becoming more relaxed and trusting of one another.[137]

The Arctic Council, lacking international legal personality (i.e., it is not an international organization), does not speak with a single voice internationally and has in fact no instrument through which it can speak. The chair is not authorized to provide an "Arctic Council view" but only speaks for his or her own state.[138] Even in matters where the Arctic Council might be regarded as the most important regional body, such as the negotiations for a mandatory Polar Code for shipping at the International Maritime Organization, there was no Arctic Council representation or official Arctic Council position per se, but each Arctic state represented itself. That being said, the development of the code drew significantly on the work of the PAME working group's Arctic Marine Shipping Assessment.[139]

The Arctic Five
The five Arctic littoral states have occasionally met outside of the Arctic Council framework. Ministers of Canada, Denmark, Norway, Russia, and the United States met in Oslo in 2007; Ilulissat, Greenland, in 2008; and Chelsea, Québec, in 2010, to discuss the legal framework for the Arctic Ocean. These meetings have no formal organizational basis in a treaty or declaration of cooperation. The Ilulissat meeting culminated in a declaration that was a broad declaration of state sovereignty in the Arctic, an endorsement of the law of the sea as the governing framework for the Arctic Ocean, and a message to non-Arctic states that a treaty based on the Antarctic model of environmental protection and internationalization would not be accepted in the North.[140]

These meetings were controversial not only for the other three Arctic states, who felt unduly excluded from what they saw as their rightful place at the table through the Arctic Council, but also among the permanent participants, who were excluded not only from the process of the talks but also from the outcome. The commitment to the law of the sea prioritizes state sovereignty and sovereign rights over maritime zones and does not even mention the interests of indigenous and other coastal communities. More recently, the Arctic Five led the discussions on fisheries management in the central Arctic Ocean.[141]

The Barents Euro-Arctic Region (BEAR)
The Barents Euro-Arctic Council (BEAC) was created in 1993 by the Kirkenes Declaration.[142] BEAC brings together Sweden, Finland, Norway, Demark, Iceland, the Russian Federation, and the EU Commission to reduce military tension, tackle environmental challenges, and raise living standards in Russia in the aftermath of the Cold War.[143] Attempts to improve the standard of living in the Russian western Arctic were also intended to ease the demand for western migration.[144] There are a further nine observer states, of which Poland is the only other former Warsaw Pact country.[145]

BEAC itself is a forum for national-level cooperation: the foreign ministers of each state and the EU meet every second year. Between meetings, a committee of senior officials (similar to the Arctic Council's SAOs) maintains the momentum. At the subnational level, the Barents Regional Council (BRC) is a forum for cooperation among fourteen regional governments and indigenous institutions. Much of the cooperation, especially on indigenous issues, is a de facto subsidy from Norway (and to a lesser extent Sweden and Finland) to Russia.[146] BEAC has also facilitated cooperation between the EU and Russia when more direct links were suspended and the EU imposed sanctions following the Crimea annexation.

BEAC has four working groups, BRC three, and together they have six joint working groups. These focus on environmental challenges, sustainable development and infrastructure, culture, education, and other issues. A Working Group of Indigenous Peoples, with representatives of Sami, Nenets, and Vepsian peoples, advises both the BEAC and BRC. Originally focused on environmental projects and on creating cross-border business opportunities and partnerships, it is now more involved in student and cultural exchanges and health care programs.[147]

Other Regional Forums

It is necessary to mention briefly a number of other regional forums even if these cannot be analyzed in depth. The only pan-Arctic of these is the Conference of Arctic Parliamentarians, which is a biannual gathering of delegations from the eight Arctic parliaments, alongside representatives from the EU Parliament and the permanent participants. Observers also attend this meeting. It is a discussion body and not a parliament in its own right: it cannot pass any laws or regulations for the Arctic, but it can make policy statements in the hope of influencing the national parliaments as well as the Arctic Council.

Like BEAC, the Council for Baltic Sea States was established post–Cold War to enhance regional cooperation on the environment, culture, education, infrastructure, development, and similar issues. The Nordic Council is much older, established in 1952 between the five Nordic states. It is composed of members of the national parliaments of each state and complemented by the Nordic Council of Ministers—a meeting of representatives of the governments of each state. (The ministry taking part at any given meeting will depend upon the issue at hand—for example, health, education, etc.) At subregional and substate levels, the West Nordic Council consists of six representatives from each of the parliaments of the Faroe Islands, Greenland, and Iceland and promotes cooperation in matters of culture and development. It has close ties to the Nordic Council and is probably better viewed as a Nordic rather than an Arctic body.

At the level of regional government, the Northern Forum was established in 1991 as a gathering of substate governments from Canada, China, Finland, Japan, Mongolia, Norway, Russia, and the United States. Today it also includes Akureyri municipality, in Iceland, and Gangwon Province, in South Korea, although there are no longer Mongolian and Norwegian representatives. Its goals are mostly development focused, with the aim of cooperation to improve the welfare of Northern peoples.

During the Cold War, NATO treated the Arctic as an extra-cold battleground. There was no direct conflict, but the strategic targeting of missiles across the North Pole meant that this sparsely populated zone was a militarized front line. More than twenty years since the end of the Cold War, NATO has evolved and grown but still remains essentially an international organization for military security. Its first military operation was in 1992 in Bosnia—after the collapse of the Soviet Union—and since then, it has engaged in a number of conflicts, all justified to a greater or lesser extent as humanitarian missions. Sweden and Finland, reflecting their history of careful engagement with Russia, are not members, although there are occasionally calls domestically to join. Russia, understandably, opposes further expansion eastward. Russia, Finland, and Sweden are all part of NATO's "partnership for peace" program, which is based on bespoke agreements between NATO and the individual states (see chapter 4).[148]

Global Forums

The United Nations (UN) takes little direct interest in the Arctic as a region per se. Of the UN's regional groups, only Russia is not in the Western European and Other group. Arctic states represent themselves at the General Assembly, while Russia and the United States each enjoy permanent membership of the Security Council (as do Arctic Council observers China, the UK, and France). While Arctic issues may come to the attention of UN institutions—for example, the Permanent Forum on Indigenous Issues, the Special Rapporteur on the Rights of Indigenous Peoples, or the human rights treaty bodies—they do not come as Arctic issues as such.

Through the UN, international treaties are agreed that often have particular bearing in the Arctic, not least among them the UNCLOS, which governs the Arctic Ocean as it does every other international maritime space.[149] The UNCLOS also contains two side agreements: one on the regional management of fisheries and the other on the exploitation of the deep seabed (the area of the seabed beyond the continental shelves of any states).

The UN is also the key forum for addressing climate change mitigation, through the United Nations Framework Convention on Climate Change (UNFCCC) and the Paris Agreement (see chapter 10).[150]

The International Maritime Organization (IMO) is a specialized agency of the UN that regulates shipping to ensure the safety of those working in the shipping industry and to protect the marine environment. As a specialized agency, it operates independently of the principal UN organs. The IMO developed the Polar Code to regulate shipping in the Arctic and Antarctic (see chapter 9). During the negotiations on the Polar Code, which is of greatest relevance to the Arctic states, the Arctic Council did not have any representation in its own name as it is not an international organization. Rather, each Arctic state presented its own position, even if on many issues they presented a common front and the negotiations were significantly informed by PAME.

NONGOVERNMENTAL ORGANIZATIONS

The indigenous peoples' organizations in the North, in particular the Inuit Circumpolar Council, the Sami Council, and RAIPON, are among the most important NGOs dealing with Arctic issues from inside the Arctic. However, the globalization of the Arctic in recent years has unsurprisingly brought it to the attention of other groups. Of these, Greenpeace is the most vocal and has made the Arctic a core issue with its Save the Arctic campaign aimed at restricting industrial development in the High North—in particular, hydrocarbon activities.[151] This campaign, which at the time of writing had more than twice as many signatures as the Arctic has inhabitants, does not have wide support *in* the Arctic and is viewed as an unwelcome intrusion on what should be matters for Arctic peoples. Many Arctic residents, indigenous and nonindigenous, are opposed to oil and gas development, but they do not want to be told what is best for them by millions of people who have never set foot north of the Arctic Circle. Greenpeace's campaign is based on a call for the Arctic to become an environmental sanctuary comparable to Antarctica. However, Antarctica is an uninhabited continent, and Arctic communities feel that their interests and wishes are not being considered. As Alyson Bailes incisively put it, a "stay-away agreement is thousands of years too late."[152] The World Wildlife Fund (WWF), less vocal but with more than five million paid-up members, works more quietly with the Arctic states and with industry to promote environmentally sound practices. Like Greenpeace, WWF would like to see Arctic hydrocarbons remain in the ground but employs softer lobbying techniques with local decision makers.[153] WWF conscientiously sends delegates to Arctic Council and working group meetings, where it has observer status.

CORPORATE INTERESTS

Business in the Arctic ranges from the sole trader/craftswoman selling to tourists to multinational oil companies. The different types of economic activities and the agents behind them are explored in more detail in chapters 5 and 6. With the world's insatiable demand for natural resources turning its attentions to the North, it is unsurprising to see major international hydrocarbon and mining firms attempting to curry favor with Arctic governments. Russia and Norway have state-owned hydrocarbon corporations with long experience, albeit run along rather different lines. In Canada and the United States, the preference is for private operators to take the lead. In the other Arctic states, the multi-million-dollar investment necessary before these kinds of projects can get off the ground and the years between the first explorations and commercial returns mean that even where the states establish their own state companies, they will be dependent on international partners.

International investors can exercise significant influence on local and national governments to ensure favorable conditions for their activities. For example, they lobby for flexible employment laws and less onerous environmental standards or monitoring. Corporations should not be criticized for this: they exist to make a profit, and if they do not make a profit, their shareholders will ask why. Their *primary* responsibility is toward shareholders and not the people they employ or in whose lands they operate. This is why governments must regulate them carefully to ensure that human rights and environmental standards are upheld.[154]

The Arctic Economic Council was established in 2014 to promote business and economic development in the Arctic. It is an offshoot of the Arctic Council but not a subsidiary body of it; in other words, it provides information to the Arctic Council, but its reports do not require Arctic Council endorsement. Of the voting membership, there are eighteen indigenous representatives (from six indigenous organizations) and twenty-four from business organizations (principally shipping and natural resource extractive companies). This demonstrates that even in the nonstate world, the inclusion of indigenous peoples is becoming a norm in Arctic governance.

OTHER STAKEHOLDERS

Other stakeholders in the Arctic include scientific and research institutions and universities. The International Arctic Science Committee (IASC) is the leading NGO representing researchers and research institutes dealing with the Arctic and provides opportunities for cooperation and coordination. Established in March 1998 and including representatives from both Arctic and non-Arctic states, IASC is an observer at the Arctic Council. Another observer is the University of the Arctic, which, despite its name, is not a degree-granting institution in its own right but rather a virtual network of Arctic universities and further education colleges based in all eight Arctic states (including Greenland and the Faroe Islands). Only universities and colleges located in the Arctic states may become full members, but the University of the Arctic has associate members from elsewhere. Nations around the world also have Arctic or polar-themed research institutes, not least those striving to show their commitment to Arctic research to justify the coveted Arctic Council observer status.[155]

CONCLUSIONS

The complexity of actors in the Arctic illustrates how the society of states and global society interact. The discourses and practices between them affect policy and can lead to new rules for governing activities in the Arctic. The late James N. Rosenau said the world was "bifurcated" into a state-centric world and a multicentric one made up of individuals, mass movements, firms, and NGOs.[156] The worlds compete and cooperate within their spheres and between worlds. Each brings a different perspective, a different way of talking about issues, goals, and aspirations. The players in the Arctic are no exception in the multilayered pattern of global politics.

FURTHER READING

Arctic Governance in an Era of Transformative Change: Critical Questions, Governance Principles, Ways Forward. Report of the Arctic Governance Project, April 14, 2010. http://www.arcticgovernance.org/agp-report-and-action -agenda.156784.en.html. Also available in French and Russian.

Axworthy, Thomas S., Timo Koivurova, and Waliul Hasanat, eds. *The Arctic Council: Its Place in the Future of Arctic Governance.* Toronto: Gordon Foundation, Munk School of Global Affairs and Arctic Centre, 2012.

Berg-Nordlie, Jo Saglie, and Ann Sullivan, eds. *Indigenous Politics: Institutions, Representation, Mobilisation.* Colchester, UK: ECPR Press, 2015.

Bertelsen, Rasmus Gjedssø, Xing Li, and Mette Højris Gregersen. *Chinese Arctic Science Diplomacy: An Instrument for Achieving the Chinese Dream?* Abingdon, UK: Routledge 2017.

English, John. *Ice and Water: People, Politics and the Arctic Council.* Toronto: Allen Lane, 2013.

Graczyk, Piotr, and Timo Koivurova. "The Arctic Council." In *Handbook of Politics in the Arctic*, edited by Leif Christian Jensen and Geir Hønneland, 298–327. Cheltenham, UK: Edward Elgar, 2015.

Grøn, Caroline Howard, Peter Nedergaard, and Anders Wivel, eds. *The Nordic Countries and the European Union: Still the Other European Community?* Abingdon, UK: Routledge, 2015.

Heininen, Lassi. "Northern Geopolitics: Actors, Interests and Processes in the Circumpolar Arctic." In *Polar Geopolitics: Knowledges, Resources and Legal Regimes*, edited by Richard C. Powell and Klaus Dodds, 241–58. Cheltenham, UK: Edward Elgar, 2014.

Hønneland, Geir. *Arctic Euphoria and International High North Politics.* Basingstoke, UK: Palgrave Macmillan, 2017.

Hønneland, Geir. "Cross Border Cooperation in the North: The Case of Northwest Russia." In *Russia and the North*, edited by Elana Wilson Rowe. Ottawa: University of Ottawa Press, 2009.

Hønneland, Geir, ed. *The Politics of the Arctic.* Cheltenham, UK: Edward Elgar, 2015.

Hough, Peter. *International Politics of the Arctic: Coming In from the Cold.* Abingdon, UK: Routledge 2013.

Hovgaard, Gestur, Beinta í Jákupsstovu, and Hans Andrias Sølvara, eds. *Vestnorden: Nye roller I det internationale samfund* [The West Nordic: New roles in the international community]. Torshavn, Faroe Islands: Faroe University Press, 2014.

Jakobson, Linda, and Seong-Hyon Lee. "North East Asia Eyes the Arctic." In *The New Arctic Governance*, edited by Linda Jakobson and Neil Melvin. Oxford: Oxford University Press, 2016.

Koivurova, Timo, Tianbao Qin, Sébastien Duyck, and Tapio Nykänen, eds. *Arctic Law and Governance: The Role of China and Finland.* Oxford: Hart Publishing, 2017.

Laruelle, Marlene. *Russia's Arctic Strategies and the Future of the Far North.* Abingdon, UK: Routledge, 2013.

Liu, Nengye, Elizabeth A. Kirk, and Tore Henriksen, eds. *The European Union and the Arctic.* Leiden, Netherlands: Brill, 2017.

Lunde, Leiv, Yang Jian, and Iselin Stensdal, eds. *Asian Countries and the Arctic Future.* Singapore: World Scientific, 2016.

Lynge, Aqqaluk, and Marianne Stenbaek, eds. *Inuit Arctic Policy.* 2010. Available at http://polarconnection.org/inuit-arctic-policy-inuit-circumpolar-council-2010.

Nord, Douglas. *The Arctic Council: Governance within the Far North.* Abingdon, UK: Routledge, 2016.

Nord, Douglas. *The Changing Arctic: Creating a Framework for Consensus Building and Governance within the Arctic Council.* Basingstoke, UK: Palgrave Macmillan, 2016.

Rosing Olsen, Rupaarnaq. *Qaannat alannguanni: Kalaallit Nunaanni naalakkersuinikkut oqaluttuarisaanermit 1939–79* [In the shadow of the kayaks: Greenland's political history 1939–79]. Nuuk, Greenland: Forlaget Atuagkat, 2002. Also in Danish as *I skyggen af kajakkerne: Grønlands politiske historie 1937–79.* Nuuk, Greenland: Forlaget Atuagkat, 2005.

Shadian, Jessica. *The Politics of Arctic Sovereignty: Oil, Ice and Inuit Governance.* Abingdon, UK: Routledge, 2014.

Stokke, Olav Schram, and Geir Hønneland. *International Cooperation and Arctic Governance: Regime Effectiveness and Northern Region Building.* Abingdon, UK: Routledge, 2007.

Suliatsinnik Oqaluttuaq: Fortællingen om vort arbeide [The story of our work]. Nuuk, Greenland: Inuit Issittormiut Siunnersuisoqatigiiffiat, Kalaallit Nunaat/Inuit Circumpolar Council, 2017.

Thór, Jón Th., Daniel Thorleifsen, Andras Mortensen, and Ole Marquardt. *Naboer i Nordatlanten: Færøerne, Island og Grønland. Hovedlinjer i Vestnordens historie gennem 1000 år* [Neighbors in the North Atlantic: The Faroe Islands, Iceland and Greenland. Principles of West Nordic history over 1000 years]. Torshavn, Faroe Islands: Faroe University Press, 2012.

Zagorski, Andrei. "Russia's Arctic Governance Policies." In Jakobson and Melvin, eds., *The New Arctic Governance.*

4

Securities in the Arctic

SECURITY OR SECURITIES?

SECURITY COMES IN a number of guises. Its forms can be grouped into two main categories: national and human. National security means the security of the territorial state and the people within from external invasion or unwanted interference. Military forces deter or meet such threats through preparedness. States also obtain security through cooperation in international institutions, through alliances, and through arms control. The term "human security" came into use at the end of the Cold War by the United Nations as a response to the wide array of threats to individuals from many sources. The end of the Cold War was a hopeful time when many thought the world could turn from national security in the form of military power and focus on the well-being of individuals and their communities.[1] Human security is closely linked to international human rights law. It concerns ways to address the most serious threats to individuals and communities. "Human" security broadens the idea of security considerably, perhaps almost to a limitless degree. Thus some states, like Canada, limit its use to immediate threats to Canadian inhabitants. At heart, however, the idea is broader and asks: Are individuals and/or their communities secure, including from their own governments?[2]

The different kinds of security are linked.[3] Certainly, a minimum of national security is essential for human security: people cannot be secure if they live under a shadow of invasion, civil war, or terrorism. However, the reverse is not true: a state can be secure—even very secure—while its inhabitants are not. A state can also become less secure if its citizens are reluctant to interact with government for fear of being a target of investigation or if hunger, unemployment, or inequality reduce the creativity of a nation or, worse, lead to civil unrest. Beyond the state and people is the emerging insecurity of climate change. Climate change affects all the securities; in fact, the US Defense Department considers climate change the single most important security problem facing the United States because of it many likely effects.[4]

Security is not the same idea as safety. If one tries to be safe at home, one might have a fire extinguisher or avoid leaving clutter on the floor. To be secure in the home, however, people put locks on their doors and also rely on external sources of protection, such as the legal right to exclude others and a reliable police force or neighbors to call on in case of an emergency. Beyond this, security also means that one can speak one's language and practice a religion or express political views. Societal security means that a community is free to create, express, change, or preserve customs considered central to identities. Even more broadly, human security is interested in the well-being of individuals. Human agency makes for more security and thus tends to be more bottom-up, as people make local choices or assert claims that they should have a say in building security.

National security is also social, though it is managed from a top-down perspective—the national government downward toward individuals at home (and outward toward other states). During major wars and often in peacetime, citizens are drafted to serve in the military on the grounds that all citizens owe this to the government and other citizens. National security relies on all of us paying taxes. The objective in investing in defense and diplomacy is that the very existence of military security institutions renders their activation unnecessary.

Securities Are Interwoven

Alyson Bailes argued that civil disasters like oil spills or cruise ship accidents in the Arctic require governments to develop a common regulatory regime or to demand significant self-governance by firms.[5] Achieving that outcome requires specific answers to difficult questions. Are the coast guards and other emergency personnel available to help, and how long would it take for them to reach the crisis location? Is safety equipment available? Who pays for accidents?[6]

A rescue of a foundering cruise ship would be especially problematic. One recent study of the effectiveness of equipment designed to keep people warm in the event of an accident in cold waters indicated that equipment that should have worked for five days barely lasted one day.[7] This could trigger a crisis for seafarers or cruise tourists and anyone hoping to rescue them. The distances and small populations in the Arctic complicate any rescue, and yet the first responders to offshore emergencies are likely to be local people and not professional coast guards. Even if accomplished in time, a tiny Arctic village would be hard-pressed to feed and care for the passengers and crew of a cruise ship. The local people might in turn be left in crisis because local stockpiles for the community would be depleted. States have international and domestic laws on these topics, but only recently has much specific attention been paid to readiness in the Arctic. Testing plans and equipment to respond to emergencies takes time, but it is essential.

Human security focuses on gaps in the fundamental capacity of individuals to live in a community. It seeks more individual- and community-focused ideas for security and emphasizes bottom-up approaches to building security, the ones most likely to affect the inside of homes rather than the edges of states. Can one get medical care? How does one cope with the persistence of tuberculosis in northern Canada or Greenland? Is there enough food, and is it culturally appropriate and nutritionally adequate? (See box 4.1.)[8]

Cultural and national security values clash and cause security problems for individuals. Nowhere is this clearer than with respect to the security of indigenous peoples. Where indigenous people would like to use their land's natural resources, whether for traditional practices or modern industries, they discover people far away from the Arctic want to keep the region free of such use. Efforts to suppress whaling or seal hunting, with repercussions for indigenous hunters, emerge from Western assumptions about animal rights or animal welfare that fail to consider indigenous perspectives or the values that indigenous peoples attach to animals, including spiritual values.[9] Heather Nicol and Lassi Heininen put it this way: "One of the greatest unacknowledged threats to the Arctic region, besides the race for natural resources as a result of climate change may be the continuing way in which competitive southern geopolitical and geoeconomic discourses concerning northern development serve to effectively 're-colonise' the north and re-marginalise its peoples."[10]

BOX 4.1 | Food Security

A crucial factor in human security is access to adequate food. Huet, Rosol, and Egeland reported that over 60 percent of Inuit Canadian families are affected by food insecurity.[a] Adequate food serves the many cultural needs of a community.[b] People are food secure if they have access to safe and nutritious food at all times; they are food insecure if they do not have access—either because of lack of available food or lack of money to obtain adequate food. Even if they have resources to hunt and fish, people may be barred from subsistence activities by hunting and fishing restrictions imposed from outside, often on an environmental basis with little consultation with the affected communities. Traditional food supplies can be affected by inadequate management of predator species: in Sweden, measures to protect wolves have led to an increase in the wolf population and hence pose a threat to reindeer as well as sheep that are left to graze freely in the summer months. Improved consultations with subsistence hunters and herders could reduce these difficulties without worsening animal management. The food example also illustrates how security in one category can end up connected to others. Developments on the land, such as roads and renewable energy projects, can disrupt migration routes and in turn open an area to further development. Roads also improve access to jobs, education, and medical care.

Arctic communities require external assistance to address the environmental threats to food caused by actions thousands of miles away from the Arctic. Mercury, lead poisoning, and persistent organic pollutants (POPs) arrive in the North and contaminate the food chain (see chapter 10).[c] Climate change alters the availability of food from the land and sea. Too much ice on the land can kill off reindeer, causing a food, culture, and economic catastrophe.[d]

The substitution of traditional foods with a Western diet is not the easy solution. Crops cannot usually be grown nor animals farmed on tundra, permafrost, or ice. Substitute food must therefore be imported. The distances involved result in irregular deliveries, high prices, and low quality, especially of fresh food. Further, growing reliance on Western foods has led to an increase in noncommunicable diseases in the North, such as diabetes and cardiovascular problems. Food is not only a physical necessity; to indigenous Arctic communities, it has spiritual significance and plays a major part in holistic well-being and health.[e] It is not a simple matter of counting calories but of connection to nature and community cohesion, for example, through customs of sharing.

[a] C. Huet, R. Rosol, and G. M. Egeland, "The Prevalence of Food Insecurity Is High and the Diet Quality Poor in Inuit Communities," *Journal of Nutrition* 142, no. 3 (2012): 541; cited in Arja Rautio, Birger Poppel, and Kue Young, "Human Health and Well-Being," in AHDR II, 309. See also "Feeding Nunavut," accessed April 16, 2018, http://www.feedingnunavut.com.

[b] See, for example, Bill Hess, *Gift of the Whale: The Inupiat Bowhead Hunt, a Sacred Tradition* (Seattle: Sasquatch Books, 1999).

[c] Rautio, Poppel, and Young, "Human Health and Well-Being," 310.

[d] See E. Carina H. Keskitalo, "Climate Change, Vulnerability and Adaptive Capacity in a Multi-Use Forest Municipality in Northern Sweden," in *Community Adaptation and Vulnerability in Arctic Regions*, ed. Grete K. Hovelsrud and Barry Smit (Dordrecht, Germany: Springer), 285–311, esp. 296–99; see also Anna Stammler-Gossmann, "'Translating' Vulnerability at the Community Level: Case Study from the Russian North," in *Community Adaptation*, 131–62, esp. 149–50.

[e] Carl M. Hlid et al., "Human Health and Well-Being," in *Arctic Human Development Report*, ed. Joan Nymand Larsen and Gail Fondahl (Akureyri, Iceland: Stefansson Arctic Institute, 2004), 160.

MAKING HUMANS SECURE

Most people, most of the time, establish the conditions for their own security. They get jobs or live by traditional means. They have families and educations. They move to a new place or stay where they are among people they know. The state (here meaning government in its many forms) has a role to play in creating the conditions that make it possible for people to secure themselves and their communities. A UN handbook on how to assess human security says families and communities should be able to secure themselves rather than wait for external help.[11] The handbook suggested seven areas where human security might be impaired enough to make individuals and communities feel and be insecure. Table 4.1 is a version of the UN's table of basic types and illustrative threats, revised to be more Arctic-relevant.

Social infrastructure that facilitates economic opportunities, the rule of law, enforcement of property and contracts, policing, and national security efforts contribute to human and societal security. Sometimes government steps in to assist those who cannot ensure their own security, due to disability or age, for example. National and subnational governments provide education, health, employment, and environmental programs.

In other settings, the state needs to empower people with enough political security to make decisions that will secure themselves.[12] Political security is the capacity to make choices not just through elections but also through meaningful participation in making choices that will affect how one lives and works. It requires more devolved decision making rather than less, if only because the rapid pace of climate change requires immediate local responses first and the slower national and international ones later.[13] It might even mean the capacity to say no or yes to industrial projects.

Cultural security is also essential to human well-being, especially for heavily outnumbered minorities. Environmental changes in the region affect the culture.[14] Alaskan elders are concerned about changes in animal migrations, language loss, landscape change (including the availability of permafrost ice cellars), loss of traditional knowledge, costs of food, unpredictable and extreme weather events, and arrival of new animals like porcupines and insects.[15] Unsurprisingly, minority leaders seek ways to retain control over the development and evolution of their cultures in the Arctic.[16]

Table 4.1   Types of Security in the Arctic

Type of Security	Examples of Threats
Economic	Persistent poverty, unemployment. Rural indigenous populations are on average much poorer than people in larger towns. Poverty increases the likelihood of illness (health security).
Food	Hunger, poor-quality food, unavailability of traditional foods. Poor-quality imported food is common in the Arctic. Store-bought food is very expensive, due to transportation costs, and of lesser quality as it must be preserved for long life. Traditional foods become unavailable owing to environmental change and regulation.
Health	Infectious diseases (e.g., tuberculosis), noncommunicable diseases (e.g., heart disease, diabetes, depression), contaminated or poor-quality food, lack of access to health care services, inadequate sanitation.
Environmental	Environmental degradation, resource depletion, pollution, extreme weather, coastal erosion (including existential threats to entire villages).
Personal	Violence (including domestic violence), harassment, terrorism, abusive employment conditions.
Community	Pressure to assimilate, forced relocations, rapid demographic changes (e.g., sudden shifts in numbers of migrant workers), intercommunity tensions, loss of native languages, restrictions on religious expression. Young people often still have to leave families, and many choose never to return. Forced migration and residential schools were common among earlier generations and contributed to the destruction of culture, exposure to racism, and prohibition of native languages or religious practices.
Political	Political repression, lack of access to democratic process, restrictions on freedoms of expression and association. Experiences vary widely, especially for indigenous peoples.

Source: Adapted from UN Trust Fund for Human Security, *Human Security in Theory and Practice* (New York: United Nations, 2009), 7.

Logics of Security

The logics of securities differ. Theories of geopolitics tend to see things in grand strategy terms as large powers vie with each other for access to resources, strategic control of vital transportation routes, and preparation for potential militarized conflicts. National security in the Arctic is strong; none of the Arctic states faces the fear of extinction by another state in the region. Human security requires looking inside states and at the well-being of individuals relative to policies and assets as well as links to global actors like firms or environmental NGOs. The linkages between people, issues, resources, and security are more complex in human security than in national security—and more immediate.

| BOX 4.2 | Human Security vs. National Security |

Many citizens are happy to pay the price of national security by supporting defense infrastructure through national taxation. In 2015 the US Army placed a $241 million order for twenty-two Black Hawk helicopters (just over $10 million per helicopter).[a] Meanwhile, in Alaska, the coastal village of Shishmaref is going underwater.[b] The price to move the six hundred people who live in the village is $180 million, or $300,000 per person. According to the US Army Corps of Engineers, it would cost even more to attempt to protect the village from the waves and rising water. Alaska set aside $8 million for all tribal climate adaptation programs. Shishmaref's residents cannot pay for the move. Multiple securities are at stake in these two cases. The villagers want the societal security of maintaining their collective identity as a village and keeping their culture alive. The military seeks to defend US interests abroad and potentially defend the United States as a whole against attack. Which is more important and to whom? Whose security is more at risk?

[a]John Keller, "Army Places $241.7 Million Order with Sikorsky to Build 22 New UH-60M Black Hawk Helicopters," *Military and Aerospace*, March 4, 2015, http://www.militaryaerospace.com/articles/2015/03/light-military-helicopter-market-to-decline-over-the-next-15-years-says-forecast-international.html.
[b]Christopher Mele and Daniel Victor, "Reeling from Effects of Climate Change, Alaskan Village Votes to Relocate," *New York Times*, August 19, 2016, https://www.nytimes.com/2016/08/20/us/shishmaref-alaska-elocate-vote-climate-change.html.

Consider box 4.2 on the serious problem facing a number of communities in the Arctic—the erosion of the coastline that puts villages at risk. Individual and community security is center stage. Addressing the immediate threat is costly, but not significantly more costly than spending on defense for threats that might or might not exist.

Current Strategies to Understand and Manage Securities

Human securities demand a move from large-scale national and international security concerns to ones simultaneously local and comprehensive.[17] Human security is geopolitics at a small scale, tied to pasts and places in the direct experience of the people who live there. For example, reindeer herders and Alaskan coastal Inuit have detailed knowledge of the landscape and the animals on it. Their knowledge includes an individual and community-wide mental "database" of past conditions that influenced the lives of people, animals, and land. Natural scientists and policy makers often attempt to understand small pieces of the world. In contrast, indigenous knowledge is more holistic, is empirically based, and comes from generations of observations that led to robust strategies for living in the Arctic. Human security approaches that include local people and their knowledge of a locale alongside Western scientific approaches produce rounder, more holistic knowledge. Holistic knowledge, in turn, is more likely to yield insights into what is going on and thus make for better social responses.

Because national security dominates most conceptions of security, it is common to think of solving domestic problems within a national security framework.[18] National security usually reduces local, community, and individual control over decisions about how to live. Governments can draft citizens to serve, ration supplies for the population, and take over civilian towns for the war effort. National security creates us-versus-them thinking and raises abstract threats and risks so that plans and equipment are ready in advance. Sometimes the national security approach can be temporarily effective in crises like natural disasters, but this may be at the cost of not dealing with the *causes* of the crisis or of encouraging communities to find solutions for the future. Box 4.3 uses the concept of securitization to highlight the liabilities of applying national security approaches to human security.

NATIONAL SECURITY

No "hot" military conflict in the Arctic has happened since World War II. Then, Allied convoys ran to and from Murmansk to supply the Soviet Union in the fight against the Axis powers. Other Arctic regions were occupied by the Nazis or the Allies (see chapter 2). After the war, security in Western Europe came primarily from the North Atlantic Treaty Organization (NATO). Iceland joined the North Atlantic Treaty Organization (NATO) in 1949 (notwithstanding public protests) and from 1951 to 2005 hosted a US naval air base at Keflavík to provide security for Iceland, which has no military.[19] In 2016 the US Navy began preparations to return to Iceland on a reduced scale.[20] The United States occupied Greenland in April 1940 and opened military bases in Greenland in 1941, following an agreement with the Danish ambassador, who had never recognized the German-directed puppet regime in Copenhagen. The United States has a military presence in Greenland to the present day. Norway was used by the Germans for submarine bases and to invade the Kola Peninsula in the USSR. Similarly, Finnish Lapland was first invaded by the USSR and then occupied by the Germans, who used the region as a staging ground for German attempts to invade and cut off the Kola Peninsula. It is not surprising that the geostrategic impor-

---

BOX 4.3 | **A Potential Danger: Securitization**

One of the dangers of the term "human security" is that it may fall victim to a process called securitization. Securitization is when someone declares a person, place, or object a threat. If that claim takes hold, then local input and participation in decisions may be curtailed.[a] The "key idea underlying securitization is that an issue is given sufficient saliency to win the assent of the audience, which enables those who are authorized to handle the issue to use whatever means they deem most appropriate."[b] In other words, securitization combines the politics of "threat design with that of threat management."[c] For example, after the 9/11 attacks on the United States, much blood and treasure were put into combating terrorism. It has allowed the US government to divert funds from areas that support deep human security, through economic, social, and environmental programs, to defense and what became called homeland security. Results would likely have been very different if the attacks had been construed as a regular crime or a public health challenge. How might this happen in the Arctic? The US military has declared climate change an existential threat to the United States and other places.[d] At most, a military approach to climate change can help in cases of short-term disaster relief, but it is not a solution for living on a daily basis. Broader, robust strategies for addressing climate change would enhance a wider range of human securities.

[a]Barry Buzan, Ole Wæver, and Jaap de Wilde, *Security: A New Framework for Analysis* (London: Lynne Rienner, 1998).
[b]Thierry Balzacq, Sarah Léonard, and Jan Ruzicka, "'Securitization' Revisited: Theory and Cases," *International Relations* 30, no. 4 (2016): 494–531, esp. 495.
[c]Ibid.
[d]US Navy, Climate Change Roadmap, April 2010, http://www.navy.mil/navydata/doc uments/CCR.pdf; Department of Defense, Climate Change Adaptation Roadmap, June 2014, http://www.acq.osd.mil/ie/download/CCARprint.pdf.

---

tance of the Kola Peninsula for Russia remains. Russia has much of its submarine-based nuclear deterrence fleet there, and its naval doctrine incorporates strategic routes for its Northern Fleet to break out of the region for service elsewhere in the Atlantic. The doctrine also aims to deny NATO fleets access. The aim of these military activities is not particularly about conflict arising in the Arctic but rather about deterrence and the possibility of war elsewhere in the world, especially in Europe.

As the post-WWII period hardened into the Cold War confrontation between the USSR and the United States, some military writers thought the next war would erupt in the Arctic. Longtime air power advocate Henry H. "Hap" Arnold, Army Air chief of staff, said, "If there is a third war, its strategic center will be the North Pole."[21] The Distant Early Warning system (DEW line) was built in Alaska and Canada and additional stations in Greenland and Iceland to give warning of any Soviet bomber and missile strikes. Submarines prowled under the ice. The Cold War saw Russia and the United States make many probes of each other's defenses.

There were also nuclear accidents due to the military activity. For the United States, most of them happened over US territory, but some happened abroad. For example, the United States lost four nuclear weapons in an aircraft accident in Greenland in 1968, contaminating the area with radiation. A part of one bomb has still not been recovered.

Probes and submarine activity still go on in the Arctic, which raises security concerns and accident risks. The Novaya Zemlya archipelago has been used for missile tests since the 1950s. In October 2017 Russia tested missiles through its Arctic airspace in both directions—toward the Barents Sea, to the west, and toward Kamchatka, on the Pacific.[22] NATO has announced some new commands based on functions rather than geography.[23] Most of the Arctic states are modernizing their defense systems after significant declines in expenditures immediately following the Cold War.

The Arctic states, however, have tried to find ways to minimize the risk of accident and reduce concerns over activities that could increase tensions. The Norwegian and Russian admirals in the Barents routinely talk to each other to improve transparency. Pursuant to a 1997 agreement, NATO and Russia created the Permanent Joint Commission (PJC) to discuss topics of mutual interest.[24] In 2002 the PJC was replaced by the NATO-Russia Council.[25] In 2017 the council met three times to discuss Ukraine, Afghanistan, and transparency and risk reduction.[26] Both NATO and Russia inform each other of major military exercises, a practice that dates to the end of WWII. In a related vein, actions on the civilian side of aviation could be misinterpreted for military ones, so both sides inform each other about launches of rockets for nonmilitary uses.[27]

In October 2015 the Arctic Eight established the Arctic Coast Guard Forum to facilitate cooperation between coast guards.[28] It operates through the thick and thin of relations between Russia and the other states.

How Secure Is National Security in the Arctic?
In no way do the authors of this book think hot conflict is the future of the Arctic. Cooperation and communication dominate in the region, creating deep security. However, it is also true that Arctic states pay

attention to each other, prepare and maintain forces for combat, and gauge intentions and adjust their defense posture as needed. For example, in 2018 the United States Navy decided to reestablish the Second Fleet in the Atlantic, which had been disestablished in 2011, in light of Russian and Chinese activity and to reassure NATO allies.[29] Both the United States and Russia are continental powers with interests along all their land and maritime borders, as well as toward the rest of the world. Rising powers can destabilize or stabilize national security in a broad international system sense. Narrower activities like security dilemmas, arms racing, and deterrence could happen. Any hot conflicts between the Arctic states, however, would be more likely to erupt elsewhere in the world.

Power and Hegemonic Transitions: The Rise of China

The rise of China presents a possible systemic source for instability or stability in the Arctic. Especially for realist theorists, the Great Powers define the international system. During the Cold War, Russia and the United States created a bipolar international structure and each was hegemonic, setting the norms within its sphere. When new powers arrive on the scene, others have to manage or respond to the rising power. Power transition theory argues that when a rising power is dissatisfied with its status, war is more likely.[30]

China has risen carefully, and the United States and other states have engaged primarily in mutual adjustment. China has been an effective participant in Arctic governance, contributing to dialogue and scientific work in the region. Thus, it seems China and its international competitors have made it through the power transition without the use of force between Great Powers.

A different abstract theory in international relations has to do with hegemonic transition. In this concept, ideas matter most, though material power usually supports those ideas. The issue in a hegemonic transition is how a very powerful state will use its power to structure world politics. Hegemony, as Ian Clark put it, is "power with a purpose."[31] The United States is considered a hegemon, and after WWII its purpose was to encourage democracy and international free trade. It acted on these goals while developing a significant military to deter Soviet efforts to spread communism. The problem with having a vast military is that it becomes a powerful lobby at home and all too easy to use in response to any problem arising abroad. China has a simpler purpose: it wants to trade and invest internationally and will not interfere in another state's internal affairs, including on human rights.

China's nuanced 2018 policy on the Arctic suggests it will choose where, among international institutions/regimes, it will pursue its Arctic interests. China emphasizes international law and China's participation in international organizations.[32] China is building its new Belt and Road Initiative (BRI) to improve trade and secure natural resources, and the maritime routes of the Arctic are part of it (see box 6.1 in chapter 6). It has a deepening relationship with Russia. While a new partnership with Russia changes calculations for other powers, it could prove a boon to cooperation in the Arctic. Russia can look east to replace economic opportunities it lost after annexing Crimea. China will not ask difficult questions about the legality of that action. China hardly wants conflict in the Arctic and is very concerned about the effects climate change will have in China. Its support to Russia may, therefore, facilitate increasing cooperation in the Arctic.

Geostrategy

Geostrategy looks at geography and resources to understand better the interests of states and how they translate into defense strategies. This viewpoint suggests that the Arctic Eight (plus China and other important states outside the Arctic) have many reasons to cooperate or at least not to escalate military tensions in the Arctic. China may want uranium or other rare earth minerals from the Arctic states that are essential for modern electronics; other states may move to block too strong a hold on those resources over fears of military application (uranium) or economic dominance. Security concerns over resources may also prompt cooperation. Much of the current Russian Arctic strategy is about securing the region for planned economic development. An orderly Arctic with rules and the capacity to enforce those rules on sovereign land territory and outward into the ocean is very much in the interests of the Arctic Eight and other states.[33]

Russia has the most to lose if the Arctic becomes a zone of high stress or conflict. Major Russian rivers flow from the south to the Arctic Ocean (for example, the Ob, the Yenisei, and the Lena). A warmer and more open Arctic Ocean offers an opportunity to better connect and develop economically the Russian interior and to link the Far North communities to internal and external markets. For shipping between Russia or Canada and Asia or Europe to become reality, the region needs to be secure *and* peaceful. Both the 2008 and the 2013 Russian Arctic strategy documents emphasize these points.[34] Heininen, Sergunin, and Yarovoy summarized the link between military forces and the Arctic as follows:

"The Arctic Group of Forces is charged not simply with defending territory but also with protecting Russia's economic interests in the region," and that includes modernization.[35]

Economic power is one measure of state power, a matter of interest to realist and liberal thinkers alike. Better infrastructure in the coastal Arctic and further inland would contribute to that power and improve human security. Seen in this light, Russia's recent efforts to reopen some of its old radar, coast guard, scientific, and military bases in the North make good, and not necessarily threatening, sense, especially in light of its plans to develop the Northern Sea Route (NSR).[36] That said, it has increased and modernized its naval and airpower presence in the region since 2008. It has probed the defenses of a number of Arctic states, though the number of its tests of other nations' defenses does not come close to the numbers during the Cold War.[37]

Russian (and American) calculations of "how much is enough"[38] might require alteration as China builds its blue water navy.[39] While China also needs a peaceful Arctic for trade and will not benefit from conflict, its growing and modernizing navy could begin to look threatening to Russia and has gotten the attention of the United States. After a rendezvous with Russian Navy vessels, China sent a naval convoy through the Bering Straits on the US side in September 2015 and said it would use the Russian side of the Straits in due course. The Chinese actions were according to law, as explained in chapter 9. China has also sent an icebreaker across the central Arctic Ocean sailing north of the NSR, which could signal to Russia that China is looking for a high seas route in the long term, thus avoiding the NSR and Russian jurisdiction. That could reduce the NSR's commercial viability, while complicating Russia's security environment. On the other hand, China is investing in Arctic Russia, and China could simply be hedging its bets while encouraging Russia to focus on the effective development of the NSR for Arctic trade.

Russia faces the problem that five of the other Arctic states are in NATO: Denmark (including the Faroe Islands and Greenland), Norway, Iceland, Canada, and the United States. NATO is intended to be a defensive alliance. Russia, however, has long argued NATO expansion eastward after the end of the Cold War was unwarranted and unfriendly, taking in former Warsaw Pact countries that had been under the Soviet sphere of influence. Sweden and Finland periodically weigh the option of joining NATO but have so far remained outside. Sweden, Finland, and Russia each have a special Partnership for Peace cooperative arrangement with NATO to keep information as transparent as possible.

There are credible reports that Russia has used disinformation campaigns in Sweden and Finland to discourage joining NATO.[40] In addition, Denmark (but not the Faroe Islands or Greenland), Finland, and Sweden are all in the EU. The Treaty on European Union requires each member state to come to the aid of the others in the event of attack or other crisis.[41] The EU has no real mechanism to do this, though it is developing one called "permanent structured cooperation."[42] The EU essentially relies on NATO; for example, one response from the EU and NATO to Russian behavior was creating a new headquarters in Helsinki, Finland, devoted to hybrid security threats (e.g., cyberattacks, security in the Mediterranean, etc.).[43]

Security Dilemmas
Every sovereign state has the right to have military forces, exercise its forces, and move them around on its own territory. Each one can legally sail and fly military aircraft in much of the ocean and the sky.[44] Each state can invite another state to conduct exercises or even build bases on its territory or choose to join an alliance. The US media talks about Russian exercises in the north on Russian territory neighboring Finland and Norway, but not about US military exercises on bases and posts in the United States or in allied countries neighboring Russia.

The use of force as well as hardware updates and increases in troop levels can raise questions about intention. Doubt about intentions often leads to security dilemmas. A security dilemma arises when a state begins to fear for its security relative to another state. For example, state A decides to hedge its bets, and it increases its spending on the military to address the perceived threat from State B. State B might not have had aggressive intentions. At this point State B's officials may note State A's behavior and increase military capacity. The response from State B confirms State A's fears. State A builds more arms, and that increases the alarm of State B. At that point, the very expensive and possibly dangerous process of arms racing might start. A security dilemma can be tested for its reality (is it safe to ignore another country's military acquisitions or not?). State B could simply not respond to an early instance of State A increasing arms, when the risks of being wrong about State A's intentions are low. Alternatively, it might exercise diplomacy to reduce tensions. In 2014, then prime minister Harper of Canada visited the Arctic during Canada's annual military exercises there and said the country had to be on guard against the Russians. In October 2016 Canada's Prime Minister Trudeau reversed the security discourse of the Harper government and promised to work more with Russia, a classic way to evaluate and possibly stop the security dilemma dynamic.[45]

Booth and Wheeler have argued that the security dilemma is a result of states answering two questions.[46] The first is the "Dilemma of Interpretation." Is the other's action to increase capacity defensive or offensive (actively directed against other states) in nature? It is plausible that Russia believed in at least unfriendly intentions from the West as it saw NATO expand into former Soviet Bloc states.[47] The United States dismissed Russian concerns for its security and offered the NATO-Russia Council.[48] Weak at the time, Russia accepted. It complained again in 2007 as NATO and EU expansion continued. In 2008 the financial crisis ravaged the Russian economy. This pattern of events caused some in Russia to believe there was a deliberate strategy to prevent its recovery. From the US/EU perspective, Russia's concerns were unwarranted: there was no threat to Russia by EU or NATO enlargement, and everyone suffered from the 2008 financial crisis, including the United States.

If Russia had concerns regarding the expansion of NATO, Russia's annexation of Crimea and Russian-backed rebellion in eastern Ukraine changed NATO perceptions of Russian intentions. Sanctions have been the main consequence for Russia, which have greatly affected the Russian economy, including with regard to international investment and cooperation in Arctic hydrocarbon development. Geopolitics would suggest that Russia does not harbor offensive intentions in the Arctic. Stated Russian military doctrine says the Arctic is a zone of cooperation. The rebuilding of Russian Arctic bases and modernizing weapons were announced years ago, during a period of considerable cooperation, suggesting defensive intent and possible dual use to support commercial navigation.

The second question involves the "Dilemma of Response," which comes into play when a state interprets another state's actions as offensive in nature. In that case, the latter state needs to decide whether to signal deterrence or reassurance. Most European states and the United States are using a mix of signals to reassure and to deter Russia from aggression in Europe, especially toward Ukraine and the Baltics. Trudeau's emphasis on cooperation was an instance of reassurance to the Russians. The 2015 Arctic Coast Guard Agreement is an exercise in reassurance/trust-building to promote cooperation. In January 2017 the United States reinforced its Baltic Sea allies, notably Norway and Poland, by sending US troops along with other NATO troops.[49] This constitutes deterrence of the Russians because (as the United States argued in the Cold War) the prospect of dead Americans signals US commitment. It is also reassurance to its allies. Sweden has made it clear it would assist Europe in the event of a natural disaster or attack and has new plans to make its own society resilient. By this they mean assisting, but not joining, NATO; increasing capability through improved human security; and updating plans and capabilities in national security. These Swedish policies are intended as a deterrent to Russia.[50]

Nevertheless, it probably raises Russian concerns about response. Gorbachev's Murmansk speech that opened the door to better cooperation in the Arctic included this remark: "The Soviet Union duly appreciates the fact that Denmark and Norway, while being members of NATO, unilaterally refused to station foreign military bases and deploy nuclear weapons on their territory in peacetime. This stance, if consistently adhered to, is important for lessening tensions in Europe."[51] Today, about three hundred US troops are on regular rotation to Norway: not quite a permanent base, but foreign troops nonetheless.

Seen in that light, increased US support to NATO could signal a threatening situation to Russia, perhaps even in the Arctic. At the same time, Russian actions on its southern borders and in Syria, its increased probes of Scandinavian defenses, not to mention its cyberactivities, have raised concern about Russian intentions. There is some evidence in academic studies that neighboring democracies are less likely to perceive a threat from each other than is the case between neighbors that consist of one democracy and one nondemocracy.[52] In recent years, Russia has stepped back from earlier reforms for more democracy and free expression. The likelihood of higher threat perceptions in Europe and the United States rises as a consequence. Russia might build more arms, and the spiral of mistrust and misunderstanding of a security dilemma could begin and trigger arms racing. Responses to Russian activities have prompted deterrence and reassurance.

Arms acquisition by a neighbor that has a shared land border with another state is more likely to provoke a response than one that happens across an ocean.[53] Russia has by far the best-equipped navy for Arctic operations. Its icebreaker fleet is aging and creaking, but unlike the United States, it at least has the ships to operate in the Arctic. After Russia, Finland and Sweden have the next most icebreakers.[54] Scandinavian countries cannot hope to stop a concerted military effort by the Russians, but they can deter the Russians. The Arctic Ocean limits the threat from Russia to the United States and Canada (and vice versa).

In contrast, Canada only has the (friendly but powerful) Americans to worry about on its landward side. The Nordic states are near to or border on Russia, so Russian actions to increase arms or to gather intelligence by flying or sailing near these countries pose a significant dilemma to them regarding intentions and response. However, even there, the threat is not likely over the Arctic region itself but over NATO activities elsewhere or in the Baltic Sea.[55]

From Security Dilemmas to Arms Racing

Security dilemmas do not always trigger wars or even low-level skirmishes, even if both sides suspect offensive intentions. Often they translate into arms races. At present, there is little evidence of any arms racing between NATO and the Russians, though all have been modernizing equipment. The tentative growth in arms might indicate an emerging arms race in light of growing fears over intent, but whether the fears would be directed to the Arctic is another matter; cooperation increases security. Similarly, not all arms races turn into hot war. The cost of arms races lies in the diversion of resources away from other state interests, including measures to enhance human security.

On the whole, quantitative arms races are more likely to lead to armed conflict, while qualitative ones rarely do.[56] This is because qualitative improvements are less obviously offensive than sheer numbers of weapons or military personnel. Finger-pointing is the more likely outcome from replacing older equipment with newer technology, though difficulties interpreting the meaning of a more accurate or longer-range system might heighten the problem of the security dilemma. Qualitative improvements are also harder to see, count, or compare. Whether weapons are dual use can further confuse the situation. Many technologies can be both peaceful and warlike. Is a drone a security threat or a useful tool for science and cooperation? Icebreakers and ice-capable ships are for trade and rescue but also essential for Arctic military operations.

Lasserre, Le Roy, and Garon argued in 2012 that there was no arms race in the Arctic, and their assessment still holds. They define an arms race as a two-part process. One part requires "abnormal growth rates in the military outlays of countries in a region."[57] There is no abnormal growth in the Arctic. There was a massive decrease in Russian assets in the region after the end of the Cold War (and a general decrease in military spending after the Cold War by all parties). Moreover, the kind of military technologies useful in the Arctic are primarily navy or air force. These technologies entail a very long acquisition process, so countries plan many years in advance. A new weapons system might become operational at a time when tension is elevated, but it would have been commissioned, developed, and produced at a much earlier time, possibly when the acquisition raised no concerns. Thus, the increase in arms now in progress in the Arctic states is at least partly explained as part of earlier decisions to modernize old systems.

The second part of Lasserre, Le Roy, and Garon's definition of an arms race requires that *regional* tensions must drive the increase: "Build up must be reciprocated, not driven by *exogenous or domestic factors* [emphasis added] that coincidentally bring about simultaneous increases."[58] One should distinguish older, planned acquisitions with new levels of expenditures and, even then, consider the events or commitments that drove the decision. Iraq, Afghanistan, Syria, and the "war on terror" account for most of the increases for the United States and some NATO states.[59] Some Russian increases are partly due to Syria. It is not an increase that is Arctic-specific.

It is possible, however, that Russia's increased tests of air and sea space have prompted Nordic states to plan increases in their arms acquisitions. The extent of Norwegian alarm at Russian behavior may be easier to gauge in a few years as expenditures and types of weapons become clearer. Then analysts can better determine whether the increases are in response to Russian actions or part of earlier acquisition decisions. Reinstitution of the draft for men and women in Sweden as part of their resiliency approach to security indicates growing alarm over Russian activities, particularly in the Baltic.[60] Nevertheless, four thousand one-year conscripts look more like symbolic precaution than preparation for impending conflict.

As Alyson Bailes put it, "Russian actions and gestures made in the northern theatre may have little or nothing to do with the Arctic as such. When they reflect strategic rivalry with the US, NATO, or other world powers, any response directed at Russia may more appropriately and effectively be made outside of the Arctic."[61] Strong military facilities in the Arctic do not mean the military assets are intended for use in the Arctic.[62]

One way to gauge whether an arms race has begun is to look at expenditures. Table 4.2 shows military expenditures by the Arctic Eight in five different years in constant 2016 millions of US dollars. (Using constant dollar figures facilitates comparisons over the years without the vagaries of exchange rates, inflation, etc.) The United States spends more on defense than the other Arctic states combined in each of the years. That is not surprising given that the United States spends more than the next six top spenders in the world combined: China, Russia, Saudi Arabia, India, France, and the UK. The American expenditures could look threatening (and did in some quarters) but were caused by factors extraneous to the Arctic or the US-Russia relationship, like Afghanistan,

Table 4.2   Arctic States' Military Expenditures 2012–2017 (millions in constant 2016 US dollars)

State	2012	2014	2015	2016	2017
Canada	16,260	15,275	17,561	18,132	19,837
Denmark	3,883	3,405	3,370	3,593	3,701
Finland	3,485	3,327	3,402	3,415	3,516
Iceland	0	0	0	0	0
Norway	5,452	5,821	5,779	5,997	6,330
Russia	53,317	59,929	64,593	69,245	55,327
Sweden	4,974	5,300	5,357	5,429	5,470
United States	715,838	618,341	603,625	600,106	597,178

Note: The year 2013 was omitted due to unavailable constant dollars data.
Source: Stockholm International Peace Research Institute (SIPRI), Military Expenditures Database, Budgets in Constant 2016 US$ Millions, 2018, https://www.sipri.org/databases/milex.

Iraq, and Syria. In constant dollars, US defense expenditures declined over the period, partly due to force drawdowns and efforts to reduce the deficit. There were modest incremental increases in the budgets of other Arctic states, with the exception of Russia. Spending in the Arctic region would be less. For example, of the total US defense budget, Alaska got less than 1 percent in fiscal year 2015, though that amount contributed 6.1 percent of Alaska's state GDP.[63]

In the past, there was an increase in the US share of defense spending at the end of the Cold War (1991), because the Soviet Union/Russia dropped its expenditures dramatically. In absolute dollars, however, the defense budget of the United States also fell. (It was called the peace dividend at the time.)[64]

There was another increase in the US share starting around 2002—the year after the 9/11 terrorist attacks. The 2002 US increase was a real increase. It was caused by the decision to go into Afghanistan after 9/11. The decline in 2013 partly reflects US drawdown of forces.[65] In other words, there was no massive increase in spending or arms building due to an arms race with anyone; the increases were attributable to operational uses of force.

In sum, there is limited evidence of a security dilemma in the works in the Arctic and next to no evidence of an arms race. Cooperation and avoiding escalation of tensions seem the main strategy. Michael Byers has used complex interdependence as a framework to speculate on why cooperation is able to succeed in the Arctic through the use of liberal international relations theory (see box 4.4).

BOX 4.4	Complex Interdependence

In 2017 Michael Byers explored why the Arctic States have succeeded in keeping the peace and surviving various crises and disagreements.[a] He proposed an older idea from international relations theory: "complex interdependence," first laid out by Keohane and Nye.[b] If states have overlapping interests and memberships in organizations and intergovernmental forums, they are more likely to find a venue to discuss things when normal channels are constricted by a disagreement. Byers outlines the many different places where Arctic states can discuss issues of mutual interest. The Arctic Eight cooperate in search and rescue, they inform each other of military activities, and they meet at the Russia-NATO Council. The availability of venues outside the Arctic also promotes cooperation. Similarly, interstate interaction at the Arctic Council may open diplomatic doors to address tensions outside of the North.

[a]Michael Byers, "Crises and International Cooperation: An Arctic Case Study," *International Relations* 3, no. 4 (2017): 375–402.
[b]Robert Keohane and Joseph Nye, *Power and Interdependence*, 4th ed. (Boston: Longman, 2012).

Hot Conflict in the Arctic? Two Unlikely Scenarios

Actual fighting between the Arctic Eight is very unlikely and thus more suitable for a novel than a textbook. Still, all militaries plan for "just in case" scenarios, and two are offered here. One is through an accident at sea or in the air; the other is through spillover from conflicts elsewhere in the world that then spread.

One potential trigger for a crisis in the Arctic in which military forces confront each other is from increasing use of military probes underwater and near national airspaces. States deliberately sail or fly very close to another's border to check on the target's response and to collect intelligence; it is normal (and legal) practice. The probes happening now are nowhere near the levels of the Cold War. But sometimes planes crash and submarines sink. For example, submarines could have collisions at sea as they attempt to find each other through sound, heat, and other electromagnetic-radioactive signals. There have been post–Cold War accidents or near misses with submarines in the Arctic before.[66] If the past is any guide, small crises or accidents might increase tension but do not lead to war. Accidents in the past have, if anything, led to improved communications and cooperation between the United States and the USSR/Russia.

Spillover fighting from conflict originating outside the Arctic is another plausible, if unlikely, trigger for the use of force in the Arctic between the Arctic Eight. Even then, most of the action would be elsewhere rather than risking the national territories of the Arctic states. No doubt the sanctions against Russia have delayed Russia's plans for Arctic oil and gas. Thus, a reason for strong Russian cooperation in the Arctic may grow weaker. Russia needs subassemblies in order to repair industrial and defense systems and is starting to build the parts at home or with Chinese investment.[67] Nevertheless, Russian interests in the Arctic still support cooperation, which is matched elsewhere. For example, the EU's European External Action Service (EEAS) has sought to keep Arctic affairs in the Arctic and Ukrainian affairs in Ukraine.[68] As noted earlier, NATO and Russia talk to each other through, among other initiatives, the Partnership for Peace.

CONCLUSIONS

The national security conflict viewpoint radically undervalues the strength of cooperation in the Arctic and the efforts by Arctic states to improve the security of people. There is little evidence that conflict is likely or that arms racing is going on in the Arctic. Arctic states are interested in the lives of their citizens and in peaceful relations. That suggests, for national security, a need for renewed commitments to transparency through confidence-building arms control measures made during the Cold War, and continued cooperation, such as through the Coast Guard Agreement. Arms control measures were crucial to the Cold War staying cold rather than becoming a hot war between the USSR and the United States. As we have seen, the Arctic Council's efforts to include other states and indigenous and transnational actors are all ways to improve Arctic security, national and human.

The interwoven nature of securities in the Arctic means that building assets to support human security will assist in realizing national security. Heininen, Sergunin, and Yarovoy conclude the following:

> Increasing competition for trade routes, maritime zones and natural resources continues to drive a military build-up in certain coastal states and the intensification of NATO military activities in the region. In contrast with the Cold War era, when the global confrontation between the superpowers or military blocs defined military decision-making, the current military efforts by Arctic states are about protecting economic interests and asserting national sovereignty over maritime zones and trade routes.[69]

The US Department of Defense, in its climate change roadmap, put it this way:

> Decreases in Arctic ice cover, type, and thickness will lead to greater access for tourism, shipping, resource exploration and extraction, and military activities. Land access—which depends on frozen ground in the Arctic—will diminish as permafrost thaws. These factors may increase the need for search and rescue (SAR) capabilities, monitoring of increased shipping and other human activity, and the capability to respond to crises or contingencies in the region. Difficult and unpredictable weather conditions, large distances, and scarce resources make emergency response in the Arctic difficult. Arctic operations are expensive and dangerous for military forces that are unprepared for the austere operating environment. DoD continues to evaluate the need for specific Arctic capabilities.[70]

Seen in this light, better transparency and cooperation between governments of states and the people of the Arctic will increase the quality of securities in the region.

FURTHER READING

Bailes, Alyson. "Security in the Arctic: Definitions, Challenges and Solutions." In *The New Arctic Governance*, edited by Linda Jakobson and Neil Melvin, 13–40. Oxford: Oxford University Press, 2016.

Bergh, Kristofer, and Ekaterina Klimenko. "Understanding National Approaches to Security in the Arctic." In Jakobson and Melvin, eds., *The New Arctic Governance*, 41–75.

Broadhead, Lee-Anne. "Canadian Sovereignty versus Northern Security: The Case for Updating Our Mental Map of the Arctic." In *Handbook of Politics in the Arctic*, edited by Leif Christian Jensen and Geir Hønneland, 281–97. Cheltenham, UK: Edward Elgar, 2015.

Clark, Ian. "China and the United States: A Succession of Hegemonies?" *International Affairs* 87, no. 1 (2011): 13–28.

De Bourmont, Martin, and Dan De Luce. "The Head of the U.S. Coast Guard Isn't Afraid to Talk about Climate Change," *Foreign Policy*, May 4, 2018.

Doel, Ronald E., Kristine C. Harper, and Matthias Heymann, eds. *Exploring Greenland: Cold War Science and Technology on Ice*. Basingstoke, UK: Palgrave Macmillan, 2016.

Forbes, Bruce. "Cultural Resilience of Social-Ecological Systems in the Nenets and Yamal-Nenets Autonomous Okrugs, Russia: A Focus on Reindeer Nomads of the Tundra," *Ecology and Society* 18, no. 4 (2013): 36–51.

Heininen, Lassi, Alexander Sergunin, and Gleb Yarovoy. *Strategies in the Arctic: Avoiding a New Cold War*. Research Report to the Valdai Discussion Club, 2014. http://vid-1.rian.ru/ig/valdai/arctic_eng.pdf.

Hoogensen Gjørv, Gunhild, Dawn R. Bazely, Marine Goloviznina, and Andrew J. Tanentzap, eds. *Environmental and Human Security in the Arctic*. Abingdon, UK: Routledge, 2014.

Hossain, Kamrul, Dele Raheem, and Shaun Cormier. *Food Security Governance in the Arctic-Barents Region*. Cham, Switzerland: Springer, 2018.

Huebert, Robert. "The Arctic and the Strategic Defence of North America: Resumption of the 'Long Polar Watch.'" In *North American Strategic Defense in the 21st Century: Security and Sovereignty in an Uncertain World*, edited by Christian Leuprecht, Joel J. Sokolsky, and Thomas Hughes, 174–86. Cham, Switzerland: Springer, 2018.

Huebert, Robert. "The Transformation of Canadian Arctic Sovereignty and Security: From Myth to Reality?" In *Modern Canada: 1945*, edited by C. Briggs and Don Mills. Oxford: Oxford University Press, 2014.

Kraska, James, ed. *Arctic Security in an Age of Climate Change*. Cambridge: Cambridge University Press, 2011.

Nicol, Heather, and Lassi Heininen. "Human Security, the Arctic Council and Climate Change: Cooperation or Coexistence," *Polar Record* 50, no. 11 (January 2014): 80.

Serguinin, Alexander. "Is Russia Going Hard or Soft in the Arctic?" *Wilson Quarterly* (Summer/Fall 2017), https://wilsonquarterly.com/quarterly/into-the-arctic/is-russia-going-hard-or-soft-in-the-arctic.

US Department of Defense. *National Security Implications of Climate-Related Risk and a Changing Climate*. July 2015, http://archive.defense.gov/pubs/150724-congressional-report-on-national-implications-of-climate-change.pdf?source=gov delivery.

Zhang, Yongjin. "China and Liberal Hierarchies in Global International Society: Power and Negotiation of Normative Change." *International Affairs* 92, no. 4 (2016): 795–816.

5

Arctic Economies
and Resources

★ ★ ★

THIS CHAPTER EXPLAINS the main features of Arctic economies, the different ways that the people who live there make a living, and the different industries. The following chapter then shows us how the Arctic economies tie into global economic processes. This chapter should also be reconsidered when considering issues of human rights, indigenous rights, and environmental protection explored later in the book.

Contrary to some portrayals of the North as a backward region relying on subsidies from southern capitals, the Arctic as a whole punches well above its weight in terms of production and productivity. Per capita productivity in the Arctic taken as a whole rivals that of the United States and exceeds that of all the other Arctic states.[1] That is without taking into account the wealth produced in the North that does not enter the formal market—the subsistence economy, the goods and services that people harvest, produce, and share among themselves absent any exchange of cash. However, despite the vast resources of the North, the benefits of Arctic production are not equitably shared between the people of the North, and much of the wealth leaks out of the region altogether.[2] Some of the communities in the Arctic, especially indigenous communities, are among the poorest in the developed world.

This chapter will begin with a brief introduction to some basic terms from economics that help to frame a discussion of the Arctic's economies and resources. The following sections describe the different types of Arctic resources and the different kinds of Arctic economies, respectively. Next, the chapter explains competition between different industries and considerations regarding the social impacts of different approaches to resource management in the Arctic. The different interest groups and their influences on Arctic resource governance are then introduced. The penultimate section examines the implications of climate change before some concluding comments are presented to round off the discussion. A number of case studies are presented by way of illustration to bridge the gap between the abstract and theoretical explanations and the experiences of those living and working in the Arctic.

The main findings are as follows: The Arctic is not a struggling, underdeveloped region reliant on subsidies from the South but is instead resource-rich. However, the benefits of Arctic production are not necessarily staying in the Arctic and, if they do stay, are not distributed evenly. Arctic traditional activities and modern industry are both pivotal to Arctic economies; traditional subsistence activities and large-scale resource extraction may be in competition, but they need not necessarily be so. The key to vibrant Arctic economies that contribute to human welfare (rather than just to state or corporate coffers) is in the power of the local inhabitants to make decisions about what resources will be tapped and how to strike the balance between different stakeholders and different industries, traditional and modern.[3]

PILLARS OF ARCTIC ECONOMIES

The Arctic is characterized by three main pillars: the traditional economy, which involves subsistence and local production for local consumption; the formal economy, which is largely based on large-scale resource exploitation; and transfers from central government.[4] These are all ideal types and none exists in a pure form.[5]

The Subsistence Economy

A subsistence economy is a system in which people provide for their own needs directly from the natural resources around them and within their own communities through exchange in an informal setting. It is marked by the absence of money, lack of interaction with external groups, and no industrialization. People take what they need from nature and use it; there may be some craft work, such as construction of homes, boatbuilding, and manufacture of hunting tools, but this is directed at immediate needs and not as goods for trade or profit.

Although subsistence activity rarely provides for all the needs of a contemporary Arctic family, it remains a very important factor in Arctic economies and human well-being, not only for indigenous families.[6] In

Alaska, town dwellers consume around 10kg (22 lbs.) of subsistence foods every year, but their counterparts in the countryside consume around 170kg (375 lbs.).[7] Nevertheless, despite the importance of local products, Alaskans still now import around 95 percent of the food they consume from outside the region.[8] Traditional hunting, fishing, gathering, and consumption of subsistence foods in the Arctic are not only about material well-being but have a strong cultural and spiritual component.[9] The sharing traditions of the Inuit in respect to hunted food also create a kind of welfare net where those unable to directly meet their own basic needs can obtain nourishment. Inuit sharing is not a simple matter of discretionary kindnesses from one family to another but is instead structured normatively: it is *required* to provide assistance, and refusing to do so would be considered wrongful.[10] This can create tensions between those expected to provide and those seeking support.

The informal nature of the subsistence economy makes it very difficult to measure in dollars and cents, but nonetheless, it is important to attempt to measure subsistence activity in order to get a realistic picture of overall Arctic production. Further, if subsistence activities are not measured, it is impossible to compensate adequately should an alternative use of the land or ocean hamper them.[11]

The Formal Economy

The formal economy describes trade that takes place through recognized exchanges in the open market—usually involving money. Market economies, discussed in an international context in chapter 6, are characterized by their reliance on market forces: supply and demand. The formal economy is the most easily measurable aspect of any economy, as each exchange has a price. This also means that it is fairly easy to compare the value of goods and services in the formal economy against one another. It is this part of the economy that is the basis for calculations of states' gross domestic product (GDP). Similarly, gross regional product (GRP) is based on the formal economy of a region. Between the pure subsistence and monetarized formal economy, there is a barter economy in which people exchange goods and services directly (e.g., providing meat in exchange for childcare).

However, if, as in the Arctic, there are significant subsistence and bartered activities that are not measured through the formal market, GDP and GRP are unreliable indicators of the actual wealth created by a society.[12] Furthermore, they tell us nothing about the welfare of the people living in a society, because they provide only a total figure and do not demonstrate how resources are shared and whether benefits even remain in the region at all.[13]

The Transfer Economy

In all economies, there are children, disabled, sick, elderly, and other people who do not have capital or labor to sell but still have needs to be met. There are many different views about how those people should be protected, from a reliance on family to government-led provision. Inuit communities have traditionally met these needs through sharing of hunted and fished foods. Where support is provided by a government, paid for through taxation, this is called the *transfer economy* (also sometimes called the welfare economy). The transfer economy includes direct payments to people (e.g., unemployment benefits, sick pay, disability allowances, and pensions) as well as provision of services (e.g., childcare, schools, hospitals, and government offices).

Today, subsistence, formal, and transfer economies are intertwined in mixed economies. With increasing urbanization of the Arctic (the gradual migration of people from tiny villages to larger settlements), there are fewer immediate opportunities for subsistence activities and they become more costly (in terms of time, equipment, and fuel needed for transport). Traditional activities become partly commercialized, for example, through the selling of surplus fish, meat, and furs to urban dwellers and the sale of handicrafts to tourists. The transfer economy moderates the inequalities and even destitution of some people that would result from reliance solely on market exchange, and in turn, it provides cash that then enters the formal economy.

Economic Sectors

Economies are also broken down into sectors to describe different kinds of economic activities. The "primary sector" describes the taking of natural resources—for example, hunting, mining, logging, and so forth. A subsistence economy will largely be concerned with the primary sector, though there will be some elements of the secondary sector. The "secondary sector" is about adding labor to the natural resources to transform them in some way—for example, manufacturing, home building, boatbuilding, clothes making, and so on. The "tertiary sector" is known as the service sector: here people are no longer taking or making things but offering their labor to one another. This includes caring work, education, entertainment, banking, transport, and similar activities. There has been a gradual shift in the wealthiest economies (measured by GDP) of the world from the primary sector, through the secondary sector, to the tertiary sector. In the United States, around 70 percent of workers are engaged in the tertiary sector. In the Arctic, there is a proportionately larger primary sector, almost no secondary sector, and a tertiary sector that is closely linked to the transfer economy.[14]

THE THREE *D*s

To appreciate the nuances of Arctic economies, the three *D*s should be kept in mind: decoupling, dependency, and diversification.

Decoupling
Decoupling of the economy describes the situation where a society produces what it does not consume and consumes what it does not produce. This is a central characteristic of colonial economies and is common to the formal economy in most Arctic regions.[15] The hydrocarbons, minerals, wood, and commercial fisheries in the Arctic serve mostly markets to the south. Meanwhile, contemporary Arctic societies do not rely wholly on what they can produce themselves but supplement the subsistence economy with imported food, clothing, building materials, and so on. Even subsistence activities today rely on imported tools such as boats, snowmobiles, fuel, GPS, and modern camping gear and clothing.

Dependency
Decoupling triggers dependency. A dependent economy is one that is reliant on economic decisions and patterns that take place elsewhere and over which the local population has little influence, a point to which we return in the following chapter. All but the most isolated subsistence economies today are dependent to some extent on outside economic and political decisions, as they are all interlinked. The large-scale extraction activities in the Arctic as well as the transfer economy are all heavily dependent.[16] Decisions regarding natural resource extraction are made based on global prices that in turn fluctuate according to international supply and demand. The transfer economy is subject to political decisions made in federal capitals far to the south. Dependency in this technical sense should not be interpreted to suggest that Arctic regions are net recipients, relying on subsidies from the south. In fact, even if only the formal economy is measured, ignoring subsistence production, Arctic production per capita is higher than the Arctic states' averages: with only 0.15 percent of the world's population, the Arctic produces 0.6 percent of measured global production.[17] Arctic economies overall grew at an enviable average of 3.5 percent every year between 2000 and 2010.[18] The Russian Arctic is the main engine of this performance, producing more than 71 percent of all market-measured activity in the Arctic in 2010.[19] However, the second *Arctic Human Development Report* warns that, precisely because of the dependency of Arctic production on global markets, this trajectory is

at risk, as after a sustained period of rising commodity prices, they are now entering a period of decline.[20]

Decoupling and dependency together create the conditions for leakage. This means that the benefits of the economic activities in the Arctic do not stay there but leak south.[21] This happens for a number of reasons. First, because of the huge up-front costs of development, large-scale resource extraction activities require external investment, usually from multinational companies or state-owned companies, with decision making taking place hundreds or thousands of miles from their Arctic operations. Profits from their investments remain in the control of the companies to benefit their shareholders, including federal or central governments. Special agreements are needed, alongside good governance, to ensure that local populations benefit (sometimes through local taxation; sometimes through negotiated impact benefit agreements). Second, given the low population density of the regions where most large-scale natural resource extraction takes place, labor is often brought into the region. Transient workers spend a portion of their wages to maintain themselves in the North but usually spend the bulk of their earnings to support family in the South or take it with them when they leave.

Diversification

Diversification, or rather lack of same, renders economies even more vulnerable to dependency. Most large-scale Arctic industries lack flexibility: they require high up-front investment and cannot respond quickly to changes in global demand. A gold mine cannot respond to a collapse in the price of gold by producing diamonds instead; oil and gas fields cannot be converted into hydropower. If an operation closes altogether, employees cannot easily walk into a new job suiting their skills: there is limited transferability of skill sets and poor transport links between settlements and job opportunities.

Finally, the Arctic is an inescapably high-cost region, which explains the lack of a secondary sector (manufacturing).[22] Industrial development is expensive compared with more densely populated, southerly regions of the Arctic states (except Iceland, which is propped up by low energy costs). Distances from global markets and global labor forces make it costly to bring the necessary resources and human capital in and expensive to ship products out. The construction season is short, owing to dark and hostile winters. Population sparseness and lack of infrastructure create a vicious circle as each new project requires original investment in transport facilities (roads, ports, or airports), communications, and essential services for workers (housing and health care).

ARCTIC RESOURCES

Natural resources—the basis for the primary economy—can be classified with regard to two simple distinctions: renewable and nonrenewable, and onshore and offshore. The reason to distinguish onshore and offshore resources is based on the different legal principles that apply. States have *sovereignty* over their land territories but, beyond twelve nautical miles, only *sovereign rights* over the exclusive economic zone and continental shelf.[23]

Renewable resources include all living resources as well as renewable energy (e.g., wind, tidal, solar, hydro, geothermal, and biomass).[24] Box 5.1 explains Iceland's renewable energy market. Onshore, of most importance in the Arctic are hunting, herding, and renewable energy. Settled agriculture is very important culturally, economically, and politically in Iceland and is also historically and culturally important in South Greenland. The sheep farming landscape of Kujataa became a UNESCO World Heritage site in 2017.[25] Agriculture is limited above the tree line for obvious reasons. Forestry is an important export sector in Scandinavia. Offshore, fisheries are central to both subsistence and formal economies while marine mammals remain very important in many indigenous communities and are commercially hunted in Iceland, Norway, and the Faroe Islands. The Arctic is estimated as the source of more than 10 percent of the global fish catch.[26] Some economies—for example, Greenland's—are highly dependent on living marine resources, and within that sector, there is limited diversification.[27]

| BOX 5.1 | Marketing Renewable Energy in Iceland |

Iceland is well known for its cheap renewable energy. Today, renewable energy meets most of Iceland's energy needs. Transport is still mostly dependent on hydrocarbons, but electric cars are increasingly popular.

Hydropower (where energy is converted from the kinetic energy of moving bodies of water—for example, glacial rivers) provides three-quarters of Iceland's electricity.[a] Geothermal power (where energy is converted from the heat released naturally from Iceland's subterranean network of volcanoes) accounts for about one-quarter of Iceland's electricity generation.[b] However, geothermal energy

[a]"Electricity," Orkustofnun (National Energy Authority of Iceland), accessed April 11, 2017, http://www.nea.is/hydro-power/electric-power.
[b]"Electricity Generation," Orkustofnun, accessed April 11, 2017, http://www.nea.is/geo thermal/electricity-generation.

is even more important as a source of heat—a crucial resource in an Arctic State! Around 90 percent of Icelandic households are heated directly by geothermal energy.[c]

With a population of only 350,000, there is a limit to how much electricity Iceland can actually use. The National Energy Authority has therefore looked into ways in which its abundance of clean energy can be marketed to bring revenue into the country. The most obvious but technically challenging method is to sell energy directly—for example, by transmitting it through cables to the EU via Scotland.[d] The EU considers it a key infrastructure project ("project of common interest"). However, the up-front costs in developing such a cable are discouraging, and an abundance of energy for Iceland may not seem to be quite so abundant in the context of a market of half a billion EU inhabitants. Moreover, direct sales of electricity trap Iceland in the primary sector. Selling its valuable natural resource (power) directly means that all the added value and employment related to manufacturing or services benefits another country.

Therefore, Iceland has sought to attract investment from high-energy consuming industries in Iceland. The most significant of these is the aluminum processing industry, which today consumes nearly 70 percent of all Iceland's electricity.[e] To put this in perspective, residential use of electricity is less than 5 percent. Aluminum production has not been without controversy, however, as the promotion of the aluminum industry has meant flooding of hitherto wilderness sites in order to construct the necessary hydroelectric dams; the price paid by the aluminum companies for electricity is secret; the environmental and human rights track record of aluminum companies elsewhere in the world is a cause for concern; and some of the aluminum produced in Iceland is likely to end up used in the arms industry.[f]

Iceland is also exploring the possibility of hosting server farms for use in cluster computing. High-end, international information technology firms require thousands of computers to work together to store, exchange, and deliver information at the click of a button anywhere in the world. Iceland can offer relatively cheap and, just as important, reliable electricity.

[c]"Direct Use of Geothermal Resources," Orkustofnun, accessed April 11, 2017, http://www.nea.is/geothermal/direct-utilization/nr/91.
[d]See "Submarine Cable to Europe," Landsvirkjun, accessed February 14, 2018, https://www.landsvirkjun.com/researchdevelopment/research/submarinecabletoeurope.
[e]"Energy Statistics in Iceland 2013," Orkustofnun, accessed April 11, 2017, http://os.is/gogn/os-onnur-rit/orkutolur_2013-enska.pdf.
[f]Alcoa Inc., the owner and operator of Iceland's aluminum plants, makes no secret of its design and delivery of products to the arms industry; see, for example, "Defense and Space," Arconic, accessed April 11, 2017, https://www.alcoa.com/defense/en/home.asp.

Nonrenewable resources are the backbone of the formal economy in the Arctic, but they have different histories and serve different priorities in different places.[28] Hydrocarbon exploration began in Arctic Canada in the 1970s, but there is currently only one production license. Here, oil and gas are viewed as a commercial good—something to be developed by corporations for private benefit.[29] In Norway, hydrocarbon development has been extensive in the Barents for more than three decades.[30] Hydrocarbons are a public good; oil and gas production constitutes around 30 percent of government revenues and underwrites a generous welfare state and social policies. Nearly all of this is for export, as Norwegians' domestic energy needs are principally met by hydroelectricity.[31] Greenland has yet to discover a commercially viable hydrocarbon resource notwithstanding explorations dating back to the 1970s and surging after the Self-Government Act in 2009. For Greenland, hydrocarbon (and mining) potential is very much a strategic good: the independence of Greenland depends on financial security, and right now extractive industries are seen as an essential factor in establishing that.[32] Extractives are also a strategic good in Russia, where oil was first refined in 1745 in the Komi Republic.[33] The Russian economy fundamentally depends on them: hydrocarbons constitute 70 percent of exports and 52 percent of national GDP.[34] The Arctic Zone contains 95 percent of Russian gas and 70 percent of its oil but only 1.6 percent of its population.[35] Russia's carefully crafted legal regime preserves the monopolies of its own state-owned corporations.[36] In Alaska, hydrocarbon development is a mix of commercial and public good. Hydrocarbons are governed according to largely commercial premises, and profits are privately held; but royalties and other revenues from oil and gas constitute 87 percent of the state budget and allow Alaskans to pay no state tax and even receive an annual dividend.[37]

Table 5.1 displays the share of gross regional product by sector in each Arctic country. Most Russian hydrocarbon production is onshore. Depletion of more easily accessible fields is driving attention toward the Russian continental shelf off its north coast, but most production is still coming from fields discovered decades ago rather than new finds.[38] Of the Russian Arctic's gross regional product, 56.9 percent comes from mining and hydrocarbon exploitation; another 4.4 percent is attributable to processing. Alaska and northern Canada are the only other Arctic regions that come close, with 33.2 percent and 27.2 percent, respectively, from mining and hydrocarbon production. Nevertheless, Alaskan oil peaked in 1988, and the promise of offshore reserves has not yet borne fruit.[39] The Trump administration has expressed intentions to open up the Arctic

Table 5.1 Distribution by Percent of GRP for Arctic Regions, 2005

	United States	Canada	Finland	Iceland	Norway	Russia	Sweden	Denmark
Fishing	0.6	0	0.1	4.7	5.0	0.6	0	10.5
Mining and petroleum	33.2	27.7	0.8	0.1	1.0	56.9	7.5	3.2
Other resources	0.1	0.4	4.7	1.4	0.9	1.3	3.0	2.4
Resource processing	2.0	0	13.3	4.8	5.2	4.4	7.2	5.8
Construction	5.4	8.0	6.8	9.6	6.9	5.0	5.4	7.2
Public sector	26.9	28.7	24.8	23.8	40.5	9.1	32.6	29.9
Other services	31.3	34.8	37.7	50.1	37.4	22.1	36.6	38.9
Remainder	0.5	0.4	11.8	5.5	3.1	0.6	7.7	2.1

Source: Table reproduced with permission from Larsen and Fondahl, eds., *Arctic Human Development Report II.*

National Wildlife Refuge to hydrocarbon activities, but it is not self-evident, irrespective of environmental concerns, that it would be commercially viable.[40] The public sector accounts for between 23 percent and 40.5 percent in the other Arctic regions but in Russia is under 10 percent.

Reliance on the primary sector, especially nonrenewable resources such as hydrocarbons and minerals, in a global market is a risky business. The economy becomes strongly decoupled, and leakage is endemic. Despite their much higher per capita production than any other Arctic region, the people of Arctic Russia have the worst health outcomes, education, and disposable incomes.[41] With reference to the previous chapter, we can say that Russian Arctic residents have comparatively less human security than those in other Arctic states. Resource extraction is also vulnerable to climate change: 93 percent of current gas and 75 percent of current oil production in Russia is on permafrost.[42] As this melts, the structures built upon it become unstable.

The primary sector (including both renewable and nonrenewable resources) is exposed to sudden and uncontrollable price shifts. This is a greater problem for nonrenewable activities, which require long-term planning and heavy front-loading of costs, than for fisheries, which can more easily convert from one stock to another. Offshore Arctic oil is probably only commercially viable if the price remains at least $110 per barrel.[43] When the price of a barrel of oil reached the dizzy heights of $115 on June 23, 2014, expectations were high that offshore Arctic oil would soon become a commercial reality. Less than seven months later, the price dropped to under $50/barrel and nearly four years later had not recovered. Competition from unconventional hydrocarbons such as shale oil and gas extracted from more temperate regions may be more attractive in the short term.[44] In the longer term, sincere efforts to mitigate climate change and a shift toward renewable energy sources could mean that offshore Arctic oil and gas stay in the shelf. The International Energy Authority estimates that the majority of renewable energy production will be competitive, subsidy-free, by 2040.[45] This may seem like the distant future, but hydrocarbon projects take decades to move from prospecting to commercial production.

ARCTIC ECONOMIES

Duhaime and Caron have grouped the Arctic economies according to three main patterns: the North American model, the Scandinavian model, and the Russian model.[46] (These three patterns are discussed again in chapter 6.) Their categorization is based on six key social indicators: the ratio of female to male inhabitants, life expectancy, infant mortality, the proportion of inhabitants with a university degree or higher, personal disposable income (income per person after direct taxation), and the ratio of people of working age to children and older inhabitants (dependency ratio).[47]

The North American Arctic scores highly on all indicators, but this disguises limited redistribution and high inequality. Although *average* disposable income may be high, it is not equally shared, meaning that there are some very well-off people and lots of people living in poverty.[48] Further, North American families have expenses for services that would be provided or at least heavily subsidized by the state through taxation in Nordic countries. These include early-years childcare, university education, social housing, and, in Alaska, health care. Therefore, although disposable income may look high, the actual part of it that is available once these needs are met is lower than would be the case for a family with the same nominal disposable income in a Nordic country. "Given the same income, the Scandinavians' standard of living is higher, since it is supported by generous social benefits."[49] For these reasons, average disposable income is not a very reliable indicator to estimate the true economic security of individuals and families.[50]

The Scandinavian model[51] scores high on infant mortality, life expectancy, education, and gender balance, and medium on disposable income and the dependency ratio. In contrast to the North American Arctic, although average incomes are lower, high rates of redistribution and strong public services as well as closer gender parity in paid employment mean that inequality is less marked. In other words, there is less of a gap between the best- and worst-off, and people have to use less of their disposable income to pay for essential services.[52]

Of all the Nordic countries, Greenland performs less well: there are significantly more men than women (owing to female emigration), health indicators are weaker, disposable income is significantly lower (though money income is supplemented by extensive subsistence activities—for example, hunting and fishing), and the dependency ratio is higher.[53]

Russia's impressive productivity is not reflected in the standard of living of the people who live in the Russian North—in particular, indigenous peoples who continue to fare poorly relative to ethnic Russians.[54] A significant gap also persists between the material well-being of rural and town dwellers.[55] The Russian North scores poorly on all six indicators, although more recent studies indicate that in at least some regions, health outcomes and household incomes are improving.[56] The collapse of the Soviet model and the rush to privatization increased inequality, unemployment, and poverty and reduced social safety nets and public services.[57] The wealth produced in the Russian Arctic is concentrated and exported southward (i.e., leakage occurs).

COMPETITION BETWEEN DIFFERENT SECTORS

Stereotypes of the Arctic depict traditional, indigenous livelihoods against modernization: the subsistence fisherman against the trawler, the herder against the mining company, or the hunter against the logger. In these portrayals, the indigenous are viewed romantically as vulnerable people in need of protection, as defenders of nature who require shelter from globalization, or as backward peoples resisting the unstoppable tide of economic progress. The multinational extraction firms are viewed as vultures, swooping in to steal resources, threatening the pure existence of the indigenous communities with blatant disregard for the "wilderness" in which they operate, or as pioneers, overcoming the challenges of a hostile region to pursue development and growth for the good of civilization.[58] These pictures are extremes but are not uncommon perceptions of Arctic resource use among those living farther south.[59]

The reality is, of course, much more nuanced. Resource competition exists between indigenous people living in the same communities: they can overfish or keep more reindeer than are sustainable on the land; they can disagree about the protection of areas for spiritual reasons. Indigenous people have different views regarding large-scale resource developments: many work closely with and for multinationals to exploit minerals, hydrocarbons, and forests, believing that they will bring much needed income, jobs, and infrastructure.[60] Industrial developments do not necessarily diminish traditional lifestyles but can even facilitate the conditions to preserve them, by providing the cash income necessary to pay for hunting and fishing equipment, investing in traditional arts, maintaining populations against outward migration, and building teaching tools in their native languages.[61] Large-scale industries may also be in competition with one another: the same land cannot be used for both mining and wind farms.

Resource use conflicts are not limited to the land. Offshore activities can also come into competition with one another. Shipping can be obstructed by offshore oil and gas facilities (although in the Russian North, extractive industries and commercial shipping are mutually supportive).[62] Shipping itself disturbs living marine resources, for example, through noise pollution; hydrocarbon activities (especially seismic testing) also contribute to ocean noise. Noise can travel thousands of kilometers underwater and is believed to disturb marine mammals and possibly fish as well.[63] The use of military sonar has been connected to physical injuries in the ears and brains of whales and triggers behavioral changes, such as reduced singing and changes in migration routes, that in turn have consequences for breeding and feeding.[64] This kind of interference has consequences for fishers and hunters living in coastal communities hundreds of kilometers away. In 2017, the Inuit inhabitants of Clyde River, Nunavut, won a legal challenge to stop offshore seismic testing because of its potential impacts on their rights to food, culture, and traditional economic activities.[65] The Baffinland Mines case in box 5.2 is another example of a successful indigenous challenge to industrial activity.

The potential for an oil spill is also a major concern for Arctic fisheries—both commercial and subsistence. In the High Arctic, almost all local foodstuffs are connected to the sea—one cannot grow crops on tundra. Even the perception of contamination can have major consequences. Indigenous communities may be reluctant to consume marine produce that they view as tainted; importing countries will pay less for Arctic fish that they can no longer market as "clean."[66]

SOCIAL IMPACTS OF LARGE-SCALE RESOURCE EXTRACTION

Many communities welcome large-scale resource development for the advantages that it can bring: income through payments to local and regional government; jobs for local people; construction of roads, airports, housing, and even schools and health-care centers. With attention, communication, and democratic engagement, traditional and globalized economic activities can operate side by side and even promote one another. The questions are whether large-scale projects come at too high a cost and whether the benefits are equitably distributed.[67] The first *Arctic Human Development Report* compared two very similar reindeer cooperatives in the Nenets Autonomous Okrug in Northern Russia and how they fared in light of oil development that took place on traditional herding lands. Owing to a different organizational structure and a more proactive approach to negotiations with the oil companies, the members of Erv were substantially better off than those of Kharp.[68] This indicates that community leadership—which in turn requires institutional support from federal and state agencies and law—is an important factor in ensuring that the benefits of resource extraction are shared among the

BOX 5.2 | Baffinland Mines

The case of Baffinland Iron Mines Corp. in Nunavut demonstrates the connections between large-scale resource extraction, transportation, environmental protection, animal conservation, and indigenous rights. It is not enough for a company to recover deposits from the ground; they must be able to transport them to international markets. Nunavut (population 32,000) has no local market for the iron ore extracted. In 2015 the company sought permission to increase production. Local concern was not so much with the extraction itself but the plan to introduce year-round shipping of the iron ore, supported by icebreakers. The Nunavut Planning Commission rejected Baffinland's application because the necessary icebreaking had not been adequately studied vis-à-vis its impacts on living marine resources and the communities relying on them. The proposal was rejected on human rights grounds because it would have made it impossible for the Inuit to travel as before on the surface of the winter ice and to pursue traditional hunting activities during the winter. Moreover, the Nunavut Planning Commission recognized the spiritual significance of the ice in the Inuit worldview, holding that "ice is an essential part of life in the North. For people, for polar bears, for seals and other animals in the North, ice is a bridge—both metaphorically to the past and present Inuit values and activities, also actually as a fact. Ice physically links Inuit to their culture and values."[a] Baffinland Mines developed an alternative plan, proposing rail transport during the winter months, but this has also been challenged by representatives of the local community, Pond Inlet Hamlet, as well as the Mittimatalik Hunters and Trappers Organization.[b] This would require modification of the North Baffin Regional Land Use Plan, which involves a lengthy process of consultation and negotiation, as well as a new environmental impact assessment.[c]

[a]Lisa Gregoire, "Nunavut Regulatory Org Says No to Baffinland," *Nunatsiaq News*, April 9, 2015, http://www.nunatsiaqonline.ca/stories/article/65674nunavut_regulatory_org _says_no_to_baffinland.
[b]Nick Murray, "Baffinland Iron Mines' Phase 2 Plan Gets Sent Back to Nunavut Planning Commission," CBC News, December 20, 2016, http://www.cbc.ca/news/canada/north /nirb-baffinland-phase-2-planning-commission-1.3904189; Jim Bell, "Baffinland Railway May Be 'Dead,' Pond Inlet Group Declares," *Nunatsiaq News*, January 8, 2018, http://nun atsiaq.com/stories/article/65674baffinland_railway_may_be_dead_pond_inlet_group _eclares.
[c]Qikiqtani Inuit Association, "NPC Decision on Baffinland's Phase II Project," March 20, 2018, https://qia.ca/npc-decision-on-baffinlands-phase-ii-project.

people on whose territories the developments take place. Cornell and Kalt have also found that indigenous communities do better when they have more local control.[69] Projects must be carefully managed to ensure that the potential negative impacts are minimized.

Large-scale extraction activities require a substantial labor force that is usually weighted heavily toward the construction phase, declining once commercial extraction is underway. Indigenous and other local people may not have access to these newly created jobs for a number of reasons. Small, local communities may not have sufficient numbers of persons with the right skills and interests to take these jobs, especially in highly specialized industries. Incoming corporations may insist, as a condition of investment, that they bring their own labor force with them that is not subject to the state's collective bargaining agreements.[70] This means that a temporary labor force—foreign, without local language skills, and usually male—is often imported into the region. The lack of permanent ties, family, and community support networks creates the conditions for antisocial behavior and even the trafficking and sexual abuse of local women and girls.[71] To support the construction phase, housing and health-care services are also required.

License agreements for large-scale resource activities often include quotas for local labor, to try to reduce local unemployment and to ensure that the wages are recycled into the local economy. The new industries may also offer higher wages with which other employers cannot compete. However, when the available, qualified workforce is small, when local people take the new jobs, there is a consequent shortage of workers to fulfill essential public services such as education, health care, and maintenance of buildings and roads. Wage disparities also contribute to an increase in inequality between families, creating internal divisions in the community.

Once the construction phase is complete, the need for labor will drop suddenly, or at least the *type* of labor required will change. Transient workers will usually leave, but this will not be sufficient to offset a spike in unemployment among local workers. The community may be left with redundant housing that it must either maintain at its own expense or allow to fall into dereliction, creating an environmental and physical safety hazard.

Where the resource sought is nonrenewable, these projects—oil, gas, minerals—will come to an end. Unemployment will take a further spike, and the necessary skills and equipment to return to traditional activities may be lost.

Governments can reduce leakage by building in a preference for local subcontractors for government contracts. For example, the government of Nunavut facilitates a bid preference of up to 25 percent.[72] Even if prices are more expensive, a local company can win a contract based on extra points for Inuit ownership, local incorporation, and so forth.

INTEREST GROUPS AND INFLUENCES INSIDE AND OUTSIDE THE ARCTIC

It is not only international corporations that have an eye on the Arctic; governments, international governmental organizations, international nongovernmental organizations, news outlets, and concerned citizens are all paying more attention to the Arctic. Box 5.3 explains the controversy over whaling in the Arctic. While "Big Oil" surveys the prospects of harvesting defrosting reserves, pressure groups are firing around petitions to rescue the Arctic from this very fate. Greenpeace's Save the Arctic campaign is probably the best known of these in recent times.[73] Although many groups in the Arctic are also against drilling, they object equally strongly to the Greenpeace campaign.[74] More important than protecting the environment or indigenous traditions for their own sakes is local control over decision making and economic development. Some indigenous and other local communities perceive these NGO campaigns that originate in the South as a modern-day colonialism where people who have never set foot in the Arctic tell them what is good for them. Nevertheless, sometimes small communities work with international NGOs to pursue shared ends because the NGO has the resources to fund litigation.[75]

THE IMPACTS OF CLIMATE CHANGE ON ARCTIC RESOURCES

Indigenous people in the Arctic are concerned about climate change with around three-quarters of Inuit interviewed viewing it as a concern for their communities.[76] The Arctic climate change paradox is that the rapid warming in the Arctic makes it easier to exploit the hydrocarbons in the region, the consumption of which will further contribute to increasing global warming. Besides hydrocarbons, warming temperatures in the Arctic present economic opportunities, including shipping, mining, and settled agriculture. One of the coalition parties in the 2013–2017 Icelandic government described "climate warming" controversially in 2015 as "creating new and exciting opportunities," with particular importance

BOX 5.3 | Whaling in the Arctic

Whaling is an industry in which certain Arctic populations are pitted against more numerous and politically powerful populations holding a competing ethical view. Whaling has gone on for thousands of years in some parts of the Arctic and is at the spiritual heart of many indigenous Arctic communities.[a] It is culturally important to nonindigenous whalers in the Faroe Islands, Iceland, and Norway and can even become a matter of national pride: not giving in to pressures from outside. International concerns about whaling arose owing to overexploitation and a resultant collapse in the stocks of some species at the beginning of the twentieth century, when whaling vessels sailed thousands of kilometers from Europe to the Arctic and the Antarctic. Although whale meat was consumed around Europe, the big prize was the oil that was produced from whale blubber and found in the heads of sperm whales. Beside heating and lighting oil, whale oil was used in margarine, and baleen was used to make corsets. So, in an ironic twist of fate, the savior of whales could be said to be the oil industry!

In 1946 the International Convention for the Regulation of Whaling was agreed and the International Whaling Commission (IWC) established.[b] The IWC was originally intended to be a scientific body to review stocks and manage whaling in a sustainable manner. The clue is in the title of the treaty, which is to preserve *whaling* not *whales*. However, through the latter part of the twentieth century, as the demand for train oil vanished in response to the ready availability of hydrocarbon-based substitutes, popular Western views on whaling shifted and the IWC became deadlocked between whaling states and states that believed that whaling should be prohibited entirely.[c] A moratorium on commercial whaling was agreed upon in 1982 and came into force in 1985–1986. Norway never accepted it, and Canada withdrew from the convention altogether (even though it has banned commercial whaling since 1972). Iceland, having initially accepted the moratorium, changed its mind in 1992, withdrew from the convention, and reapplied with a reservation regarding the moratorium.[d] Indigenous subsistence whaling was never prohibited, and the IWC recognizes it in Alaska, Chukotka, Greenland, and Bequia (St. Vincent and the Grenadines).

[a]See, for example, Bill Hess, *Gift of the Whale: The Inupiat Bowhead Hunt, a Sacred Tradition* (Seattle: Sasquatch Books, 1999).
[b]International Convention for the Regulation of Whaling, 1946, 161 U.N.T.S. 72.
[c]See Malgosia Fitzmaurice, "The International Convention for the Regulation of Whaling and the International Whaling Commission—Conservation or Preservation—Can the Gordian Knot Be Cut (or Untangled)?" *Yearbook of Polar Law* 5 (2013): 451.
[d]International Convention for the Regulation of Whaling Schedule, as amended by the commission at the 65th Meeting, September 2014, para. 10.

for Icelandic farming.[77] Nevertheless, climate change presents a number of risks to Arctic communities, from the melting of the permafrost to the reduction of coastal sea ice that has protected coasts from sea storms and erosion.[78] Mitigation of climate change (i.e., taking measures to minimize the rise in temperature and associated consequences) is very difficult, as it requires concerted and coordinated international action to reduce emissions of greenhouse gases. The transaction costs (the costs of getting everybody together to agree on measures) are huge.[79] Those responsible for climate change are not those who will suffer the most from its consequences in the Arctic, in low-lying Pacific islands, in hot and dry climates facing increasing droughts, and in the paths of more unpredictable, extreme weather events.

The decisions that lead to climate change are made far away from the Arctic. This means that people in the Arctic can do little themselves to mitigate it. Even as they campaign for international action, communities focus instead on adaptation: accepting that some human-caused climate change is already upon them and taking measures to minimize the negative impacts. Adaptation can benefit from regional cooperation to share knowledge and technology, protect populations, and deal with transboundary climate impacts. However, for those on the front line of climate change, local knowledge and experience in the face of change is key: it is the local people who will innovate and adapt—as they have done through all sorts of change over the centuries.

Renewable and nonrenewable, industrial and traditional resource activities in the Arctic are climate-sensitive.[80] With regard to hydrocarbons, the costs of onshore exploitation are likely to rise owing to unstable permafrost that threatens structures and pipelines and complicates waste disposal. Offshore, reduced ice extent and thickness facilitate easier access, but new risks would be present from higher waves and an increase in storms and icebergs.[81] The construction season, important for mining, is likely to lengthen, but construction standards now have to take into account the potential for permafrost melting and some existing structures becoming unstable.[82] Ice roads—roads created each winter over the ice that connects Arctic settlements—will have a shorter usable season.[83] More water and faster flow will create more potential for hydroelectric power generation; but storage and dam safety may be at risk from increasing rainfall and meltwater.[84]

At the same time as land transportation is rendered more difficult (owing to a shorter season for ice roads), shipping by sea becomes more attractive, making it easier to deliver resources to international markets.[85] As access for large vessels improves, climate change presents dangers for smaller fishing vessels from increasing storm frequency and intensity. Sea ice cover remains unpredictable from year to year, and even from week to week, undermining forward-planning of deliveries that remains essential for competitiveness.[86] Freshwater transport (i.e., along rivers) may be more attractive.[87] Easier access for large vessels brings not only cargo ships but also cruise ships, but the search-and-rescue facilities are not adequate should a ship hit an iceberg or be irreparably damaged in a storm.

Warming climates increase the growing season for agriculture and forestry. The boreal forest is likely to gradually expand northward, and new or better-quality products may become possible. However, climate change can also bring invasive species (species that are not native to the Arctic) that can upset the sensitive ecosystems. New predators, new insects, and new diseases all pose a threat. The reproductive and migratory patterns of Arctic species—birds, mammals, and fish—may all change in unpredictable ways. If reindeer and caribou follow new routes, their herders and hunters face competition from landowners reluctant to allow them access and who may be using the land for other purposes (including settled agriculture and forestry). Traditional hunting and fishing on ice becomes dangerous or even impossible: dogsleds cannot be taken out on unstable ice, but there may still be too much ice for small boats to pass safely. Arctic fisheries are further explored in box 5.4.

BOX 5.4 | **Arctic Fisheries and Climate Change**

The Arctic is estimated as the source of over 10 percent of the global fish catch.[a] Some economies—for example, Greenland's—are highly dependent on living marine resources, and within that sector, there is limited diversification.[b]

Changing sea temperatures, climatic patterns, ocean acidification, and shifting ocean currents are likely to have a direct but unpredictable effect on marine species in the Arctic.[c] In the event of a general

(continued)

---

[a]Gunnar S. Eskeland and Line Sunniva Flottorp, "Climate Change in the Arctic: A Discussion of the Impact on Economic Activity," in *The Economy of the North 2006*, ed. Solveig Glomsrød and Iulie Aslaken (Oslo: Statistics Norway, 2006), 83.

[b]David Michelsen, ed., *Greenland in Figures 2012* (Nuuk, Greenland: Statistics Greenland, 2012), 13, 21. In Greenland, prawns constitute over 54 percent of revenues and halibut 22 percent. Lumpfish (8.6 percent) and Atlantic cod (9.4 percent) are the only other significant fishing sectors. See also Joan Nymand Larsen, "Climate Change, Natural Resource Dependency, and Supply Shocks: The Case of Greenland," in *The Political Economy of Northern Regional Development, Volume I*, ed. Gorm Winther et al. (Copenhagen: Norden, 2008), 208 and 211.

[c]Eskeland and Flottorp, "Climate Change in the Arctic," 83, figure 6.3. Atlantic cod appears to be particularly sensitive; see Yereth Rosen, "Warming Waters Pose Dangers to

BOX 5.4 | *Continued*

rise in temperature, cold-water species such as shrimp are expected to decline or move farther north.[d] However, shrimp are increasingly discolored by "blackspot" (melanosis) as they migrate north, reducing their price at market.[e] The shrimp will also face increased competition from stocks moving in from farther south (e.g., cod, herring, tuna, and mackerel),[f] but some species may thrive if predator or competitor species migrate elsewhere.[g] On balance, owing to limitations at the bottom of the food chain, a significant overall increase in fish stocks is not expected.[h] Introduction of viruses from southern waters that could not previously have thrived and algae bloom in warmer waters also pose a threat, in particular to farmed fish.[i]

These changes create challenges for international management of commercial fishing, as the finely balanced interests of states and international fisheries must be renegotiated. Stocks moving across Exclusive Economic Zones (EEZs) or in and out of high seas areas mean that catch allocations cannot simply be based upon historic data. Tonnage is also no reliable indicator of viability if reproductive cycles change: there is a risk that based on historic data and fishing seasons, fish will be taken before they have had adequate opportunity to mature and spawn.[j] Yet vested interests in the fishing sector, magnified in many states by the transferability of quotas leading to consolidation in the hands of a few individuals, make it even more difficult to reach agreement when stock patterns change. Possessing both financial capital and personal connections to governments, a small network of quota owners can bear a disproportionate influence on the political process, creating barriers to fisheries reforms.

Arctic Cod, Research Finds," *Arctic Dispatch News*, September 28, 2016, http://www.adn.com/article/20150502/warming-waters-pose-dangers-arctic-cod-research-finds.

[d]Sedentary species and demersal fish can adapt less quickly to changes in ocean temperature (i.e., they cannot simply swim elsewhere) and are at risk of abrupt decline; see Lars Thorstrup and Rasmus Ole Rasmussen, eds., *Climate Change and the North Atlantic* (Torshavn, Faroe Islands: NORA, 2009), 14.

[e]Narenda Narain, Norma Barreto Perdigão, and Masayoshi Ogawa, "Occurrence of Black Spots in Shrimps under Physiological Conditions," accessed April 11, 2017, http://nsgl.gso.uri.edu/flsgp/flsgpw88002/flsgpw88002_part4.pdf.

[f]Eskeland and Flottorp, "Climate Change in the Arctic," 83; Larsen, "Climate Change, Natural Resource Dependency, and Supply Shocks," 211; and Thorstrup and Rasmussen, *Climate Change and the North Atlantic*, 14.

[g]Compare the increase in shrimp, crab, and lobster as the cod collapsed in 1960s Greenland fisheries; see Lawrence C. Hamilton, Benjamin C. Brown, and Rasmus Ole Rasmussen, "West Greenland's Cod-to-Shrimp Transition: Local Dimensions of Climatic Change," *Arctic: Journal of the Arctic Institute of North America* 56, no. 3 (2003): 271, 272–73, and 275.

[h]Protection of the Marine Environment Working Group, *The Arctic Ocean Review: Phase I Report (2009–2011)* (Akureyri, Iceland: Arctic Council, 2011), 30–31.

[i]Ibid., 84.

[j]See chapter 8 for an explanation of the international regime for fisheries management.

Large-scale commercial fisheries may find it easier to adapt, bene-fiting from economies of scale and likely state subsidies, which facil-itate readier adaptation.[k] They may become more rather than less profitable over the medium term. However, traditional fishing may become more dangerous, if not impossible, in some cases. For exam-ple, indigenous ice fishing using dogsleds is precluded when the ice is too thin, yet the same sea may still have sufficient loose ice and icebergs to render fishing too dangerous for small boats. As species move to new and unfamiliar zones, small-scale fishers can no longer rely on their traditional knowledge regarding the location of produc-tive fishing grounds and of the marine environment, a fortiori when the environment around them is swiftly changing. Aside from the dangers of unpredictable weather and unfamiliar waters, moving far-ther from the shores and from established search-and-rescue centers poses a direct threat to human life.

[k]Protection of the Marine Environment Working Group, *The Arctic Ocean Review*, 14.

CONCLUSIONS

Arctic economies are diverse and complex, but they share a number of features. Subsistence activities remain important in almost all areas, and not only for indigenous people. The Arctic contains an abundance of natural resources that the industrialized South views with anticipation, but it remains a challenge to convert the potential into profitable enter-prise and even more of a challenge to ensure that those profits benefit the people living in the North. Dependency is a problem, reducing the power of local people to regulate their own economies and welfare.

Traditional activities are relatively flexible in response to supply and demand, especially where these serve local markets (both formal and informal). The international market in natural resource exploitation is instead inflexible, determined by global prices and belabored with high up-front costs, infrastructural deficiencies, limited labor supply, and transport difficulties. However, the traditional and the modern exist side by side, and efforts must be made to ensure that they complement one another as far as possible.

Climate change—caused by decisions made far from the Arctic—presents new issues. Undoubtedly, some people will profit from some of the opportunities that open up in the Arctic, but concerted efforts are required to ensure that the most vulnerable are protected from the nega-tive impacts of climate change, many of which are already visible on the sinking permafrost and disappearing coast.

The following chapter will examine more closely the position of Arctic economies within the global market and the international forces that influence resource management.

FURTHER READING

A Circumpolar Inuit Declaration on Resource Development Principles in Inuit Nunaat 2011, http://www.inuitcircumpolar.com/declarations.html.

Fakhri, Michael. "Gauging US and EU Seal Regimes in the Arctic against Inuit Sovereignty." In *The European Union and the Arctic*, edited by Nengye Liu, Elizabeth A. Kirk, and Tore Henriksen, 200–235. Leiden, Netherlands: Brill, 2017.

Hennig, Martin, and Richard Caddell. "On Thin Ice? Arctic Indigenous Communities, the European Union and the Sustainable Use of Marine Mammals." In Liu, Kirk, and Henriksen, eds., *The European Union and the Arctic*, 298–341.

Hunter, Tina. "Russian Arctic Policy, Petroleum Resources Development, and the EU: Cooperation or Coming Confrontation." In Liu, Kirk, and Henriksen, eds., *The European Union and the Arctic*, 172–99.

Kristoffersen, Berit. "Drilling Oil into Arctic Minds? State Security, Industry Consensus and Local Contestation." PhD diss., University of Tromsø, 2014.

Lajeunesse, Adam, and P. Whitney Lackenbauer. "Chinese Mining Interests and the Arctic." In *Governing the North American Arctic: Sovereignty, Security and Institutions*, edited by Dawn Alexandrea Berry, Nigel Bowles, and Halbert Jones, 74–99 (Basingstoke, UK: Palgrave Macmillan, 2016).

Larsen, Joan Nymand, and Gail Fondahl, eds. *Arctic Human Development Report*. Akureyri, Iceland: Stefansson Arctic Institute, 2004.

Larsen, Joan Nymand, and Gail Fondahl, eds. *Arctic Human Development Report: Regional Processes and Global Linkages*. Akureyri, Iceland: Norden, 2014.

Lindahl, Karin Beland, Anna Zachrisson, Roine Viklund, Simon Matti, Daniel Fjellborg, Andreas Johansson, and Lars Elenius, *Konflikter om gruvetablering: Lokalsamhällets aktörer och vägar till hållbarhet* [Conflicts about mining: Local communities, actors and paths to sustainability]. Luleå, Sweden: Lånsstyrelsen Norbotten, 2017.

Olsen Siegstad, Mia, and Mads Fægteborg. *"Ajorpoq"—vi får ingen svar!* [We get no answers!]. ICC Grønland, in collaboration with the NGO-koalitionen for bedre Borgerinddragelse, 2015.

PAME. Arctic Offshore Oil and Gas Regulatory Resource. Accessed April 13, 2014. https://pame.is/index.php/projects/resource-exploration-and-development/mre.

Pelaudeix, Cécile, and Ellen Margrethe Basse, eds. *Governance of Arctic Offshore Oil and Gas*. Abingdon, UK: Routledge, 2017.

Sejersen, Frank. "Mega-Industrialising in Greenland." In *Rethinking Greenland and the Arctic in the Era of Climate Change*. Abingdon, UK: Earthscan, 2015.

6

The Political Economy of the Arctic

★ ★ ★

THE LAST CHAPTER discussed features of Arctic economies through the lens of natural resources. This chapter explores the Arctic economies from an international political economy perspective. Arctic economies are analyzed in the context of globalized flows of goods, services, and finance. These flows are partially managed by global economic institutions that arose after World War II. Most of these institutions were created between the United States, Canada, and noncommunist countries, some of which had seen their territories destroyed by the war.

US (and Canadian) territory had largely been spared any destruction and American Gross National Product (GNP) had grown during WWII. Melvyn Leffler explains, "In 1945, the United States had two-thirds of the world's gold reserves, three-fourths of its invested capital, half of its shipping vessels, and half of its manufacturing capacity."[1] Western leaders drew lessons from the interwar period and concluded that trade protectionism and competitive devaluation of currencies during the Great Depression had contributed to the outbreak of WWII. The United States used its gold reserves and strong dollar to recapitalize and stabilize Western Europe and Japan.[2] The International Monetary Fund (IMF) and the World Bank are two results. After an effort to create an international trade organization by treaty failed to pass in the US Senate, states relied on a limited set of tariff reductions that had been negotiated in 1947 as the General Agreement on Tariffs and Trade (GATT).[3] Additional rounds of tariff reduction talks were held until 1994 when states agreed to create the World Trade Organization (WTO).[4] Regional economic organizations—most notably, what would later become the

European Union (EU)—appeared, as did regional free trade agreements like the North American Free Trade Agreement (NAFTA).[5]

Even though the Arctic is quite productive, relative to population, Arctic regions vary considerably and even the most productive have limited influence on the global scene. The problem of dependency on outside decisions extends from the domestic economy to their relationships with the global economy. As Mark Nuttall put it, "Future strategies for Arctic environmental protection and sustainable development would benefit from moving beyond an Arctic-centered perspective in an attempt to conceptualise economic, social and environmental linkages between the Arctic and other regions of the globe."[6] What economic strategies have Arctic states chosen to interact with the larger world? What are the consequent economic threats and opportunities?

Arctic communities do not control decisions over prices, investment, labor, or terms of trade. States have some legal control over labor through immigration rules, but these are determined at the national level. If we extract the Arctic from its various *national* links, we find it represents a minor, resource-dependent periphery in both the national and the global economy in *absolute* economic terms. For example, in 2014 Iceland fishing (not all of it from Arctic waters) provided roughly 11 percent of Iceland's GDP and at 23 percent is second only to tourism for generating foreign exchange revenues.[7] If one takes in the entire maritime cluster that includes processing and new maritime technology, then the contribution to the GDP is around 25 to 30 percent.[8] Yet Iceland's share of the global catch is roughly 1.3 percent (still impressive for its size).[9] Norway ranks fifteenth in global oil production, but very little of it comes from the Arctic. Canada has no oil production in the Arctic. The United States is the third-largest producer of oil, but Alaska's North Slope only yields 5 percent of American production. Studies on the future of oil and gas disagree on whether the Arctic will ever be a notable source of hydrocarbons. One Norwegian study suggested that Arctic natural gas would drop as a percentage of world production from 22 percent to 10 percent by 2050 and that most of the production would be from Russia.[10] Some analysts have argued that drilling for Arctic oil might be too risky and have suggested that stocks in firms that spend on this activity may prove excessively speculative.[11]

Being peripheral to the global economy does not mean the people and communities of the Arctic are powerless. Arctic communities can also leverage globalization to their advantage. Florian Stammler, an anthropologist specializing in reindeer herding in the Yamal/Nenets region of Russia, says it is impossible to understand reindeer herding without its connection to the outside world. For example, the herders have adapted their own traditional strategies and rules to trade velvet reindeer horn to workers on hydrocarbon development projects.[12] Thus, one small and local market intersects with a global market. At the same time, expansion of natural resource extraction and energy projects to feed into the global economy breaks up access to reindeer pastures or migration routes. Zojer and Hussain argue that large-scale natural resource extraction may prove a greater threat to reindeer herding than climate change.[13] The connections between the local, regional, national, and global economies can prove quite complex.

ECONOMIC GLOBALIZATION AND MODERN CAPITALISMS

The previous chapter discussed three intersecting types of economies in the Arctic (subsistence, formal, and transfer). In this chapter we are primarily interested in the formal economy and in three flavors of market capitalism: neoliberalism, state capitalism, and the Nordic model. The Arctic Eight encourage private business. Due to a mix of international trade rules, intra-European trade rules, and the spread of neoliberal ideas, governments of the Arctic Eight have made going into business easier.[14] Thus, all of the Arctic Eight states have essentially capitalist market economies, but they vary in how much control the state has over the market and in how they promote human security by protecting workers and the environment from the downsides of capitalism.[15]

Markets often need governments to intervene in highly risky situations. For example, the problem of floods is so extreme that in the United States, flood insurance comes from the US government because private insurance firms withdrew.

As firms and markets grow, consumers and workers need protection from the market, so the state intervenes to soften or redirect the negative effects of market forces. For example, tourism is a $1.3 billion dollar business in Alaska and around $110 million of that goes to the purchase of indigenous art. The US Federal Trade Commission has a "tips" guide on how to distinguish genuine indigenous art from cheap replicas and where to make a complaint in the case of deception.[16] This is one way the US government interferes with a free market to help consumers, artisans, and the state of Alaska.

In international trade, the role of the national government matters a great deal because states do the negotiating. Differences in domestic regulations shape trade, banking, currency, and investment preferences. In recent years, the general aim of free trade negotiations has been to give a larger scope to private firms and to limit the capacity of states to interfere in private decisions. Firms often lobby for governments and international organizations for regulation to gain or prevent advantages relative to rivals (e.g., through subsidies or trade protection). Positive public outcomes can arise from lobbying when, for example, firms find sound environmental solutions to problems in their production and seek national or international rules that will give their innovations a boost.[17]

Trade is a strategic topic, and states seek outcomes that will make their goods and services more competitive abroad. Yet it is not a realist zero-sum game; in trade there are often positive sum games where multiple parties win.

Three Flavors of Capitalism

The United States was the first liberal state in modern international relations, though it drew on liberal economic ideas from the United Kingdom. It encouraged small-scale private enterprise and allowed much labor mobility for free men. American constitutional law allows states to regulate intrastate trade, but only the US government can impose an external tariff. Some US states regulated economic activity in their territories, with limitations based on noneconomic values—for example, requiring stores to close on Sundays; others tried ways to make business better or easier—for example, by limiting liability or by facilitating information sharing. The Chicago Board of Trade promoted the innovation of allowing the sale of futures for buyers and sellers of agricultural products.[18] National parks were set aside for the public, state governments regulated utilities, and money became more regulated. US states tried out "radical" ideas like unemployment and old-age insurance.

In the early 1980s, the United States began to move away from its mixed concern with competition and social protection and toward neoliberalism.[19] Neoliberalism emphasizes deregulation, privatization, and reducing government intervention in the market. The guiding principle in this approach is to let the market govern itself in order to improve the economy and release the creativity of entrepreneurs. This has meant reducing regulations and using free trade agreements to limit the possibility of subnational governments and states implementing different (stricter) rules on labor, health and safety, or environmental protection. Whether these changes have negative effects on labor or environment is unclear. One study on whether Canada would have to lower its labor protection to compete with the United States showed that this would not be necessary unless the American competitive advantage was due to the lower labor protections in the United States.[20] Others say free trade agreements, especially those that reduce nontariff barriers, could build on the high standards of the United States and the EU that give their products a competitive advantage in some areas. A race to the social bottom to be competitive need not happen, but there does need to be clarity on how to encourage mutual recognition of high standards. People have doubts about free trade partly because of the way the agreements have been negotiated: too much behind closed doors, with too little public discussion, and with too little democratic control.[21]

More broadly, neoliberalism has meant turning public spaces and resources into private property, even though taxpayers sometimes had originally funded the public goods. Moreover, if things go wrong in the market, firms quickly seek government tax dollars and assistance. Taxpayers, workers, and consumers end up footing the bill when markets fail. Put differently, neoliberal approaches create a situation where profits are privatized (when markets are good) but losses are socialized (when markets crash).[22]

Other states and subnational governments adopted neoliberal ideas. For example, British Columbia once kept small logging towns solvent for decades through an appurtenance rule that required any logs cut in an area (i.e., appurtenant) to be milled there. The rule created a reasonably stable local economy with stable jobs and slowed logging.[23] Appurtenance rules, however, were a regulatory burden for Canadian firms and constituted a nontariff barrier for international trade, because investors would have to follow the appurtenance rule even if there were cheaper milling options elsewhere. The cheapest way to process wood was to cut it and transport it quickly to modern, large-scale plants. Cheaper timber meant cheaper timber-based products. Large-scale timber processing, however, was not efficient in a broader social sense if one wanted to keep small towns healthy by providing jobs and moderating the speed of harvesting the trees. Once the appurtenances rule was eliminated and logs were milled elsewhere, small, rural towns declined. Some logs are shipped out to Asia and milled en route. To pick a different industry, jobs in small communities are similarly lost when fish are caught and processed on a factory ship while it sails to another country for sale and resale. The resources are taken, but little of the added value of the product that would improve the local community remains in their places of origin.

State capitalism is another possibility. Russia, while a market economy, still gives a very strong role to state-owned firms, notably in oil and gas, as explained in the previous chapter. F. Joseph Dresin, from the Wilson Center, writes:

> There are three criteria for state capitalism: substantial state ownership in enterprises; direct government involvement in those enterprises; and an otherwise capitalist system where most enterprises are privately held and operate in market conditions. Russia meets them all . . . the state owns two-thirds of the market capitalization in the Russian stock

market. However, that ownership is mainly limited to four industries: energy (oil, gas, and electricity), banks, defense industries, and transportation. There is little state ownership in most other sectors in the Russian economy, including consumer goods, non-defense manufacturing, agriculture, insurance, and services.[24]

The Russian government strongly assists state firms by making credit available at preferential rates. Due to budgetary concerns partly caused by economic sanctions, the Russian government began to sell off some of its interests in state-owned firms. For example, it reduced the government control in Rosneft, which dominates oil and gas efforts in western Siberia and in the Laptev Sea, by nearly 20 percent in 2016.[25]

Yet another approach, the Scandinavian model, discussed in terms of social indicators in chapter 5, offers vigorous competition among private firms. As noted in the last chapter, these states have an exceptionally strong, tax-based set of social welfare programs. People in Nordic countries pay high taxes (especially compared to the United States) but have access to health care, childcare, job (re)training, assistance to the poor, and higher education at low or no out-of-pocket cost at the point of access.[26] Globalization has put pressure on this model, but keeping the social protections is deemed a critical part of responding to the risks and opportunities it brings.[27]

Economic Development National Strategies

The variation in underlying national approaches to the public/private economic interface among Arctic states affects how the states navigate the global economy.

In the 1960s, the Norwegian government set up a sovereign investment agency now called the Government Pension Fund Global. This state-owned investment entity takes a portion of the financial gains from resource extraction and invests it, to be drawn upon when the market is low or when the resource is exhausted. The Norwegian government may take 4 percent of the fund per year, but never did so until early 2016, when it took more than $100 million (out of more than $800 billion) because of a sustained low hydrocarbon price.[28]

If oil prices return to higher levels, Norwegian Arctic oil may become attractive once more. Norwegian public policy, however, favors a move to renewable energy, at least for itself, and, as noted earlier, the pension fund has been divesting from hydrocarbons.[29] Norway's extraordinary efforts to reduce CO_2 by developing alternative energy sources reduces its own hydrocarbon dependency and gives Norway technological innovations that could "green" up other parts of the Norwegian economy and perhaps other countries as well. In addition, the Pension Fund provides a cushion for reductions in oil sales, and its investment clout can affect the market. In 2017 the "fund's average holding in the world's listed companies was 1.4 percent."[30] The combination of renewables and the Pension Fund help Norway follow its preferred policy on oil.

Unlike Norway, the US state of Alaska traded its oil and gas wealth for the shorter-term satisfaction of Alaskan residents. Alaska sends checks every year to its permanent residents.[31] Like most other oil-producing states, it did not invest the money for the long haul, and the checks fluctuate with international markets. When oil revenues are down, as they were for some time after the 2008 financial crisis, Alaska experienced depressed family incomes and reduced oil/tax receipts to its state government.

When Iceland became fully independent of Denmark in 1944 (it had been a sovereign nation since 1918), it was an agricultural community of small farmers and fishers—that is, a subsistence economy. Bertelsen, Justinussen, and Smits claim obtaining independence before the establishment of the welfare state proved an advantage because, unlike Greenland, Iceland did not have to try to maintain high social welfare standards while building its independent economy.[32] However, one of Iceland's first moves as it strove for independence was to establish its own university in 1911, an investment in human capital. Iceland now has four full-fledged universities and three university centers. By contrast, the University of the Faroe Islands was founded in 1965 and the University of Greenland in 1987. Canada still has no university in its three Arctic territories.

Independent Iceland did not immediately begin any large-scale energy projects but harnessed its natural resources (geothermal energy and hydropower) for municipal and agricultural uses.[33] Today, as we saw in box 5.1 in chapter 5, it is selling its energy resources on a global market by inducing industrial investment locally and potentially by exporting electricity through a subsea cable. Strong gains in human capital and the unique hydrogeology of Iceland opened the door to international niches in which the country can be competitive.

The Faroe Islands chose a strategy focused on the prospect of hydrocarbon resources that has produced jobs and improved the capacity of the Faroese to compete globally—even though they never struck commercial oil. First, the Faroe Islands set up a Faroese competence fund. Those seeking to explore for offshore hydrocarbons contributed 117 million kroner ($16 million USD/€15.7 million) so that the islands could educate the population in a wide array of competences, not solely for work in the hydrocarbon industries. This fund has supported many different kinds of projects, including the arts, information technology, and oil and gas. Second, the state required that any people or equipment destined for the oil rigs would go through a Faroese port. This created enough demand for infrastructure to support the building of harbors, airports, and associated services through public/private investment. Third, would-be investors were obliged to guarantee equal opportunity in bidding on contracts for Faroese businesses, thus ensuring that Faroese firms would have a chance to compete against the international giants. Bertelsen, Justinussen, and Smits conclude the following:

> Since the oil business is highly regulated and, for insurance reasons, cannot compromise on safety standards, requirements to suppliers are extremely high. In the first exploration rounds, very few Faroese companies qualified to participate at all. However, the same sets of demands have served to push and motivate Faroese businesses to continuously develop and upgrade their competencies in terms of international training and certification.[34]

Despite extracting no oil commercially themselves, Faroese firms now provide training and win contracts on activities elsewhere in the world. They have a thriving oil industry, even without the oil.

Diversification offers a way to cope with the opportunities and risks of a globalized world. Arctic countries and regions hope to develop green and blue economic assets: environmentally friendly "green" assets and new ways to use the "blue" ones of the ocean, such as algae farming or products from algae.[35] Others advocate for diversification through the creative fields in the arts and design.[36]

FINANCE AND BANKING

Globalization of Arctic economies makes it difficult to identify the ultimate owners and beneficiaries of industries in the Arctic. With complex ownership structures of international firms, it is not always easy to discover who has the power to make the major investment decisions, let alone where they are made. Company names are often misleading. London Mining, for example, which has invested in Greenland, is (at the time of writing) Chinese-owned.[37] Oil platforms may be leased by one firm from another. Large investment funds control stock in many firms. Governments and private firms, as we have seen, may co-own a large project. Norway's sovereign wealth fund owns stock in corporations all over the globe.

In investment finance, global money tends to flow to (or at least through) New York and London. Thus, investors and firms with cash to store or to raise go to those places. For a time, Iceland positioned itself as an international banking center—with disastrous results, when the country found itself massively overleveraged when the global economy collapsed in 2007–2008. One of Iceland's problems was its attempt to do international banking when it had the world's smallest population to have its own currency and a poorly staffed supervisory authority. The banks could not cover payments to international creditors or depositors, and there was a run on the banks. The government attempted a bailout, and the value of the Icelandic kronur collapsed until it ceased to be traded at all, which led in turn to a huge inflation spike (since most consumer goods are imported). Loans in Iceland (including mortgages) were nearly always index-linked (i.e., they went up with inflation as well as interest), so people's debts and monthly repayments rocketed. Thousands found themselves in negative equity, and tens of thousands could no longer meet monthly bills. To slow the exodus of savings and investments, the Icelandic government introduced capital controls (that were only lifted in 2017) and called in the IMF.[38]

In contrast, China has a vast foreign exchange reserve because China sells goods to the West and is paid in foreign currency. It is not, as yet, a center for global banking because the Chinese Renminbi is not yet a fully tradable currency.[39] That means people cannot buy it on the market due to government currency controls. However, the country took a step toward convertibility when it became the sixth currency to be allowed as a reserve currency in the IMF on October 1, 2016.[40]

China may not yet be significant for international banking, but it is a major direct investor around the world. The Chinese government and firms are turning the foreign exchange reserve into improved infrastructure at home, state-approved direct investments in other countries, and innovative approaches to building institutions with developing countries.[41] It is actively working with others to build new international institutions for financing development, such as the Asian Infrastructure Investment Bank (AIIB) to support economic developments in Asia. The six European Arctic states are all members/investors in the AIIB. China's investments in the Arctic itself are tiny compared to elsewhere (in 2016 Chinese foreign direct investment [FDI] in the United States hit a high of 51.09 billion or 12 percent of the total FDI in the United States), but its patient and creative funding of infrastructure and natural resources projects means it will likely continue to be a big player in the Arctic.[42] The downside to the spending is unsustainable levels of debt. In 2017 Moody's lowered China's credit rating, and the IMF issued a warning.[43] China has a plan to reduce debt. Whether that plan, if executed, would have effects in the Arctic is unclear. In 2018 the IMF warned about rising global debt and noted that only the United States expected further growth in debt relative to GDP.[44]

FREE TRADE

Free trade today is more than reducing tariffs; its proponents seek to harmonize regulations and thus make doing business easier. Free trade regulations, however, change entire economies and affect democratic government processes. On the one hand, goods may get less expensive; money can flow more readily. On the other, critics of free trade have focused on how it weakens labor protection and increases the capacity of firms to undermine environmental, health, and safety rules though investor-state dispute resolution. Some argue that free trade costs jobs—a justification used by President Trump for threatening to leave NAFTA in 2017. A more accurate statement would be that free trade costs the jobs of the less educated in wealthier countries, given that a nation's advantage in trade is usually in whatever it has in greatest supply: capital (the United States) versus labor (Mexico).[45] A good social safety net can mitigate some of those losses, but in the United States, social protections are relatively weak compared to Europe. Trump also asserted a number of anti–free trade claims, announced withdrawals from new agreements under negotiation (and sometimes asked to rejoin them later—without success), and imposed tariffs in 2017–2018 on long-time allies and on China.[46]

The Arctic states are part of this institutionalized, globalized trade system. Projects that began as regional initiatives to reduce trade barriers in Western Europe, North America, and Latin America now encompass the globe. China joined the WTO in 2001. Russia joined over a decade later, in 2012. Iceland and Norway are not part of the EU but have a very strong relationship to the EU through the European Free Trade Association formed in 1960. In 1994 the EU, Iceland, Norway, and Liechtenstein deepened ties with the EU and each other through the European Economic Association by accepting many of the rules of the EU regarding free movement of goods, services, persons, and capital.[47] Other Arctic states also make regional trade agreements. Russia has made bilateral free trade agreements with former Soviet states in central Asia as well as Belarus and Vietnam.[48] Iceland entered a free trade agreement with China in 2015, the first European country to do so.[49] Denmark, Sweden, and Finland may not make trade agreements, as that is an area of EU sole competence. There are no free trade agreements between Russia and the other Arctic states.[50]

NAFTA

New policies and new organizations are hard to craft and may or may not work as intended. When the North American Free Trade Agreement (NAFTA) was being negotiated in the early 1990s, there were concerns about its effects on workers' rights and the environment. The parties negotiated an additional side agreement on environmental protection. The side agreement set up the Commission on Environmental Cooperation (CEC) as well as processes by which the parties could contest practices that injured the environment.[51] Though well intentioned, the side agreement has not worked especially well. Few of the articles that could be used to protect the environment from harm from trade have been used.[52] The CEC has not lived up to promises. For example, it did good work in creating maps on habitats at sea, but it has not built on that information to assess the impact of NAFTA on the vast ocean areas stretching from the Arctic Ocean to the Atlantic and the Pacific where the three states have sovereign rights (see chapter 8).[53]

NAFTA, however, had considerable success in integrating the three economies—a point that became all too clear when Trump announced and then implemented tariffs on a range of goods from many trading partners in 2018. The North American continent, for better or for worse, is increasingly integrated. The automobile industry in particular has spread production out between the three NAFTA members.[54] One cannot build a car in a single country from parts and materials made only in Canada or Mexico or the United States. Nevertheless, President Trump campaigned on a promise to negotiate a better deal for the United States under NAFTA. He put tariffs on goods from both Mexico and Canada in ways that breached current NAFTA and WTO rules. Trump's initial NAFTA stance was popular with many of his supporters because they thought free trade had decimated blue-collar jobs in the United States and depressed wages for low-skilled workers. Many corporate lobbyists were concerned because the firms (and shareholders) they represent benefited from the free flow of materials, financial flows, and larger markets. Negotiations between the NAFTA partners began in 2018. At the start of 2018, negotiations were stalled primarily on three key issues: automobiles, dispute settlement, and labor standards.[55] In April 2018 the United States reintroduced an earlier idea of a termination option in five years if any one of the partners wanted to quit.[56] At the time of going to print (September 2018), the United States and Mexico had a tentative draft bilateral deal, but negotiations with Canada to reform NAFTA were ongoing.

While it is not clear how each of the three possible outcomes for NAFTA—terminated, radically changed, or tweaked—would affect the Arctic, leaders in the Canadian Arctic are concerned. The premier of the Yukon Territory in Canada, Sandy Silver, lobbied in Washington to emphasize the importance of NAFTA to the Yukon. According to Yukon Party leader Stacey Hassard, the Yukon exported $200 million worth of mostly copper and other metals to the United States. It imported $50 million, primarily in fish and petroleum. It also has a large import/export relationship with Mexico, exporting $2.3 million, with an emphasis on drilling and boring tools, while importing $35 million, mostly truck machine parts and fire extinguishers.[57]

Supply and Value Chains

The examples of metals, truck parts, fish, and fire extinguishers illustrate that everyday life and work are dependent on global linkages. Supply chains move things around. A supply chain is the set of steps it takes to get products made and delivered. A value chain is how one adds value to a process or product through production or marketing or service. Economic integration due to NAFTA has made the three involved countries rely on materials and goods in these chains. The effects and nature of supply and value chains have only recently gotten attention outside of business publications as the economic effects of them grow.

Royal Greenland catches, prepares, boxes, and ships fish from Greenland. It is owned by the government of Greenland. There are natural and legal limits on how much of any fish can be taken from the oceans to maintain a sustainable fishery. To keep its operations efficient, it needs to match supply and demand for cod. That means knowing whether to buy cod from elsewhere in the world to keep its food processing going or whether to buy a processing plant in another country. Royal Greenland both imports and exports cod on a globe-spanning basis. Its aim is diversification in species caught, to manage fluctuations in fish populations and quotas, technology, and access to large markets.[58]

Statistics Denmark, along with statistical offices in other Nordic countries, has begun to collect data and study how value chains affect their economies. Imports do not necessarily harm domestic producers, because firms that trade "also generate the most domestic backward linkages for each unit of value added that they produce and export, high-lighting complementarities between imports and strong domestic supply chains that can drive export success."[59] The trading firms buy supplies and services from the domestic economy as part of their supply chains.

Possibly the positive relationships between supply chains, domestic economies, and international trade could be leveraged to promote human security in the Arctic. Canada has studied costs of supplying food to Arctic communities to address the food insecurity discussed in the security chapter. The supply chains are complex, and the distances and low population levels make supply very costly.[60] That is one view of moving materials from the south to the north. It might be possible to find less expensive chains or other interventions where supply chains are unlikely to form. Backward mapping of what would be needed to improve supply chains can show where infrastructure is

Map 6.1   Royal Greenland: Main Supply Chain Flow for Cod

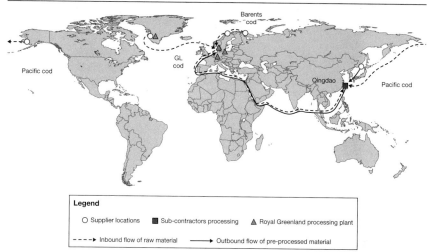

Legend

○ Supplier locations   ■ Sub-contractors processing   ▲ Royal Greenland processing plant

- - - -▶ Inbound flow of raw material   ——▶ Outbound flow of pre-processed material

Source: Mathias Maegaard Mikalsen, "Royal Greenland Optimizes Its Supply Chain," *Implement Consulting Group*, November 13, 2015.

needed in order to take advantage of growing supply chains. At the same time, supply chains may impair human security. They can mask labor exploitation or human trafficking.[61]

Russian oil and gas development has long relied on partnerships with international oil companies.[62] Due to sanctions imposed by many governments, Russia has turned to China for billions in funding for a liquefied natural gas project in the Yamal and for drilling services in the Kara Sea.[63] China is also involved as a final market and in many value chain steps along the way:

> Located deep within Russia's Arctic zone, the project has been subject to sanctions targeting Arctic development generally and Novatek [the Russian firm in which the Russian government has a majority share] specifically. As a result, the project's ability to move forward has been largely dependent on China's participation throughout the value chain, including as an upstream equity partner, strategic investor, lender of last resort, LNG buyer, tanker operator, and even equipment supplier.[64]

China has a clearly outlined plan for building its supply chains and the economies through which those chains run: the Belt and Road Initiative (BRI) (see box 6.1). The BRI includes an Arctic extension through the Northern Sea Route. Whether and how quickly China can accomplish its initiative depends partly on the relationship of BRI to the reduction of its debt load.

BOX 6.1	The Belt and Road Initiative

China has built a railroad to Europe through Central Asia. China ships goods and materials around the world and is helping to build port facilities in many countries. Its interest in the Northern Sea Route (NSR) across the northern coast of Russia has grown as the Arctic ice has weakened. China is trying to secure its supply and value chains both for potential cost savings and as a hedge against political instability destabilizing other routes. Development of Arctic resources is strategically crucial to the Russian economic plan, and this depends upon increased shipping through the NSR (see chapter 8). China's influence grows with its trade and funding, thus the investment is also sound strategic thinking for China.

The Belt and Road Initiative (BRI)[a] brings many benefits to Russia. However, it could also change Russia's behavior in the Arctic. Greater economic wealth would enhance its national power and its influence in international economic discussions. China is keenly interested in how climate change will affect the country, while Russia has not shown great concern. Possibly China can encourage stronger environmental efforts by Russia. And it could force Russia to make difficult diplomatic decisions. China could put pressure on Russia to pay greater attention to China's interests. China, due to the other elements of the BRI, would have more options for trade and shipping by land or sea than Russia; thus China has both economic and political leverage. On the other hand, Russia may be able to eliminate or reduce the effects of economic sanctions with China's investments. The sanctions have hurt Russia and Europe. The China factor makes the sanctions less effective and thus might induce European states to weaken their sanctions.

[a]See Marc Lanteigne, "One of Three Roads: The Role of the Northern Sea Route in Evolving Sino-Russian Strategic Relations," *Norwegian Institute of International Affairs*, Policy Brief 2 (2015), https://www.files.ethz.ch/isn/187750/NUPI%20Policy%20Brief%20 2-15-Lanteigne.pdf; and Nengje Liu, "Will China Build a Green Belt and Road in the Arctic?" *RECIEL* 27 (2018): 55.

A Perfect Trade Storm Hits Canadian Inuit

The use of trade to achieve political goals in the Arctic is not limited to the globe-spanning activities of China. Box 6.2 discusses how the EU seal ban fits into the international trade regime. The EU seal ban exemplifies how perceptions, trade rules, and the supply-chain nexus between indigenous hunters and nonindigenous exporters combined to destroy livelihoods in the Arctic.

BOX 6.2 | The EU Seal Product Ban

Public concern about the welfare of marine mammals in Europe triggered the EU ban on imports of seal products in 2009.[a] The EU has no jurisdiction to determine whether people living in non-EU countries may hunt seals or not, but it is permitted under international trade law to restrict imports in certain circumstances. The Netherlands and Belgium had already banned seal product imports, but because of the single market and the open borders in the EU, it was impossible to prevent products being imported first into neighboring member states and then carried across into the Netherlands and Belgium. The EU therefore banned almost all imports of products derived from seals (in practice, this is mainly sealskin), with an exception made for products that "result from hunts traditionally conducted by Inuit and other indigenous communities and which contribute to their subsistence."[b] However, even with this exemption, the market for sealskins in Europe was irrevocably destroyed because the Canadian Inuit hunters sold the skins to nonindigenous firms that then sold the skins in Europe. The Inuit hunt needed the larger commercial hunt to subsidize processing and shipping costs. Owing to the ban, the Inuit hunters could not effectively sell the skins from their hunts to Europe. The nonindigenous commercial Canadian sealers were hit even harder, as they were entirely prohibited from exporting to Europe.

The ban on seal products was not based on concerns regarding the health of seal populations, as none of those hunted were in any danger of collapse. (Some seal populations had in the past been hunted to endangerment by distance-water fleets, especially in the Antarctic and the Bering Sea, but this was never a result of indigenous hunting.) Some arguments were made regarding animal welfare and the manner in which seals are killed: about 90 percent are shot; the rest are killed with a hakapik, a club with a spike that is aimed at the seal's head. This latter manner of killing the seal may be graphic, but it involves the direct contact of the hunter with the animal, is

(continued)

[a]Regulation No. 1007/2009 of the European Parliament and of the Council on trade in seal products; see, for example, Dorothée Cambou, "The Impact of the Ban on Seal Products on the Rights of Indigenous Peoples: A European Issue," *Yearbook of Polar Law* 5 (2013): 389; and Nikolas Sellheim, "The Neglected Tradition? The Geneses of the EU Seal Products Trade Ban and Commercial Sealing," *Yearbook of Polar Law* 5 (2013): 41; Nikolas Sellheim, "Legislating the Blind Spot: The EU Seal Regime and the Newfoundland Seal Hunt" (PhD diss. University of Lapland, 2016), http://lauda.ulapland.fi/handle/10024/62393; and Martin Hennig and Richard Caddell, "On Thin Ice? Arctic Indigenous Communities, the European Union and the Sustainable Use of Marine Mammals," in *The European Union and the Arctic*, ed. Nengye Liu, Elizabeth A. Kirk, and Tore Henriksen, 296–341 (Leiden, Netherlands: Brill, 2017).
[b]Regulation No. 1007/2009, para. (i).

| BOX 6.2 | *Continued* |

quick, and enables the hunter to determine whether the animal has been killed cleanly or whether it requires another blow.

The WTO upheld the EU's ban in principle (requiring some minor modifications) on the basis of "public moral concerns."[c] In the end, the ban is not legitimized based on actual animal welfare issues but rather on what the public in Europe perceives to be animal welfare issues.

For many people living in the Arctic, both the sealing case and the whaling controversy in chapter 5 display a failure to understand the economic, social, historical, and environmental aspects of hunting of marine mammals. In both cases, pressures from far outside the Arctic attempt to define what Arctic peoples may or may not do with the resources around them based on quite different economic realities. The outsiders seem to say, "We no longer need this; so you cannot have it."

[c]*European Communities—Measures Prohibiting the Importation and Marketing of Seal Products*, Reports of the Panel, World Trade Organization, November 25, 2013, WT/DS400/R and WT/DS401/R; and *European Communities—Measures Prohibiting the Importation and Marketing of Seal Products*, Reports of the Appellate Body, May 22, 2014, WT/DS400/AB/R and WT/401/AB/R.

RECENT NEOLIBERAL TRADE NEGOTIATIONS

As neoliberalism took hold in the 1990s, the United States and others moved to eliminate nontariff barriers (NTBs) to trade, such as the appurtenance rule discussed earlier, agricultural subsidies, or "buy United States/EU/Canada" rules. This trend in free trade—that goes beyond reducing direct tariffs on goods—has raised concerns about transparency, human rights, the environment, and how far to let private actors control decisions over what has been the public sphere. The logic of neoliberalism expressed itself in the most recent set of free trade negotiations: the Trans-Pacific Partnership (TPP), the Transatlantic Trade and Investment Partnership between the United States and EU (TTIP), and the Comprehensive Economic Trade Agreement (CETA) between Canada and the EU.

CETA and CPTPP

In 2017 newly inaugurated President Trump pulled the United States out of TPP negotiations. The remaining parties continued without the United States, the agreement was signed March 8, 2018, and the ratification process has begun. The treaty agreed upon is the Comprehensive and Progressive Agreement for Trans-Pacific Partnership (CPTPP).[65] It includes Canada and various states with Pacific coasts. Trump halted TTIP negotiations, and these show no signs of restarting. Meanwhile, CETA, between the EU and Canada, entered provisionally into force in September 2017, shortly after Trump announced his intention to quit or reform NAFTA.[66]

Both CETA and CPTPP are relevant to the Arctic. They retain some of the neoliberal approach to trade but with more concern for human rights and a greater willingness to limit the capacity of firms to litigate disputes. These small changes suggest both that states are learning to solve problems without the United States and that their solutions differ from what the United States had sought to include. CPTPP changed intellectual property rules, notably by limiting the amount of time pharmaceuticals can maintain a patent, which will better protect human health. Investment dispute changes mean "investors' ability to litigate disputes under investment agreements and investment authorizations—which are used mostly for mining and oil investments—will be more limited relative to TPP."[67] The EU pushed for some social protections and got them in CETA. Canada has also pledged to join four International Labour Organization protocols and has discussed new processes to consult with devolved indigenous governments before agreeing to a treaty.[68]

CETA limits the practice of setting aside a portion of jobs for local people, though there is an exception for hiring indigenous people and businesses.[69] CETA also has a labor chapter in it. CETA aims to make investment easier, but this goal met with considerable public disapproval. Two features in particular generated opposition: CETA allows firms to bid on government contracts in each other's territories. The ability to bid might well bring in investment, but it also encourages privatization of public services and reduces local control. Moreover, it appeared that once privatized, services would be very difficult to renationalize even if the private contractors failed to deliver. In the final version of CETA, the governments kept the possibility of private firms taking over public services but made it easier to return activities to public management.

Even greater scorn was directed at rules proposed on investor-state dispute resolution. These would give more power to firms over governments and were believed to favor firms over other interests.[70] In the end, the EU and Canada approved the treaty but rejected the original investor-state dispute chapter. Ultimately, the parties changed their approach to dispute resolution by agreeing to a permanent court rather than arbitration. Each member state of the EU must ratify the agreement before it can come into force indefinitely (and before the dispute resolution provisions become effective). The national parliaments of EU member states, however, must vote on the revised agreement.

Parliamentary approvals add a measure of democratic accountability, but the process will take a number of years to complete.[71]

CETA Impacts

In an effort to understand the impact of a free trade agreement—and perhaps mitigate negative aspects that concern the public—the EU has developed an impact assessment process. The EU's processes help to see where positive, negative, and unclear impacts might occur and allow the EU to find measures to soften the negative social and environmental impacts of free trade on workers, on the environment, and on third parties outside the agreement.[72]

Impact on Small and Medium Enterprises

Trade agreements clearly facilitate trade and investment for large firms, so it is possible that large natural resource firms will do well with CETA. Less clear are its impacts on small and medium-sized enterprises (SMEs). In the EU and the United States, two-thirds of all private sector employment is in SMEs, and they accounted for around 85 percent of new jobs.[73] Only a small percentage of American SMEs participate in international trade—on the order of 408,000 firms in the United States out of a total of thirty million SMEs.[74] But they account for 98 percent of US firms engaged in trade. The value of their trade is 30 percent of the US total, with large firms providing the bulk of value. Free trade can be good at creating jobs, and SMEs that engage in it are less likely to go out of business and more likely to grow faster. SMEs often lack the knowledge to take advantage of new opportunities, which may account for the tiny percentage of them that engage in international trade. The majority of companies in the Arctic fall into the SME category. If SMEs make widespread use of trade opportunities, then CETA could produce jobs as well as less expensive products.

Social Impacts

The EU seeks to negotiate trade agreements that support democracy, human rights, and environmental protection and set the stage for sustainable development. There are specifics in CETA that suggest attention to those goals. Chapter 22, "Trade and Sustainable Development," introduces a Civil Society Forum to review progress and comment on issues to the governments. It will also advise on labor protections (chapter 23) and the environment (chapter 24). The forum, however, is only required to meet once a year. The agreement clearly states that the two parties could continue to implement environmental rules. Canada and the EU agree not to use the agreement to reduce labor protections, and Canada commits to consultation with its indigenous peoples on implementation.[75] There is no Arctic-specific section in the CETA analysis, so it is unclear whether the agreement will help or hinder indigenous and human rights or improve environmental sustainability. Leona Aglukkaq, then chair of the Senior Arctic Officials, conservative MP for Nunavut and federal minister of the environment until voted out in 2015, was optimistic about the benefits of CETA and expected it to make fish easier to sell and infrastructure investment easier to acquire.[76]

CONCLUSIONS

Globalization creates new relationships between states, firms, and people. More liberal trade rules have done much to drive globalization. Arctic leaders and residents have reasons to care about how trade agreements are negotiated and what they include. Trade agreements can encourage infrastructure development and improve local lives. The possibility of using supply and value chain thinking may improve the economic conditions found in some parts of the Arctic. However, free trade agreements can also weaken human rights, indigenous rights, and democratic decision making. The efforts to improve social protections in CETA while opening the Canadian and EU economies more to each other may better balance the public interest with private interests than earlier free trade deals. If the investor court in CETA proves better able to moderate the power of corporations, it may be copied in other agreements as a preferred method of dispute resolution. Similarly, the limits on intellectual properties in CPTPP may spread and trim back the extensive protections long pressed for and often achieved by the United States. An indigenous chapter is under discussion within the NAFTA negotiations.[77] Those discussions may not lead to implementation, but their very existence suggests a turnaway from neoliberal dogma. In sum, the inclusion of labor, permanent investment courts, new approaches to intellectual properties protection in CPTPP and CETA, and at least talk of a chapter on indigenous rights may signal a willingness to moderate the neoliberal approach to economic affairs.

FURTHER READING

Ágústsson, Hjalti Ómar, and Rachael Lorna Johnstone. "Practising What They Preach: Did the IMF and Iceland Exercise Good Governance in Their Relations 2008–2011?" *Nordicum-Mediterraneum* 8, no. 1 (2013), https://nome.unak.is/wordpress/08-1.

Anderson, Torben M., Bengt Holmström, Seppo Honkapohja, Sixten Korkman, Hans Tson Söderström, and Juhana Vartiainen. *The Nordic Model: Embracing Globalization and Sharing Risks*. Research Institute of the Finnish Economy. Helsinki: Taloustieto Oy, 2007.

Baker, Betsy. "Assessing Assessments of NAFTA's Marine Environment: The Commission for Environmental Cooperation Meets the World Ocean Assessment." In *NAFTA and Sustainable Development: History, Experience, and Prospects for Reform*, edited by H. Kong and L. Wroth, 191–203. Cambridge: Cambridge University Press, 2015.

Bertelsen, Rasmus Gjedssø. *Knowledge-Based Institutions in Sino-Arctic Engagement: Lessons for the Belt and Road Initiative*. Basingstoke, UK: Palgrave Macmillan, 2018.

Bertelsen, Rasmus Gjedssø, Jens C. Justinussen, and Coco Smits. "Energy as a Developmental Strategy: Creating Knowledge-Based Energy Sectors in Iceland, the Faroe Islands, and Greenland." In *Handbook of Politics in the Arctic*, edited by Leif Christian Jensen and Geir Hønneland, 3–25. Cheltenham, UK: Edward Elgar, 2015.

Frieden, Jeffry, and Lisa L. Martin. "International Political Economy: Global and Domestic Interaction." In *Political Science: The State of the Discipline*, edited by Ira Katznelson and Helen V. Milner, 118–46. New York: W. W. Norton, 2003.

Jónsson, Ásgeir, and Hersir Siguregeirsson. *The Icelandic Financial Crisis: A Study into the World's Smallest Currency Area and Its Recovery from Total Banking Collapse*. Basingstoke, UK: Palgrave Macmillan, 2016.

Lanteigne, Marc. "'Have You Entered the Storehouses of the Snow?' China as a Norm Entrepreneur in the Arctic." *Polar Record* 53, no. 2 (2017): 117–30.

Murtagh, Aisling, and Patrick Collins. "Northern Peripheries and Creative Capital and Its Role in Contributing to Regional Development in Nordic Regions." *Arctic Yearbook*, 2017, https://www.arcticyearbook.com/toc2017.

Stammler, Florian. *Reindeer Nomads Meet the Market: Culture, Property and Globalisation at the "End of the Land."* Vol. 6 of Halle Studies in the Anthropology of Eurasia. Münster: LIT Verlag, 2009.

7

Human Rights and the Rights of Indigenous Peoples in the Arctic

WHEN THE UNITED NATIONS (UN) Charter was negotiated in 1945, there were hopes to include a human rights chapter, but the need for a treaty to be agreed upon swiftly to secure lasting international peace and security took precedence. Nevertheless, the idea of human rights—innate rights that all people have simply by virtue of being human, rights that they hold against their own states, rights that curtail the power of their governments—gained traction in the shadows of the atrocities of World War II. A complex web of binding and nonbinding global and regional instruments has emerged since then.

There are three main sources of human rights and indigenous rights norms in the Arctic: the UN system, the Council of Europe system (relevant to the six European states), and the Inter-American system (relevant to the United States and Canada). There is only one binding treaty devoted to indigenous rights—ILO Convention 169 on Indigenous and Tribal Peoples (ILO C169)[1]—but indigenous communities and individuals are also protected under general human rights instruments. The Universal Declaration of Human Rights (UDHR) and the UN Declaration on the Rights of Indigenous Peoples (UNDRIP), being declarations, are not formally binding on states but are politically powerful instruments.[2]

The UDHR is so fundamentally connected to the UN and its origins that no state would be willing to admit that it pays it no regard.[3] It is "in some sense the constitution of the entire regime."[4] Much of the UDHR is now considered as reflecting customary international law and therefore has, over time, become binding on states. The UDHR was the basis for the development of a number of treaties. The two most important of these are the International Covenant on Economic, Social and Cultural Rights (ICESCR) and the International Covenant on Civil and Political Rights (ICCPR).[5] These were both agreed in 1966 and together cover the contents of the UDHR and convert it into binding obligations for their states parties.[6] The ICCPR has been ratified by all the Arctic states and the ICESCR by all but the United States (see table 7.1). There are a further seven core human rights treaties and nine optional protocols (see box 7.1).

This chapter explains the conceptual differences between human rights and indigenous rights and explores the main regimes and instruments for their protection in the Arctic: the UN and the regional systems of Europe and the Americas. It then provides a closer study of some of the main human rights and indigenous rights challenges in the region.

HUMAN RIGHTS OR INDIGENOUS RIGHTS?

The traditional individual rights approach protects individuals (including members of minorities) *within* the dominant culture of the state; but indigenous rights protect the group's right to exist *outside*, in some respects, of the dominant culture; in short, they aim at ensuring the group can continue to exist at all.[7] Persons who identify as indigenous enjoy all of the human rights that their states have accepted, on the same basis as everyone else.[8] However, indigenous peoples also enjoy certain rights because of their indigenous status, including both individual rights and collective rights.[9] These include rights to self-governance, land and resource management, education, language, and culture. Arctic indigenous peoples are also minorities in their states and enjoy certain rights by virtue of that status.[10]

The indigenous groups in each Arctic state were discussed in chapter 3. But how do we recognize a community as indigenous in a manner that is legally relevant and would entitle them to exercise indigenous rights? No single, authoritative definition of indigenous peoples exists in international law. Even the UNDRIP avoids giving a definition and suggests that it is up to the community itself to identify as indigenous or not.[11] However, it cannot only be a matter of self-identification because then any group of individuals could claim indigenous status and the rights and protections that emanate from that status. Nor can it simply be left up to states to determine whether or not indigenous peoples reside within their borders. Otherwise, they could effectively deny indigenous peoples their rights by denying their indigenousness. ILO C169 does not provide a conclusive definition either, but is intended to apply to groups who

Table 7.1   Human Rights and Indigenous Instruments by Arctic State

	ICCPR	ICESCR	CERD	ILO C169	ECHR	ACHR	UDHR	UNDRIP	ADRIP
Canada	P	P	P	NP	N/A	NP	E	E	R
Denmark (Kingdom of)	P	P	P	P	P	N/A	E	E	N/A
Finland	P	P	P	NP	P	N/A	E	E	N/A
Iceland	P	P	P	NP	P	N/A	E	E	N/A
Norway	P	P	P	P	P	N/A	E	E	N/A
Russia	P	P	P	NP	P	N/A	E	E	N/A
Sweden	P	P	P	NP	P	N/A	E	E	N/A
United States	P	NP	P	NP	N/A	NP	E	E	R

Note: P = Party (binding on the state); NP = Not Party (not binding on the state); N/A = Not Applicable (not in region); E = Endorses as political but not legally binding instrument, may be conditional; R = Does Not Endorse politically or legally

BOX 7.1	Human Rights Treaties, Protocols, and Instruments

UN Declarations
- UDHR: Universal Declaration of Human Rights 1948
- UNDRIP: United Nations Declaration on the Rights of Indigenous Peoples 2007

ILO Treaty
- ILO C169: Indigenous and Tribal Peoples Convention 1989

Council of Europe
- ECHR: European Convention on Human Rights 1950

Organization of American States
- ADRDM: American Declaration on the Rights and Duties of Man 1948
- ACHR: American Convention on Human Rights 1969
- ADRIP: American Declaration on the Rights of Indigenous Peoples 2016

UN Human Rights Treaties[a]	Monitoring Committee
CERD: International Convention on the Elimination of All Forms of Racial Discrimination 1965	Committee on the Elimination of Racial Discrimination
ICCPR: International Covenant on Civil and Political Rights 1966 ICCPR-OP1: Optional Protocol to the International Covenant on Civil and Political Rights 1966 (creating a communications procedure) ICCPR-OP2: Second Optional Protocol to the International Covenant on Civil and Political Rights 1989 (prohibiting the death penalty)	Human Rights Committee
ICESCR: International Covenant on Economic, Social and Cultural Rights 1966 OP-ICESCR: Optional Protocol to the International Covenant on Economic, Social and Cultural Rights 2008 (creating a communications procedure and permitting inquiries)	Committee on Economic, Social and Cultural Rights

UN Human Rights Treaties[a]	Monitoring Committee
CEDAW: Convention on the Elimination of All Forms of Discrimination Against Women 1979 OP-CEDAW: Optional Protocol to the Convention on the Elimination of All Forms of Discrimination Against Women 1999 (creating a communications procedure and permitting inquiries)	Committee on the Elimination of Discrimination against Women
CAT: Convention against Torture and Other Cruel, Inhuman or Degrading Treatment or Punishment 1984	Committee against Torture
OP-CAT: Optional Protocol to the Convention against Torture and other Cruel, Inhuman or Degrading Treatment or Punishment 2002 (to inspect prisons in states parties)	Subcommittee on Prevention
CRC: Convention on the Rights of the Child 1989 OP-CRC-AC: Optional Protocol to the Convention on the Rights of the Child on the involvement of children in armed conflicts 2000 OP-CRC-SC: Optional Protocol to the Convention on the Rights of the Child on the sale of children, child prostitution and child pornography 2000 OP-CRC-Comm: Optional Protocol to the Convention on the Rights of the Child on a communications procedure 2011 (creating a communications procedure and permitting inquiries)	Committee on the Rights of the Child
MWC: International Convention on the Rights of All Migrant Workers and Members of Their Families 1990	Migrant Workers Committee
CRPD: Convention on the Rights of Persons with Disabilities 2006 OP-CRPD: Optional Protocol to the Convention on the Rights of Persons with Disabilities 2006 (creating a communications procedure)	Committee on the Rights of Persons with Disabilities
CED: International Convention for the Protection of All Persons from Enforced Disappearances 2006	Committee on Enforced Disappearances

[a]For current information on which states are parties to which treaties and protocols, see "Status of Ratification Interactive Dashboard," Office of the High Commissioner for Human Rights, http://indicators.ohchr.org.

have distinct social, cultural, and economic conditions (in contrast to the dominant community of the state in which they live) and have their own systems for recognizing membership of the group; and/or to groups who descend from precolonial times and have maintained at least some of their traditional social, economic, cultural, or political institutions.[12] Self-identification is also regarded as "a fundamental criterion."[13]

One of the most influential definitions of indigenous peoples comes from Jose R. Martinez Cobo, the first UN Special Rapporteur on Discrimination against Indigenous Populations. He enumerated the following criteria in 1986 (see also the summary in box 7.2 and the discussion of the Greenland situation in box 7.3):

> Indigenous communities, peoples and nations are those which, having a historical continuity with pre-invasion and pre-colonial societies that developed on their territories, consider themselves distinct from other sectors of the societies now prevailing on those territories, or parts of them. They form at present non-dominant sectors of society and are determined to preserve, develop and transmit to future generations their ancestral territories, and their ethnic identity, as the basis of their continued existence as peoples, in accordance with their own cultural patterns, social institutions and legal system.
>
> On an individual basis, an indigenous person is one who belongs to these indigenous populations through self-identification as indigenous (group consciousness) and is recognized and accepted by these populations as one of its members (acceptance by the group). This preserves for these communities the sovereign right and power to decide who belongs to them, without external interference.

BOX 7.2 | **Who Is Indigenous?**

The following criteria are the main factors in identifying an indigenous people. It is not necessary that every factor be present in every case:

- Self-identification (this is essential)
- Historical continuity to precolonial and/or preindustrial society
- Connection to land; usually traceable to direct ancestors
- Distinct cultural, religious, and/or linguistic tradition
- Politically nondominant within the state
- Desire to maintain traditions and not to assimilate with the dominant population

BOX 7.3 | Are the Greenlanders an "Indigenous People"?

From the eighteenth century until 1953, Greenland was considered a colony of the Kingdom of Denmark. However, in 1953, Denmark incorporated Greenland as a county and removed it from the UN list of colonies.[a] On ratifying ILO C169 in 1996, the Kingdom of Denmark declared: "There is only one indigenous people in Denmark in the sense of Convention 169, viz. the original population of Greenland, the Inuit."[b] Most recently, under the 2009 Self-Government Act, the Kingdom of Denmark recognized the Greenlanders as a "people." Colonial peoples have stronger rights to self-determination compared with indigenous peoples—in particular, a right to full independence—and Denmark has provisionally accepted the Greenlanders' right to become independent at a time of their own choosing.[c]

Views of Greenlanders as to whether they are indigenous or not are very mixed. Some argue that they should retain the protections they enjoy as indigenous people based on cultural and historical traditions as well as their close relations with other Inuit across the North American Arctic. The Inuit Circumpolar Council has an active Greenland chapter. However, others argue that now so much power is exercised by the self-government in Nuuk, with only a few matters reserved to Copenhagen, that it makes no sense to talk about indigeneity, as the Greenlandic Inuit are neither a numerical minority nor oppressed in their political community. As a practical matter, both Copenhagen and Nuuk governments share the view that the Self-Government Act constitutes full implementation of the UNDRIP.[d]

However, there are also two minorities within Greenland that might be seen as distinct indigenous communities: the Inughuit or Thule people of the Northwest, and the East Greenlanders. Their traditions, language, and clothing are all quite distinct from those of the majority West Greenlandic population. Therefore, if Greenland becomes independent, it may decide to recognize these two minorities as indigenous peoples within the new nation-state. They are undoubtedly "linguistic minorities" and would enjoy protection on that basis.[e]

[a]For a full history from a Danish perspective, see Erik Beukel, Frede P. Jensen, and Jens Elo Rytter, *Phasing Out the Colonial Status of Greenland, 1945–1954: A Historical Study* (Copenhagen: Museum Tusculanum Press, University of Copenhagen, 2010).

[b]Report of the committee set up to examine the representation alleging nonobservance by Denmark of the Indigenous and Tribal Peoples Convention, 1989 (No. 169), made under article 24 of the ILO Constitution by the National Confederation of Trade Unions of Greenland (Sulinermik Inuussutissarsiuteqartut Kattuffiat: SIK) (*SIK v. Denmark*), GB.277/18/3; GB.280/18/5, para 20.

[c]Act no. 473 of June 12, 2009, on Greenland Self-Government, chapter 8, article 21. If the Greenlanders opt for independence, negotiations commence between the Greenland government and the Danish government. The final agreement must, however, be approved by both Greenland and Danish Parliaments (Inatsisartut and Folketing) as well as by referendum in Greenland.

[d]Ministry of Foreign Affairs of Denmark, Danida, *Review Report: Strategy for Danish support to indigenous peoples 2001–2010* (Copenhagen: Ministry of Foreign Affairs of Denmark, 2011), 8.

[e]See ICCPR, article 27.

HOW DO HUMAN RIGHTS IMPACT DECISION MAKING?

All humans have human rights. They do not have to be earned; one does not have to deserve them; and they cannot be lost.

While Arctic governments seek to protect the well-being of their citizens, a protective or welfare model is not the same as a "rights-based" approach. It is always desirable that development be pursued in harmony with the social and economic interests of those peoples most likely to be affected. However, when viewed as a matter of *law*, and not just political expediency, the discourse changes significantly. A welfare or development model still leaves the power in the hands of the states who can choose to grant support—or choose to withhold it. "To enjoy something only at the discretion of someone else, especially someone powerful enough to deprive you of it at will, is precisely *not* to enjoy a *right* to it."[14] However, if someone holds a right to something, they do not have to beg for it; there is no shame in demanding it; and it cannot be easily retracted on a political whim.[15]

There are also pragmatic incentives for states to uphold human rights law: they face a risk of legal action through international human rights mechanisms, as will be illustrated below, as well as through domestic laws that have been passed to implement the international standards. Most Arctic states consider themselves leaders in human rights and seek to influence human rights protection elsewhere in the world; if their own record is under attack, they lose their credibility.

Similarly, we can hope that businesses operating in the Arctic—for example, in the large-scale extractive industries—try to ensure that their operations do no harm to local populations. Irrespective of corporate goodwill, if an activity is found to be unlawful, it can be halted, and compensation will be payable to affected parties. Even if a developer ultimately wins a case, lengthy litigation brings major costs for industry in terms of direct legal expenses, workforce hours, inactive hardware, and idle employees. Therefore, it is essential for all concerned that adequate pre-project analysis be conducted in respect to human rights and the rights of indigenous peoples. Box 5.2 in chapter 5 presented the case study of the Baffinland Mines project in which the Nunavut Planning Commission issued its first nonconformity decision when it rejected an already revised proposal of Baffinland Mines to ship ore through the winter from Milne Inlet to Baffin Bay. Also in Canada, in 2011, a consortium of oil companies proposed seismic testing in Baffin Bay and the Davis Strait. Permission was granted by the National Energy Board in 2014, but the Hamlet of Clyde River brought a legal challenge. It finally won its case at the Supreme Court in 2017 based on the oil companies' lack of consultation with the affected communities as required under constitutional law.[16]

UNITED NATIONS INSTRUMENTS AND MECHANISMS

The UN has three dedicated institutions for the observance and protection of the rights of indigenous peoples (see box 7.4). Besides these, there are nine monitoring committees and a subcommittee (also called human rights treaty bodies) to review state performance and advise states on implementation of the human rights treaties (see box 7.1). Some of the human rights optional protocols, such as the first optional protocol to the ICCPR, create mechanisms for receipt and review of communications from those who believe their rights have been violated. Others introduce substantive protections (in which case they can be ratified by states that are not party to the parent treaty) such as the optional protocols to the Convention on the Rights of the Child on the Sale of Children and on

---

BOX 7.4 | **Three UN Bodies on Indigenous Rights and Issues**

There are three main forums for addressing indigenous issues at the United Nations.[a]

The *UN Permanent Forum on Indigenous Issues* has existed since 2002 as an advisory body to ECOSOC (the UN's Economic and Social Council). Half of its sixteen independent experts are appointed by governments and half by indigenous organizations from around the world (including the Inuit Circumpolar Council). It provides advice and recommendations to ECOSOC, disseminates information about indigenous issues and rights, and promotes integration of indigenous issues through the other UN bodies. It includes an Arctic Caucus.

The *Expert Mechanism on the Rights of Indigenous Peoples* was created in 2007 and operates under the UN Human Rights Council. It has five independent experts whom the Human Rights Council directs to conduct research on indigenous peoples.

The *Special Rapporteur on the Rights of Indigenous Peoples* (as of 2014, Victoria Tauli Corpuz, from the Philippines) prepares reports along thematic and/or country grounds and investigates alleged violations. She (or he) seeks permission to make visits to countries to evaluate indigenous rights and well-being. Recent missions to Canada, the United States, Sápmi (the Sami homeland in Norway, Sweden, and Finland), and Russia have resulted in critical reports.[b]

[a]For a fuller account, see S. J. Rombouts, "The Evolution of Indigenous Peoples' Consultation Rights under the ILO and U.N. Regimes," *Stanford Journal of International Law* 53 (2017): 169.
[b]The reports can be found in full at "Country Reports," UN Human Rights Office of the High Commissioner, accessed March 2, 2018, http://www.ohchr.org/EN/Issues/IPeoples/SRIndigenousPeoples/Pages/CountryReports.aspx.

Children in Armed Conflict.[17] The United States is party to both these protocols even though it has not ratified the Convention on the Rights of the Child (CRC).[18]

All of the committees receive and review reports from states parties and hold discussion sessions with state representatives to examine their performance and make recommendations for improvements. They also make general comments and recommendations that are addressed to all states.[19] They are often thematic (explaining individual articles or addressing protection for vulnerable groups) but can also address structural questions regarding states' obligations under the treaties—for example, on reporting obligations or state responsibility. In some cases, they deal with emerging issues that are not addressed explicitly in the conventions but are implicit. Some treaty bodies can undertake inquiries if there are grounds to consider that serious and systematic violations are taking place. Individuals can submit communications (letters of complaint) if they believe their rights have been violated in respect to eight treaties, as long as their state is a party to the treaty *and* has accepted the communications procedure.[20]

At the heart of international human rights law is the principle of equality: all persons, irrespective of race, gender, social status, religion, political beliefs, wealth, or other criteria, enjoy the same human rights. The ICCPR and ICESCR both require that all people within a state's jurisdiction enjoy human rights on the same basis and make an additional provision on gender equality.[21] The Convention on the Elimination of All Forms of Racial Discrimination (CERD) and the Convention on the Elimination of All Forms of Discrimination against Women (CEDAW) are both based on nondiscrimination approaches. The CRC prohibits discrimination against children but also provides additional protections, recognizing the innate vulnerability of children and their inability to take care of themselves. It also requires that special attention be paid to the resources available to indigenous children through the media; that education of children promote understanding, peace, tolerance, equality, and friendship, including in respect to indigenous people; and that indigenous children be free to practice their culture, religion, and language.[22]

Because indigenous peoples are also racial minorities in their states (or, if a majority in numerical terms, they are a historically marginalized and ethnically distinct group), the CERD provides important protections for them. In 1997 its monitoring committee, the Committee on the Elimination of Racial Discrimination, issued a General Recommendation explaining the CERD's significance for and application to indigenous peoples.[23] It emphasized in particular the land and resource rights of indigenous peoples and called on states to recognize and promote indigenous culture, language, and history; facilitate sustainable development of indigenous communities; ensure that indigenous individuals did not face discrimination; and ensure that decisions affecting indigenous peoples were only made with their informed consent.

The International Labour Organization predates the UN but is now one of its specialized agencies. As its title suggests, its main focus is to promote the rights and welfare of workers around the world, but it is also the only institution that has created a binding international treaty dedicated to indigenous peoples. ILO C169 was agreed in 1989, but so far only twenty-two states have agreed to become bound by it. In the Arctic, Norway (with regard to the Sami) and the Kingdom of Denmark (with regard to Greenland) are the only two states parties. Finland has taken some steps toward ratification, but it has been a protracted process. The treaty requires states parties, among other things, to recognize the land and resource rights of indigenous peoples.[24] Trade unions and industrial associations can bring representations to the ILO's Governing Body if they believe a state is not upholding its obligations under an ILO convention, including under ILO C169.[25] In 2001 the Greenland SIK trade union brought a petition complaining about the displacement of the Inughuit from Uummannaq in 1953 to make way for the US airbase.[26] The petition was unsuccessful because the Governing Body held that Denmark had taken adequate steps to settle the dispute domestically in line with the convention.[27] One important aspect of the case, however, was the recognition that the displacement of the Inughuit was a continuing act.[28] In other words, the wrong done to the Inughuit was not a onetime action in 1953 but was ongoing, as the Inughuit are still unable to return to their ancestral home. Although forced relocations were not prohibited by international law in 1953, measures that prevent indigenous peoples from returning to their homelands today can violate contemporary international law.

The UNDRIP was agreed as a resolution of the UN General Assembly on September 13, 2007, after more than two decades of difficult negotiations between states and indigenous representatives. Indigenous leaders played a key role in its drafting, and it would not have been sent to a vote had they not supported the text. However, ultimately, it was the member states of the UN that agreed to it.[29] At the UN General Assembly, each state has one vote. Of those who attended the session, 143 states voted in favor, 11 abstained, and 4 voted against (Australia, Canada, New Zealand, and the United States).[30] These four have since come out in support of the UNDRIP.[31] Russia abstained at the vote, and its position on the UNDRIP remains ambiguous: it has said it will take the UNDRIP into account when it develops new legislation so far as the declaration is compatible with the Russian constitution.[32] Presumably, if some tension exists between the UNDRIP and the Russian constitution, the latter will take precedence.

The discussion in the UN General Assembly as well as the later statements of endorsement from Australia, Canada, New Zealand, and the United States make it quite clear that states do not regard the UNDRIP as binding in its entirety and that they consider much of it to be "aspirational"—in other words, to contain provisions that are politically and morally desirable but not creating obligations for states.[33] On the other hand, some states have already taken measures to incorporate the UNDRIP into domestic law, and a former Special Rapporteur on the Rights of Indigenous Peoples considers it the "yardstick" against which to measure state performance.[34]

In the "honeymoon period" of the Trudeau leadership of Canada following his election in October 2015, earnest commitments were made about repairing some of the historic wrongs that had been committed against Canada's native peoples, including the Inuit.[35] Trudeau's election followed a damning 2014 report by a Truth and Reconciliation Commission that had been specially appointed to document the history of residential schools for aboriginal children, propose measures to heal the ongoing intergenerational trauma, and restore trust between aboriginal Canadians and the government.[36] Trudeau endorsed all of the commission's recommendations, including that Canada unequivocally endorse the UNDRIP and implement it.[37] This has not proven quite as straightforward in practice as Trudeau's election promises might have indicated.[38]

Much of the UNDRIP is already binding either as a matter of customary law (e.g., on the rights of indigenous peoples to consultation before decisions affecting them are made) or under the treaties discussed above, especially ILO C169, the ICESCR, and the ICCPR.[39] The UN human rights monitoring committees that supervise the treaties are now referring to the declaration in their discussions with states. For example, the Committee on the Elimination of Racial Discrimination recommended to the United States, even before the United States had endorsed the UNDRIP, "that the declaration be used as a guide to interpret the state party's obligations under the Convention relating to indigenous peoples."[40] It advised Canada to implement a national action plan to "implement" the UNDRIP.[41] The UNDRIP is being cited in domestic proceedings in states and has even found its way into debates of the International Whaling Commission.[42]

THE COUNCIL OF EUROPE

All six European Arctic states are members of the Council of Europe and parties to the European Convention on Human Rights (ECHR).[43] The ECHR is broadly similar in scope to the ICCPR of the UN. Each of the eight hundred million residents of the Council of Europe's member states has the right to apply to the European Court of Human Rights if he or she believes his or her rights have been violated. The implementation of the court's judgments is supervised by the institutions of the Council of Europe, which can ultimately expel a member state if it refuses to comply with the ECHR. The European Court of Human Rights has been relatively conservative with regard to indigenous rights, mostly because of a reluctance to recognize group rights as opposed to individually held rights.[44] Nevertheless, it is very important in upholding traditional civil and political rights of relevance in the Arctic, such as freedom of expression; the right to privacy, family life, and the protection of the home; and the right to property (which is not included in either the ICCPR or the ICESCR).

THE INTER-AMERICAN SYSTEM
OF HUMAN RIGHTS PROTECTION

The Inter-American system is more complicated than the European one in the Arctic. Neither the United States nor Canada has acceded to the American Convention on Human Rights (ACHR),[45] which means that the Inter-American Court of Human Rights does not have jurisdiction to consider communications from Northern Canadian or Alaskan residents. However, both Canada and the United States are members of the Organization of American States (OAS), and one of the key instruments within that system is the American Declaration of the Rights and Duties of Man (ADRDM).[46] The Inter-American Commission on Human Rights reviews the human rights performance of all members of the OAS and holds that they must uphold the rights and freedoms in the ADRDM. Individuals, groups, and NGOs can send petitions to the commission, which can inquire and make recommendations.[47] The Inter-American Court of Human Rights and the Inter-American Commission on Human Rights have decided a number of cases in Latin America pertaining to indigenous peoples and have repeatedly upheld the rights of indigenous peoples to their continued existence, traditional practices, cultural and economic activities, and land and resources. To the extent that these findings reflect the ADRDM, they are applicable in Canada and the United States as well. In June 2016 the OAS concluded the American

Declaration on the Rights of Indigenous Peoples (ADRIP).[48] Much of the ADRIP mirrors the UNDRIP—for example, on rights to self-government and management of resources, with deference to the priority of state sovereignty—but it has a few provisions that go beyond.[49] Although the ADRIP was agreed by consensus, Canada and the United States both distanced themselves from it and stated their preference to concentrate on the UNDRIP.[50] At the present time, the UNDRIP is therefore of more relevance in the North American Arctic.

RESPONSIBILITY FOR HUMAN RIGHTS AND THE RIGHTS OF INDIGENOUS PEOPLES

States can violate human rights and the rights of indigenous peoples in a myriad of ways. For example, Arctic states have forced aboriginal children from their families to send them to schools thousands of miles from their homes, and they have granted resource rights that have destroyed indigenous culture and livelihoods. However, in many other cases, rights violations are not a result of state action or policy but are at the hands of nonstate actors—for example, when industry pollutes the land, river, and resources of local inhabitants. Individuals also violate the rights of one another; domestic violence is a good example of this.

States are intrinsically responsible for the conduct of their own organs and others they hire to act on their behalf.[51] However, states can also be held indirectly responsible for the activities of nonstate actors (e.g., corporations and individuals).[52] This is because a state's *failure* to act is also a form of "conduct." In law, an omission is a kind of action. A state that allows corporations to abuse the rights of workers or pollute the territories and natural resources of local inhabitants has violated international law. In fact, all the Arctic states have relatively strict regimes governing industrial activity, especially in the extractive sectors, but they do not implement them equally effectively, owing in some cases to lack of resources and in others to lack of will. Furthermore, some human rights require positive state action to be realized, even in the absence of any direct interference from another. The duty to ensure adequate food requires the state to take measures whenever someone under its jurisdiction cannot access food, even if no one else can be considered blameworthy.

This is an area where the concept of due diligence is very important. Due diligence in international law simply means adequate care. If a state has not taken adequate care to prevent human rights violations, this again is a form of conduct for which it can bear international responsibility. The concept of due diligence is common to many areas of international law and will be examined once more in the context of international environmental law.[53]

The UN treaty bodies have interpreted states' obligations under the various human rights treaties according to a tertiary framework of responsibilities to respect, protect, and fulfill. This model was first outlined by Henry Shue and Asbjørn Eide in the 1980s.[54] The duty to respect means that states' organs must refrain from actions that could harm human rights. The duty to protect is to take measures (exercise due diligence) to prevent nonstate actors, including corporations and individuals, from infringing on human rights. The duty to fulfill is another obligation of due diligence: to take measures to ensure that basic rights are guaranteed, even if no individual or institution can be blamed for their failure.[55]

A state is not *always* responsible every time there is a violation of human rights. If a state has exercised due diligence but there has nonetheless been a human rights violation (e.g., a murder that could never have been anticipated or prevented by the state's organs), then the state is not responsible for that outcome. The state is always the respondent (defending party) in human rights complaints before the international human rights institutions we have considered above: the regional courts and commissions and the UN human rights treaty bodies.

In the twenty-first century, there have been increasing efforts to develop direct corporate responsibility for human rights under international law. Corporations and individuals that violate human rights can be taken before domestic courts under criminal or civil law; indeed, the state is *obliged*, as an aspect of due diligence, to investigate and bring proceedings if there are grounds to believe a violation has taken place.[56] Since 2002, the International Criminal Court has been able to prosecute individuals for violations of the most fundamental norms of humanitarian law: genocide, crimes against humanity, war crimes, and the crime of aggression (planning, preparation, initiation, or execution by a person in a leadership position to use armed force against another state).[57]

In 2011 the UN Human Rights Council adopted the UN Guiding Principles on Business and Human Rights (UNGPs) that had been developed by Special Representative John Ruggie.[58] The UNGPs rely on the language of corporate responsibility *to respect* human rights, but the principles themselves indicate that corporations are required to take positive measures to minimize human rights violations to which they are connected—for example, "the responsibility to respect human rights requires that business enterprises . . . seek to prevent or mitigate adverse human rights impacts that are directly linked to their operations, products or services by their business relationships, even if they have not contributed to those impacts."[59]

HUMAN RIGHTS AND INDIGENOUS ISSUES IN THE ARCTIC

Human rights and the rights of indigenous peoples are both very wide fields of international law and it is not possible to give a full account with regard to Arctic peoples. Instead, some key concepts will be explored, but readers are encouraged to closely read the UNDRIP, ILO C169, and all of the other aforementioned UN and regional human rights instruments. Readers should also reflect on the historic abuses of indigenous peoples when considering this section.

The Right to Self-Determination and Political Participation

"The right to self-determination is the heart and soul of the declaration" of the UNDRIP.[60] Article 3 of the UNDRIP declares: "Indigenous peoples have the right to self-determination. By virtue of that right they freely determine their political status and freely pursue their economic, social and cultural development."

Heavily contested through the drafting process, it was a triumph of sorts for this article to even appear at all. Its meaning remains contested to this day. Self-determination is an inherently vague concept, but it is quite clear that self-determination for indigenous peoples in the UNDRIP does not amount to the right to full political independence (i.e., a right to become an independent state), as it does for colonial peoples. Article 46(1) provides that

> Nothing in this Declaration may be interpreted as implying for any state, people, group or person any right to engage in any activity or to perform any act contrary to the Charter of the United Nations or construed as authorizing or encouraging any action which would *dismember or impair, totally or in part, the territorial integrity or political unity of sovereign and independent States* [emphasis added].

If self-determination for indigenous peoples is not independence, then what is it? Article 4 gives further clarification: "Indigenous peoples, in exercising their right to self-determination, have the right to *autonomy or self-government* in matters relating to their *internal and local affairs*, as well as ways and means for *financing* their autonomous functions" (emphasis added).

Article 4 can be read not only as a description of the indigenous right to self-determination but as an attempt to *contain* that right. Self-determination is *only* a right to autonomous government vis-à-vis internal affairs, including resource management and economic, social, and cultural development. It is pointedly not a right to secession or separation. Also implicitly excluded are rights to exercise jurisdiction over nonmembers of the indigenous community or to negotiate with foreign states. However, article 4 is a minimum floor, and states may always grant indigenous peoples greater powers under their own constitutional arrangements.

While indigenous populations can exercise jurisdiction, even criminal jurisdiction, over their own members, there are still limits. Indigenous populations must still respect the basic human rights of their members, and states have duties to protect indigenous individuals from abuse within their own communities. For example, an indigenous group would not be permitted to whip children, even if it argued that this was a traditional cultural practice. They may, however, have a system of governance that does not appear to Western eyes as democratic—for example, giving elders power over decision making in the community, or employing "judges" in tribal councils that are close to the parties and draw on their personal knowledge (as opposed to the independence we expect in Western courts).

Self-determination of indigenous communities in the Arctic is expressed in different manners in different states. The Greenlanders enjoy the highest degree of autonomy by far, although, as discussed above in box 7.3, they may be better seen as a colonial people rather than an indigenous people.

As we saw in chapter 3, Alaska is complex because of the many layers of government (federal, state of Alaska, tribal, regional corporations, and native villages). The Alaskan Native Claims Settlement Act (ANCSA) was about title to land and property and did not address sovereignty or self-determination. The act (of the federal government, rather than a treaty between nations) purportedly extinguished aboriginal title to land and converted around 12 percent of Alaskan land into fee simple (ownership in the common law tradition) for native Alaskans. The system was (and is) incongruent with indigenous organizational and land-use traditions and is a tool of assimilation: trying to make Alaskan natives order their affairs according to mainstream American laws and values. The UN Special Rapporteur on the Rights of Indigenous Peoples noted that more than forty years later, ANCSA "continues to define realities for indigenous peoples in their ability to maintain the subsistence and cultural patterns that have long sustained them" and was "struck by indications about how the economic and cultural transformations accelerated by ANCSA have bred or exacerbated social ills among indigenous communities."[61] Two boroughs—the North Slope and the Northwest Arctic boroughs—contain a majority of indigenous people, but they are not native governments per se; rather, they are municipal governments that happen to have a majority of indigenous voters.[62]

The three territories of the Canadian Arctic enjoy a degree of autonomy but are not full provinces (see chapter 3). The Inuvialuit settlement region straddling the boundary between Yukon and the Northwest Territories, established in 1984, was the subject of a land claim agreement in 1984.[63] Its population of fewer than six thousand persons controls (through the Inuvialuit Regional Corporation) around thirty-five thousand square miles (land and water). Its powers principally relate to resources rather than self-governance more broadly, but it is charged with preserving Inuvialuit culture and protection of the environment. After nearly two decades of negotiations with the Inuit Tapiriit Kanatami (representing the Canadian Inuit), in 1993 the Nunavut Land Claims Agreement and Nunavut Act cut in half the Northwest Territories and led to Nunavut becoming the only territory with an Inuit majority in the population in 1999 (more than 80 percent).[64] Nunavut has extensive powers of self-governance and resource management. While elected territorial governments are elected based on residence rather than indigenous status, various provisions in the Nunavut Act are designed to ensure that the Inuit have control over their affairs. For example, there is a provision that requires proportional representation in the civil service, but at the time of writing, Inuit only constitute around half of the civil service.[65] Inuit regions of Quebec (Nunavik) and Newfoundland (Nunatsiavut) also enjoy limited autonomy, in particular over resource management.

Norway's Finnmark Act was intended to implement ILO C169.[66] Finnmark is governed in part by the Finnmark county municipality (elected by all residents of Finnmark) and in part by the Board of the Finnmark Estate (see chapter 3). The Finnish constitution respects the right of Sami to language, culture, and traditional activities. The Sami Parliament of Finland is the principal indigenous organ and governs language and culture in the Sami homeland (Enontekiö, Inari, Utsjoki, and part of Sodankylä municipalities). However, most Finnish Sami today live in other parts of Finland, which makes it difficult to provide cultural and linguistic services, and many people who self-identify as Sami are not legally recognized as such and hence cannot vote in Sami parliamentary elections. Sweden's Sami Parliament manages reindeer herding and allocation of resources, promotes Sami culture and language, and seeks increased self-determination and control over natural resources. However, the Swedish Sami Parliament cannot pass laws and does not have jurisdiction over any particular territory.

Russian indigenous peoples enjoy the least degree of indigenous self-government. President Putin has said that indigenous cultures are an even more valuable resource than hydrocarbons—but this is not borne out in practice.[67] Autonomous regional government is based on geography rather than indigenous or nonindigenous identity and is subject to a strong federal hand.[68] This means that where the indigenous are a minority in their homeland, they have very limited control over their political affairs. Appointments to leadership positions are often influenced or even dictated by Moscow. Russian law provides some protections for indigenous individuals and groups. For example, they have a right to compensation if their lands are expropriated, but they do not possess mineral rights or veto power to prevent commercial development on their territories that interferes with their traditional activities.[69]

All Arctic inhabitants are entitled to take part in the general democratic political life of their states, although this was not always the case. Canadian Inuit were only granted the right to vote in 1950, and other native Canadians in 1960.[70] Today, indigenous peoples around the Arctic enjoy the right to stand for election and vote on the same basis as other citizens in national and regional government, to freedom of expression (including a free press), and to freedom of association (including political parties, trade unions, indigenous organizations, and other NGOs). Since around 2006, Russia has been taking measures that restrict the operation of NGOs.[71] In 2012, it suspended the Russian Association of Indigenous Peoples of the North (RAIPON), preventing it from participating in the Arctic Council meeting of the Senior Arctic Officials before reinstating it under new direction in 2013 (see chapter 3). On the basis of the same law (and categorizing it as an NGO), in 2015, Russia closed the office of the Nordic Council.[72] Managing elections and facilitating the conditions necessary for a free press is also challenging in the Arctic owing to vast distances between small settlements and poor communications infrastructure. Nevertheless, a state cannot exclude rural inhabitants from elections on the grounds that it is too expensive to provide a polling station!

Land and Resource Management

Self-determination of indigenous peoples means that they exercise authority over their own members; but for it to be meaningful, it must also incorporate land and resource rights: Where and over what does an indigenous people exercise self-determination? "Land" in this context is not only terra firma but, according to ILO C169, includes "the total environment of the areas which the peoples concerned occupy or otherwise use," including areas not physically or permanently occupied but "to which they have traditionally had access for their subsistence and traditional activities"—for example, coastal and ocean regions of hunting and fishing.[73] ILO C169 requires states to recognize indigenous "ownership and possession" of lands (so understood).[74] It also requires states parties to "respect the special importance for the cultures and spiritual values of the peoples concerned of their relationship with the lands or territories, or both as applicable, which they occupy or otherwise use, and in particular the collective aspects of this relationship."[75]

Aside from ILO C169, indigenous land and resources are protected under the UNDRIP.[76] As ethnic minorities, indigenous persons are also protected under article 27 of the ICCPR, which provides the following: "In those States in which ethnic, religious or linguistic minorities exist, persons belonging to such minorities shall not be denied the right, in community with the other members of their group, to enjoy their own culture, to profess and practise their own religion, or to use their own language."[77]

The Human Rights Committee (monitoring the ICCPR) has interpreted "culture" relatively broadly under this provision to include traditional economic activities, such as Sami reindeer herding and indigenous fishing, even when they are conducted on a commercial basis.[78] It has also recognized the spiritual connection to land as an aspect of indigenous culture entitled to protection under article 27.[79]

Land and resource rights are protected for indigenous and nonindigenous inhabitants of the Arctic under the rubric of rights to property, privacy, and protection of the home.[80] The right to property under the ACHR explicitly includes a right of communities to hold property in common. In the Awas Tingni case, the court also recognized that for some communities, including the Awas Tingni indigenous community, land is not just a thing to be used but has a spiritual and cultural aspect.[81]

Indigenous peoples must never be forcibly removed from their ancestral homes.[82] In circumstances where such a historic wrong has occurred, they have a right to return or, if this is impossible, they should be granted an alternative location, selected in consultation with the community affected.[83] If an indigenous community loses access to its lands through force or threat, this does not extinguish its claims.[84] In the meantime, if indigenous territory or resources are in the legal ownership of a private party, the state must take measures to ensure that

they are not irreparably damaged, pending restoration to the indigenous community.[85] This means that in such cases, the state must not
permit logging, mining, hydrocarbon drilling, or wildlife destruction
that would interfere with the indigenous claims.

In its examination of the *Case of the Saramaka People v. Suriname*,
the Inter-American Court of Human Rights held that the land and
resources of tribal and indigenous communities are fundamental to their
identity and survival:

> Members of tribal and indigenous communities have the right to own
> the natural resources they have traditionally used within their territory
> for the same reasons that they have a right to own the land they have
> traditionally used and occupied for centuries. Without them, the very
> physical and cultural survival of such peoples is at stake. Hence the
> need to protect the land and resources they have traditionally used to
> prevent their extinction as a people. That is, the aim and purpose of
> the special measures required on behalf of the members of indigenous
> and tribal communities is to guarantee that they may continue living
> their traditional way of life, and that their distinct cultural identity,
> social structure, economic system, customs, beliefs and traditions are
> respected, guaranteed and protected by States.[86]

This statement of the importance of land and resources to indigenous peoples is just as important in the Arctic as it is in Suriname. Canada and
the United States could anticipate a similar view from the Inter-American
Commission on Human Rights, and the ILO Governing Body is likely to
pay heed to this case in its interpretations of ILO C169.

Many land claims by indigenous peoples have been settled with their
respective national and provincial governments and, the Alaska Native
Claims Settlement Act aside, these almost always include a degree of
self-government. Some of these were examined above and in chapter 3.
In 1980, the Alaska National Interest Lands Conservation Act recognized the rights of rural dwellers (indigenous and otherwise) to subsistence activities, but this was struck down by the Alaskan Supreme Court
in 1989 as unlawful discrimination between rural and town dwellers.[87]
There is no special recognition of or protection for traditional indigenous subsistence activities, and the Special Rapporteur on the Rights
of Indigenous Peoples concluded that in Alaska, "subsistence activities
are subject to a state regulatory regime that allows for, and appears to
often favour, competing land and resource uses such as mining and other
activities, including hunting and fishing for sport, that may threaten natural environments and food sources."[88]

The Right to Culture

Minorities (including indigenous peoples) enjoy a right to culture under the ICCPR, and this naturally goes beyond economic activities to include all sorts of cultural expression. Indigenous peoples are further protected by ILO C169, which requires states to have "due regard" for indigenous culture, and the UNDRIP, which requires cultural protection.[89] Reflecting the tragic history of attempts to destroy indigenous cultures and destroy indigenous societies, by virtue of, among other wrongs, mandatory residential schooling of indigenous children and curtailment of indigenous expression and association, the UNDRIP prohibits the forced assimilation of indigenous peoples.[90] The right to culture is also protected for all persons under the ICESCR.[91]

Industrial Development and Rights to Participation

Reflecting the principle of self-determination of indigenous peoples and as a means to ensure their substantive rights, certain procedural rights come into play. Indigenous peoples unquestionably enjoy a right to consultation in good faith before any decisions are taken that affect them, including industrial developments that impact their territory or resources.[92] The UNDRIP takes this further with the second most debated provision in the declaration (the most debated being the right to self-determination). It requires not only consultation but free, prior, and informed consent (FPIC):

> States shall consult and cooperate in good faith with the indigenous peoples concerned through their own representative institutions in order to obtain their free and informed consent prior to the approval of any project affecting their lands or territories and other resources, particularly in connection with the development, utilization or exploitation of mineral, water or other resources.[93]

Interpreted literally, this gives indigenous peoples a veto over such developments: consultation must result in consensus or it may not go ahead.[94] This is certainly the interpretation that indigenous organizations place upon it and was in fact the interpretation that the United States indicated when originally voting against the declaration.[95] Shortly after having promised to implement the UNDRIP, including FPIC, the Canadian government indicated that it interpreted the provision only as an obligation to *seek* consent in good faith but not necessarily to obtain it.[96] Canadian case law has not (yet) recognized an indigenous veto and only time will tell how the concept of FPIC is incorporated into domestic law and process.[97] An obligation to obtain consent would be a major barrier to extractive industries in northern Canada. The UNDRIP is not a binding document, and this particular provision has been repeatedly contested by states, so it cannot be said to reflect customary international law. However, the UN human rights treaty bodies have been giving FPIC more and more support in their discussions with states parties, so it is now potentially an evolving principle under treaty law.[98] During reviews of states' reports under the treaties, the Committee on the Elimination of Racial Discrimination and the Committee on Economic, Social and Cultural Rights have both referred to the principle.[99] The Human Rights Committee also upheld the requirement for FPIC in its review of a communication concerning Ángela Poma Poma, an indigenous llama farmer in Peru, under article 27.[100] In addition to the FPIC standard, the committee also held that for the development to be lawful, there must be indigenous participation in planning, and any interference in Ms. Poma Poma's cultural rights must be proportionate.[101] Peru had complied with none of these conditions.[102] The Human Rights Committee concluded that FPIC would be necessary whenever an activity has a "substantial negative impact."[103] All the Arctic states are parties to the ICCPR and hence bound by the provisions according to which this case was decided. The Inter-American Court of Human Rights (later followed by the African Commission on Human Rights) has also upheld the requirement of FPIC if activities present a likelihood of "major impact."[104]

Indigenous peoples whose land or resources are damaged through industrial activities are entitled to compensation; but even in the absence of any measurable damage, they are entitled to share the benefits of development under ILO C169.[105] This provision has also been supported by the Inter-American Court, the African Commission, and the Committee for the Elimination of Racial Discrimination.[106]

Nonindigenous people in the Arctic also enjoy certain rights to participate in decision making with regard to industrial development, though their rights are not as extensive as those enjoyed by indigenous communities. The most important treaty in this respect is the Aarhus Convention, which gives rights to all members of the public, including interest groups, to obtain environmental information and, if they are potentially affected by a development, to participate in the decision-making process.[107] It does not matter if a person lives inside or outside the state borders where the development is to take place: the person must have the same access to information, participation, and remedies.[108] In the Arctic, the Kingdom of Denmark (excluding Greenland), Finland, Iceland, Sweden, and Norway are all parties.[109] The European

Union is also a party and, through a directive, has implemented its provisions throughout the European Economic Area (the European Union plus Iceland, Liechtenstein, and Norway).[110] Former president Medvedev of Russia stated in 2011 that Russia intended to become a party to the Aarhus Convention, but no further steps have since been taken, and President Putin has not expressed further support.[111]

Under the ECHR, states must disclose information to potentially affected persons regarding environmental pollution that could impact the right to life or family life.[112] The ACHR is more generous, and the right to freedom of information includes a right to *obtain* information as well as to impart it.[113] Information can be sought on broad public interest grounds, as the person seeking the information does not even need to be personally affected.[114] However, Canada and the United States are not parties to the ACHR, and the ADRDM is less broadly worded.

Economic and Social Rights

Major challenges remain in almost all Arctic states in guaranteeing economic and social rights, such as the right to adequate food and housing, the right to the highest attainable standard of physical and mental health, the right to freely chosen work, and the right to education.[115] Chapter 4 explored this from the perspective of human security. Many of these rights pivot on state responsibilities to fulfill human rights: to take measures to ensure certain standards are upheld even if no person can be said to have acted in such a way as to have directly violated such rights. When food security is viewed not only as a matter of social justice but as a *human right*, the pressure on states to take measures to ensure adequate food has greater resonance. Adequate food requires not only the provision of a basic minimum of calories but must be "culturally appropriate."[116] This supports, prima facie, the maintenance of traditional activities and access to country foods (subsistence foods), as long as the community, indigenous or otherwise, seeks this.

Many of the human rights challenges in the Arctic are a result of political choices—for example, privatization, depletion of the welfare state, and centralization of services. However, other difficulties in fulfilling economic and social rights in the Arctic do not arise from lack of state will or interest but rather from the sparsity of population settlements, economies of scale, and limited human resources. It is not possible to provide a senior school or fully equipped medical center in every Arctic village; sometimes it is not even possible to provide a teacher or a doctor in a community. There may be a national shortage of qualified professionals—sometimes quite deliberately so in order to maintain a closed profession and protect wages—but remote communities are nearly always the most susceptible. Teachers and doctors cannot be forcibly moved to fill rural positions without violating their own human rights to freely choose their professions and residence. Local and especially indigenous individuals in the North may lack educational opportunities: there is still no university in the whole of Arctic Canada. Advancements in distance education and telemedicine hold promise but still require a great deal of investment and can never substitute entirely for face-to-face provision. A doctor cannot remove a marble from child's nose over an internet chat, even when the internet connection is fast and stable. In many parts of the Arctic, internet access is slow, intermittent, and very expensive; without improved communications infrastructure, distance education and telemedicine are of limited utility.

The Nordic states (excluding Greenland) perform rather better on economic and social rights than Russia or the North American Arctic. Part of the reason for this is political commitment in these states to a welfare model that is no substitute for a rights framework but in many cases will protect economic and social rights (see chapter 5). However, the Nordic states (again, except Greenland) do not have such vast geographical territories to cover or, as a result, such long distances between human settlements.

CONCLUSIONS

A rights-based approach to Arctic governance and development helps to ensure that the decisions taken *for* the Arctic are taken *by and for* the people whom they will affect most. The Arctic is not a wilderness but a home, and the peoples whose home it is are not just *a* consideration but the *primary* consideration when a rights-based framework is used.

The protection of indigenous rights and human rights in the Arctic is in many areas far ahead of standards elsewhere in the world. Arctic indigenous leaders have been pioneers in the international indigenous rights discourse, and the role of the permanent participants at the Arctic Council ensures that their voices are central to the major international decision-shaping discourses in the Arctic. Innovative forms of indigenous self-government have been developed, implemented, studied, and revised in the Arctic. They provide experience on which indigenous peoples and their states around the world can draw to develop self-government regimes elsewhere. Economic and social rights are relatively strong in the Nordic countries, and civil and political rights are defended robustly in seven of the eight Arctic states.

FURTHER READING

Anaya, James, and Siegfried Weissner. "The UN Declaration on the Rights of Indigenous Peoples: Towards Re-empowerment." *Jurist Forum*, October 3, 2007. http://www.jurist.org/forum/2007/10/un-declaration-on-rights-of-indigenous.php.
Cameron, E. S. "Securing Indigenous Politics: A Critique of the Vulnerability and Adaptation Approach to the Human Dimensions of Climate Change in the Canadian Arctic." *Global Environmental Change* 22 (2012): 103–14.
Charters, Claire, and Rodolfo Stavenhagen, eds. *Making the Declaration Work: The United Nations Declaration on the Rights of Indigenous Peoples*. Copenhagen: International Work Group for Indigenous Affairs, 2009.
Corpuz Tauli, Victoria. *Report of the Special Rapporteur on the Rights of Indigenous Peoples*. September 15, 2017. UN Doc. A/HRC/36/46 (on indigenous peoples and climate change).
Dunbar-Ortiz, Roxanne, Dalee Sambo Dorough, Gudmundur Alfredsson, Lee Sweptson, and Petter Wille, eds. *Indigenous Peoples' Rights in International Law: Experience and Application. A Book in Honor of Asbjørn Eide at Eighty*. Copenhagen: Gáldu and International Work Group for Indigenous Affairs, 2015.
Gordon Foundation. *IBA Community Toolkit*. Accessed April 13, 2018. http://gordonfoundation.ca/resource/iba-community-toolkit.
Green, Carina. *Managing Laponia. A World Heritage Site as Arena for Sami Ethno-Politics in Sweden*. Uppsala Studies in Cultural Anthropology 47. Uppsala, Sweden: Acta Universitatis Upsaliensis, 2009.
International Law Commission, Committee on the Implementation of the Rights of Indigenous Peoples. Accessed April 13, 2018. http://www.ila-hq.org/index.php/committees.
Lalonde, Suzanne, and Ted L. McDorman, eds. *International Law and Politics of the Arctic Ocean: Essays in Honour of Donat Pharand*. Leiden, Netherlands: Brill, 2015.
Lennox, Corinne, and Damien Short, eds. *Handbook of Indigenous Peoples' Rights*. Abingdon, UK: Routledge, 2016.
Michanek, Gabriel, and Tore Henriksen (guest), eds. "Extractive Industries in the North: What about Environmental and Indigenous Peoples Law?" Special issue, *Nordisk Miljörättslig Tidskrift* [Nordic Environmental Law Journal] 1 (2014).
Oude Elferink, Alex, Erik Molenaar, and Donald Rothwell, eds. *The Law of the Sea and the Polar Regions: Interactions between Global and Regional Regimes*. Leiden, Netherlands: Brill, 2013.
Øverland, Indra. "Indigenous Rights in the Russian North." In *Russia and the North*, edited by Elana Wilson Rowe, 165–85. Ottawa: University of Ottawa Press, 2009.
Pulitano, Elvira, ed. *Indigenous Rights in the Age of the UN Declaration*. Cambridge: Cambridge University Press, 2012.
Richardson, Benjamin, Shin Imai, and Kent McNeil, eds. *Indigenous Peoples and the Law: Comparative and Critical Perspectives*. Oxford: Hart Publishing, 2009.
Webber, Jeremy, and Colin M. Macleod, eds. *Between Consenting Peoples: Political Community and the Meaning of Consent*. Vancouver: University of British Columbia Press, 2010.

Westra, Laura. *Environmental Justice and the Rights of Indigenous Peoples: International and Domestic Legal Perspectives.* Abingdon, UK: Earthscan, 2008.

Zadorin, Maksim, Olga Klisheva, Ksenia Vezhlivtseva, and Daria Antufieva. *Russian Laws on Indigenous Issues. Guarantees, Communities, Territories of Traditional Land Use: Translated and Commented.* Rovaniemi, Finland: University of Lapland, 2017.

Zaikov, K., A. Tamitskiy, and M. Zadorin, "Legal and Political Framework of the Federal and Regional Legislation on National Ethnic Policy in the Russian Arctic." *Polar Journal* 7, no. 1 (2017): 125–42.

8

Law of the Sea in the Arctic

THE ARCTIC OCEAN is the heart of the Arctic, both geographically and figuratively. Like all other oceans of the world, it is governed by the international law of the sea, a tradition stretching back centuries to efforts to reduce tensions between European colonial powers who sought to control crucial trade routes to Africa, Asia, and the New World. The second part of the twentieth century saw great efforts to develop and codify the law of the sea in treaties through international conferences. The first lasted for two months in 1958 and resulted in four important conventions: on the Territorial Sea and the Contiguous Zone; on the Continental Shelf; on the High Seas; and on Fishing and Conservation of the Living Resources of the High Seas.[1] A second conference was called in 1960 to address two outstanding issues—the breadth of the territorial sea and the extent of fisheries jurisdiction—but no consensus emerged and no new treaty was agreed.[2] The third UN Conference on the Law of the Sea lasted for an impressive nine years (1973–1982) and resulted in one of the most comprehensive international treaties ever to be agreed: the UN Convention on the Law of the Sea of 1982 (UNCLOS).[3] It took another fourteen years and a separate implementing agreement for enough states to accept it formally (i.e., to ratify or accede) for it to come into force.

THE UN CONVENTION ON THE LAW OF THE SEA (UNCLOS)

The UNCLOS's seventeen parts with more than three hundred articles and nineteen annexes are nevertheless not exhaustive of contemporary law of the sea. In 1994 an implementing agreement regarding the Area beyond national jurisdiction (the deep seabed beyond any state's continental shelf) was agreed; it effectively amended part XI of the UNCLOS. In 1995 another implementing agreement on the management of fish stocks was agreed, which built upon part V of the UNCLOS.[4] Negotiations have begun on a third implementing agreement to conserve and to sustainably use biodiversity in the high seas.[5] Meanwhile, states that have not ratified the UNCLOS are still bound by the provisions in the 1958 conventions that they have ratified as well as by customary international law, which today mostly mirrors the UNCLOS.

Seven of the Arctic states have ratified the UNCLOS; the exception is the United States. Its recalcitrance was originally based on concerns about the "common heritage of mankind" principles that had been endorsed at the third conference and that appeared to the Reagan administration to be unnecessarily communistic.[6] Every president from Bush Sr. to Obama (alongside shipping firms, corporations, government agencies like the Department of Defense and the Department of State, and environmental groups) has supported accession to the UNCLOS. (At the time of this writing, President Trump seemed disinclined but had not pronounced explicitly on the matter.) The barrier is the Senate: only thirty-four senators are required to block accession, and sufficient numbers object to multilateralism in general and the jurisdiction of international courts and tribunals in particular. Accession to the UNCLOS would strengthen, not weaken, American rights to maritime resources and shipping, but domestic political pressures stand in the way. As a party, the United States would likely have a judge on the International Tribunal for the Law of the Sea (ITLOS) and an expert on the Commission on the Limits of the Continental Shelf (CLCS).

Nevertheless, aside from part XI (of limited importance in the Arctic), Reagan endorsed the substantive provisions of the UNCLOS as customary international law, and the United States follows them in practice—for example, on the definitions of maritime zones.[7] The United States is also a party to the Fish Stocks Agreement and all four conventions from 1958, and it has signed, but not ratified, the 1994 Agreement on the Area. At their meeting in Ilulissat in May 2008, the five Arctic Ocean littoral states—Canada, the Kingdom of Denmark, Norway, Russia, and the United States—all expressed their commitment to follow the law of the sea in managing the Arctic and rejected calls for an Arctic-specific general treaty.[8] The UNCLOS is without doubt the key to understanding the relative authority of states to the offshore resources, living and nonliving, in the Arctic.

MARITIME ZONES

The provisions of the UNCLOS that define jurisdiction in the oceans and carve up rights to resources are widely accepted as customary international law. Figure 8.1 shows how the oceans are carved up.

Figure 8.1   Maritime Zones

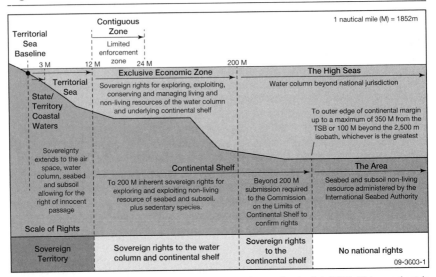

Baselines

All coastal states are surrounded by *baselines*. Any waters inside the baseline are called internal waters and are equated to land: this means that the coastal state can regulate entry or forbid entry altogether to foreign vessels.[9] In this respect, the baseline is analogous to a land border with a neighboring state.

The presumption is that the baseline is the low-water line of the shore.[10] Ice shelves that hang off of coasts are not taken into account and are considered "sea" for this purpose.[11] States are permitted to draw "straight baselines" across bays and fjords and around fringes of islands as long as the lines follow the "general direction of the coast."[12] In the Arctic, only the United States relies on the low-water mark exclusively, and the other states all employ the straight baseline method.[13] This has the effect of pushing their maritime zones a little farther seaward. Canada and Russia have also drawn long, straight baselines based on claims of "historic title."[14] As we will examine in the following chapter, these have not been widely accepted by other states.

The Territorial Sea and the Contiguous Zone

It was finally agreed in the UNCLOS that territorial waters could extend from the baseline up to a maximum of twelve nautical miles (nm) seaward.[15] Nearly every state has declared a 12 nm territorial sea, but Greenland is one of the few exceptions with only a 3 nm territorial sea that was never extended after the UNCLOS came into force.[16] Given the length of the sparsely populated Greenland coast, it does not have the resources to ensure security and supervision of vessels and protection of the marine environment to 12 nm (or even to 3 nm in many places), and there are no obvious advantages to Greenland in extending its jurisdiction, given that its exclusive rights to the marine resources in the Exclusive Economic Zone and on the shelf are secured in any case. In the United States, the state of Alaska exercises jurisdiction (and can enjoy the royalties of resource development) up to 3 nm, and the federal government exercises authority beyond that.[17]

Within the territorial sea (and in the airspace above), the coastal state enjoys sovereignty, which is largely comparable to that which it enjoys over its terra firma, with one exception: states must permit innocent passage of foreign vessels up to their baselines (but not beyond into internal waters).[18] Ships exercising this right must be both *in passage* (i.e., they are in continuous movement through the territorial sea) and *innocent* (e.g., they are not engaged in military maneuvers, taking resources such as fish, dumping waste, unloading goods or persons, etc.).[19] They have a right to sail but not to stop and engage in any other activity. Submarines are obliged to sail on the surface, displaying their flag.[20]

States have the right to declare a contiguous zone, up to 24 nm from the baseline, in which they may exercise jurisdiction over vessels to uphold customs, fiscal, immigration, and sanitary laws or regulations.[21] Around half of coastal states in the world have claimed a contiguous zone.[22] In the Arctic, only Iceland and Greenland have not.

The Exclusive Economic Zone (EEZ)

Up to a distance of 200 nm from the baseline, a coastal state can declare an exclusive economic zone (EEZ).[23] "Rocks which cannot sustain human habitation or economic life of their own" have a territorial sea but no EEZ or continental shelf.[24] In practice, states have claimed EEZs and continental shelves around remote, unpopulated, and inhospitable islands with little protest.[25] However, in the 2016 *South China Sea* case, a panel of five judges gave a restrictive definition of "island," incorporating a functional test that many Arctic islands, including Jan Mayen (a Norwegian-held island northeast of Iceland), would struggle to meet. Taiping Island/Itu Aba, which possesses a natural source of potable water as well as "multiple buildings, a lighthouse, a runway, and port facilities," has been used historically by fishermen who even established agriculture on it, and it is currently used by military personnel of Taiwan.[26] The panel nevertheless considered it a "rock" because it could not, in their view, "in its natural form have the capability of sustaining human habitation or an economic life."[27] The status of a feature as a rock as opposed to an island "is to be determined on the basis of its natural capacity, without external additions or modifications intended to increase its capacity to sustain human habitation or an economic life of its own."[28] Numerous "islands" in the Arctic and the Antarctic would fail such a test, being incapable of independently sustaining human habitation or economic life.

Within the EEZ, up to the territorial sea, foreign vessels enjoy full freedom of navigation, but the coastal state enjoys the resources of the water column. These are considered "sovereign rights," to distinguish them from the full "sovereignty" that states enjoy on their territory and territorial seas. In the EEZ, these include most obviously living marine resources (fish and mammals) but also energy (wave power or building of wind turbines).[29] Only the coastal state is permitted to build artificial structures or islands in the EEZ, but these should not interfere with shipping.[30] Other states should in theory be allowed to conduct marine scientific research in the EEZ (though not the territorial sea), but they should seek permission from the coastal state, and this is not always forthcoming, especially from Russia.[31]

Today, based on the UNCLOS, about one-third of the world's oceans are now enclosed within the EEZs of states, and these areas contain 95 percent of all commercial fish stocks.[32] Coastal states are not only entitled but required to exploit the fish within the EEZ, following the principle of "maximum sustainable yield," which means that they should take (or permit to be taken) as much fish as is compatible with the natural reproduction of the stocks.[33] The coastal state must establish, based on scientific data, a total allowable catch and, according to the UNCLOS, if it is unable to fish up to that maximum, it should allocate the surplus to other states.[34] However, since the setting of the total allowable catch is at the discretion of the coastal state, there is never in practice any "surplus" that is shared with other states, and coastal states do not need to accept the jurisdiction of any international court to resolve a dispute over this requirement.[35] Coastal states are exclusively entitled to catch marine mammals within their own EEZs, but they are not obliged to, and marine mammals are not subject to the maximum sustainable yield principle.[36]

Fish, however, swim about. Stocks can be shared between the EEZ of more than one state or may straddle across the EEZ (or EEZs of more than one state) and the high seas. Further, some species of fish are highly migratory and travel hundreds of miles, traversing the EEZs of multiple states and the high seas. Neighboring or opposite states with shared stocks are required to reach agreements on how to manage the resources, and they are encouraged to do so through regional fisheries management organizations (RFMOs).[37] Stretching into the Arctic from the Atlantic are the North Atlantic Fisheries Organization and the North-East Atlantic Fisheries Commission. The Joint Norwegian-Russian Fisheries Commission manages the Barents fisheries. The United States has a number of joint management regimes with Canada and works closely with Russia through the Intergovernmental Consultative Committee. Straddling stocks and highly migratory species are complicated because while they are in the high seas, all states have, in principle, rights to take them, irrespective of how far away their own territory may be. As for shared stocks, states engaged in fisheries of straddling stocks or highly migratory species are also required to settle and allocate the catch through agreement between themselves or through an RFMO.[38]

The provisions in the UNCLOS regarding fishing of shared and straddling stocks are insufficiently specific to govern the complexity of managing one of the world's most important food resources. In 1995, following two years of negotiations, the Fish Stocks Agreement (FSA) was opened for signature and ratification.[39] All the Arctic states are parties to the FSA, including the United States.[40] The FSA is built around twelve principles to encourage sustainable and equitable exploitation of straddling stocks and highly migratory species (see box 8.1). Particularly emphasized is the precautionary approach (discussed further in chapter 10).

The Continental Shelf

All coastal states have sovereign rights (not sovereignty) over the seafloor, extending from their territories and everything on or below it, known as the continental shelf. If the EEZ is the "wet bit," the continental shelf is the "hard bit." In the absence of an adjacent or opposite state within 200 nm, the continental shelf extends to 200 nm from their

BOX 8.1	The Twelve Principles of the Fish Stocks Agreement

The principles of the Fish Stocks Agreement are expressed in Article 5. They are:

a) To promote long-term sustainability of straddling and highly migratory fish stocks and promote optimum utilization
b) To determine measures based on best scientific evidence to produce maximum sustainable yield
c) To apply the precautionary approach
d) To take an ecosystem approach (examining fishing's impacts on associated and dependent species) when assessing fishing impacts
e) To conserve and manage species in light of the ecosystem approach to prevent any species becoming seriously threatened
f) To minimize pollution, waste, discards, and catch of nontarget species
g) To protect biodiversity in the marine environment
h) To prevent or eliminate overfishing
i) To take into account artisanal and subsistence fishers
j) To share data
k) To promote and conduct scientific research and technology to support conservation and management
l) To monitor, control, and survey activities

baselines, irrespective of the geomorphology of the seafloor.[41] Unlike the territorial sea, contiguous zone, and EEZ, a state need not claim the continental shelf but enjoys it automatically. This is because the idea is that the continental shelf is an extension of land—it is *terra*, not *mare*.

The continental shelf in some cases will continue beyond 200 nm (the outer continental shelf), and this is the case over most of the Arctic Ocean floor.[42] The rules for establishing an outer continental shelf are contained in article 76 of the UNCLOS and are notoriously opaque. The easiest way to make sense of them is to consider two kinds of rules: First, there are *formula lines*, based on the geomorphology or shape and substance of the ocean floor. These define the furthest extent of the continental shelf as geologists would understand it. Second, there are *constraint lines*, which are based on policy considerations and set an outer limit.[43]

There are two formula lines. Both require identification of the foot of the continental slope—the point at which the angle of the seafloor changes swiftly.[44] States can simply add 60 nm from this point (the *Hedberg* Rule).[45] However, they may choose to apply the *Gardiner* Rule, in which case they must establish the composition of the ocean floor. This is more complex, time-consuming, and costly for the coastal state, but it can be more generous.[46] A thick layer of sediment[47] collects at the foot of the slope and lies on top of the hard rock. States may expand their continental shelf to the point at which the thickness of this sediment is 1 percent of the distance to the foot of the slope. For example, for an extra 100 nm from the foot of the slope, the sediment should be 1 nm thick. For an extra 200 nm from the foot of the slope, the sediment should be 2 nm thick and so on.[48]

The constraint lines are then applied to prevent unduly expansive continental shelves. The simpler rule is a maximum of 350 nm from the baseline.[49] The alternative rule is a maximum of 100 nm beyond the 2,500 m isobath (i.e., 2,500 meters depth).[50] Therefore, if the sea is relatively shallow, a state's outer continental shelf can extend well beyond 350 nm from the baseline. This is the case in much of the Arctic Ocean, in particular off the Russian flank.

Never allowing things to remain this simple(!), a distinction is then made between submarine ridges, submarine elevations, and oceanic ridges.[51] Oceanic ridges are not part of the continental shelf.[52] Submarine ridges are limited by the 350 nm constraint (the isobath constraint may not be applied to them).[53] Submarine elevations can carry either the 350 nm constraint or the isobath constraint.[54] Coastal states are allowed to select the combination of formula and constraint lines that is most advantageous.

In principle, the outer continental shelf attaches automatically and need not be claimed, but states that are parties to the UNCLOS are nevertheless obliged to submit mapping and geological data regarding the ocean floor to the UN Commission on the Limits of the Continental Shelf (CLCS), which is empowered to make "recommendations." In practice, this means the CLCS either approves the state's submission (in which case the recommendation is "final and binding" for that state) or it asks the state to provide more data (a polite way of saying it is not convinced by the data submitted). Russia was the first state to submit in 2001 but was asked by the CLCS for further information. It resubmitted its Arctic data in 2015.[55] Norway submitted with regard to the northeast Atlantic and Arctic in 2006, and the CLCS approved its data in 2009. (Norway does not contest the North Pole itself.) The finality of the CLCS recommendations for the coastal state means that even if the baseline shifts through erosion or accretion, the limit of the outer continental shelf will not be readjusted.[56]

The United States, not being party to the UNCLOS, probably does not have the option of submitting its data to CLCS to secure a recommendation. The Americans are nonetheless gathering data to support their (potential) rights to an outer continental shelf and, in the absence of a turnaround in the Senate and the necessary two-thirds majority to ratify the UNCLOS, can be expected to make a unilateral declaration in due course. It is likely that other states will protest this, because the extended continental shelf is part of the package deal that is the UNCLOS, and other states will argue that the United States cannot have the benefits of the outer continental shelf without the responsibilities (including sharing) that come with it. However, the International Court of Justice has confirmed that the CLCS process is a formality and that the outer continental shelf accedes automatically to the coastal state even in the absence of a CLCS recommendation.[57] Nevertheless, only a recommendation by the CLCS can give finality and stability to the coastal state's outer continental shelf limits.[58]

Coastal states enjoy monopoly rights over their continental shelves, meaning that they can exclude any other state from exploiting the resources on or under them. These resources include surface and subsurface minerals, subsurface hydrocarbon deposits, and sedentary living marine resources. Sedentary species are defined as "organisms which, at the harvestable stage, either are immobile on or under the seabed or are unable to move except in constant physical contact with the seabed or the subsoil."[59] In other words, they either crawl along the seabed (like crabs) or are immobile on it (like coral). Unlike the EEZ, there is no obligation on states to harvest any resources, living or nonliving, from the continental shelf, let alone to share any surplus that they cannot utilize themselves. Further, unlike for living marine resources of the EEZ, there is no obligation under the UNCLOS to conserve them either.[60] Other states are permitted to lay cables and pipelines, though the coastal state must approve their course and may set reasonable requirements to protect its economic interests and prevent pollution from pipelines.[61]

With regard to nonliving resources taken from the outer continental shelf, article 82 requires states to make "payments or contributions in kind" to the International Seabed Authority, which administers the Area (see below) for "equitable" distribution, "taking into account the interests and needs of developing states, particularly the least developed and the land-locked among them." (This is one of the provisions to which the

United States persistently objects.) The payments and contributions are rather low: nothing for the first five years and then between 1 percent and 7 percent of annual production value thereafter. Although a few scattered leases exist beyond 200 nm, there is not yet any commercial exploitation, so no contributions are due. This provision is regarded as one of the key compromises in the UNCLOS, between the expansion of coastal state resource monopolies over the oceans and the interests of the international community of states as a whole. Should the United States exploit its purported outer continental shelf without having first acceded to the UNCLOS, it is unlikely to be willing to make these payments. This is one of the objections of other states to the United States having an outer continental shelf at all.

In the Arctic, the carve-up of the Arctic Ocean floor has received much media attention but is of more symbolic than economic interest. Even if the proclaimed Canadian, Greenland, and Russian outer continental shelves overlap, there are unlikely to be significant hydrocarbon resources beyond 200 nm, and any that are out there are going to be extremely costly and technically difficult to tap.[62]

Durham University's IBRU Centre for Borders Research maintains a detailed map of the maritime zones of the Arctic states, including contested areas, along with a detailed explanation (see map 8.1).

The High Seas

Beyond the EEZ are the high seas. These are global commons in which all states are entitled to sail, fish, conduct science, lay cables and pipelines, and build artificial islands or other constructions, and over which their planes may fly.[63] Nevertheless, to avert a tragedy of the commons, high seas fishing is not permitted to become a free-for-all. States must cooperate with one another to ensure the conservation of living marine resources in the high seas, and they usually do this through an appropriate RFMO.[64] Nearly all of the world's high seas are now governed by an RFMO, but there is one large exception: the central Arctic Ocean. Beyond 200 nm northward of the Greenland, Canadian, Alaskan, Russian, and Norwegian baselines is an area of high seas approximately the size of the Mediterranean. Currently, there are no commercial fisheries northward of the 200 nm EEZ of the coastal states, not least because it is largely ice-covered and no interesting stocks have yet been discovered there.

According to the FSA, states having a "real interest" should work together.[65] The difficulty is that when there are *no* fisheries, there is plenty of disagreement about who, if anyone, has a "real interest." Another

Map 8.1   The Durham Map

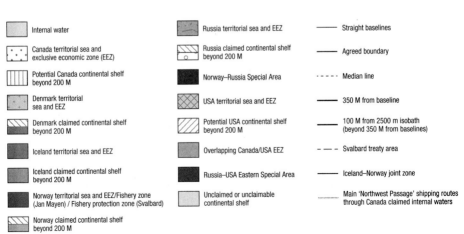

Internal water	Russia territorial sea and EEZ	Straight baselines	
Canada territorial sea and exclusive economic zone (EEZ)	Russia claimed continental shelf beyond 200 M	Agreed boundary	
Potential Canada continental shelf beyond 200 M	Norway–Russia Special Area	Median line	
Denmark territorial sea and EEZ	USA territorial sea and EEZ	350 M from baseline	
Denmark claimed continental shelf beyond 200 M	Potential USA continental shelf beyond 200 M	100 M from 2500 m isobath (beyond 350 M from baselines)	
Iceland territorial sea and EEZ	Overlapping Canada/USA EEZ	Svalbard treaty area	
Iceland claimed continental shelf beyond 200 M	Russia–USA Eastern Special Area	Iceland–Norway joint zone	
Norway territorial sea and EEZ/Fishery zone (Jan Mayen) / Fishery protection zone (Svalbard)	Unclaimed or unclaimable continental shelf	Main 'Northwest Passage' shipping routes through Canada claimed internal waters	
Norway claimed continental shelf beyond 200 M			

Source: IBRU, Durham University, UK. A full-color version of this map and commentary is available at https://www.dur.ac.uk/ibru/resources/arctic.

problem can arise if a state ceases fishing in the relevant area for a prolonged period: it might cease to have a real interest and be expelled from the RFMO.[66] This encourages states to continue fishing to maintain their legal interest, even if it is not commercially profitable or environmentally sustainable. The five littoral Arctic Ocean states (Canada, the Kingdom of Denmark, Norway, Russia, and the United States) agreed to a moratorium in 2015 on commercial fishing by their fleets in the central Arctic Ocean pending scientific studies to determine the status of any stocks.[67] Aware that a moratorium agreed between themselves cannot bind other states, they invited five other participants whom they considered as having a "real interest" to talks that concluded in December 2017. They agreed to establish a joint program on scientific research and monitoring and to desist from commercial fishing until sufficient scientific evidence indicates that it can be conducted sustainably and an RFMO has been set up.[68] Indicating the influence of the indigenous bodies involved in the talks, the research and monitoring program will consider indigenous and local knowledge alongside scientific data according to Western methods.[69] The parties to the agreement are the five Arctic Ocean littoral states plus China, Iceland, Japan, South Korea, and the European Union.[70]

The Area beyond National Jurisdiction

One more maritime zone remains: "the Area" beyond national jurisdiction. The Area is the ocean floor beyond the outer continental shelf of any coastal state. Thus, the high seas lie over both the outer continental shelves of coastal states and the Area. It is governed by part XI of the UNCLOS, which is based on the principle of "common heritage of mankind"—that the deep ocean floor belongs to all peoples, not just those with sufficient technology and capital to harvest its resources.[71] The International Seabed Authority has been established by the UNCLOS to govern the extraction of mineral resources on or under the deep ocean floor. It does not, however, govern living marine resources, cables and pipelines, or artificial islands.

The participation of developing states in the economic exploitation of the Area is to be promoted (though the UNCLOS does not specify by whom);[72] developers must transfer technology to the Authority's business arm (the Enterprise) and developing states;[73] and the Authority must take into account the onshore production of minerals in developing states if their economies are likely to suffer from a sudden influx of competing minerals from the Area onto the market.[74] This all proved sufficiently controversial to a number of developed states, led by the United States, to trigger an implementing agreement that effectively negated some of its provisions on the sharing of benefits and technology with developing states.[75]

Once the outer continental shelf in the Arctic is definitively carved up, there will be very little Area left in the Arctic Ocean. The two small zones in the central Arctic Ocean (see map 8.1) are likely to be too deep and too far out to offer any commercially interesting resources. In fact, even under the temperate waters of the South Pacific, efforts to exploit the polymetallic nodules on the ocean floor have yet to bear commercial success. Any exploitation would almost certainly require some kind of joint development with a coastal state's outer continental shelf.[76]

DELIMITATION BETWEEN ADJACENT OR OPPOSITE STATES

So far, we have considered maritime zones by looking at their distance from the coastal states' baselines. The determination of zones by reference to the coastal baseline is called delineation. For the territorial sea and EEZ, this is based on arithmetic; for the outer continental shelf, complex geology and math are required. However, it is also necessary to consider delimitation—that is, how to establish boundaries between opposite or adjacent states. In the Arctic, around half of all maritime boundaries have been settled (a rate substantially above the global average), and where they have yet to be defined, interim cooperative agreements are in force.[77]

Historically, both the Soviets and the Canadians promoted a "sector line" theory to divide up the Arctic Ocean—that is, they called for the Arctic to be divided following straight lines of longitude extending from the states' more southerly land and maritime borders and converging on the North Pole. This view has since fallen out of favor and is unlikely to be resurrected, given the priority now given to the UNCLOS.[78] With regard to the territorial sea, where the distance between two states is less than 24 nm, the UNCLOS prefers a median line—the halfway point between the adjacent or opposite coasts—though states can, of course, agree otherwise and special circumstances including "historic title" can be taken into account.[79] With regard to the EEZ and the continental shelf (including the outer continental shelf), opposite and adjacent states should reach an equitable agreement. If they cannot reach an agreement, they can ask the International Court of Justice, the ITLOS, or an arbitral tribunal to decide for them.[80] State practice and judicial decisions support negotiated solutions with the median line as the starting point.[81] A sector line would be theoretically possible if the states concerned all agreed upon it, but since they do not, it cannot be supported.[82]

When it comes to the outer continental shelf, much is made in the media of a "land grab" (even though it is not land) or assertions of sovereignty (when what is at stake are sovereign rights, a much lesser concept). The CLCS cannot and will not review submissions if any other states object. It is an entirely technical body staffed by "experts in the field of geology, geophysics or hydrography,"[83] not government officials or lawyers. It is most certainly not a dispute resolution body. The CLCS concerns itself only with delineation, not delimitation.[84] Boundaries between states are settled through negotiation and occasionally litigation.[85] It will not examine the data regarding the central Arctic Ocean floor until some sort of agreement is reached between the concerned states. Most likely this will be by agreement on the delimitation (boundary lines) between their respective shelves, in which case the CLCS's role is to provide recommendations on the delineation of the outer limits of those shelves. This means that the states will agree on the boundary lines to apply between themselves first, and then the CLCS will determine the boundary between the coastal states' respective shelves and the Area. However, it is also possible for the states to make a joint submission, allowing the CLCS to delineate the outer limits of the shelves before the states have decided where the boundaries lie between themselves.[86] In that case, the CLCS will examine the ocean floor and determine where all the states' outer continental shelves end and the Area begins; the coastal states then delimit (draw the boundaries) and divide up the continental shelf between themselves.

In 2010, after forty years of on/off negotiations and allegations of illegal fishing by the Russian fleet, the Norwegians and Russians finally settled the maritime boundary in the Barents Sea.[87] The impetus that finally led to the delimitation of the maritime boundaries was almost certainly the prospect of hydrocarbon reserves, but the agreement also settled the parties' respective fisheries jurisdictions in the EEZs. Fisheries had previously been jointly managed, and a bilateral fisheries commission continues to govern the area.[88]

The maritime boundary between the Soviet Union and the United States was agreed in 1990; but while the United States quickly ratified the treaty, the Soviet (now Russian) Duma has never done so—a result of their own domestic politics and concerns about cession of power to a foreign (and periodically hostile) state.[89] This means that it is not strictly binding on Russia. Nevertheless, both states have an interim agreement to follow the terms of the treaty "pending the entry into force," and in fact they both uphold it.[90]

Still to be settled is the maritime boundary between the United States and Canada in the Beaufort Sea. Canada takes the view that the boundary line should extend from the land border of Alaska and the Yukon and follow the 141st parallel due north: a sector line. This is based on an 1825 delimitation treaty between Russia (which then possessed Alaska) and the United Kingdom (which then possessed Canada) that specifies the border.[91] However, the United States takes the view that this only applies to the land border and that the maritime border should follow the usual principles of the law of the sea—in particular, the equidistance line.[92] Unsurprisingly, each side's own position would give it a larger EEZ, hence the overlap. However, if the outer continental shelf is taken into account, their positions are reversed: the sector line favors the United States and the equidistance line favors Canada.[93]

Since the United States is not party to the UNCLOS and since Canada has excluded compulsory jurisdiction on maritime boundaries, neither party can force the dispute before a court or tribunal for a binding settlement.[94] In practice, nearly all boundaries, particularly between the Arctic states, are settled through peaceful negotiations rather than adversarial litigation in any case. The two states are already taking steps to negotiate a settlement, beginning with scientific and technical discussions and in time moving toward the more political process of drawing a line on the map.[95] This need not necessarily be based on a simple equidistance line but, considering the costs and challenges of offshore development in the Arctic, could include a joint development zone for hydrocarbon developments on the continental shelf.[96] It is even possible for Canada and the United States to agree to different boundaries with regard to the EEZ and the continental shelf, though this is rare in state practice. Meanwhile, although Canada and the United States have both offered licenses for hydrocarbon exploration in the area, no exploration or development has been allowed pending agreement.[97]

Maritime Zones around the Svalbard Islands

The Spitsbergen Treaty preceded the twentieth-century advances in the law of the sea, the agreement of a number of important treaties, and crystallization of customary international law regarding maritime zones.[98] Norway has declared a 12 nm territorial sea around the islands but accepts the rights of the treaty parties to nondiscriminatory access to resources in that area (essentially fisheries). However, Norway claims that the 200 nm fisheries protection zone (beyond the territorial sea) is entirely under its own jurisdiction with no obligation to share resources with the treaty parties, and it asserts that the continental shelf around Svalbard is in fact part of the same shelf that joins the main Norwegian coast and hence is exclusively Norwegian, too. Other parties to the Spitsbergen Treaty have protested Norway's interpretation, arguing that the EEZ and continental shelf around Svalbard is subject to the same sharing provisions as the islands themselves.[99]

STATES' OR PEOPLES' RIGHTS OVER THE SEAS

The law of the sea focuses unabashedly on states. Humans and peoples do not feature in the UNCLOS, nor have they been much considered in the historical development of the law of the sea. Indeed, the sea in some ways might appear easier to manage from an international relations perspective because of the lack of permanent human population.

If we are to be serious about indigenous sovereignty (rather than mere rights of ownership or use over territory), then we need to address whether that sovereignty can extend offshore. So far, no state is willing to consider this possibility and therefore customary law (as well as the UNCLOS) both agree that only states enjoy territorial waters, EEZs, and continental shelves. Indigenous communities may have certain concessions under domestic law, but the international law of the sea does not recognize them. The insistence of the five Arctic Ocean littoral states in the Ilulissat Declaration on the priority of the law of the sea for managing the Arctic (following a meeting to which indigenous representatives were not invited) was an implicit rejection of any indigenous sovereign rights in the marine Arctic. However, as demonstrated in chapter 7, indigenous peoples have rights to marine areas and marine resources that they have traditionally used that curtail states' exploitation of their maritime zones if activities would negatively impact traditional indigenous resources.

THE INTERNATIONALIZATION OF THE ARCTIC OCEAN AND SEAS

If all of the Arctic's resources are so neatly packaged up and allocated among the Arctic states, why is there so much interest from afar? All states have rights of navigation, explained in more depth in the following chapter, through the Arctic seas. Fisheries on the high seas are open to ships from all states, but in the Arctic Ocean, these are not yet of any commercial interest. Probably for the first time in hundreds of years of large-scale fishing activity by humans, states are working together *before* fishing commences to research the stocks and determine if and when sustainable fishing can take place and on what basis.

On land and in the territorial sea, the state enjoys sovereignty, which means it has exclusive rights to determine if, when, and by whom natural resources will be consumed, be they living or nonliving. In the oceans (the EEZ) or under the oceans to the edge of the Area (the continental shelf), coastal states have exclusive sovereign rights to the resources therein. Other states may be interested in the great treasures the Arctic is said to hold, but they will only be able to take part in any hoped-for bonanza with the Arctic states' agreement and cooperation. In practice, this usually means joint development with a domestic company, obligations to train and hire local workers and retain domestic contractors, and hefty royalties to ensure that an equitable share of the economic benefits of the resource developments flow to the home state. In the case of Greenland, foreign companies are obliged to work with Nunaoil, Greenland's fledgling state oil company, not only to share revenues but also to provide training and experience for Nunaoil's Greenlandic employees. Further, although Nunaoil works together with the foreign firms and earns a share of any profits, it does not contribute to the costs of the projects or share liability should something go wrong (i.e., it is a wholly "carried partner").[100]

In countries like Greenland and Iceland, foreign money—and technological expertise—is essential to any large-scale developments of hydrocarbons or minerals. The United States, Russia, and Norway have economies large enough and sufficient experience that they can, if they want, go it alone. Nevertheless, Russian hydrocarbon firms Rosneft and Gazprom work regularly in cooperation with other firms and have a strong historical record of joint ventures with Norway's Statoil and France's Total. In the eye-wateringly expensive world of offshore Arctic oil and gas development, cooperation between competing firms from different countries is the only way to have any chance of producing hydrocarbons at a competitive price. Recent Western sanctions against Russia (in response to Russia's intervention in Ukraine and annexation of Crimea) have made it more difficult for firms registered in the EU to work in the Russian hydrocarbon industry, as there is a ban on the transfer of advanced technology necessary for Arctic offshore drilling or shale exploration.[101] As seen in chapter 6, Russia looks for alternative sources of investment and skills, and the natural choice is its powerful neighbor to the south that prides itself on not interfering in other states' political affairs: China.[102] China's huge economies of scale, long-term planning, and financial muscle, accompanied by a fast-growing economy's insatiable demand for natural resources means that Chinese firms, both private and state-owned, are involved in natural resource exploration and extraction throughout the Arctic. These investments and activities are in all cases governed by the home state. It is the home state, the Arctic state, that sets the conditions and the price for their activities. However, the imbalance in experience and resources between the small Nordic states (except Norway) and long-established multinational firms (and in some cases, their powerful parent state) presents a challenge at the negotiating table to ensure that the state's and its population's interests are adequately protected.

Indirectly, the Arctic Council system provides shelter for the small Arctic states and their indigenous peoples. This is because to become, and remain, an observer state at the Arctic Council, a non-Arctic state must maintain excellent relations with all the Arctic states and, in practice, also the permanent participants.[103] All the observer states, new and old, go to great pains to defer to Arctic state sovereignty and sovereign rights to govern their natural resources.[104]

CONCLUSIONS

This chapter has shown that far from being an ungoverned frontier, the Arctic Ocean has an abundance of law governing resource allocation in and under itself. The remaining question for this chapter is how well these norms are followed in practice and to what extent they can be enforced.

In general, the law of the sea is very well followed, at least with regard to the issues addressed in this chapter. For example, no state proclaims a territorial sea in excess of 12 nm or an EEZ beyond 200 nm from the baseline. States do not generally try to take resources from one another's maritime zones, though we will see in the next chapter disagreements regarding the status of straits and some states take inadequate steps to prevent illegal, unauthorized, and unreported fishing.[105] The littoral states, in particular Russia, have much to gain from following the principles of the UNCLOS, and challenging or even defying the rules that apply in one context risks undermining the whole system.[106]

One factor that promotes compliance in the law of the sea is that the UNCLOS contains compulsory dispute settlement procedures. In other words, if two or more states disagree about the implementation of the UNCLOS, one can force the other(s) to court to sort it out.[107] Even if applications to the International Court of Justice, the ITLOS, or arbitral tribunals are relatively rare in practice (at least, given the quantity of obligations and squabbles between states about their application), the possibility that an issue might be taken to a court for a binding ruling is a powerful incentive for states to follow the rules in the first place and negotiate constructively if there is a genuine disagreement about what they require in any given case.

Maritime boundary disputes are fairly common subjects of litigation but still require one of the parties to initiate proceedings. States can be patient if there is no immediate payoff. The disagreement between Norway and Russia over the maritime boundaries in the Barents took forty years to resolve and was only settled when both sides thought there were profits to be made from the exploitation of the hydrocarbons under the sea.[108] The matter was never litigated and both sides followed an interim cooperative agreement on fisheries management until the time was ripe for a permanent solution.

Neither being party to the UNCLOS nor (since 1984) accepting the general jurisdiction of the International Court of Justice, the United States cannot be brought before an international court on these issues. Nevertheless, it upholds the law of the sea and does not, for example, abuse its military power by drilling for oil on Norway's continental shelf: something a naive realist understanding of international relations struggles to explain. International law constrains the conduct of even the strongest states and even where there is no obvious or immediate consequence of breach.

All in all, the political bluster and media representations of a hotly disputed Arctic are not reflective of the constructive and mutually respectful relations on the ground and at sea.

FURTHER READING

Bertelsen, Rasmus Gjedssø. *The International Political Systemic Context of Arctic Marine Resource Governance*. Cham, Switzerland: Springer, 2018.

Brekke, Harald. "Defining and Recognizing the Outer Limits of the Continental Shelf in the Polar Regions." In *Polar Geopolitics: Knowledges, Resources and Legal Regimes*, edited by Richard C. Powell and Klaus Dodds, 38–54. Cheltenham, UK: Edward Elgar, 2014.

Byers, Michael. *International Law in the Arctic*. Cambridge: Cambridge University Press, 2013.

Byers, Michael. *Who Owns the Arctic?* Madeira Park, BC: Douglas and McIntyre, 2010.

Churchill, Robin. "The Exploitation and Management of Marine Resources in the Arctic: Law, Politics and the Environmental Challenge." In *Handbook of Politics in the Arctic*, edited by Leif Christian Jensen and Geir Hønneland, 147–84. Cheltenham, UK: Edward Elgar, 2015.

Henriksen, Tore, Geir Hønneland, and Are Sydnes. *Law and Politics in Ocean Governance: The UN Fish Stocks Agreement and Regional Fisheries Management Regimes.* Leiden, Netherlands: Martinus Nijhoff, 2006.

Jensen, Øystein. "The Seaward Limits of the Continental Shelf beyond 200 Nautical Miles in the Arctic Ocean: Legal Framework and State Practice." In Jensen and Hønneland, eds., *Handbook of Politics in the Arctic*, 227–46.

Liu, Nengye. "The European Union's Potential Contribution to the Governance of the High Seas Fisheries in the Central Arctic Ocean." In *The European Union and the Arctic*, edited by Nengye Liu, Elizabeth A. Kirk, and Tore Henriksen, 274–95. Leiden, Netherlands: Brill, 2017.

McDorman, Ted L., and Clive Schofield. "Maritime Limits and Boundaries in the Arctic Ocean: Agreements and Disputes." In Jensen and Hønneland, eds., *Handbook of Politics in the Arctic*, 207–26.

Molenaar, Erik. "Adapting Governance and Regulation of the Marine Arctic." In Powell and Dodds, eds., *Polar Geopolitics: Knowledges, Resources and Legal Regimes*, 74–89.

Norman, Emma S. *Governing Transboundary Waters: Canada, the United States, and Indigenous Communities.* Abingdon, UK: Earthscan, 2015.

Oude Elferink, Alex G., and Donald R. Rothwell, eds. *The Law of the Sea and Polar Maritime Delimitation and Jurisdiction.* Leiden, Netherlands: Martinus Nijhoff, 2001.

Rothwell, Donald R. *The Polar Regions and the Development of International Law.* Cambridge: Cambridge University Press, 1996.

Rothwell, Donald R. "The Polar Regions and the Law of the Sea." In Powell and Dodds, eds., *Polar Geopolitics: Knowledges, Resources and Legal Regimes*, 19–37.

Rothwell, Donald R., and Tim Stephens. *The International Law of the Sea.* 2nd ed. Oxford: Hart Publishing, 2010.

Tanaka, Yoshifumi, "Reflections on Arctic Maritime Delimitations: A Comparative Analysis between the Case Law and State Practice." *Nordic Journal of International Law* 80 (2011): 459–84.

9

Arctic Shipping and Navigation

ISSUES OF SOVEREIGNTY have come to prominence as the Arctic opens to increased shipping. Legal disputes over who controls the waterways of the Northwest Passage (NWP) and the Northern Sea Route (NSR), long frozen in a literal as well as a figurative sense, take on a new relevance. Arctic shipping is fundamentally connected to the global economy. As we saw in chapter 5, communities depend on imported goods, and the natural resources from the Arctic must be transported to market. Three potential transit shipping routes are opening up and are of interest from an international relations perspective. These are the NWP (through the Canadian Archipelago), the Northeast Passage (from the Norwegian Arctic across the Russian North Coast to the Bering Strait, including the NSR), and the central Arctic or Transpolar route (over the top between the Bering Strait and the North Atlantic through the Norwegian Sea or the Greenland Sea).[1] The immediate attraction to cargo shipping companies is the shorter distances between Asian, North American, and Northern European ports (see table 9.1). None of these routes is in fact a single line but, in practice, will be responsive to prevailing ice and weather conditions. For example, the NSR is defined by Russia as any sea area north of the Russian coast within the EEZ, stretching from the Kara Gate, or north of the Novaya Zemlya islands near Norway, to the Bering Strait in the North Pacific.[2] The NWP includes multiple courses within the northern Canadian archipelago.

Table 9.1   Comparison of Shipping Distances between Common Cargo
            Shipping Ports (in nautical miles)

Route	Panama Canal	Suez Canal and Malacca Strait	Northwest Passage	Northeast Passage
Hamburg–Seattle	17,110	29,780	15,270	13,459
London–Yokohama	23,300	21,200	15,930	13,841
New York–Shanghai	20,880	22,930	17,030	19,893
Rotterdam–Shanghai	25,588	19,550	17,570	15,793
Rotterdam–Vancouver	16,350	28,400	14,330	13,445

Source: Figures taken from Willy Østreng, "Geopolitics and Power Constellations in the Arctic," in *Shipping in Arctic Waters: A Comparison of the Northeast, Northwest and Trans Polar Passages*, ed. Willy Østreng et al. (New York: Springer 2013), 50, table 2.1.

The following discussion will explain the current status of shipping in the Arctic, the practical and economic considerations that constrain its growth, and the balance of rights and responsibilities of different parties. It analyzes the arguments over the contested status of "international straits" in the NWP and NSR in light of their geographical features and historic use and the measures applied to limit pollution and reduce the risk of a major accident. Arctic fisheries were examined in the preceding chapter.

FREEDOM OF NAVIGATION

The principle of the freedom of the seas, the idea that the seas belong to everyone and cannot be owned by individuals or by states, goes back to the 1608 treatise of Dutch scholar Hugo Grotius, *Mare Liberum.*[3] Through the twentieth century, while sovereign rights to ocean resources were gradually demarcated, packaged, and granted to coastal states, as we saw in the previous chapter, the rights of all states and their ships to navigation were protected. This means that all states, even landlocked states, have navigational interests to defend. However, the right to navigation is accompanied by obligations to protect and preserve the marine environment.[4] Rights and responsibilities are allocated to flag states, coastal states, and port states (see box 9.1).

Coastal states have limited rights to control navigation that takes place close to their shores and, in ice-covered areas, they may introduce environmental protection measures to a distance of two hundred nautical miles (nm).[5] Port states (states where foreign ships come to harbor) also have certain rights to check ships while they are docked. However, the responsibility lies principally upon the flag states. Every vessel that ventures beyond a state's baselines must be registered to a particular

---

BOX 9.1 | **Essential Definitions**

- **Flag state**: The state in which a vessel is registered (i.e., whose flag it flies).
- **Coastal state**: The state in whose maritime zone (territorial sea or EEZ) a ship is located.
- **Port state**: The state in whose harbor a vessel is docked.
- **Cabotage**: Transport that begins and ends within the same state (e.g., Murmansk to Dudinka within Russia); includes fishing vessels.
- **Destinational shipping**: Transport that either begins or ends within an Arctic state and serves a non-Arctic state (e.g., Murmansk to Rotterdam or vice versa); includes cruise ships and some fishing vessels.
- **Intra-Arctic shipping**: Transport that begins in one Arctic state and ends in another Arctic state (e.g., Murmansk to Narvik).
- **Transit shipping**: Transport that neither begins nor ends within an Arctic state (e.g., Shanghai to Rotterdam), possibly with stops at Arctic ports en route; usually cargo but could (in theory) include transit passenger services.

---

state: the flag state. Registration gives a ship nationality, without which any other state can stop and search it at any time.

ARCTIC SHIPPING TODAY

Shipping covers a wide variety of usages of the sea: cargo, fishing and hunting (indigenous, small-scale, and industrial), transport of persons (local people, migrant workers, and tourists), and scientific research voyages. The Protection of the Marine Environment Working Group (PAME) of the Arctic Council is developing a ship traffic database that the working group aims to make public in 2018.[6] Meanwhile, older figures can be found in its Arctic Marine Shipping Assessment Report showing the total number of vessels in 2004 to be around six thousand, of which cargo and fishing vessels constitute by far the largest share.[7] The greatest factors in the *increase* in Arctic shipping in the 2010s come not from cargo shipping but from the increase in tourism, research, and government support vessels.[8]

The majority of long-distance shipping in the Arctic is destinational. This includes deliveries to local communities, exports from the Arctic, science voyages, tourism, and pelagic fisheries.

As the ice retreats, especially in summer, with the result that there is much less multiyear ice, major shipping companies and shipping nations around the world are keeping one eye on the North in the hope that it may one day offer alternative or supplementary routes for transit shipping (between Asia and Europe or North America). Meanwhile, Arctic tourism—something that has occurred since the nineteenth century—is becoming more popular.[9] Alarm about the impacts of cruise tourism is not new: already in the early twentieth century, Alaskans were complaining about tourists viewing their coast from afar and taking photos but failing to interact with local communities or learn about their cultures.[10] Stiff competition between cruise ship operators and popular desires to visit what is marketed as an undisturbed wilderness have led to a sharp spike in the number of cruise voyages in the Arctic, without a corresponding increase in accident prevention measures or search-and-rescue services. It is not the existence of Arctic shipping per se that causes concern but rather the rate of growth and the capacity of Arctic communities to manage it safely and sustainably.

The Northern Sea Route

The NSR is a crucial trade route for the Russian Arctic settlements, and its development is closely connected to resource extraction in the Russian North.[11] NSR activity collapsed with the Soviet Union, having reached heights of around six million tons per year in the 1980s (before foreign vessels were permitted) and falling by 75 percent by the year 2000.[12] With the growth of Russian Arctic production and its centrality to the Russian economy as a whole, development of the NSR to support cabotage and destinational shipping is a key pillar of Russian Arctic strategy.[13] Today, most shipping is cabotage and destinational, with the bulk of traffic at the western end, between Murmansk and Dudinka. (See box 9.1 for definitions of cabotage, destinational, intra-Arctic, and transit shipping.) Use and development of the NSR is pivotal to the success of the Chinese-backed Yamal Liquefied Natural Gas (LNG), a project nearly four hundred miles north of the Arctic Circle to extract and liquefy natural gas and transport it to Asian markets through the NSR.[14] The economic feasibility of the Yamal project requires considerable infrastructural investment in the NSR and year-round access and is part of China's broader Arctic Belt and Road Initiative.[15]

In 2015 Prime Minister Medvedev discussed plans to increase transit shipping twentyfold by 2030.[16] President Putin has attempted to market the NSR as a genuine alternative to the existing, crowded, and sometimes unstable routes:

204 ★ Chapter 9: Arctic Shipping and Navigation

> This route is almost a third shorter than the traditional southern one. I want to stress the importance of the Northern Sea Route as an international transport artery that will rival traditional trade lanes in service fees, security and quality. States and private companies that choose the Arctic trade routes will undoubtedly reap economic advantages.[17]

The NSR's feasibility as a through-transit route is nevertheless uncertain, and year-to-year variations make it difficult to forecast a general trend. Raw figures from the NSR Administration count forty-one transits in 2011, forty-six in 2012, and seventy-one in 2013.[18] On closer inspection, Malte Humpert calculated that in 2013, only forty-one of these voyages were full transits, and of these, only thirty carried cargo.[19] A total of 1,190,000 tons was transported, and this was mostly oil, iron ore, and other nonrenewable resources, but many vessels traveled back empty.[20] In 2014, however, transit shipping declined dramatically. The NSR authority counted thirty-one transits, but only twenty-three ships made a full transit, carrying a total of 274,000 tons (23 percent of the 2013 figure).[21] In 2015 the figures were lower still: eighteen passages, of which seven were full transits and the rest intra-Russian shipping (i.e., cabotage).[22] Only six carried cargo and one carried passengers; two were rescue missions and the rest carried ballast or nothing at all.[23] The year 2015 included a novel transit cargo: fin whale meat from Iceland was transported through the NSR from Tromsø to Osaka in Japan, in an effort to avoid attention from antiwhaling protestors in the Netherlands.[24] The vessel was registered in St. Kitts and Nevis. Nineteen passages were registered in 2016, of which six were full transits, carrying coal (two), paper pulp, general cargo, and another whale-meat shipment. One vessel transited empty. Aside from differences in ice cover, shipping in connection with natural resource extraction may also have fallen in response to the economic sanctions imposed by the United States, Canada, the European Union, and others in the wake of the Ukraine crisis. The proportions of Russian and foreign-flagged ships also vary between years, but Russian vessels dominate, with the exceptions of 2012 and 2016 (see table 9.2).[25]

In context, these numbers are very small indeed: in 2014 nearly twelve thousand ships transited the Panama Canal carrying around a quarter billion tons of cargo.[26] The Suez Canal saw more than seventeen thousand transits carrying nearly one billion tons.[27] Arctic transit shipping is still very much at an experimental stage, and little can be derived from the early figures.

Russia administers the NSR through the Northern Sea Route Authority and charges high fees for its services. In late 2017, it was

Table 9.2   Vessels Transiting the Northern Sea Route, 2011-2016

Year	Total Vessels	Complete Transits (neither departure nor destination within NSR)	Russian Flagged	Non-Russian Flagged	Share Russian Flagged (%)
2011	41	19	26	15	63
2012	46	40	18	28	39
2013	71	41	46	25	65
2014	31	23	25	6	81
2015	18	7	10	8	56
2016	19	6	7	12	37

Source: Data from "Transit Statistics," NSR Authority Information Office, accessed April 13, 2017, http://www.arctic-lio.com/nsr_transits.

reported that the Russian nuclear power company Rosatom would take over management from the NSR Administration as part of a measure to consolidate its hold on Arctic infrastructure and development strategy, though it cannot yet be determined what practical impact, if any, this change will have.[28] The permit system was slow but is becoming more flexible: the usual period of notice used to be four months, but now one month or even just fifteen days in some cases will suffice.[29] From 2009 onward, the pricing system for the NSR was also made more flexible and responsive to market conditions; the fee is now effectively negotiable, but actual fees paid are commercial secrets.[30] The usual permission is only for *transit*: ships must seek additional permission if they are engaged in tourism, scientific research, or, of course, fishing, or if they plan to go into port. The Russian regulations also apply to warships and other government vessels. Russia justifies its NSR regulations based on environmental considerations and sovereignty claims (as shall be explained in more detail below), but a key motivation for the NSR regulations is economic: the fees subsidize the domestic use of the route.

Arctic Marine Tourism
Polar tourism is becoming "hot" as companies market a "last chance" to see the ice, flora, and fauna before they are lost. Byers has called this, disparagingly, "extinction tourism."[31] The Arctic is also sold as a premium destination precisely because of the absence of tourists, its relative inaccessibility, the expense of getting there, its mythical challenges, and its exclusiveness: few of one's friends will have similar stories to tell. Hence, one sales pitch in Greenland has shifted from "Come and see Greenland before it melts" to (without irony) "Come see Greenland before mass tourism ruins it."[32] Cruise tourism allows companies to visit the

most secluded spots while bringing their hotel facilities and staff with them. The largest cruise ship to date in the NWP was the 250-meter-long *Crystal Serenity* in the summers of 2016 and 2017, carrying 1,070 passengers and 655 crew members on each voyage. With prices ranging from just under $22,000 USD to more than $120,000 USD (with your own personal treadmill), the trip sold out both years. However, smaller ships had already brought cruise tourism through the NWP, and cruise ships are a common site around Greenland, Iceland, and through the northeastern Arctic.

For the foreseeable future, Arctic cruises will be seasonal (i.e., summer only). This means that cruise ships carrying thousands of passengers will not necessarily have to be ice-strengthened. Cruise companies can be registered anywhere in the world, and their ships are not always flagged to the state of the cruise company's headquarters. This can make it difficult to regulate as the presumption is that the flag state regulates and monitors its vessels in accordance with international standards, and experience shows that not all flag states are equally diligent in this respect (the concept of "flags of convenience"). Nevertheless, lessons can be learned from Antarctic cruise operators who have worked closely with the Antarctic Treaty System to ensure high standards of safety and environmental protection.[33] The tour operators have a premium product to sell to an elite market, and therefore it is in their interests to take all possible measures to minimize adverse impacts. In 2003 the Association of Arctic Expedition Cruise Operators (AECO) was established to provide an equivalent industry body in the North, and this introduced its own mandatory safety and environmental protection guidelines for its members.[34] Membership is self-selective, however, and none of the five largest cruise operators are currently members.[35] Aggressive competition and easier access to the Arctic (compared to the Antarctic) create a greater risk of a race to the bottom in standards. However, insurance companies, seeking to minimize their own risk, can lead the way by making strict standards a condition for insurance coverage.

Local economies can benefit from Arctic cruise tourism through port and landing fees, and tourists buy souvenirs and snacks, but cruise passengers sleep and eat on their ships, so it creates very little employment and limited tourist spending.

SEA ICE AND OTHER CHALLENGES TO ARCTIC SHIPPING

Arctic shipping is responsive to climate change. Were the Canadian archipelago and the northern Russian seas covered by an impenetrable ice blanket, there would be no shipping. However, changes to the ice cover and predictions of an Arctic Ocean that may even be ice-free in summer within the lifetimes of many of the readers of this book (maybe even the authors of this book!) have reawakened dreams about northern alternatives to the Panama and Suez Canals. Different kinds of ice on the ocean pose different challenges to shipping.[36]

Predicting the future ice cover in the Arctic is a difficult business; the factors are many, and while the general direction of ice cover is indisputably declining (taking a forty-year view), the maximum (winter) and minimum (summer) extent and thickness of ice vary from one year to the next.[37] None of the models to date suggest that the Arctic Ocean will be completely ice-free in the immediate future; but there may be open water through the Arctic Ocean *in late summer* within a few decades. If this occurs, there will be no multiyear ice: all ice will melt and reform within a year and hence will not be able to thicken. Meanwhile, transit shipping will be made more attractive by improvements in ship construction, port infrastructure, and local production (i.e., increasing the need for destinational shipping).

Nevertheless, less ice does not necessarily mean easier voyages. The ice cover will be replaced by huge icebergs, sea ice ridges, higher waves (as these have a larger area over which to form), and more extreme weather events. Changes to the ice cover even change the basis for legal regulation: article 234 of the UNCLOS allows coastal states to introduce more stringent environmental controls on ships within 200 nm of their baselines over seas that are ice-covered "for most of the year" (see below). If the ice season falls below six months of the year in an area, this provision may no longer be applicable.

Even within seasons, use of the NSR varies widely in response to ice cover, especially at the beginning of the season (when ships must wait for suitable ice conditions).[38] Unpredictability is the greatest hurdle to the commercial potential of the NSR. Freight shipping companies usually operate a just-in-time model for deliveries as this reduces manufacturers' inventory costs but puts pressure on the shipping company to arrive on cue or face stiff financial penalties.[39] Just-in-time shipping depends on the advance planning and reliability of delivery estimates. While manufacturers do not wish to pay the costs of storage of raw materials or components that they are not ready to use, neither do they wish to pay a labor force that is standing idle waiting for essential goods. The imbalance of cargo is also problematic: it is expensive to bring a vessel empty on a return voyage. Insurance companies may be reluctant to insure valuable cargo in untested waters or may impose costly requirements.[40] Port facilities are few and far between, and in order to handle a significant increase in shipping, they would need improvements in waste management, repair services, salvage, search and rescue—and the personnel to work in them. Ships' crews need reliable weather and ice information. Communications are improving in the Arctic, but the location of the relevant satellites (relative to Earth) are such that they are unable to reach the Poles and less efficient systems have to be used.[41] Hydrographic charts are woefully incomplete, presenting a risk to the safety of shipping. Even if the NSR Administration continues to invest in the necessary research, it will be some years before sufficient data is available.[42]

GLOBAL INTEREST IN ARCTIC TRANSIT SHIPPING

The major world shipping companies are displaying caution and continue to invest in traditional routes.[43] The Suez and Panama canals offer reliable services in temperate conditions, with established navigational information, repair, search and rescue, and crew services. Nicaragua is now constructing its own canal to offer yet another route. China and Russia may also invest in an improved rail network from the Pacific Coast to Europe to rival the NSR.

Currently, the costs mean that transit shipping is still economically unattractive, but the issue remains one of economies of scale: if more ships use the route, the NSR Administration can reduce the tariff per vessel and the price per ton of cargo will fall, port services will be enhanced, and experience will contribute to safer shipping.[44]

Both Russia and China can afford to play a long-game: they can run at a loss in the short term in order to establish their respective interests and rights. Russia must keep the route open to service its local communities, but it can afford to take a loss now in order to promote future transit shipping to subsidize the essential local services. China can send occasional ships to corroborate its status as a near-Arctic state with valid interests to defend, including freedom of navigation.[45] China's economic planning is based on an assumption of world population growth at the predicted rates coupled with improvements in the standard of living in developing countries. Hence, according to this model, demand for goods—for which China is the world's workshop—will follow on an unstoppable, upward trajectory. Under these circumstances, the NSR is not an alternative trade route but an additional one that in the future may become necessary to handle the increased volume of cargo transport that China anticipates. Nevertheless, this model cannot be taken at face value. There might be limitless demand, but there cannot be infinite supply in a world that has a natural limit of resources. The increase in demand is driven by the global South rather than relatively saturated European and North American markets, so the NSR will only be relevant if shipping to existing markets moves north to make space in established routes for the new markets.

Japan is also eyeing the NSR and is seeking "possible economic chances for the use of the Arctic Sea Route and for the development of resource [*sic*]."[46] Japan intends to be an active contributor to science and technology in this regard (for example, on sea ice prediction and weather forecasting) and also seeks to "participate actively in the international debates regarding the drafting of new rules."[47]

CONSTRAINTS TO FREEDOM OF NAVIGATION

Freedom of navigation varies depending on how far a ship is from the nearest coastal state's baseline. Landward of the baseline, saltwater areas are treated in the same way as land, and states may forbid others from access (with some exceptions in international straits).[48] Within the territorial sea, ships from other states enjoy innocent passage, but beyond the territorial sea (i.e., in the EEZ) other states enjoy freedom of navigation as they do on the high seas (though they may not take resources or conduct marine scientific research without permission). Innocent passage (within the territorial sea of another state) must be continuous and must take place on the surface (i.e., submarines may not pass submerged and there are no rights of overflight). The coastal state can introduce requirements (for example, to promote safety, protection of navigational aids, prevention of pollution, conservation of living resources, and state security), but it may not normally apply special requirements on ship design, construction, or personnel as these would interfere with freedom of navigation.[49]

Beyond the territorial sea but within the EEZ (i.e., from 12 to 200 nm from the baseline), coastal states have very limited powers to restrict navigation. However, the aforementioned article 234 of the UNCLOS provides:

> Coastal States have the right to adopt and enforce non-discriminatory laws and regulations for the prevention, reduction and control of marine pollution from vessels in ice-covered areas within the limits of the exclusive economic zone, where particularly severe climatic conditions and the presence of ice covering such areas for most of the year create obstructions or exceptional hazards to navigation, and pollution

of the marine environment could cause major harm to or irreversible disturbance of the ecological balance. Such laws and regulations shall have due regard to navigation and the protection and preservation of the marine environment based on the best available scientific evidence.[50]

This provision only applies where the seas are in fact ice-covered for most of the year. Regulations may go beyond the internationally agreed standards that would otherwise apply, but they must be in good faith: based on scientific evidence, genuinely intended to protect the environment, nondiscriminatory, and paying due regard to the freedom of navigation of other states. Government vessels from other states cannot be obliged to comply.[51] Measures taken under article 234 are, theoretically at least, subject to compulsory dispute resolution, meaning that a flag state that considers article 234 measures to be excessive could bring the coastal state to an international tribunal to settle the matter.[52]

Beyond 200 nm, in the high seas, only the flag states have jurisdiction.

ARCTIC CONTROVERSIES: STRAIGHT BASELINES AND THE QUESTION OF "INTERNATIONAL STRAITS"

As explained in the previous chapter, a normal baseline follows the low-water line of the coast, but states can draw straight baselines if the coastline is jagged, contains deep bays or fjords, or is surrounded by a fringe of islands.[53] Norway, Russia, Denmark (Greenland), Iceland, and Canada all have Arctic coasts of this kind and have drawn straight baselines. Canada and Russia's baselines enclose, respectively, the entire NWP and important parts of the NSR as internal waters, excluding the right of innocent passage that would apply otherwise in a territorial sea or the freedom of navigation that applies in the EEZ.[54] Canada's longest baseline is 99.5 nm long.[55]

While codifying states' rights to draw straight baselines, the UNCLOS also provided that where *new* baselines of this nature are introduced, the rights of flag states to navigate through such areas are protected. If a straight baseline "has the effect of enclosing as internal waters areas which had not previously been considered as such, a right of innocent passage as provided in this Convention shall exist in those waters."[56] For this reason, both Canada and Russia claim that the seas within their baselines are "historic waters," considered to be internal waters even before they formally published their straight baselines (Russia in 1984; Canada in 1985).[57] Therefore, both states exclude the right of innocent passage for foreign vessels. Even if their baselines are accepted (and they are highly contested),[58] there is still a possibility that internal waters (as well as territorial seas) contain "international straits."[59] In that case, a right of transit passage exists through the strait, which is more generous than innocent passage.[60] If an equally convenient route is available seaward of a relevant island, only innocent passage applies.[61] Transit passage differs from innocent passage by allowing submarines to pass submerged, extends also to aircraft, cannot be suspended by the coastal state, and grants fewer rights to the coastal state to pass restrictive environmental regulations.[62]

The disagreement in the Arctic pivots on whether the NWP and relevant parts of the NSR constitute international straits and hence give ships from other states rights of transit passage. An international strait exists where a narrow stretch of water that is used for international navigation joins two areas of either high seas or EEZ. International straits are therefore defined by both geographical and functional considerations. The geographical factor can be determined with a map and a measuring tape. It is a narrow, navigable channel, usually fewer than 24 nm wide, between coasts pertaining to the same state (e.g., the mainland coast and an island or between two islands of the same state), which joins two larger bodies of water (e.g., EEZs).[63] The NSR includes a number of geographical straits, the four most important being the Dmitry Laptev Strait, the Sannikov Strait, the Vil'kitskii Strait, and the Shokalshy Strait.[64] Canada's straight baselines purportedly close off the entire NWP as internal waters.[65]

The functional test is more controversial. To constitute an international strait, the stretch of water must, according to the UNCLOS and going back to the *Corfu Channel* decision in 1949, be "used for international navigation."[66] Disagreements arise over how to interpret this provision. In *Corfu Channel*, the International Court of Justice had said that a strait did not have to be the only or even the principal route for navigation.[67] During the first UN conference on the law of the sea, the word "normally" was dropped as a qualifier before "used for international navigation" in the text of the 1958 Convention on the Territorial Sea and the Contiguous Zone (a predecessor to the UNCLOS).[68] Nevertheless, there must be evidence of *some* traffic and, in *Corfu Channel*, the Court examined the raw number of transits as part of the process of determining that the Corfu Channel was indeed a strait.[69]

A further disagreement regarding interpretation pertains to the relevant date to assess "use" of the strait. Some Canadian jurists argue that it is the date at which the straight baselines were drawn that is relevant.[70] According to this view, if these disputes are to be solved, it has to be determined if, in 1985 (when Canada declared its straight baselines[71]), the NWP was already used for international navigation, and in 1964, if Russia's NSR was similarly used. Alternatively, the date might be 1994 when the UNCLOS came into force.[72] In either case, the key here is *international* use. Both areas have long been used for cabotage to serve local populations, and in the Canadian case, the permanently frozen waterways have been treated similarly to land by the Inuit population since time immemorial. However, if there was no international use as of right (i.e., without obtaining permission) prior to these dates, then the states' straight baselines are conclusive and the straits inside of them are not, according to this view, "international" straits.

Others take the view that the purpose of the UNCLOS was to put an end to many of the preexisting disagreements by creating a universal framework for all states based on geography first and foremost rather than historic military might. Then UN secretary-general Javier Pérez de Cuéllar declared when the UNCLOS was opened for signature that "international law is now irrevocably transformed, so far as the seas are concerned."[73] The preamble to the UNCLOS begins by specifying its purpose "to settle, in a spirit of mutual understanding and cooperation, all issues relating to the law of the sea."[74] This would support the argument that current or potential use and usefulness is key: if a strait *is now* or *can be* used for international navigation, then it is an international strait.

The US government has vociferously and persistently claimed that potential use is sufficient and that therefore the NWP and the straits within the NSR are international straits.[75] If the US position is accepted, foreign vessels do not have to seek permission of either Canada or Russia to travel through. The United States is supported, at least vis-à-vis the NWP, by the European Union, which collectively controls the largest merchant shipping fleet in the world.[76] In its 2009 *Council Conclusions on Arctic Issues*, it indicated its support for "the right of innocent passage and transit passage, and [that the EU] will monitor their observance."[77]

The *principle* is much more important to the Americans than its practical application to either the NWP or the NSR.[78] This demonstrates once again how Arctic governance is inextricably tied to global issues. John Negroponte, from the US Department of State, stated in 1986 that freedom of the seas is a top national priority and the American position is unchanged.[79] President Bush's 2009 Directive on Arctic Region Policy reasons as follows: "Preserving the rights and duties relating to navigation and overflight in the Arctic region supports our ability to exercise these rights throughout the world, including through strategic straits."[80] The principle is repeated in the May 2013 National Strategy for the Arctic Region.[81] The United States is concerned about the precedent that would be set in other, more volatile regions of the world if it bows to Russia and Canada's straight baselines and the enclosure of these straits without protecting the right to transit passage.[82] For the Americans (as indeed for all the Arctic states), the general law of the sea applies in the Arctic, and it must be governed by the same standards as other marine areas.[83]

Assessment of the Claims
Are the Straits in the NWP "International"?

The history of the use of these sea routes demonstrates that while both routes have been used for decades, they have been used almost exclusively by ships of the coastal state. When the baselines were drawn and published, there had been negligible international use (i.e., use by foreign flagged vessels) of these routes without explicit permission.[84] (When voyages take place with the consent of the coastal state and according to the coastal state's regulations, this supports the coastal state's claim to sovereignty because it is evidence that the flag state recognizes the coastal state's authority.)

The first navigators were the indigenous hunters and explorers.[85] Within the Canadian archipelago, where the ice rarely melted, Inuit lived and hunted on the ice as on land without clearly differentiating between the two. British interest in transit shipping through the NWP originates in the late fifteenth century, but the first significant attempt was Cook's voyage, which began west of Canada in 1778.[86] Cook was followed by Franklin's doomed expedition in 1845 (starting this time from the east), and the various searches for the remains of Franklin's ship and crew led to the production of the first maps of the NWP and the Canadian Arctic islands.

The first transit occurred in 1906, led by Amundsen, who sailed the *Gjoa* from east to west through the passage. The reverse feat was not accomplished until 1942, led by Larsen. Nearly all the non-British/Canadian shipping was with the express consent of the Canadian authorities.[87]

The first challenge came in 1969 when private oil firm Humble Oil (now Exxon) sent the US-registered SS *Manhattan* through the NWP. It was carrying only water, not oil, but the purpose of the voyage was to test whether the NWP could provide a practical route for hydrocarbon transports.[88] The US position was that the ship would not enter even the territorial sea of Canada (which at that time was only 3 nm wide) and that no permission of Canada was necessary. Nonetheless, Canada responded by granting a permission that had not been sought and even provided icebreaker services (which proved essential on a number of occasions[89]). Thus were both states' legal positions (and faces) saved.

The *SS Manhattan* voyage was followed by a transit of the US Coast Guard icebreaker, the *Polar Sea*, in 1985. The American icebreaker needed to travel from the Thule base (Northwest Greenland) to Seattle, and the NWP looked like an attractive option. Again, Canada granted the permission that had not been sought, and both states agreed that the voyage was "without prejudice" to their respective legal positions.[90] Canada then declared straight baselines around the entire archipelago.[91] The following year, Canada passed the Arctic Waters Pollution Prevention Act in a provocative exercise of jurisdiction.[92] The act introduced strict pollution prevention standards extending 100 nm outward, well beyond the standards accepted under international law at the time.[93] Canada received a "drawer full of protests" from other states.[94]

Through the Cold War, US and Soviet submarines entered the NWP.[95] Nevertheless, if such transits were covert (and the entire purpose of submarines is that they travel covertly), they would not add to the case for international usage of the straits: only open use by international vessels that goes unprotested by the states concerned can contribute to the relevant state practice.[96] Canada cannot be said to have acquiesced to transits about which they did not know and could not have known.[97]

The first commercial freighter transit through the NWP took place in 2013, from Vancouver, in western Canada, to Pori, in Finland. The specially constructed *Nordic Orion* carried coal to a Finnish steel company.[98] The transit was not only quicker and shorter than the alternative Panama Canal route, but a fully laden *Nordic Orion* would have been too large to pass through the relatively shallow Panama Canal in any case.[99]

Pharand counts a total of forty-three foreign transits of the Northwest Passage for the entire twentieth century and a further twenty-six between 2000 and 2005.[100] To put this in context, nearly eighty thousand ships transit the Strait of Malacca every year: more than one every seven minutes.[101]

Does the NSR Contain International Straits?

Exploration of the Northeast Passage has a much longer history, dating back at least to the eleventh century. Russian exploration and the search for an Atlantic-Pacific transit route began in earnest in the seventeenth century. In 1648 the Dezhnev voyage from Kolyma to the

Chukchi Peninsula demonstrated conclusively that there was no existing land link between Russia and Alaska. Vitus Bering, after whom the
strait takes its name, sailed the *Sviatoy Gavriil* from Chukchi to the
Bering Strait in 1725. Partial transits through the Northeast Passage
between the Kara Sea and western Siberia became more common in
the nineteenth and early twentieth centuries. The first full transit took
place under Eduard Toll's captaincy in 1878–1879.[102]

Following these initial explorative ventures, the Protection of the
Marine Environment Working Group of the Arctic Council identifies
four periods in the development of the NSR, between the Kara Gate and
the Bering Strait qua regular shipping route (see table 9.3).

Table 9.3   Development of the Northern Sea Route

Period	Characteristics
1917–1932	Exploration and settlement of coastal areas, including destinational shipping (deliveries to communities; periodic exports of local resources).
1932–1950s	Regular navigation and investment in infrastructure (fleets and ports); increase in destinational shipping; the NSR is officially declared in 1935.
1950s–1970s	Use of the NSR as a regular transportation line in summer and autumn for destinational shipping; further investment in the fleet.
1970s onward	Development of the NSR into a year-round transportation route.

Source: Based on information from PAME, *Arctic Marine Shipping Assessment* (Akureyri, Iceland: Arctic Council, 2009), 44.

One might also divide the fourth period in two: the still very heavy
Soviet use of the NSR between 1970 and 1991 and increasing moves to
internationalize it post-1991. In 1967 Viktor Bakaev, then minister of
merchant marine, suggested that the NSR had potential as a transit route,
but nothing more was said for more than two decades.[103] It was not until
Gorbachev's famous Murmansk speech that the first move was made
toward opening the NSR to international transit shipping.[104] The first
foreign goods (on a Russian-flagged ship) were transported in 1989.[105]
Foreign vessels were invited to use the NSR in 1991—subject to Soviet/
Russian conditions—and the first of these was the French-flagged *Astro-
labe*.[106] The Soviet Union collapsed soon afterward. (The two events are
not connected!) The first Russian regulations for navigation on the NSR
were introduced the same year.[107]

There is, therefore, a clear historic case to claim that the various
straits within the NSR have been used for navigation. However, this

is almost entirely Soviet navigation and not international. Navigation by foreign-flagged vessels has almost exclusively been with the express consent of the Soviet or Russian authorities.[108] In 1965 the United States sent its Coast Guard icebreaker, *Northwind*, toward the Vil'Kitskii Strait.[109] The Soviets considered the vessel to be a warship, which they did not believe had a right to innocent passage in what was their territorial sea.[110] The Soviet response was unequivocal: they would "go all the way" if the American vessel dared to enter the strait that the Soviets maintained was under their exclusive jurisdiction (i.e., internal waters). The United States blinked first and the *Northwind* changed course.[111] In 1967 another two American icebreakers, *Edisto* and *Eastwind*, traveled eastward on a planned Arctic circumnavigation. The planned route would have taken them north of the Soviet islands of Novaya Zemlya and Severnaya Zemlya. Ice cover made passage impossible, and the Americans advised the Soviet authorities of their intention to enter the Vil'Kitskii Strait. The Soviets forbade entry, and once more, the Americans turned back, protesting the Soviet position and insisting on their right to navigate (i.e., denying that the strait contained internal waters) but, nonetheless, unwilling to provoke the Soviets at the height of the Cold War.[112]

A voyage by a Greenpeace vessel, *Solo*, to gather evidence of nuclear dumping offshore of Novaya Zemlya in 1992 ended with the ship being fired upon in the Kara Sea after it sent an inflatable to take water samples on the edge of the territorial sea. (Taking water samples is neither "innocent" nor "passage" and requires coastal state permission, even in the EEZ.) However, the *Solo* had already traveled for two days within the Kara Sea without incident, indicating Russian acceptance of its freedom of navigation within the NSR.[113] A more aggressive response met the unauthorized voyages into the NSR of the Greenpeace vessel *Arctic Sunrise* in fall 2013. Greenpeace had applied three times for authorization to enter the NSR and was refused each time on (spurious) technical grounds.[114] The vessel nevertheless entered the Kara Sea in August 2013 to draw attention to their Save the Arctic campaign (which, inter alia, argued for a ban on any offshore hydrocarbon activity in the Arctic), was boarded by the Russian Coast Guard, and threatened with the use of force. It then left the NSR area.[115] A month later, Greenpeace submitted another application to enter the NSR, which was likewise refused.[116] The *Arctic Sunrise* reentered the Kara Sea anyway and headed toward the Prirazlomnaya oil platform. Russian authorities boarded and seized the vessel and arrested the crew. However, neither of these journeys can be viewed as straightforward disputes about transit passage rights and straits. Russia defended its responses with reference to the rights of the coastal state to defend the marine environment in ice-covered waters and against the breach of the safety zone around the Prirazlomnaya oil platform, including attempts by the Greenpeace protestors to climb onto the platform.[117]

Managing the Disputes: Agreeing to Disagree

Canada and Russia remain vigilant. Even if the routes are not *today* international straits, should Canada and Russia cease to enforce their regulations in their respective straits and turn a blind eye (acquiesce) to foreign transits, a right of transit passage could still emerge in the future.[118]

The disputes must be understood in light of the global picture; as mentioned above, the principle of freedom of navigation in straits is more important to the United States and others than is the practical value of Arctic shipping, especially on the Canadian side. The United States and Canada also cooperate around the issue: they entered a bilateral treaty in 1988 according to which each cleverly reserved its position on the status of the waters around the Canadian Arctic archipelago.[119] The United States agrees to seek consent from Canada for any icebreaker voyages conducting marine scientific research in the NWP, which it recognizes as the territorial sea and EEZ of Canada. (Vessels are always required to obtain consent to conduct such research in the EEZ of another state.) Canada, for its part, pledges to grant its consent to such vessels, but it interprets this as consent *to navigate in the NWP* and not only to conduct marine scientific research. In practice, all US government vessels claim to be conducting marine scientific research and hence seek the requisite permission, which is always forthcoming. Therefore, US vessels can use the NWP, but Canada has not surrendered sovereignty. Meanwhile, Canada also raises the issue of national security, arguing that it is in both American and Canadian interests that the NWP be recognized as Canadian to reduce the risk of terrorists using the route to enter North America untraced.[120] This is another factor promoting de facto cooperation.

The United States also supports Canada's mission to protect the marine environment of the NWP. While on the one hand, the United States formally protests the lawfulness of Canada's NORDREG (shipping notification regulations in Canada's northern EEZ and internal waters; see below), claiming that only the International Maritime Organization (IMO) has the authority to set such requirements on a mandatory basis, the United States complies with them on a voluntary basis.[121]

On the NSR, Russian authority to permit—and exclude—foreign vessels in the straits is symbolically important, but Russia nevertheless justifies the strict NSR regulations (including advance notification and expensive icebreaker support) with reference to article 234—the EEZ north of Russia being "ice-covered" for most of the year.[122] However, article 234, as we saw above, gives the coastal states limited authority, and measures taken under it do not apply to government (including military) vessels.[123]

Most other states have refrained from the diplomatic fray. Even states like Japan and China, with the most to gain from the commercialization of the NSR, have not taken a strong position. In China's case, its priority seems to be quiet, mutually beneficial cooperation in the NSR (including investment in extractive projects that depend on the NSR) and a wait-and-see approach to the NWP.[124] China has its own guidebook on shipping in the NSR.[125] China must also be wary of establishing precedents that could be used against some of its own controversial baselines.[126] It is no coincidence that four of the six new observer states at the Arctic Council are major shipping nations: China, Japan, Singapore, and South Korea.

ENVIRONMENTAL AND HUMAN SECURITY: VESSEL-SOURCE POLLUTION AND SAFETY AT SEA

Even on the high seas, all states, including landlocked states, have responsibilities to protect and preserve the marine environment and must regulate their ships accordingly.[127] The Arctic is not, unfortunately, pristine or unaffected by pollution, but it contains areas of sensitive biodiversity that are vulnerable to a rapid increase in shipping.[128] Human safety and welfare is also a concern on the seas, and the Arctic and Antarctic offer the harshest conditions on Earth.

Should an accident occur, it is the coastal state—and in practice, the nearest local community—that will be responsible for search and rescue and be left holding the bill. The profits from the cruises will mostly benefit cruise companies with headquarters thousands of miles away from their Arctic activities, while a significant portion of the risk is borne by the communities they visit. Russia has a number of icebreakers that can be sent out in an emergency (albeit moving slowly over vast distances), and its northern ports have some rescue equipment and trained personnel. The NWP has many fewer resources at its disposal. It is the Canadian and US authorities—Coast Guards and local port authorities—that must acquire rescue equipment and train local people as first responders. It is the local people, especially fishers and hunters, who are most likely to be first on the scene; they maintain and manage the nearest harbors, they have the closest boats, and they are monitors and interpreters of real-time weather, ice, sea, and wildlife conditions. When a whale-watching boat, *Leviathan II*, sank suddenly in October 2015 off the Vancouver coast (in apparently calm conditions), it was a First Nations Ahousaht fisherman who saw the flare and raised the alarm. It was his boat that rescued more than half of the survivors, with most others being rescued by other boats from his village and the broader district.[129]

Local communities will be called on to provide emergency accommodation, heating, food, clothing, and possibly medical care to passengers of varying ages and states of health. When the *Clipper Adventurer* became grounded in calm conditions in the NWP in 2010, the Canadian Coast Guard had time to reach it and transfer its nearly two hundred passengers and crew to safety. They were taken to Kugluktuk, whose population of 1,400 had a few hours to prepare accommodation and supplies before the rescued passengers were flown onward to Edmonton.[130] The *Crystal Serenity* carried more than 1,700 souls in 2016 and 2017—more people than the entire population of Kugluktuk. Cruise passengers from around the world also bring dangers of contagious diseases and alien species attached to their clothing—especially via Velcro and similar fastenings—to which isolated communities have little natural resistance.[131]

Shipping interferes with the marine environment, and although some impacts can be minimized, many cannot be entirely avoided.[132] Pollution from ships represents a relatively low share of all ocean pollution—almost certainly less than 12 percent. Most ocean pollution comes from land-based sources.[133] Shipping's contribution to oil pollution is notably higher; a 2007 assessment of pollution by oil at sea estimated that around 37 percent could be attributed to regular shipping, with 13 percent arising from accidents (including shipping accidents) and 50 percent from land-based sources.[134]

At current levels, Arctic shipping is not considered to pose a significant threat (unless there is an accident), but that can change if transit shipping or cruise tourism grows exponentially or if cowboy operators join the scene.[135] Nevertheless, that is no reason for failing to take measures to reduce pollution from ships. It is easy to recall the consequences of major accidents—the *Exxon Valdez*, the *Amoco Cadiz*, or the *Atlantic Empress*—but incidents like these are the source of only around 10 percent of all ship-based pollution.[136] The majority of ship-sourced pollution comes from ordinary operations.

Shipping is also a major factor in atmospheric pollution, with global consequences that are not restricted to the oceans. Most ships run on non-renewable fuels that release carbon into the atmosphere and contribute to climate change. In the short term, the consumption of diesel also creates black carbon (soot), which is dispersed locally. The black carbon then lies on the ice, discoloring it. As the ice is less bright, it absorbs more of the sun's energy, leading it to melt more quickly and creating a localized, increased global warming effect.[137] Black carbon in the air is also indicated in increased rates of respiratory diseases, such as asthma, in nearby settlements.[138] As ships travel, they release discharges directly into the sea, ranging from the human waste of their crews and passengers to oil and oily sludge.[139] The oil so released enters the food chain. Other impacts on marine fauna include ship-strike of marine mammals and birds[140] and the effects of noise pollution, which are believed to interfere with the behavior of marine mammals and possibly fish.[141] The movement of icebreakers as they crush the ice is particularly noisy.[142] Cargo and cruise ships, traveling thousands of kilometers, also bring with them alien species—that is, they transport lifeforms from one area of the ocean to another, mostly through attachment to the hull of the ship or by the transfer of ballast water.[143] This creates a risk for Arctic biodiversity because these new species can change the ecosystem balance and threaten the niche of indigenous Arctic species. The cumulative effects of shipping must also be borne in mind: while each ship may be insignificant for the marine environment and biodiversity, a rapid increase in the number of cruise or cargo vessels could amount to a significant threat.

The aforementioned impacts are a part of normal shipping operations; but the Arctic conditions create increased risks of accidents, and the Arctic is ill-equipped to respond to these and to minimize their impact.[144] The weather, wave, and ice conditions are rivaled only in the Antarctic, where there is some experience of tourist shipping and fishing but no transit cargo shipping. The limited port infrastructure and search-and-rescue capacities of the Arctic coastal states also make responding to an accident much more complex and time-consuming. In the event of a major oil spill, the onset of darkness makes cleanup more difficult, and cleanup of oil in ice-infested waters is as yet untested (fortunately!). The sinking of the *Selendang Ayu* and loss of six lives in 2004 near the Unimak Pass demonstrates how quickly things can go awry and the difficulties of rescue in adverse weather conditions.[145]

International and Domestic Efforts to Control the Impacts and Reduce the Risks

Shipping is an area in which there is an abundance of law and regulation. There is very little that is specific to the Arctic, but the Polar Code that came into force in January 2017 was developed specifically to govern Arctic and Antarctic shipping.[146] It is not possible to examine closely every instrument that governs maritime human and environmental safety; this section paints a general picture by introducing the kinds of issues that international agreements and regulations can govern.

The UNCLOS provides that states shall cooperate through the "competent international organization" to agree to international rules and standards to reduce pollution from ships and establish routing systems to reduce the risk of accidents.[147] The competent international organization to which this article refers is the IMO. The main responsibility to regulate and monitor ships falls on the flag states, but there are limited powers of coastal and port states to introduce measures to limit risks. Coastal states have fairly broad powers in their territorial seas as long as they do not introduce requirements that would effectively interfere with innocent passage. So coastal states can prohibit discharges of waste in the territorial sea, but they cannot introduce requirements for ship construction.[148] Beyond the territorial sea, coastal states may only introduce requirements that are congruent with "generally accepted international rules and standards."[149] The internationally agreed rules are, therefore, a floor, or minimum, for flag states but a ceiling, or maximum, for coastal states in their EEZs. States can also set slightly stricter requirements on vessels entering their ports (which are internal waters).[150] Ports are always under the sovereignty of a state, which can refuse the entry of foreign ships and enjoys certain powers to check discharges, bring legal proceedings against ships if evidence of a violation comes to light, and prevent a ship from leaving port if there is reason to believe there is a risk of pollution.[151]

International shipping standards govern discharges and emissions from ships; standards of ship construction, design, equipment, crew qualifications; navigational regulations, such as shipping lanes and areas to be avoided; contingency planning and preparedness; and liability and insurance requirements.[152] Ships must also report their whereabouts to prevent accidents and facilitate easier search and rescue should the need arise, and cruise ships are subject to special rules to ensure passenger and crew safety. In response to a request of a coastal state or states, the IMO can designate "Particularly Sensitive Sea Areas" (PSSAs) within one or more EEZs if the areas in question are of ecological, socioeconomic, or scientific importance and vulnerable to impacts from shipping.[153] Under the MARPOL treaty and its annexes, "special areas" can be created with stricter rules to prevent pollution by oil, noxious liquids, and/or refuse.[154] Unlike the PSSAs, these can extend also into high seas areas, but it is possible for MARPOL special areas and PSSAs to overlap. None have yet been introduced in the Arctic. Under some international treaties, other forms of marine protected areas can be created, which limit shipping.[155] More than a dozen treaties are in force through the IMO and regional arrangements. That does not by itself indicate, however, that the law is adequate to protect the unique Arctic marine environment.

The Arctic Search-and-Rescue Agreement and the Agreement on Marine Oil Pollution Preparedness and Response

The first treaty to be negotiated through the Arctic Council mechanisms was the Agreement on Cooperation on Aeronautical and Maritime Search and Rescue in the Arctic in 2011.[156] It is not a treaty *of* the Arctic Council (which does not have the capacity to agree treaties) but rather a treaty of the eight Arctic states. It builds on two global treaties and does not create new legal rights and obligations, but it does promote trust and make it politically easier for one state to allow a rescue vessel from another state into its waters in an emergency.[157] The marine Arctic is divided into eight zones, for each of which one state has primary responsibility, and this arrangement makes it easier for them to seek assistance from one another. Based on the treaty, the Arctic states have held joint practice exercises.

The 2013 Agreement on Cooperation on Marine Oil Pollution Preparedness and Response similarly divides the marine Arctic into eight zones for the purposes of oil spill cleanup.[158] Like the former agreement, it does not add greatly to the provisions of other global treaties, but its "non-binding operational guidelines" clarify and simplify processes for requesting assistance and allow for expedition or waiver of the usual visa and customs requirements to allow personnel and equipment to be moved quickly in an emergency.[159] In 2015 a non-treaty-based framework for oil spill prevention was adopted, dealing both with production and shipping of oil.[160]

The permanent participants contributed to the negotiation process for these treaties, but they are not parties to them. Their effective implementation will, however, require each state to coordinate search-and-rescue and cleanup facilities and processes with local communities.

The Polar Code

In November 2014 the IMO adopted the International Code for Ships Operating in Polar Waters (Polar Code).[161] This supersedes nonbinding Guidelines for Ships Operating in Polar Waters (2009), which in turn followed the Guidelines for Ships Operating in Arctic Ice-Covered Waters (2002).[162] To avoid the difficulties and delay of securing a new treaty, the Polar Code was implemented through amendments to the MARPOL and Safety of Life at Sea (SOLAS) conventions that came into force in 2017.[163] The Polar Code establishes minimum standards for design and construction of ships in Arctic or Antarctic waters, and each ship must apply for a certificate indicating its resilience. Category A ships are expected to be able to travel in medium first-year ice, including some older ice; Category B ships should be able to operate in thin first-year ice, with some older ice; and Category C ships can operate in less challenging conditions. The Polar Code also promotes maritime safety through minimum standards for equipment, training of crew, and search-and-rescue capabilities (though there are doubts about whether adequate equipment even exists[164]). Ships must carry a *Polar Water Operational Manual* containing detailed information regarding the ship's capacities and intended to help the crew and shipowners make informed decisions in adverse conditions. The environment is further protected through special rules that restrict the discharge of oil, noxious substances, sewage, and garbage. Some aspects of the Polar Code remain nonbinding.[165] Nevertheless, given the risks involved, shipowners and charterers may find that they cannot obtain adequate insurance if they do not adhere to the nonbinding recommendations.

Unlike in the Antarctic, there is no ban on heavy fuel oil in the Arctic. Heavy fuel oil is controversial because, in the event of a spill, it tends to emulsify (mix with the seawater in such a way that it is very difficult to separate) and does not evaporate as quickly as lighter alternatives. This complicates cleanup as the volume to be recovered is substantially increased. Burning of heavy fuel oil also releases more greenhouse gases. The alternative distillate fuels are more expensive, so without a legal ban, it is unlikely that shipping companies will voluntarily renounce heavy fuel oil.

The emphasis is usually on flag state responsibility to implement international standards within its domestic legal regime and to monitor and enforce these accordingly. The flag of a vessel often bears no relation to the nationality of its owners, and not all flag states are equally diligent. Flag states may fail to monitor and enforce the international standards (or even fail to ratify the relevant treaties). This gives rise to the problem of states that have open registries—"flags of convenience"—allowing any ship to obtain the nationality of such a state, subject to a fee but with no genuine connection or effective oversight. Nengye Liu explains that flagging to another state is not only a matter of evading strict supervision but in some cases may be a response to practical and economic concerns, including tax laws.[166] In theory, flag states have obligations of due diligence, meaning that other states could make a claim against flag states that fail to supervise their ships adequately; but in practice, this has never happened.[167] This is why port state authority is necessary: all ships have to dock at some point. Coastal states have limited powers, but Canada and Russia have both introduced standards that are stricter than the generally agreed international requirements and standards in their ice-covered EEZs on the basis of article 234 of the UNCLOS. Iceland has no ice-covered waters and Norway only a small area; neither have straits. The United States could introduce measures north of Alaska but has so far elected not to do so based on policy considerations: it seeks to defend the maximum freedom of navigation. The United States also has straits, but these are not ice-covered.

The link between the rights of transit passage in international straits and article 234 is unclear. Were Canada and Russia to lose the battle over the straits in their self-declared internal waters, they would rely on article 234 to continue to apply environmental and probably even vessel management regulations. The United States and others might argue, however, that the right of transit passage in international straits takes precedence over article 234 and would therefore deny the authority of Canada and Russia to pass regulations that go beyond the international standards.[168]

Canada's Arctic Waters Pollution Prevention Act 1985 goes beyond the generally agreed international regulations and standards in a number of areas. It places a blanket ban on discharge of any waste, with exceptions only for emergencies and exhaust emissions. Canada also sets stricter standards on ship construction, design, equipment, and navigation. Warships and other vessels on foreign government service are exempt from administration fees but must meet the other requirements.[169] Canada further manages shipping in its Arctic waters (including the NWP) through the Northern Canada Vessel Traffic Services Zone Regulations (NORDREG). Originally framed in 1977 as voluntary guidelines, in 2010, the system became mandatory (under Canadian law) for all ships, and it entails a vessel traffic and monitoring system for all vessels within the Canadian EEZ or internal waters above the 60th parallel north and down into Hudson Bay, James Bay, Kigmallit Bay, and Ungava Bay.[170] It applies, therefore, in the EEZ outside of Canada's generous straight baselines. Ships must obtain traffic clearance from the Coast Guard to enter this zone, report on their location daily, and notify Canadian authorities when they leave it.[171]

Canada's justification for these stringent requirements is based on article 234, but there is some doubt that all the waters so covered are indeed ice-covered for most of the year.[172]

The Alaskan entrance to the NWP is not subject to any special shipping regulations, though in 2015 the Arctic Waterways Safety Committee first met with a view to evaluating the risks posed by shipping to coastal communities—in particular, subsistence activities.[173] This is a multistakeholder initiative of the US Coast Guard that brings together representatives of subsistence hunters and fishers, commercial fisheries, the hydrocarbon and mining industry, and local government.

In 2012 Russia updated its 1990 NSR Regulations with the new Law on the NSR.[174] Its regulations apply to all Russian internal waters (including the contested straits), the territorial sea, and the EEZ adjacent to Russia's north coast, from the Novaya Zemlya Straits in the west to the Bering Strait in the east. Russia sets standards that go beyond the international standards for ship construction, equipment, discharges, crews, and insurance and requires ships to seek permission to enter in advance. Russia requires mandatory icebreaker service and charges hefty fees for this as well as for the hiring of Russian pilots and provision of weather and ice information. Ships are also liable for any pollution, which means they must obtain the requisite—and expensive—insurance. Russia reserves the right to stop and inspect all ships on the NSR on suspicion of pollution or other violations of their permits, and they must follow a specified route without deviation. Permission to navigate can be suspended at any time if they do not follow the directions of the Russian authorities.

CONCLUSIONS

The law can tell us about rights and responsibilities, but the future of Arctic shipping will be determined by economics. Shipping companies and cruise operators will weigh up the costs—including the costs of meeting construction, environmental, reporting, and other obligations—against the costs of alternative routes. Destinational shipping will have a future as long as Arctic communities persist, but its extent will vary according to Arctic production and consumption (type and volume). Tourism follows market demand: in this respect, the marketing of the Arctic as a wilderness or a frontier means that, as in Antarctica, the cruise operators have a strong interest in protecting the area from environmental contamination or even a perception of contamination. The demand for Arctic cruises will fall if passengers find their scenic routes repeatedly interrupted by unsightly tankers or even an abundance of competing cruise ships.[175] On the contrary, Arctic transit shipping depends on unsentimental bottom-line comparisons with alternative transit routes and can only become commercially attractive if shipping numbers justify investment in port facilities and services. Thus, although sharing many interests (such as the need for navigational information and search and rescue), the interests of cruise operators and shipping companies are in this respect diametrically opposed. The NWP is still a long way from commercial development; the ice is extremely difficult to predict owing to the geographical complexity of the Canadian archipelago.[176] The NSR is more promising though still challenging. Laruelle estimates that building the necessary infrastructure to make the NSR a viable transit route will require another twenty years.[177]

The contested status of the Arctic straits (international or domestic waters) is unlikely to be settled in the short term, but these issues have not, at least since the Cold War, led to tensions in practice between the parties involved. The United States will continue to formally protest Canada's very broad exercise of jurisdiction but will continue to comply with Canadian regulations on a "voluntary" basis. Ships using the NSR, especially those flagged to the major shipping nations, will comply with the requirements of the NSR Administration as the latter provides an essential service and an escalation of the disagreement is in no party's interests.

A huge amount of international and domestic law governs shipping in the Arctic. Furthermore, insurance companies impose strict requirements to minimize their own exposure to risk. Nevertheless, Polar Code aside, none of the international law is tailored to Arctic conditions. Even the Polar Code may be insufficient to protect the unique Arctic marine environment or the safety of shipping crews, passengers, and local communities. The principle of freedom of navigation limits the powers of the Arctic coastal states to set stricter standards.

FURTHER READING

Arctic Ocean Review (AOR). *Final Report 2013*. Arctic Council.

Caminos, Hugo, and Vincent P. Cogliati-Bantz. *The Legal Regime of Straits*. Cambridge: Cambridge University Press, 2014.

Franckx, Erik. "De reis van het Greenpeace schip, de MV *Solo*, naar Novaia Zemlia en het internationaal recht: Enkele bemerkingen [The voyage of the Greenpeace ship, MV *Solo*, to Novaya Zemlya and international law: Some remarks]." In *Liber Amicorum Paul De Vriede* [Book in honor of Paul de Vriede], edited by C. Eliaerts, M. Flamée, and P. Colle, 803–36. Diegem, Belgium: Kluwer Rechtswetenschappen België, 1994.

Franckx, Erik. "The Legal Regime of Navigation in the Russian Arctic." *Journal of Transnational Law and Policy* 18, no. 2 (2009): 327–42.

Hansen, Carsten Ørts, Peter Grønsedt, Christian Lindstrøm Graversen, and Christian Hendriksen. *Arctic Shipping: Commercial Opportunities and Challenges.* Copenhagen: CBS Maritime, 2016.

Lalonde, Suzanne, and Frédéric Lasserre. "The Position of the United States on the Northwest Passage: Is the Fear of Creating a Precedent Warranted?" *Ocean Development and International Law* 44 (2013): 28–72.

Liu, Nengye, and Kamrul Hossain. "China and the Development of International Law on Arctic Shipping: Challenges and Opportunities." In *Arctic Law and Governance: The Role of China and Finland*, edited by Timo Koivurova, Tianbao Qin, Sébastien Duyck, and Tapio Nykänen, 233–52. Oxford: Hart Publishing, 2017.

Moe, Arild. "The Northern Sea Route: Smooth Sailing Ahead?" *Strategic Analysis* 38, no. 6 (2014): 784–802.

Molenaar, Erik, Stephen Hodgson, David VanderZwaag, Huni Heidar Hallsson, Tore Henriksen, Lena Holm-Peterson, Maxim Vladimirovich Korel'skiy, et al. *Legal Aspects of Arctic Shipping.* Brussels: DG Maritime Affairs and Fisheries, 2010.

Østreng, Willy, Karl Magnus Eger, Brit Fløistad, Arnfinn Jørgensen-Dahl, Lars Lothe, Morten Mejlænder-Larsen, and Tor Wergeland, eds. *Shipping in Arctic Waters: A Comparison of the Northeast, Northwest and Trans Polar Passages.* New York: Springer, 2013.

PAME. *Arctic Marine Shipping Assessment.* Akureyri, Iceland: Arctic Council, 2009.

Pharand, Donat. "The Arctic Waters and the Northwest Passage: A Final Revisit." *Ocean Development and International Law* 38 (2007): 3–69.

Ringhom, Henrik. "The European Union and Arctic Shipping." In *The European Union and the Arctic*, edited by Nengye Liu, Elizabeth A. Kirk, and Tore Henriksen. Leiden, Netherlands: Brill, 2017.

Rothwell, Donald R. "Arctic Sovereignty and Its Legal Significance for Canada." In *Handbook of Politics in the Arctic*, edited by Leif Christian Jensen and Geir Hønneland, 247–61. Cheltenham, UK: Edward Elgar, 2015.

Rothwell, Donald R. "International Law and Arctic Shipping." *Michigan State International Law Review* 22, no. 1 (2013): 67–99.

Schiano di Pepe, Lorenzo. "Navigazione negli stretti internazionali, nelle acque arcipelagiche, nelle zone 'ecologicamente sensibili' e nelle aree coperte da ghiacci: Cenni sull'azione applicataiva dello Stato costiero" [Navigation in international straits, in archepelagic waters, in "ecologically sensitive" zones and in ice-covered areas: Overview of enforcement by the coastal state]. In *Inquinamento Marino da Navi e Poteri dello Stato Costiero* [Ship-sourced marine pollution and the powers of the coastal state], 246–52. Turin: G. Giappichelli, 2007.

"Shipping in Polar Waters." International Maritime Organization. Accessed April 13, 2018, http://www.imo.org/en/MediaCentre/HotTopics/polar/Pages/default.aspx (including a link to the entire Polar Code).

VanderZwaag, David L. "Law of the Sea and Governance of Shipping in the Arctic and Antarctic." In *Polar Law Textbook*, edited by Natalia Loukacheva, 45–64. Copenhagen: Nordic Council of Ministers, 2010.

Zysk, Katarzyna. "Russia Turns North, Again: Interests, Policies and the Search for Coherence." In Jensen and Hønneland, eds., *Handbook of Politics in the Arctic*, 437–61.

10

Environmental Protection in the Arctic

★ ★ ★

THE CONCEPT OF SOVEREIGNTY is a recurring theme of this book. Classical approaches to international law consider state sovereignty as the basis for peaceful international relations. That view assumes that states can do largely what they want within the confines of their own borders and (in some respects) within their maritime zones (i.e., the Westphalian model). In contemporary international affairs, there are some limitations to that sovereignty: it is not absolute—and never was. The first significant limitation is that the state must uphold human rights and the rights of indigenous peoples within its territory, as was discussed in chapter 7. The second limitation is that sovereignty must be exercised by a state in a manner respectful of the sovereignty of other states: in other words, a state may not undertake activities, or turn a blind eye to activities undertaken by others under its jurisdiction, that harm the interests of other states. For example, a state must not build a factory that pours toxic waste into a river that then flows into a neighboring state, nor may it allow a private company to do the same. This principle, sometimes called the "no-harm principle" is the foundation of international environmental law.[1]

This chapter examines environmental principles and policies in the Arctic, looking in particular at the requirement for environmental impact assessments, the application of the precautionary approach, conservation of biodiversity, and sustainable development. The chapter also explains measures taken to address the most important challenges in the Arctic: climate change, long-range contaminants, and damage to the marine environment. Two short sections on human rights and the environment and on dispute settlement complete the chapter.

Everywhere on Earth is subject to anthropogenic environmental impacts, and the Arctic is in many respects *less* sullied than other regions. Huge tracts of wilderness remain. However, as we have seen through this book, there are also bustling cities and large-scale industrial activities. The Arctic is particularly vulnerable owing to the more rapid rate of climate change and a low rate of biodiversity. The small and scattered populations as well as the extreme weather conditions also make cleanup of a major pollution incident more difficult. At the time (over twenty years prior to the *Deepwater Horizon* catastrophe), the *Exxon Valdez* oil spill was considered the most damaging oil spill in modern history, and yet it was only thirty-fourth in terms of volume of oil lost.[2] The sensitive environment rendered the consequences much more severe than similar spills elsewhere.

Much pollution is of local origin—for example, from mining, processing, or abandoned nuclear hardware. According to the US Environmental Protection Agency (EPA), Alaska produces nearly three times the toxic chemicals of any other US state (largely from mining), despite having only 0.2 percent of the national population.[3] Other environmental threats in the Arctic—notably those emanating from climate change—have international sources and can only be managed through international cooperation.

Interest in Arctic environmental protection is growing not just internationally through high-profile campaigns but also domestically. In 1980, 5.6 percent of the Arctic was protected in some manner; by 2011 that had doubled to 11 percent (40 percent of which is marine).[4] By 2018, the figures were over 20 percent of land but only 5 percent of the marine environment.[5]

PRINCIPLES OF INTERNATIONAL ENVIRONMENTAL LAW

International environmental law pivots on the maxim "So use your own property not to injure that of another" (the no-harm principle).[6] In fact, it is not an obligation on states to prevent all and any harm to other states but only an obligation to take reasonable measures to prevent "significant" damage.[7]

In 1996 the International Court of Justice gave an opinion on the lawfulness of holding or using nuclear weapons and took the opportunity to pronounce upon states' environmental responsibilities toward other states, including with regard to areas beyond national jurisdiction (the high Seas, the Area, and outer space):

The Court . . . recognizes that the environment is not an abstraction but represents the living space, the quality of life and the very health of human beings, including generations unborn. The existence of the general obligation of States to ensure that activities within their jurisdiction and control respect the environment of other States or of areas beyond national control is now part of the corpus of international law relating to the environment.[8]

The Environmental Impact Assessment

The concept of the environmental impact assessment (EIA) originated in the United States.[9] Today, under domestic law, each of the Arctic states has EIA requirements, though they vary in rigor. (For example, in Russia, no EIA is required for an oil or gas pipeline.)[10] The Aarhus Convention to which the Nordic states are parties (though it is not extended to Greenland) secures rights to the public, including NGOs in some cases, to participate in assessments, to obtain information regarding developments and their potential environmental impacts, and to receive compensation if their rights are infringed.[11]

In 2010, in a contentious dispute regarding pulp mills situated on a shared watercourse that flowed south into a neighboring state, the International Court of Justice held that the EIA is a requirement of international law whenever activities pose a risk of significant impact to another state (i.e., transboundary harm).[12] The court gave further support to this obligation in another case in 2015.[13]

UNCLOS requires an EIA in respect to potential damage to the seas.[14] Onshore and offshore, the Espoo Convention provides the most important framework for transboundary EIAs in the Arctic.[15] Of the Arctic states, only Canada, the Kingdom of Denmark, Finland, Norway, and Sweden have ratified it, but Iceland, Russia, and the United States have also signed it, indicating their support in principle. In practice, they each have a system to engage with Espoo's requirements—demonstrating that international standards can be effective even when they are not strictly binding on a state.[16] Schrage claims that the "Arctic countries consider the Convention as the basis for cooperation in the Arctic area."[17] Koivurova describes it as the "primary standard for [Transboundary EIA] in the Arctic."[18]

Under the AEPS (the predecessor to the Arctic Council), a set of guidelines for EIA in the Arctic was developed to aid its member states in developing EIA systems adapted to the vulnerable Arctic environments and logistical challenges to collecting relevant information and data, including traditional and indigenous knowledge.[19] The guidelines are presented in ordinary language rather than the more technical legal language of treaties or domestic laws in order to be accessible and easier to implement by scientists and developers. They have not been widely followed (at least, not intentionally), but the Sustainable Development Working Group is currently reviewing the guidelines in the hope of giving them a new lease of life.[20]

The Protection of the Arctic Marine Environment Working Group of the Arctic Council's Arctic offshore oil and gas guidelines have been more influential.[21] They are addressed primarily to states' regulatory authorities with the intention that they should be incorporated into domestic procedures, but they are also hoped to "be of help to the industry when planning for oil and gas activities and to the public in understanding environmental concerns and practices."[22]

The requirement to conduct an EIA does not tell us what states should do with it. It might be assumed that states with better information will make a rational choice not to conduct or permit activities that are seriously damaging to their own environments. Indeed, this is likely to be true if the source of the damage and its impacts are felt by the same state; at the very least, the rational state will only permit damage that is outweighed by a project's benefits. Domestic laws may prohibit altogether projects with significant negative impacts.[23] This incentive is much reduced where harm is transboundary: states can externalize some of the true costs of their activities—that is, they benefit from the activity, but a neighboring state bears (some of) the environmental damage.[24] This is where the no-harm principle comes into play. Armed with the results of the EIA, a state may not allow a project to go ahead, knowing that significant transboundary damage is likely.[25]

The Precautionary Approach

The Seabed Disputes Chamber, a special chamber of the International Tribunal for the Law of the Sea, supports the court's position on the need for a transboundary EIA if an activity poses a risk of damage to other states or the Area, beyond national jurisdiction.[26] It has gone further, however, and is the first major international court to recognize explicitly the precautionary approach as part of customary international law.[27]

The precautionary approach is one of the most misunderstood concepts in environmental law. To be clear, it does *not* mean that in the case of any doubt about the consequences, an activity should not proceed. The Seabed Disputes Chamber endorsed the definition of the precautionary approach found in the Rio Declaration, which states: "In order to protect the environment, the precautionary approach shall be widely applied by States according to their capabilities. Where there are threats of serious or irreversible damage, lack of full scientific certainty shall not be used as a reason for postponing cost-effective measures to prevent environmental degradation."[28]

The application of the precautionary approach therefore depends on four conditions: there must be a risk of negative impacts; those impacts must be "serious" or "irreversible"; there is *some* scientific evidence pointing to the risk (i.e., it is more than a hypothesis or a risk of some unknown harm) but the evidence is inconclusive;[29] and developing states are held to lower expectations.[30] If these conditions are met, the state is *permitted* to take preventive measures but is rarely *obligated* to do so, and any measures it does take should be cost-effective. The precautionary approach says that uncertainty should not be an impediment to protective measures; but it does not say that uncertainty *requires* protective measures. The precautionary approach is certainly not a presumption against industrial activity, even in the most vulnerable of areas. It may, on the other hand, permit a state to suspend or modify free trade rules on grounds of environmental concerns.

A stricter precautionary approach could be implemented by treaty—for example, an obligation on states to take steps to reduce risks that are as yet not fully understood (e.g., the impacts on marine animals of noise pollution in the oceans from shipping, hydrocarbon activities, or wind and tidal turbines). However, the 2013 Agreement on Cooperation on Marine Oil Pollution Preparedness and Response in the Arctic addresses precaution only in the weakest of terms in its nonbinding preamble. The eight governments are "aware of the Parties' obligation to protect the Arctic marine environment and mindful of the importance of precautionary measures to avoid oil pollution in the first instance."[31]

This wording reflects the wariness of the United States (and others) to express endorsement of the precautionary approach for fear of constraining unduly industrial development. Nevertheless, the United States applies the precautionary approach in many cases, even if it uses other terms.[32]

Conservation of Biological Diversity

One of the broader limitations on state sovereignty and the power of states to do what they want within their own territories is the requirement to protect biological diversity. The Convention on Biological Diversity has an impressive 196 state parties (there are only 193 state members of the United Nations), but the United States is not among them.[33] The Convention explicitly accepts states' rights to develop their own resources, but it requires them to do so in a manner that is sustainable and protects biodiversity. The convention recognizes biodiversity as being valuable in and of itself, irrespective of any commercial value that might attach to any particular plant, animal, or genetic resource.[34] The Convention recognizes the importance of indigenous knowledge and seeks to protect the rights of indigenous peoples to free, prior, and informed consent; their intellectual property; and other property rights in this regard.[35] This is further developed in an additional protocol.[36] There are also two highly regarded sets of voluntary guidelines under the Convention. The Akwé: Kon guidelines on cultural, environmental and social impact assessment apply to projects taking place on indigenous territories and prioritize indigenous engagement in the impact assessment processes.[37] The Biodiversity–Inclusive Impact Assessment guidelines aim to mainstream biodiversity issues in the EIA process and promote a precautionary approach to development.[38]

Biodiversity has become a priority of the Arctic Council through the efforts of the Conservation of Arctic Flora and Fauna Working Group (CAFF), which produced its hefty *Arctic Biodiversity Assessment* in 2014 and is now focusing on monitoring and promoting implementation of its seventeen policy recommendations.[39] CAFF has a memorandum of cooperation with the secretariat of the Convention on Biological Diversity that seeks to enhance sharing of information and promotion of biodiversity protection initiatives.[40] CAFF also has resolutions on cooperation with a number of other international treaty secretariats, including that of the Ramsar Convention on Wetlands and the Convention on Migratory Species.[41] Under the Ramsar Convention, state parties undertake to protect wetlands of special importance, in particular those of importance to birds.[42] CAFF has been reaching out to non-Arctic states to preserve the habitats of migratory birds.[43] Some areas are also protected as World Heritage under UNESCO.[44]

Although reluctant in recent years to ratify major international environmental treaties, the United States has its own domestic regime of environmental protection and cooperates on a bilateral basis with neighboring Russia and Canada. The EPA supervises the implementation of dozens of federal laws, and the state of Alaska passes and supervises many more. One cornerstone piece of federal legislation is the Marine Mammal Protection Act of 1972 that facilitates co-management agreements between federal agencies and Alaskan native organizations.[45] It incorporates a precautionary approach in respect to human interference with the ecosystems relied on by marine mammals. Under the act, the federal agencies and Alaskan native organizations enter co-management agreements to monitor and conserve marine mammals within their ecosystems while also permitting a sustainable subsistence hunt. The United States is also increasing its efforts to implement a network of marine protected areas (MPAs) in consultation with local communities.[46] MPAs can be established to protect natural and cultural heritage or to support sustainable use strategies.

Conservation regimes are not always welcomed by those who are most affected. The Arctic National Wildlife Refuge (ANWR) demonstrates the tensions between the pro-development state of Alaska and the conservationist-minded federal agencies (see box 10.6 later in this chapter). Tensions between indigenous communities and conservation activists are also present throughout the Arctic, as elsewhere: for every photo of an indigenous person that is used by an NGO in an environmental campaign, there are dozens of less visible indigenous individuals who hold a different view. During the drafting process for the UN Declaration on the Rights of Indigenous Peoples, the risks to indigenous peoples from ill-thought-out conservation measures were raised, and at an international forum on indigenous mapping in 2004, two hundred indigenous delegates agreed that "conservation has become the number one threat to indigenous territories—an even greater threat to their right to live on their traditional land than extractive industries."[47] Species-focused protection campaigns also sometimes interfere with sustainable use, as we saw with regard to the seal product (see box 6.2 in chapter 6) and in the case of the polar bear (see box 10.1).

BOX 10.1	Protecting the Polar Bear

Even in the midst of the Cold War, the five states that border the Arctic Ocean were able to recognize the threat to the polar bear from excessive trophy hunting by hunters from outside of the Arctic. In 1973 they made the Agreement on the Conservation of Polar Bears.[a] The treaty forbade the hunting of polar bears, with limited exceptions for scientific research, population management, or by "local people using traditional methods," as permitted by domestic law or where bears had been taken "by traditional means" by the state's own nationals.[b] Polar bear skins from traditional (indigenous) hunts may be sold commercially.[c]

[a]International Agreement on the Conservation of Polar Bears 1973, *International Legal Materials* 13 (1974): 13.
[b]Ibid., article 3(1).
[c]Ibid., article 3(2).

Today, the International Union for the Conservation of Nature (IUCN) estimates that approximately twenty-six thousand polar bears live in the wild, and it classes the species as vulnerable. The bears live in nineteen subpopulations, of which eleven are stable. Eighty percent of the bears live in and around Canada.[d]

The polar bear is listed in Appendix II of the Convention on International Trade in Endangered Species of Wild Fauna and Flora (CITES) as "species not necessarily threatened with extinction, but in which trade must be controlled in order to avoid utilization incompatible with their survival."[e] Products made from a species listed in Appendix II may be traded but require an export permit to demonstrate that the animal was taken legally *and* sustainably.

The United States bans imports of any polar bear product but permits indigenous hunting in Alaska. Hunting is banned in Norway (though killing of polar bears is permitted in self-defense—a genuine concern on the Svalbard islands). Greenland and Russia do not permit sports hunting but allow limited indigenous hunting for subsistence purposes. Canada permits indigenous hunting and also allows indigenous communities to sell their quotas for sports hunting: the Inuit sell polar bear hunting tours in which they guide visitors, equip them, show them how to track bears, and allow them to shoot. The Inuit keep the meat, but the hunter is permitted to export the skin and bones. A skin can fetch $5,000 CAD and a hunting package tour up to $20,000 CAD. Approximately three hundred Canadian bears are traded internationally (out of a total global annual hunt of seven hundred to eight hundred).[f]

In March 2013 the United States led an effort to upgrade the polar bear to Appendix I of CITES—that is, as a species "threatened with extinction." This would have prevented almost all international trade or transfer of polar bear products, allowing only movement for scientific or conservation purposes but banning all international commercial transfer. Although polar bear populations have recovered from the ravages of overhunting in the twentieth century, it is well known that they are threatened by climate change—specifically, the loss of sea ice on which the polar bear relies as a base from which to hunt.[g] Therefore, it seems only common sense that they should be protected from additional threats through hunting. Nevertheless, the CITES secretariat, the IUCN, and the World Wildlife Fund (WWF) all

(continued)

[d]"Ursus Maritimus," IUCN Red List, accessed April 14, 2017, http://www.iucnredlist.org/details/22823/0.
[e]Convention on International Trade in Endangered Species of Wild Fauna and Flora, 993 U.N.T.S. 243, Appendix II.
[f]"Conservation of Polar Bears in Canada," Environment Canada, 2012, https://polarbearscience.files.wordpress.com/2013/02/conservationofpolarbearincanada-2012.pdf.
[g]"Ursus Maritimus."

BOX 10.1 | *Continued*

disagreed.[h] The legal requirements for Appendix I are not met by the current conditions of the polar bear populations, and to uplist this species could undermine the legal framework—by making the listing of species essentially a political rather than a scientific decision. IUCN and WWF both agree that the hunting of the polar bear is sustainable and that a prohibition of the export of polar bear products would not have any impact.[i] Furthermore, it is a diversion from the real threat: anthropogenic emissions that are causing rapid warming in the Arctic and sea ice melt.

The US effort to uplist the polar bear has so far been unsuccessful; it remains protected under Appendix II.

[h]Douglas A. Clark et al., "Polar Bear and CITES: A Rejoinder to Parsons and Cornick," *Marine Policy* 38 (2013): 365.
[i]"Polar Bears to Remain on Appendix II of CITES," *Polar Bears International*, March 11, 2013, http://polarbearsinternational.org/news/article-polar-bears/polar-bears-to-remain -on-appendix-ii-of-cites; "Polar Bears, WWF and CITES Trade Bans," WWF, March 12, 2013, http://wwf.panda.org/wwf_news/?207907/Polar-bears-WWF-and-CITES.

Sustainable Development

The concept of sustainable development was developed by a special commission led by former Norwegian prime minister Gro Harlem Brundtland in 1987. The Brundtland Commission defined sustainable development as "development that meets the needs of the present without compromising the ability of future generations to meet their own needs."[48]

The concept of sustainable development was at the heart of the negotiations at the 1992 Rio Conference but also colored the discussions leading to the AEPS and the first few years of its operation, prior to the creation of the Arctic Council.[49] The first four working groups of the AEPS were all environmentally oriented, but at the urging of the permanent participants, the Sustainable Development Working Group was established in 1993.

In 2015 the UN adopted seventeen sustainable development goals to be achieved within fifteen years (see box 10.2). The Arctic Council participants, especially the Nordic states, are making these a priority.[50] Their implementation in the Arctic has been the topic of dozens of conferences, including one led by the Arctic Economic Council and the Danish government in 2017.[51] Implementation of the seventeen UN goals

BOX 10.2	UN Sustainable Development Goals, 2015–2030

- No Poverty
- Zero Hunger
- Good Health and Well-Being
- Quality Education
- Gender Equality
- Clean Water and Sanitation
- Affordable and Clean Energy
- Decent Work and Economic Growth
- Industry, Innovation, and Infrastructure
- Reduced Inequalities
- Sustainable Cities and Communities
- Responsible Consumption and Production
- Climate Action
- Life below Water
- Life on Land
- Peace, Justice, and Strong Institutions
- Partnerships for the Goals

Source: "Sustainable Development Goals," United Nations, accessed February 12, 2018, https://sustainabledevelopment.un.org/?menu=1300.

in the Arctic was also the main theme of the Rovaniemi Arctic Spirit Conference the same year.[52]

Political commitment to sustainable development in the Arctic states and the Arctic Council is broad, but the concept is flexible enough that each state might have a different idea about what it means in practice. One state might emphasize development more; another might emphasize sustainability more. Even the same state is likely to have different approaches under successive governments. It is best understood as a kind of overarching concept: a commitment to sustainable development means exploiting resources in a manner that preserves or even increases the total resources for the next generation.

ARCTIC ENVIRONMENTAL CHALLENGES

Climate Change

The biggest general environmental challenge in the Arctic in the twenty-first century is anthropogenic climate change.[53] It is extremely difficult to mitigate climate change because activities in every single state around the world contribute to the problem, and dozens of states have neither the resources nor the technology to reduce their consumption of hydrocarbons, the most damaging triggers, in order of impact: coal, oil, and gas. Climate change responses call for "common but differentiated responsibilities" of states, taking into account their historic contributions to climate change as well as their capacity to mitigate and to adapt. At an Arctic Circle Forum in Edinburgh in 2017, Lord Deben explained the principle as follows:

> Climate change hits first the poor. Those of us with some chance of adaptation should remember that they have none. . . . All of us are living on the enormous advantages . . . of the industrial revolution. . . . We gained the wealth but we didn't pay the cost. It is absolutely unacceptable to say that the countries that didn't benefit should pay the cost.[54]

The parent treaty, the UN Framework Convention on Climate Change (UNFCCC), established the principle that all states should make efforts to limit anthropogenic influences on the climate, but the most developed countries (Annex I countries) have more stringent obligations.[55] It was followed by the Kyoto Protocol, which established legally binding emissions targets for the Annex I states but allowed them to "trade" emissions with other states.[56] This meant that they could meet their targets by helping a developing country reduce its emissions while taking fewer steps at home.[57] The United States under George W. Bush's leadership refused to ratify, and Canada, realizing it was never going to meet its targets and seeking to evade the financial penalties attached, withdrew from the Kyoto Protocol in 2011 under the Harper government. Fast-developing and major polluters China and India had no emissions targets in any case. A disappointing Conference of the Parties was held in Copenhagen in 2009 and resulted only in a nonbinding accord where the emphasis seemed to shift from mitigation (preventing runaway climate change) to adaptation (helping vulnerable countries cope with climate change).[58] At the end of 2015 only 14 percent of global emissions were regulated by the Kyoto Protocol.[59] For a long time it looked as though the necessary cooperation to mitigate climate change was impossible.

In December 2015 the stars aligned for a promising conference of states in Paris. An ambitious French president led delegations from around the world, including a "green"[60] Canadian prime minister ready to make his mark, a US president nearing the end of his second term, a European Union prepared to take on binding targets, and developing states ready for compromises that might hurt them in the short term but could save them in the long term by mitigating the projected change or at least slowing change long enough to give them time to adapt. The two greenhouse gas pollution giants—the United States and China—both ratified the agreement in September 2016.[61] In August 2017 President Trump formally notified the UN of his intention to withdrew the United States from the deal, and he appointed a decidedly climate-unfriendly administration. However, the withdrawal process cannot be completed within his four-year term and may not be worth the diplomatic fallout.[62] What he can do is undermine the EPA, defund climate action policies, repeal climate laws, support hydrocarbon firms, and open up more areas to hydrocarbon activities. Nevertheless, commitments by progressive states such as California and New York, as well as corporate commitments, will push the United States toward climate targets irrespective of federal priorities.[63]

The Paris Agreement rests on a trident of mitigation, adaptation, and steps to address loss or damage.[64] It locks in the 2°C target as the maximum acceptable average global warming but aims at an ambitious 1.5°C maximum.[65] This is based on a system of "nationally determined commitments."[66] Shipping is not, however, included in states' emissions targets.[67] Moreover, the obligations only begin from 2020 onward, and the pledges made at the time of the conference were not sufficient to limit warming even to a 2°C average.[68] This means a warming of 4°C or even more in some regions of the Arctic. States are encouraged to commit to tougher reductions over time but are not permitted to weaken their commitments (short of withdrawal from the agreement altogether, which is only permitted three years after its coming into force).[69] Developed countries must make cuts, and developing countries must mitigate and move "over time" toward cuts.[70] As well as cutting emissions, states should take measures to preserve carbon sinks, such as forests.[71]

States should make public adaptation plans that protect the most vulnerable people (i.e., the plans should not be a justification for forced relocations or further disenfranchising and marginalizing the poor) and must implement the plan in a manner respectful of human rights and the rights of indigenous peoples.[72] They should integrate Western scientific knowledge together with traditional and indigenous knowledge in their planning.[73] The provisions on loss or damage are rather vague, and the developed states have evaded or at least postponed any acceptance of a duty to make reparation for the damage their historical emissions cause. This topic was kicked into the long grass for further negotiations in a task force.[74]

Transparency, monitoring, and evaluation are the tools to promote compliance rather than resorting to litigation, and a twelve-member body of experts is established to facilitate implementation in a "transparent, non-adversarial and non-punitive" manner.[75]

The Arctic Council is pioneering measures to monitor and potentially reduce short-term climate forcers in the Arctic that have localized impacts (see box 10.3).

BOX 10.3 | **Short-Lived Climate Forcers**

No amount of cooperation and effort among the peoples of the Arctic alone will stop climate change impacts without commitment and change further south. However, there are some localized factors that speed up climate change; these are called short-lived climate forcers. Black carbon (or soot) and methane are two of these. Black carbon is released through incomplete combustion of carbon-based fuels. It does not travel far and dissipates in a few days or weeks. It lies on the ice and snow in the Arctic and absorbs solar radiation (whereas white ice or snow would reflect much of that solar radiation), speeding up melting, and it interferes with clouds. Black carbon also triggers and aggravates respiratory diseases like asthma for people in these areas.[a]

Methane (CH_4) stays in the atmosphere for approximately ten years, which is still short-lived in comparison to other greenhouse gases.[b] Notwithstanding its short life span, the same quantity of methane in the atmosphere will push climate change at twenty-five times the rate of carbon dioxide.[c] The Arctic Council has developed a framework to log and reduce black carbon and methane emissions; it encourages the observer states to participate alongside the Arctic Council's members.[d]

[a]See "How Black Carbon Affects the Arctic: Infographic," Arctic Institute, accessed April 14, 2017, http://www.thearcticinstitute.org/wp-content/uploads/2016/04/TAI-Infographic -Blackcarbon.pdf.
[b]*Arctic Council Task Force on Short-Lived Climate Forcers: An Assessment of Emissions and Mitigation Options for Black Carbon for the Arctic Council* (Arctic Council, 2011), 2, note 1.
[c]"Overview of Greenhouse Gases," EPA, accessed April 14, 2017, http://www3.epa.gov /climatechange/ghgemissions/gases/ch4.html.
[d]Arctic Council, *Enhanced Black Carbon and Methane Emissions Reductions: An Arctic Council Framework for Action 2015*, SAO Report to Ministers (Iqaluit, 2015), Annex 4; see also Daria Shapovalova, "The Effectiveness of the Regulatory Regime for Black Carbon Mitigation in the Arctic," *Arctic Review of Law and Politics* 7, no. 2 (2016): 136, accessed April 11, 2017; and Rachael Lorna Johnstone, "Environmental Governance through the Arctic Council: The Arctic Council as Initiator of Norms of International Environmental Law," Working Paper No. 1, Polar Cooperation and Research Centre, Kobe University, Japan, 2016, 17–18.

Long-Range Contaminants

Like climate change, many other environmental threats to the Arctic and its inhabitants are not of local origin. The Arctic food web has been contaminated by pollutants that were released in states thousands of miles from the Arctic, with major consequences for food safety and food security of many indigenous populations.

The UN Economic Commission for Europe (UNECE) developed a regional agreement on long-range transboundary air pollution (LRTAP) that came into force in 1983 (see box 10.4).[76] This agreement came about at the urging of the Arctic states in light of the impacts being felt among their indigenous Arctic populations. All the Arctic states are party to the main convention though they have not all ratified every protocol.

BOX 10.4	Long-Range Contaminants, Indigenous Activism, and International Action

Persistent organic pollutants (POPs) endure without breaking down, especially in cold temperatures, and they can evaporate, which allows them to travel vast distances. They dissolve easily in fats, bioaccumulate (become more concentrated in the first organism that consumes or absorbs them), and biomagnify (become more concentrated as they progress up the food chain).[a] This means that they are found in high concentrations in marine mammals in the Arctic even though they are rarely produced in the Arctic. Consequences in humans include cancer, birth defects, allergies, and reproductive problems. POPs are transmitted in utero.[b]

Arctic Council working groups contributed to an international regime to restrict the use of POPs. The Arctic Monitoring and Assessment Program (AMAP) was particularly active in gathering data to support the establishment of the Stockholm Convention to restrict their production and use.[c] Although indigenous activists had limited access to the UN Environment Program (UNEP), the careful structure of the Arctic Council meant that they could work closely with scientists at AMAP to build a case for international restrictions. The indigenous groups could never have funded the scientific data gathering themselves. Meanwhile, the scientists were able to integrate indigenous knowledge and incorporate their human rights approach to the issue.[d] Indigenous leaders participated in the signing ceremony of

(continued)

[a]Emily Mason and David L. VanderZwaag, "Controlling the Long-Range Transport of Persistent Organic Pollutants (POPS) into the Arctic: Progressions and Political Pairings," in *Handbook of Politics in the Arctic*, ed. Leif Christian Jensen and Geir Hønneland (Cheltenham, UK: Edward Elgar, 2015), 353.
[b]Ibid., 354.
[c]Stockholm Convention on Persistent Organic Pollutants (POPS) 2001, 2256 U.N.T.S. 119.
[d]Timo Koivurova, *Introduction to International Environmental Law* (Abingdon, UK: Routledge 2014), 16–17 and 114–16; Elana Wilson and Indra Øverland, "Indigenous Issues," in *International Cooperation and Arctic Governance: Regime Effectiveness and Northern*

BOX 10.4 | *Continued*

the convention alongside state representatives. All the Arctic states except for the United States are parties to the Stockholm Convention.

A human rights approach requires sensitivity also to the human rights of people who depend on POPs for their own health. Many developing countries, especially in Africa, continue to use DDT, one of the most notorious POPS, as it remains the most effective way to exterminate malaria-carrying mosquitos and hence preserve the lives of some of the most vulnerable populations on the planet. This means that eliminating the use of DDT overnight would have even more serious effects on the people living in malaria-stricken developing countries than its continued use has on the peoples of the Arctic.[e]

Mercury shares many of the properties of POPs. Although a naturally occurring element, its release through coal burning, mining, and industrial application (e.g., in gold mining or in batteries, pesticides, and cosmetics) creates unnatural hazards. In gas form, it persists in the atmosphere and travels to the Arctic. It also bioaccumulates. Plants absorb mercury from the air and are either eaten (in which case the mercury enters the food chain) or the plants degrade and the mercury goes into the soil, eventually draining into rivers and oceans. Warming temperatures also point to increasing releases of mercury from permafrost.[f] High levels are found in polar bears and some Arctic seals and whales.[g] In humans, mercury affects "the central nervous system, thyroid, kidneys, lungs, immune system, eyes, gums and skin."[h]

AMAP once more led data gathering (with involvement of both indigenous and Western scientific experts), which then fed into UNEP.[i] The Minamata Convention, to reduce the mining, international trade, release, and use of mercury, was signed in 2013 and came into force in 2017.[j] In the Arctic, Canada, Denmark (though not Greenland), Finland, Norway, Sweden, and the United States are parties. Russia has signed and Iceland has yet to take action.

Region Building, ed. Olav Schram Stokke and Geir Hønneland (Abingdon, UK: Routledge Advances in International Relations and Global Politics, 2007), 33; see also Olav Schram Stokke, "International Institutions and Arctic Governance," in the same volume.
[e]See generally, *Northern Lights against POPs: Combatting Toxic Threats in the Arctic*, ed. David Leonard Downie and Terry Fenge (Montreal: McGill University Press, 2003).
[f]David P. Stone, *The Changing Arctic Environment: The Arctic Messenger* (Cambridge: Cambridge University Press, 2015), 178.
[g]A. Krey, S. K. Ostertag, and H. M. Chan, "Assessment of Neurotoxic Effects of Mercury in Beluga Whales (Delphinapterus leucas), Ringed Seals (Pusa hispida), and Polar Bears (Ursus maritimus) from the Canadian Arctic," *Science of the Total Environment* 509–510 (2015): 237.
[h]"Minamata Convention on Mercury at a Glance," accessed January 23, 2018, http://cwm .unitar.org/cwmplatformscms/site/assets/files/1334/minamata_convention_on_mer cury_at_a_glance_04_16.pdf.
[i]See Froukje Maria Platjouw, Eirik Howard Steindal, and Trude Borch, "From Arctic Science to International Law: The Road towards the Minamata Convention and the Role of the Arctic Council," *Arctic Review of Law and Politics* 9, no. 2 (2018): 226.
[j]Minamata Convention on Mercury 2013, U.N.T.S., C.N. 560.2014. TREATIES-XXVII.17.

Protection and Preservation of the Marine Environment

In the ocean, beyond states' baselines, all damage is, in a sense, "transboundary"—that is, it affects other states. This is first of all a physical consideration: the water column and the creatures within it move, and hence pollution of the water or living marine resources in one state's territorial sea or EEZ can travel into the maritime zone of another state or into the high seas. However, it is also a legal consideration: all pollution or damage of the ocean is transboundary in a legal sense because the ocean is a common good. Part XII of the UNCLOS requires that states ensure their use of the oceans, including their exercise of sovereign rights, be compatible with the protection and preservation of the marine environment.[77] Any exploitation of their natural resources (including sovereign rights) must be "in accordance with their duty to protect and preserve the marine environment."[78]

HUMAN RIGHTS AND THE ENVIRONMENT

But what if a state is only damaging its own soil? For example, what if a state allows a mine to pollute a lake that is entirely within its own territory and does not affect the rights of other states? This is where international environmental law faces its limits. A state's sovereignty over its own territory allows it in some cases to severely damage its territory, even irreparably, if it chooses, just as your ownership over this book allows you to set fire to it if you wish (though we rather hope you do not! Carbon emissions!).

In some cases, human rights and the rights of indigenous peoples can provide some protection (see boxes 10.4, 10.5, and 10.6). However, this is only possible if the human and environmental interests are congruent. Through a human rights lens, the environment is only protected to the extent that it has a direct connection to human well-being. Within a human rights paradigm, the environment has an instrumental value: it is only protected if it is of some practical benefit to humans but has no recognized intrinsic value.

BOX 10.5 | **The Climate Change Human Rights Petition**

In 2005 the Inuit Circumpolar Council (ICC), led by Sheila Watt-Cloutier, submitted a petition to the Inter-American Commission on Human Rights.[a] The petitioners sought an investigation into the con-

(continued)

[a]Petition to the Inter-American Commission on Human Rights Seeking Relief from Violations Resulting from Global Warming caused by Acts and Omissions of the United States,

BOX 10.5 | *Continued*

tributions by the United States to global warming and the nation's failures to take adequate mitigation measures. They sought compensation for the damages they had suffered as a consequence. The ICC petition compiled an impressive account of the physical impacts of global warming on the Inuit way of life and argued that the United States, as the state that had contributed most to the causes of global warming, notwithstanding its knowledge of the harmful effects, bore responsibility.[b] The petition catalogued the changes in ice, permafrost, coastal erosion, flora and fauna, and weather patterns; and their impacts on human health, food management, travel, property, and culture.[c] The petitioners argued that climate change led to violations of Inuit rights to culture; use and enjoyment of their traditional lands collectively held; personal and intellectual property; health; life, physical protection, and security; subsistence; residence and home.[d] The petition was rejected by the commission on the basis that the facts alleged were not sufficient to establish a violation of the rights protected by the ADRDM.[e] However, despite having dismissed the petition, the commission held a special thematic hearing on global warming and human rights.[f] Although the ICC did not obtain its day in court, the case is important in a number of respects. The legal argument demonstrates the potential of collective claims for human rights violations based on environmental degradation. It also shows the potential for transboundary responsibility: although many of the Inuit affected were based in Alaska and under the respondent state's jurisdiction, tens of thousands more were in Canada, Greenland (Kingdom of Denmark), and Russia. The petition describes Inuit life in detail and demonstrates the continuity between contemporary Inuit life and centuries-old traditions. It also shows how closely culture, economy, health, spiritual well-being, home, and family life are woven together for the Inuit. The petition's stark illustrations of the already evident effects of a warming Arctic demonstrate the vulnerability of the Inuit to environmental changes, whether they are brought about from climate change or more localized threats to their land, waters, and resources.

submitted by Sheila Watt-Cloutier, with the support of the Inuit Circumpolar Conference, on behalf of all Inuit of the Arctic regions of the United States and Canada, Petition P-1413-05, December 7, 2005.
  [b]Ibid., chapter IV.D.
  [c]Ibid., chapter IV.C.
  [d]Ibid., chapter V.B.
  [e]Letter from the Inter-American Commission of Human Rights in respect of Petition No. P-1413-05, Sheila Watt-Cloutier et al., November 16, 2006.
  [f]Jessica Gordon, "Inter-American Commission on Human Rights to Hold Hearing after Rejecting Inuit Climate Change Petition," *Sustainable Development Law and Policy* 7, no. 2 (2007): 55.

In 2013 the Arctic Athabaskan Council (AAC) brought a petition against Canada.[g] AAC asked the commission to review Canada's failure to regulate black carbon emissions (see box 10.3). By focusing on black carbon, which can be attributed more directly to individual states and has immediate, local, climate impacts, the AAC hopes to be more successful than the Inuit challenge. However, their work has certainly been made more difficult by the failure of the Inter-American Commission to give reasons for rejecting the ICC petition.[h] The AAC petition was still pending at the time of this writing.

[g]Petition to the Inter-American Commission on Human Rights Seeking Relief from Violations of the Rights of Arctic Athabaskan Peoples Resulting from Rapid Arctic Warming and Melting Caused by Emissions of Black Carbon by Canada, April 23, 2013, archived at Earth Justice, https://earthjustice.org/sites/default/files/AAC_PETITION_13-04-23a.pdf.
[h]Don McCrimmon, "The Athabaskan Petition to the Inter-American Human Rights Commission: Using Human Rights to Respond to Climate Change," *Polar Journal* 6, no. 2 (2016): 398–416, at 412.

BOX 10.6	The Arctic National Wildlife Refuge (ANWR)

In 1960 an area of more than nineteen million acres on the North Slope of Alaska reaching the Canadian border was designated a federal protected area by the US government. In 1980 the US Congress passed the Alaska National Interest Lands Conservation Act, creating the ANWR. This vast area hosts the greatest biodiversity of any Arctic region, but it also contains oil and mineral deposits. The ANWR contains different sectors, including a few scattered villages and an eight-million-acre wilderness area. The 1002 area within the wilderness area is believed to contain commercially viable oil deposits, but any development must be approved by the US Congress rather than the Alaskan state government and legislature. Any exploration or exploitation is expected to have serious consequences for the caribou that migrate through the area.

The federal government's position has oscillated since 1980. The Republican-led Congress sought to allow drilling in 1996, but President Clinton (a Democrat) vetoed the bill. Through the twenty-first century, the positions of Congress and the presidency have swung, following more or less Republican (pro-drilling) and Democrat (anti-drilling) lines. President Trump seeks to loosen restrictions on extractives in the ANWR, but unsentimental cost versus profit calculations may limit activities.[a]

(continued)

[a]Matt Lee-Ashley, "The Energy Case against Drilling in the Arctic National Wildlife Refuge," Center for American Progress, November 13, 2017, https://www.americanprogress.org/issues/green/news/2017/11/13/442603/energy-case-drilling-arctic-national-wildlife-refuge.

BOX 10.6 | *Continued*

The anti-drilling positions in DC reflect broad environmental concerns; the federal representatives who support drilling do so in the interests of economic development and US energy security. However, the indigenous Gwich'in people who live and hunt in the area argue against drilling, not only on the basis of some abstract environmental interests but also because it will compromise their human rights and rights as an indigenous people. The Gwich'in live in Alaska and in the Yukon and Northwest Territories of Canada. Caribou are central to their diet.[b] The caribou themselves have no respect for state borders and migrate between American and Canadian jurisdiction. The two states have an agreement for joint management and protection, requiring each to obtain the consent of the other before undertaking any activity that could negatively impact the herd.[c]

This controversy demonstrates the tensions at different levels. First of all, it shows the obvious clash between industrial development and environmental protection. The interests of the Gwich'in also show us that environmental concerns have a human component: the projected impacts threaten their human rights as well as rights as an indigenous people to pursue their traditional livelihoods. Then there is the clash between the Alaskan state government, which prioritizes economic development and demands state control, and the concerns of a federal government that seeks to retain a wilderness in an area that the vast majority of American voters will never visit.[d]

[b]Julie O'Malley, "Listen to the Gwich'in," *Al Jazeera: America*, March 14, 2015, http://proj ects.aljazeera.com/2015/03/arctic-village; see also chapter 7, on the rights of indigenous and other Arctic inhabitants to resources, culture, food, and so forth.
[c]Agreement between the Government of Canada and the Government of the United States on the Conservation of the Porcupine Caribou Herd 1987, *Canadian Treaty Series* 1987: 31; see Neil Craik, "Transboundary Environmental Impact Assessment in North America: Obstacles and Opportunities," in *Theory and Practice of Transboundary Environmental Impact Assessment*, ed. Kees Bastmeijer and Timo Koivurova (Leiden, Netherlands: Martinus Nijhoff, 2008).
[d]See, for example, Nathaniel Herz, "Alaska House Leaders Take Shot at Washington State over Arctic Development," *Alaska Dispatch News*, September 28, 2016, http://www.adn .com/article/20150410/alaska-house-leaders-take-shot-washington-state-over-arctic-de velopment; and Alex DeMarban, "Obama Asks Congress to Designate ANWR Coastal Plain as Wilderness," *Alaska Dispatch News*, September 28, 2016, http://www.adn.com /print/article/20150403/obama-asks-congress-designate-anwr-coastal-plain-wilderness.

IMPLEMENTATION AND ENFORCEMENT
OF INTERNATIONAL ENVIRONMENTAL LAW

Some treaties, like the UNCLOS, contain compromissory clauses—that is, provisions that give a court or courts jurisdiction if the parties disagree. The compulsory dispute settlement provisions of the UNCLOS apply to Part XII (on protection and preservation of the marine environment) but are seldom invoked in environmental disputes. States that have made the requisite declaration recognizing the competence of the International Court of Justice to decide on any dispute between itself and another state that has made a similar declaration could bring a case before the court on an environmental dispute.[79] Among the Arctic states, Canada, the Kingdom of Denmark, Finland, Norway, and Sweden have made such declarations, but none has ever instigated an environmental case before the court.[80] Court-based dispute settlement clauses are not often found in environmental treaties, which tend instead to provide softer solutions such as monitoring mechanisms or even mere negotiations.[81] At the global level, litigation on environmental issues is rare even if it has become a little more common in recent years. Even where judicial settlement is an option, the preference is still usually for nonjudicial settlement.

The *Pulp Mills* case presented the court with an opportunity to consider the application of provisional measures—an order to one or both parties to act or desist in the interim while the court considers the merits of the case in full.[82] In this regard, the court gave rather conservative (and, for environmentalists, disappointing) rulings, holding that while provisional measures were theoretically possible, they would only apply in exceptional circumstances, where the state seeking them could establish an "imminent threat of irreparable damage"[83] or "imminent risk of irreparable prejudice to the rights of the applicant."[84]

The gaps in judicial enforcement of environmental law mean that nonbinding standards and programs, such as the Black Carbon and Methane framework and the EIA guidelines, are important. The Arctic Council and its working groups have important roles to play in translating the scientific research findings into normative expectations that states are encouraged to follow even if they are not in strictly binding form.[85] In other cases, they contribute to the creation of binding agreements (see box 10.4 on the Minamata Convention).

CONCLUSIONS

The second half of the twentieth century brought major developments in international environmental law, through intergovernmental conferences, treaties, and jurisprudence. State-level cooperation in the Arctic builds on this, especially through the Arctic Council working groups, every one of which is environmentally oriented in some way. Even when states are reluctant to ratify binding instruments, subject themselves to the threat of litigation, or unequivocally endorse emerging principles of international environmental law, they do in fact develop and implement regimes to address environmental challenges in the Arctic. The system is far from complete, but the Arctic demonstrates that environmental concerns can provide the starting point on which to build trust and cooperation. Arctic states and peoples, working together, have established environmental standards and programs both locally and internationally.

FURTHER READING

Bodansky, Daniel. *The Art and Craft of Environmental Law*. Cambridge, MA: Harvard University Press, 2011.

CAFF. *Arctic Biodiversity Assessment*. Akureyri, Iceland: Arctic Council, 2014.

Downie, David Leonard, and Terry Fenge, eds. *Northern Lights against POPs: Combatting Toxic Threats in the Arctic*. Montreal: McGill University Press, 2003.

Jessen, Henning. "Joint Approaches and Best Practices—An Integrated and Coherent EU Arctic Policy in Support of Articles 208 and 214 UNCLOS." In *The European Union and the Arctic*, edited by Nengye Liu, Elizabeth A. Kirk, and Tore Henriksen, 342–59. Leiden, Netherlands: Brill, 2017.

Koivurova, Timo. *Introduction to International Environmental Law*. Abingdon, UK: Routledge 2014.

Mason, Emily, and David L. VanderZwaag. "Controlling the Long-Range Transport of Persistent Organic Pollutants (POPS) into the Arctic: Progressions and Political Pairings." In *Handbook of Politics in the Arctic*, edited by Leif Christian Jensen and Geir Hønneland, 352–74. Cheltenham, UK: Edward Elgar, 2015.

Stone, David P. *The Changing Arctic Environment: The Arctic Messenger*. Cambridge, UK: Cambridge University Press, 2015.

Westra, Laura. *Environmental Justice and the Rights of Indigenous Peoples: International and Domestic Legal Perspectives*. Abingdon, UK: Earthscan, 2008.

11

The Future of
Arctic Governance

WE BEGAN THIS BOOK by considering the features that the Arctic shares with other parts of the world. The region faces multiple, inter-related challenges from climate change, demographic shifts, resource use questions, globalization, trade, environmental threats, and human security deficits. It is like many other places on the "periphery," in the sense that the region has little control over decisions made elsewhere that affect it. Many of these outside decisions occur in more southerly parts of the Arctic states. Seven of them contain indigenous peoples staking their own claims to sovereignty and demanding recognition of their land, resource, political, and cultural rights. The Arctic states are well-structured, wealthy states, keen to avoid conflict with one another as well as internally. The result today is that Arctic states, peoples, and organizations are pioneering new, multilayered approaches to gover-nance of the Arctic.

During the Cold War, states used the North for military facilities and sought to tap the natural resources of the region, mostly with little input from local communities, indigenous and otherwise. Today, a changing environment may speed up the development of natural resources and could also prompt more diversification of the economy through tour-ism, the arts, specialized testing, shipping, new telecommunications, and energy-intensive manufacturing. More diverse economic development tends to flourish in a climate of low military threat.[1] Economic develop-ment of natural resources directly affects long-standing uses of the Arctic by indigenous people. Today, indigenous peoples have more influence in what happens and what should happen on their traditional territories. They have rights to participation in resource governance decision making under international law and under their domestic constitutional orders as well. Thus, the domestic and international orders of states are engaged in ways that expand participation in decision making.

Sometimes real change begins to happen when people start talking differently about issues. The discourse of colonialism and discovery changed the lives of indigenous peoples and citizens of the colonial states themselves. The Cold War discourse of US–USSR competition changed lives and rules again, eventually starting a strand of cooperation to prevent dangerous miscommunications between the USSR and the other Arctic states. Cooperation in the Arctic might have begun as a low-cost and not-too-serious effort by the USSR and the United States to leave one part of the world relatively free from their conflicts elsewhere. The Arctic Council was not based and is not based on a treaty. Avoiding the constraints of a binding treat is a low-political-cost strategy. Environmental issues, the first main topics for discussion, were a useful, noncontroversial, and convenient subject for study, and scientists were already networked with each other through research collaborations. The scientists produced studies and more puzzles, and climate change made those studies ever more relevant to everyone. Indigenous peoples met, organized, litigated, campaigned, and talked to the media at home and internationally.

One can be cynical and say states invited indigenous peoples to the Arctic Council table to legitimize their actions at home, but this explanation does not match the evidence. The Sami Council and Inuit Circumpolar Council (ICC) existed long before the Arctic Environmental Protection Strategy (AEPS) or the Arctic Council. Indigenous leaders pushed Arctic cooperation onward, even when some states were reluctant: the Arctic Council would not look as it looks today without their involvement from the very start.[2] When AEPS was formed, the indigenous organizations were already sufficiently influential and organized to sit at the table with the states. Today, the actors try to shelter constructive cooperation and dialogue about the Arctic from external and domestic tensions. Yet the Arctic Council is not closed off from global affairs and includes dozens of observers. In a time of change, diversity of participation with processes to connect disparate views is critical for effective governance. Diversity allows for resiliency, and resiliency opens avenues for cooperation and continuous adaptation to change.

MATERIAL AND IDEATIONAL CONNECTIONS

World politics is theorized according to two very broad categories: material and ideational. Arctic affairs include material factors like money, technology, military forces, commercial shipping capacities, and the flow of traded goods. Perhaps more important, material factors also include the land, the sea, the ice and water, and the atmosphere. They include the flora and fauna. They even include the physical reality of human beings living in and with these other material factors.

The ideational political-legal side of world affairs is well supplied through practices and rules of international law and practices of diplomacy. It includes uses of domestic law by firms, NGOs, and individuals. Perhaps most transformative of all ideas are notions of rights, duties, due diligence, and the concept of sovereignty itself. Once indigenous peoples had little influence on the opening of a mine on their lands, but discourses about ideational concepts like law, rights, sovereignty, and justice are changing this.

ARCTIC PUZZLES FOR
INTERNATIONAL RELATIONS THEORISTS

In chapter 1, we introduced five puzzles to which we now return.

One Cannot Explain the Arctic without International Law

International law is constructed around sovereignty. Sovereign states build international law through actions and agreements. More complex international relations generally lead to more complex international law, which in turn affects internal orders. State-to-state cooperation in the Arctic is strongly tied to the law of the sea, including international rules on shipping. Meanwhile, the rights of indigenous peoples and human rights law complicate relationships between communities, individuals, and their governments. Constructivists emphasize that many states rely on international law for two reasons: to know what conduct is required of them and to evaluate the intentions and conduct of other states. Law is also a bridge between action and obligations in the sense that if a state has ratified an agreement, it indicates an intention to execute its provisions at home and thus meet its obligations to other states. Agreements may forbid activities or assign rights, as with the law of the sea. Thus, while often insufficiently included in many international relations analyses, international law has a strong influence on what states do.

The Arctic Has Weak Institutions and Strong Cooperation

The Arctic Council has been the principal forum for international cooperation in the Arctic for two decades. One might think that weak or "soft" institutions like the Arctic Council would be limited through their lack of international personality and therefore their inability to create binding obligations or enter international agreements.[3] Over time, the Arctic Council has opened up to more observers (and developed criteria for observership), commissioned dozens of scientific reports through its working groups and task forces, negotiated three binding treaties, and created a permanent secretariat in Norway—all without being an international organization (IGO) or having a treaty basis. The Arctic Council system has been able to make high-quality cooperative gains without a formal IGO structure. It is, however, worthwhile to consider how to theorize why the states have not made it a formal organization.

First, sovereignty matters in the sense that each of the Arctic Eight has significant stakes. States are inherently protective of their greatest physical assets: their lands and maritime zones. However, in the Arctic, they face shared challenges and they are sufficiently rich and strong to learn from one another without compromising their independence. The institutional weakness of the council is also a source of strength, as each member state and the council itself can respond with flexibility as new issues arise. The states can act directly on their own territories without needing authorization from an IGO. At the same time, they do not appear to their electorates as being *obligated* to do so by some "foreign" body.

Second, a weak institution allows consensus-building between states and the permanent participants. Usually, IGOs have systems of voting, sometimes with majority or qualified-majority decision making. The Arctic States—especially the two or, perhaps, three largest—are not willing to put themselves into a position where they could be outvoted and hence subject to a binding obligation to which they do not consent. The council can also be more ambitious by setting nonbinding guidelines or frameworks—for example, on Black Carbon—than the states would be willing to accept under a binding treaty framework.[4]

Third, Arctic Council states look inside their states, around the table at each other and the permanent participants, and outward to other states. The practices of states often find their way into international law for further use and elaboration by other generations of leaders and citizens. Therein lies a difficulty. Due to the Arctic Council's consensus system, the permanent participants can, most of the time, effectively block action.[5] The states accept this in the limited context of Arctic affairs—of course, always subject to their own ability to block unwanted projects or policies—but are not willing to create a precedent of *legal* equivalence of states and indigenous peoples. For this reason, the three treaties agreed through the Arctic Council are not strictly Arctic Council treaties, and only the eight states, and not the permanent participants, are parties to them. Indigenous equivalence would create a disconcerting (to states) precedent for other states and IGOs. Nevertheless, the practice of strong participation by indigenous peoples may diffuse into other systems, in which case the innovation at the Arctic Council slowly makes its way into international practice, even in nonstate, cooperative frameworks, like the Arctic Economic Council.[6]

Fourth, states, at least theoretically, act on behalf of the interests of their citizens. The internal order of states, an even messier place than the space between them, is a source of ideas, compromises, rules, and changes of heart. If there is agreement on a policy at the international level, it will have to find some support at home. Similarly, concerns at home find their way to the diplomatic table.

Fifth, states also use existing structures to facilitate their cooperation, especially when political distrust makes cooperation difficult. The strength of the cooperation shown at the Arctic Council cannot be credited just to the conduct of states. The leadership of indigenous peoples and their efforts to discuss mutual concerns on a pan-Arctic basis *prior to* the creation of the Arctic Council was crucial to cooperation between states. Arctic indigenous efforts to reach across the Cold War divide were both a trigger for and a consequence of increased trust at the state-to-state level. Novel ideas from indigenous peoples continue to challenge the thinking of states. Indigenous communities continue to press for recognition of their sovereignty over indigenous lands and waters.[7]

Finally, the presence of observers (non-Arctic states, IGOs and intergovernmental forums, and international NGOs) further reinforces the value and necessity of dialogue, if only by increasing trust through openness. The admission of six new observer states in 2013 and Switzerland in 2017 led to concerns that too many voices would reduce cooperation or that a consensus on action by the Arctic Council might encounter resistance from some observer states. Other states, however, can use informal diplomacy or raise concerns in other forums outside the Arctic. The discussion and planning of the weak but cooperative Arctic Council is more likely to drive a deepening of cooperation in the Arctic. Its policies and data will also feed into other regional discussions as other parts of the world see faster environmental changes.

The Arctic Illustrates Creative Sovereignty

Realists may see sovereignty as the cause for distrust and suspicion: power is a zero-sum game between states. Other conceptions of sovereignty lead to an expectation of cooperation. Consistent with critical constructivist theory, the practices of states in solving problems encourage learning and new ideas to take hold. Sebastian Schmidt noted that sovereignty is quite social and not immutable. As a consequence, norms can and do change, especially when there is high uncertainty: "Deliberation and experimentation by actors in environments characterized by high uncertainty can lead to the development and legitimatization of new norms that significantly alter inherited understandings of appropriate behavior."[8]

The environmental changes in the region certainly qualify the Arctic as a good example of "high uncertainty," requiring new forms of sovereignty and governance. The peripherality of the region has made it difficult to manage; thus, there is a long history of sovereignty innovations, for example, through the Svalbard Treaty.[9]

Sovereignty is permeable in interesting ways. Systems originally built for a domestic order can be internationalized through diffusion of policy, such as the US innovation of environmental impact statements that is now a requirement of international law.[10] States may also listen to their own subnational political units and propose new rules or object to the behavior of another state. For example, when the Lakota people in North Dakota objected to the construction of the Dakota Access Pipeline and the United States failed to respect their claims, the Sami Parliament persuaded the Norwegian government to remove $67 million in Norwegian government investments from firms that participate in the project.[11] The close ties between states, indigenous peoples, and academic communities in the Arctic are excellent ways for ideas to diffuse and to influence policy between and within states.

Human Security Rivals National Security in Importance

It remains to be seen how the balance between human and national security will evolve. The Arctic Council has taken steps that might lead to increased focus on human security and less on national security. The Arctic Council evaluated and set indicators for the UN sustainable development goals individually and as they related to each other during the Finnish chairmanship in 2017–2018. Virtually all of the goals were connected to human security in one form or another.[12] The Arctic Council has a Resilience Action Framework under the council's Sustainable Development Working Group.[13] The framework defines resilience as "the ability of a system to bounce back and thrive during and after disturbances and shocks."[14] The framework's guiding principles include, among other things, integrating indigenous/traditional knowledge and local knowledge alongside scientific knowledge, empowering local communities to plan for change, and developing strategies to identify risks by understanding better the relationships between different kinds of risks.[15]

Climate Change Matters in Governance Efforts

The physical-material basis for modern civilization on the planet is changing. Cities are running out of water, coastlines are more unstable, and climate changes might make weather more unpredictable and increase the frequency of extreme weather events. Our plastic and chemicals are everywhere, and there are now nearly eight billion humans, compared to four billion in 1950. There are many ideas on what to do, but they often conflict with immediate individual and political preferences. The speed of environmental change in the context of increasing human consumption and unsustainable economies creates two specific kinds of uncertainty. One is statistical. Our understanding of event probability and/or frequency will decline. That means we cannot calculate risk, which is based on known probabilities. Many public policies include risk analysis as a crucial step in deciding whether to take action or not. If the underlying probabilities have changed and will continue to do so rapidly, those policy systems may fail. Linking different changes and learning how they interact, as proposed in the Resilience Action Framework, is one way to cope with the changes. The second kind of uncertainty is the "unknown unknown." With rapid climate change, some systems might be altered radically in ways that no one has anticipated. What we do know is that the earth's climate, continents, oceans, ice, and ecosystems have changed radically in the past and continue to change now. Humans have contributed to the current changes and still have in their power the possibility of moderating the effects of change on ourselves and on the earth—but it will take an extraordinary level of international diplomacy and mutual trust.

We might take a lesson from nature in this situation of system flux. Rather than attempting to optimize one perfect way to solve a problem, nature "suboptimizes," with multiple and overlapping systems. Nature is highly inefficient in some ways, but it preserves systems over long time frames. Highly optimized systems do a few things very well and are more prone to disasters. Resilient systems do many things pretty well. When unexpected pressures (or opportunities) arise, one part in a system may fail to operate as expected, while others do better and soften the impacts of failure. The Arctic Council system of soft cooperation might not be highly optimized: it cannot impose binding obligations or sanctions for noncompliance. However, unconstrained by a treaty structure, it displays flexibility and resilience.

QUESTIONS FOR FURTHER REFLECTION

You have reached the end of this book, but it is not the end for the Arctic. The challenges of the Arctic are large and dynamic and need continual, careful, humane, and creative responses. This book ends not with conclusions but more questions.

1. Suppose the Arctic sea ice melts dramatically, perhaps only leaving a skim of ice part-time in the winter. What would life be like where you live or for people in the Arctic? Does it matter if it happens in five years or fifty years?
2. How do you think the Arctic Council will evolve? What other forums will remain or become important in Arctic governance? Is there a forum that is missing?
3. How might China influence Arctic affairs? The EU? India? Japan? Your home country?
4. People in the past have migrated in response to climatic and other environmental changes. Where should members of an Arctic community go if climate change makes it impossible to remain in their home? How could people retain their cultures in such cases?
5. Very large climate migrations are expected in other regions of the world. How would those migrations/relocations be the same or different from those that might happen in the Arctic? What if people outside of the Arctic migrate northward to escape their own environmental difficulties?
6. What do you think will be the main sectors in the Arctic economies in ten or twenty years' time? What global factors will influence developments, and how will they do so?
7. How might international trade agreements and their renegotiations affect Arctic economies? What would you change about them?
8. How do the following interrelate: human security, human rights, and sustainable development? What measures promote or hamper them in the Arctic?
9. How does a human rights perspective differ from a sovereign rights perspective for managing resources in the Arctic?

10. What do you see as the major innovations in indigenous governance in the Arctic? What are the major factors behind this? How might indigenous leadership in the Arctic influence indigenous/colonial relations elsewhere in the world?

11. Is the law of the sea regime adequate for managing offshore resources and opportunities while protecting environmental and human safety? What innovations would you recommend?

12. If you were a major insurance firm evaluating insurance for Arctic shipping, what would be your main considerations when deciding whether to offer cover, and on what terms?

13. What measures do you think are needed to protect the vulnerable Arctic environments? Are these best achieved through binding treaties or "softer" forms of cooperation?

14. Who should take the lead in mitigation of, adaptation to, and reparation for climate change?

15. How can Arctic communities promote resilience in the face of change?

Notes

CHAPTER 1: WHAT THE ARCTIC
TELLS US ABOUT WORLD AFFAIRS

1. Rebecca Pincus and Saleem H. Ali, "Have You Been to 'The Arctic'? Frame Theory and the Role of Media Coverage in Shaping Arctic Discourses," *Journal of Polar Geography* 39, no. 2 (2016): 83.

2. Arctic Monitoring and Assessment Programme (AMAP), *Snow, Water, Ice and Permafrost in the Arctic* [SWIPA]: *Summary for Policy-Makers*, 2017, https://www .amap.no/documents/doc/Snow-Water-Ice-and-Permafrost.-Summary-for-Policy -makers/1532.

3. See, for example, Arctic Council, "Telecommunication Infrastructure in the Arctic: A Circumpolar Assessment," May 11, 2017, https://oaarchive.arctic-council.org /handle/11374/1924. See also Jeremy Hsu, "An Internet Cable Will Soon Cross the Arctic Circle," *Scientific American*, June 1, 2016, https://www.scientificamerican .com/article/an-internet-cable-will-soon-cross-the-arctic-circle.

4. Torill Nyseth, "Arctic Urbanization: Modernity without Cities," in *Arctic Environmental Modernities: From the Age of Polar Exploration to the Era of the Anthropocene*, ed. Lill-Ann Körber, Scott MacKenzie, and Anna Westerståhl Stenport (Cham, Germany: Palgrave Macmillan, 2017), 59–70.

5. Treaty Concerning the Archipelago of Spitsbergen, 1920, *League of Nations Treaty Series 2* (1920), 7.

6. International Agreement on the Conservation of Polar Bears, 1973, *International Legal Materials* 13 (1974): 3. See also the IUCN website: http://pbsg.npolar .no/en/agreements/agreement1973.html.

7. The Antarctic continent is the exception, where sovereignty claims have been suspended by the Antarctic Treaty, 1959, 402 U.N.T.S. 72.

8. M. Carson and G. Peterson, eds., *Arctic Resilience Report*, Arctic Council, Stockholm Environment Institute and Stockholm Resilience Centre (Stockholm, 2016), http://www.arctic-council.org/arr, especially chapter 5. See also Christina Allard, Elsa Reimerson, and Camilla Sandström, "Contrasting Nature, Contrasting

Rights—Concluding Remarks," in *Indigenous Rights in Modern Landscapes: Nordic Conservation Regimes in Global Context*, ed. Lars Elenius, Christian Allard, and Camilla Sandström (Routledge, 2017), 223 (for a useful typology and applications of types of governance from purely state to purely private governance).

9. Scott Borgerson, "The Economics and Security Implications of Global Warming," *Foreign Affairs*, March/April 2008, 63–77.

10. Jessica Shadian, "From States to Polities: Reconceptualizing Sovereignty through Inuit Governance," *European Journal of International Relations* 16, no. 3 (2010): 485–510.

11. Michael Byers, *International Law in the Arctic* (Cambridge: Cambridge University Press, 2013), 10–16.

12. Olav Schram Stokke, "Institutional Complexity in Arctic Governance: Curse or Blessing?" in *Handbook of Politics in the Arctic*, ed. Leif Christian Jensen and Geir Hønneland (Cheltenham, UK: Edward Elgar, 2015), 344.

13. Scott G. Borgerson, "The Coming Arctic Boom: As the Ice Melts, the Region Heats Up," *Foreign Affairs* 92, no. 4 (July/August 2013): 76–89.

14. Shadian, "From States to Polities"; and K. R. Cox, "Spaces of Dependence, Spaces of Engagement and the Politics of Scale, or: Looking for Local Politics," *Political Geography* 17, no. 1 (1997): 1.

15. Nevertheless, indigenous peoples are not treated in the same way as colonial peoples (peoples in non-self-governing territories that are distant from their colonial power).

16. Frank Sejersen, *Rethinking Greenland and the Arctic in the Era of Climate Change* (Abingdon: Routledge, 2015), 18.

17. Ibid., 20–21.

18. Declaration on the Rights of Indigenous Peoples, UN General Assembly Resolution 61/295, September 13, 2007 (UNDRIP). This is explored in more depth in chapter 7.

19. Sarah Woodall, "What's in a Name? Meaning of Place Names in Greenland," April 24, 2004, https://2kalaallitnunaatigo.wordpress.com/2014/04/24/whats-in-a -name-meaning-of-place-names-in-greenland/.

20. Sejersen, *Rethinking Greenland*, 19–24.

21. See, for example, Carina Creen and Jan Turtinen, "World Heritage Bureaucracy—How It Works and How It Affects Indigenous Peoples," in *Indigenous Rights in Modern Landscapes*, ed. Lars Elenius, Christina Allard, and Camilla Sandström (Didcot, UK: Taylor and Francis, 2016), 192–93.

22. Adam Stepien, Timo Koivurova, Anna Gremsperger, and Henna Niemi, "Arctic Indigenous Peoples and the Challenge of Climate Change," in *Arctic Marine Governance*, ed. Elizabeth Tedsen, Sandra Cavalieri, and R. Kraemer (Berlin: Springer, 2014).

23. See, for example, Michael Brubaker et al., *Climate Change in Kivalina, Alaska: Strategies for Community Health* (Alaska Native Tribal Health Consortium [ANTHC], January 2011); Kivalina Strategic Management Plan (State of Alaska, 2016).

24. See, for example, Bob Reiss, *The Eskimo and the Oil Man: The Battle at the Top of the World for America* (New York: Business Plus, 2012).

25. See, for example, the State Council Information Office of the People's Republic of China, *China's Arctic Policy* (English translation), January 2018, http://english .gov.cn/archive/white_paper/2018/01/26/content_281476026660336.htm (showing

how China connects its Arctic interest and policy with its rights and obligations under international law).

26. See, for example, Jordan Branch, "'Colonial Reflection' and Territoriality: The Peripheral Origins of Sovereign Statehood," *European Journal of International Relations* 18, no. 2 (2010): 277–97 (arguing that the territoriality of the modern sovereign state emerged from contact with the New World). See also Peder Roberts and Eric Paglia, "Science as National Belonging: The Construction of Svalbard as a Norwegian Space," *Social Studies of Science* 4, no. 66 (2016): 894–911.

27. Statute of the International Court of Justice (ICJ Statute), 1945, 1 U.N.T.S. XVI, article 38(1).

28. UN Convention on the Law of the Sea 1982, 1833 U.N.T.S. 397, part VI.

29. ICJ Statute, article 59.

30. International Law Association, accessed April 17, 2018, http://www.ila-hq.org/.

31. It is not the aim of this book to explain the multifarious versions of these theories—they are like rivers that split and meander into many small streams once they hit the delta. Additional specifics on the theories will be provided as needed in the remaining chapters.

32. Richard Shapcotte, "Critical Theory," in *The Oxford Handbook on International Relations*, ed. Christian Reus Smit and Duncan Snidal (Oxford: Oxford, 2008), 327–45, offers a sophisticated start.

33. The classic article is Andrew Moravcsik, "Taking Preferences Seriously: A Liberal Theory of International Politics," *International Organization* 51, no. 4 (1997): 513–53.

34. Benjamin Miller, *States, Nations, and the Great Powers: The Sources of Regional War and Peace* (Cambridge: Cambridge University Press, 2007).

35. See Geir Hønneland, *Russia and the Arctic: Environment, Identity and Foreign Policy* (London: I. B. Tauris, 2016).

36. Timo Koivurova and Leena Heinämäki, "The Participation of Indigenous Peoples in International Norm-Making in the Arctic," *Polar Record* 42, no. 221 (April 2006): 101–9.

37. Marjo Koivisto and Tim Dunne, "Crisis, What Crisis? Liberal Order Building and World Order Conventions," *Millennium* 35, no. 3 (2010): 615–40; David Lake, *Hierarchy in International Relations* (Ithaca, NY: Cornell University Press, 2011).

38. Stephen Krasner, "Structural Causes and Regime Consequences: Regimes as Intervening Variable," *International Organization* 36, no. 1 (1982): 185–205.

39. Oran Young, *Creating Regimes: Arctic Accords and International Governance* (Ithaca, NY: Cornell University Press, 1998).

40. Ronald Mitchell, "Oran Young and International Institutions," *International Environmental Agreements: Politics, Law and Economics* 13, no. 1 (2013): 1, 6.

41. Alexander Wendt, "Constructing International Politics," *International Security* 26, no. 1 (1995): 71–81.

42. Michael N. Barnett and Kathryn Sikkink, "From International Relations to Global Society," in *The Oxford Handbook of Political Science*, ed. Robert E. Goodin (Oxford: Oxford University Press, 2011), 750.

43. Oran R. Young, "Sugaring Off: Enduring Insights for Long-Term Research on Environmental Governance," *International Environmental Agreements* 13 (2013): 87–105, 91.

CHAPTER 2: A NATURAL AND
HUMAN HISTORY OF THE ARCTIC

1. Gail Fondahl and Joan Nymand Larsen, "Introduction," in *Arctic Human Development Report: Regional Processes and Global Linkages* [AHDR II], ed. Joan Nymand Larsen and Gail Fondahl (Akureyri, Iceland: Norden, 2014), 44, figure 1.1.

2. David Ellis and Martyn Stoker, "The Faroe-Shetland Basin: A Regional Perspective from the Paleocene to the Present Day and Its Relationship to the Opening of the North Atlantic Ocean," *Geological Society*, Special Publication 397, no. 1 (2014): 11.

3. Carolyn Gramling, "As Ice Retreats, Frozen Mosses Emerge to Tell Climate Change Tale," *ScienceNews*, October 6, 2017, https://www.sciencenews.org/article /ice-retreats-frozen-mosses-emerge-tell-climate-change-tale.

4. D. S. Kaufman et al., "Holocene Thermal Maximum in the Western Arctic," *Quaternary Science Reviews* 23, no. 5 (2004): 529.

5. See Zachary Labe, "Arctic Temperatures," accessed April 19, 2018, http://sites .uci.edu/zlabe/arctic-temperatures/ (for graphs of Arctic temperatures).

6. Cheryl Katz, "New Climate Record Transforming Arctic: NOAA," *Arctic Deeply*, December 15, 2015, https://www.newsdeeply.com/arctic/articles/2015/12/16 /new-climate-records-transforming-arctic-noaa.

7. United Nations Treaty Series, chapter XXVII, 7.d, Paris Agreement 2015. See also chapter 10 of this book.

8. Peter Hannam, "'Really Extreme' Global Weather Event Leaves Scientists Aghast," *Sidney Morning Herald*, February 26, 2018, https://www.smh.com.au /environment/climate-change/really-extreme-global-weather-event-leaves-scientists -aghast-20180226-p4z1q4.html.

9. Bob Berwyn, "Polar Vortex: How the Jet Stream and Climate Change Bring on Cold Snaps," *Inside Climate News*, February 2, 2018, https://insideclimatenews.org /news/02022018/cold-weather-polar-vortex-jet-stream-explained-global-warming -arctic-ice-climate-change.

10. See, for example, Andrew Freedman, "Last Time the Arctic Was This Warm Was 120,000 Years Ago," Climate Central, October 31, 2013, http://www.climate central.org/news/the-arctic-is-warmer-now-its-been-in-120000-years-16676.

11. Intergovernmental Panel on Climate Change (IPCC), *Climate Change 2014 Synthesis Report* (Geneva: IPCC 2015), SPM 1.2 (concluding that anthropogenic drivers, including GHG emissions, are "extremely likely to have been the dominant cause of the observed warming since the mid-20th century." "Extremely likely" is defined as 95 to 100 percent probability).

12. "Record Greenhouse Gas Levels Impact Atmosphere and Oceans," World Meteorological Organization, Press Release #1002, September 9, 2014, https://pub lic.wmo.int/en/media/press-release/no-1002-record-greenhouse-gas-levels-impact -atmosphere-and-oceans.

13. Ibid.

14. "Weathering of Rocks Impacts Climate Change," *Phys.Org*, March 5, 2012, https://phys.org/news/2012-03-weathering-impacts-climate.html.

15. Dr. Janice Glime speculated that in addition to warmer water, algae could be making more CO_2. Personal communication, December 12, 2017.

16. Jennifer Bennett, "Ocean Acidification," accessed March 25, 2017, http://ocean.si.edu/ocean-acidification.

17. Kevin Schaefer, "Methane and Frozen Ground," National Snow and Ice Data Center (NSIDC), accessed March 25, 2017, https://nsidc.org/cryosphere/frozen ground/methane.html.

18. Ibid.

19. See, for example, Hajo Eicken, "Indigenous Knowledge and Sea Ice Science: What Can We Learn from Indigenous Ice Users?" in *Knowing Our Ice*, ed. I. Krupnik et al. (Berlin: Springer, 2010).

20. "Arctic Sea Ice Maximum at Second Lowest in the Satellite Record," NSIDC, March 23, 2018, http://nsidc.org/arcticseaicenews/2018/03/arctic-sea-ice-maximum -second-lowest. Arctic Sea Ice Maximum at Second Lowest in the Satellite Record.

21. "Sea Ice Features: Polynyas," NSIDC, accessed February 19, 2018, https://nsidc.org/cryosphere/seaice/characteristics/polynyas.html.

22. P. Assmy et al., "Leads in Arctic Pack Ice Enable Early Phytoplankton Blooms below Snow-Covered Sea Ice," *Science Reporter* 7 (2017): 40850.

23. Eli Kintisch, "The Great Greenland Meltdown," *Science Magazine*, February 23, 2017, http://www.sciencemag.org/news/2017/02/great-greenland-meltdown.

24. See Ólafur Ingólfsson, "Icelandic Glaciers," accessed April 18, 2018, https://notendur.hi.is/oi/icelandic_glaciers.htm.

25. "State of the Cryosphere: Ice Sheets," NSIDC, accessed April 24, 2018, https://nsidc.org/cryosphere/sotc/ice_sheets.html.

26. "Migrating 'Supraglacial' Lakes Could Trigger Future Greenland Ice Loss," Center for Polar Observation and Modeling (CPOM), May 7, 2015, http://cpom .org.uk/migrating-supraglacial-lakes-could-trigger-future-greenland-ice-loss.

27. See chapter 10, box 10.3 on black carbon and the Arctic Council initiative to monitor it.

28. See Tim Osborn and Thomas Kleinen, "The Thermohaline Circulation," accessed April 24, 2018, http://www.cru.uea.ac.uk/documents/421974/1295957 /Info+sheet+%237.pdf/320eba6e-d384-497d-b4fc-2d2c187f805e.

29. Conservation of Arctic Flora and Fauna (CAFF), *Arctic Biodiversity Assessment* (Akureyri, Iceland: Arctic Council, 2013), 68.

30. Ibid., 25.

31. Ibid., 68.

32. Ibid., 461.

33. "Billions of Juvenile Fish under the Arctic Sea Ice," Alfred Wegener Institute, October 12, 2015, https://www.awi.de/en/about-us/service/press/archive/billions-of -juvenile-fish-under-the-arctic-sea-ice.html.

34. Kevin R. Arrigo, "Melting Glaciers Stimulate Large Summer Phytoplankton Blooms in Southwest Greenland Waters," *Geophysical Research Letters* 44, no. 12 (2017): 6278.

35. Thom Hoffman, "Polar Bears Shift from Seals to Bird Eggs as Arctic Ice Melts," *New Scientist*, May 12, 2017, https://www.newscientist.com/article/2130821-polar -bears-shift-from-seals-to-bird-eggs-as-arctic-ice-melts.

36. Andrea Anderson, "Genome Sequencing Suggests Yakutsian Horses Adapted Rapidly to Subarctic," November 24, 2015, https://www.genomeweb.com/sequencing-tech nology/genome-sequencing-suggests-yakutian-horses-adapted-rapidly-subarctic.

37. IPCC, *Climate Change 2014 Synthesis Report*, SPM 1.2.

38. V. Pitulko et al., "Early Presence in the Arctic: Evidence from 45,000 Year Old Mammoth Remains," *Science* 351, no. 6270 (2016): 260–63.

39. Richard Stone, "A Surprising Survival Story in the Siberian Arctic," *Science* 33, no. 5654 (2004): 33. NB: BCE means Before Common Era (formerly BC); CE means Common Era (formerly AD).

40. Torsten Günther et al., "Population Genomics of Mesolithic Scandinavia: Investigating Early Postglacial Migration Routes and High-Latitude Adaptation," *PLOS Biology* 16, no. 1 (2018): e2003703.

41. Noel Broadbent and Jan Storå, *Lapps and Labyrinths: Saami Prehistory, Colonization and Cultural Resilience* (Washington, DC: National Museum of Natural History, 2010), 27 (for the earlier date); Thiseas Christos Lamnidis et al., "Ancient Fennoscandinavian Genomes Reveal Origin and Spread of Siberian Ancestry in Europe," *bioRxiv* 285437, March 22, 2018, doi: https://doi.org/10.1101/285437 (not yet peer-reviewed as of August 2018) (for a more recent date).

42. T. Douglas Price, *Ancient Scandinavia: An Archeological History from the First Humans to the Vikings* (Oxford: Oxford University Press, 2015), chapter 7.

43. Broadbent and Storå, *Lapps and Labyrinths*, 29.

44. Broadbent and Storå, *Lapps and Labyrinths*, 23.

45. Ingrid P. Nuse, "First Scandinavians Came from North and South," *Science Nordic*, January 12, 2018, http://sciencenordic.com/first-scandinavians-came-north-and-south.

46. CAFF, *Arctic Biodiversity Assessment*, 656.

47. Natalia Volodko, "Mitochondrial Genome Diversity in Arctic Siberians," *American Journal of Human Genetics* 82, no. 5 (2008): 1084–1100.

48. See "New Light on First Peopling of the Americas," *Popular Archeology*, July 21, 2015, http://popular-archaeology.com/issue/summer-2015/article/new-light-on-first-peopling-of-the-americas.

49. J. Victor Moreno-Meyar et al., "Terminal Pleistocene Alaskan Genome Reveals First Founding Population of Native Americans," *Nature* 553 (2018): 203.

50. "Paleo" means "old."

51. Lisa M. Hodgetts, "The Changing Pre-Dorset Landscape of SW Hudson Bay, Canada," *Journal of Field Archaeology* 32, no. 4 (2007): 353.

52. See Maanasa Raghavan et al., "The Genetic Prehistory of the New World Arctic," *Science* 345, no. 6200 (2014): 1255832.

53. Ibid.

54. See Mark A. Sicoli and Gary Holton, "Linguistic Phylogenies Support Back-Migration from Beringia to Asia," *PLoS ONE* 9, no. 3 (2014): e91722 (showing that Beringia was the likely source of both languages and that there was complicated two-way traffic across the land bridge).

55. V. M. Kotlyakov, A. A. Velichko, S. A. Vasil'ev, eds., *Human Colonization of the Arctic: The Interaction between Early Migration and the Paleoenvironment* (London: Academic Press, 2017). See also Vladimir Pitulko, "The Arctic Was and Remains an Archaeologic Enigma," *The Arctic*, July 4, 2016, https://arctic.ru/analitic/20160704/386534.html.

56. Ville N. Pimenoff et al., "Northwest Siberian Khanty and Mansi in the Junction of West and East Eurasian Gene Pools as Revealed by Uniparental Markers," *European Journal of Human Genetics* 16 (2008): 1254.

57. See Pan-Inuit Trails, accessed April 9, 2018, http://www.paninuittrails.org/index.html?module=module.paninuittrails.

58. Anna Degteva and Christian Nellemann, "Nenets Migration in the Landscape: Impacts of Industrial Development in Yamal Peninsula, Russia," *Pastoralism: Research, Policy and Practice* 3, no. 15 (2013): 1.

59. Broadbent and Storå, *Lapps and Labyrinths*, 1.

60. See, for example, "Prehistoric Period (until 1050 AD)/The Viking Age," National Museum of Denmark, accessed March 24, 2018, https://en.natmus.dk/historical-knowledge/denmark/prehistoric-period-until-1050-ad/the-viking-age.

61. See Barbara E. Crawford, "The Papar Project," accessed May 4, 2018, http://www.paparproject.org.uk/introduction.html.

62. Birgitta Wallace, "The Norse in Newfoundland," *Newfoundland and Labrador Studies* 19, no. 1 (2003).

63. Hans Christian Gulløv, "The Nature of Contact between Native Greenlanders and Norse," *Journal of the North Atlantic* 1, no. 1 (2008): 16–24 (discussing evidence that Dorset, Inuit, and Norse traded in Greenland at various times).

64. Jukka Korpela, "Finland's Eastern Border after the Treaty of Nöteborg: An Ecclesiastical, Political or Cultural Border?" *Journal of Baltic Studies* 33, no. 4 (2002): 384.

65. Anders Andrén, "'Against War!' Regional Identity across a National Border in Late Medieval and Early Modern Scandinavia," *International Journal of Historical Archaeology* 4 (2000): 315, 316.

66. See "The Christianisation of Russia (988)," accessed May 4, 2018, http://community.dur.ac.uk/a.k.harrington/christin.html.

67. Iver B. Newmann, "Entry into International Society Reconceptualised: The Case of Russia," *Review of International Studies* 37 (2011): 463–84, esp. 481.

68. Ibid., 469.

69. But see Efthymios Nicolaidis and Susan Emanuel, *Science and Eastern Orthodoxy: From the Greek Fathers to the Age of Globalization* (Baltimore: Johns Hopkins University Press, 2011): 40–54, Project Muse (on debates in the Church in Constantinople regarding secular knowledge and ancient Greek science).

70. See Marshall T. Poe, *The Russian Moment in World History* (Princeton, NJ: Princeton University Press, 2003): 38–45, 61–63.

71. Daniel Riches, "Early Modern Military Reform and the Connection between Sweden and Brandenburg-Prussia," *Scandinavian Studies* 77, no. 3 (2005): 347–64.

72. David G. Anderson, "Cultures of Reciprocity and Cultures of Control in the Circumpolar North," *Journal of Northern Studies* 8, no. 2 (2014): 11.

73. Frank Sejersen, *Rethinking Greenland and the Arctic in the Era of Climate Change* (Abingdon: Earthscan, 2015), 18.

74. European conquests of the Inca and Aztecs required more complicated legal gyrations.

75. Julie Cruikshank, *Do Glaciers Listen?* (Vancouver: University of British Columbia Press, 2005), 147.

76. Broadbent and Storå, *Lapps and Labyrinths*, 57.

77. Robert McGhee, *Arctic Voyages of Martin Frobisher: An Elizabethan Adventure* (Montreal: McGill-Queens University Press, 2001), 49–57.

78. Renée Fossett, *In Order to Live Untroubled: Inuit of the Central Arctic, 1550–1940* (Winnipeg: University of Manitoba Press, 2001), 33–39; see also Glyn Williams, *Arctic Labyrinth: The Quest for the Northwest Passage* (Berkeley: University of California Press, 2009), 18–21.

79. See Hudson Bay Company History Foundation, accessed April 24, 2018, http://www.hbcheritage.ca/history.

80. It is now a California State park; see Steven Watrous, "Outpost of an Empire," Fort Ross Conservancy, accessed May 7, 2018, https://www.fortross.org/russian-american-company.htm#Establishment%20of%20the%20California%20Settlement. See also A. A. Istomin, James R. Gibson, and V. A. Tishkov, *Россия в Калифорнии: русские документы о колонии Росс и российско-калифорнийских связях 1803–1850* [Russia in California: Russian Documents about the Ross Colony and Russian-Californian Relations 1803–1850] (Moscow: Nauka, 2005–2012) (for the historic documents on Fort Ross's operations; primarily in Russian).

81. See chapter 3; see also "Treaty with Russia for the Purchase of Alaska," Library of Congress, accessed November 24, 2017, https://www.loc.gov/rr/program/bib/ourdocs/Alaska.html (for electronic versions of all the original documents pertaining to the Alaskan purchase).

82. Josephine Peary, *My Arctic Journal: A Year among Ice-Fields and Eskimos 1891–1892*, with a new introduction by Robert M. Bryce (New York: Cooper Square Press, 2002), 193.

83. Broadbent and Storå, *Lapps and Labyrinths*, 7.

84. Johan Stromgren, "The Swedish State's Legacy of Sami Rights Codified in 1886," in *Indigenous Rights in Scandinavia: Autonomous Sami Law,* ed. Christina Allard and Susann Funderud Skogvang (Farmham, UK: Ashgate, 2015), 95–110; see also H. Eivind Torp, "Sami Hunting and Fishing Rights in Swedish Law," ibid.

85. Andrei V. Golovnev and Gail Osherenko, *Siberian Survival: The Nenets and Their Story* (Ithaca, NY: Cornell University Press, 1999).

86. Marlene Laruelle, *Russia's Arctic Strategies and the Future of the Far North* (Abingdon, UK: Routledge, 2013), 26; see also Charles Emmerson, *The Future History of the Arctic* (New York: Public Affairs, 2010), 25–60.

87. Yvon Csonka and Peter Schweitzer, "Societies and Culture: Change and Persistence," in *Arctic Human Development Report* [AHDR], ed. Joan Nymand Larsen and Gail Fondahl (Akureyri, Iceland: Stefansson Arctic Institute, 2004), 48.

88. See Marlene Laruelle, ed., *New Mobilities and Social Change in Russia's Arctic Region* (Oxford: Routledge, 2017) (on urbanization in the twenty-first-century Russian Arctic).

89. Gérard Duhaime, "Economic Systems," in AHDR, 80; Laruelle, *Russia's Arctic Strategies*, 27–28 and see, especially, 35, on "Russification."

90. See, for example, Truth and Reconciliation Commission of Canada, *Final Report,* 2015, http://www.trc.ca/websites/trcinstitution/index.php?p=890; Louise Friedberg, dir., *Eksperimentet* [The Experiment], 2010 (film).

91. Robert McGhee, *The Last Imaginary Place* (New York: Oxford University Press, 2005), 111, and 108–12, for a discussion of this move.

92. The authors are grateful to Rasmus Gjedssø Bertelsen for clarification of the following sections as well as other aspects of Nordic history.

93. "Brief History of Norway," accessed April 24, 2018, http://www.samfunns kunnskap.no/?page_id=815&lang=en.

94. Patrik Winton, "The Political Economy of Swedish Absolutism, 1789–1809," *European Review of Economic History* 16 (2012): 430–48, esp. 430 and 443.

95. Edward C. Thaden, *Russia's Western Borderlands, 1710–1870* (Princeton, NJ: Princeton University Press, 1984): 81–95 and 201–30.

96. See Johanna Lemola, "Helsinki in 1917," accessed April 24, 2018, https://www.hel.fi/kanslia/helsinkiinfo-en/uutiset/Helsinki-+in-1917.

97. Treaty of Peace with Finland 1947, 48 U.N.T.S. 253.

98. John English, *Ice and Water: People, Politics and the Arctic Council* (Toronto: Allen Lane, 2013), 99–102.

99. International Agreement on the Conservation of Polar Bears 1973, *International Legal Materials* 13 (1974): 13.

100. Mikhail Gorbachev, Speech in Murmansk, October 1, 1987, accessed April 17, 2018, https://www.barentsinfo.fi/docs/Gorbachev_speech.pdf.

101. See Tom Axworthy and Ryan Dean, "Cooperation and Geopolitics in the North Changing the Arctic Paradigm from Cold War to Cooperation: How Canada's Indigenous Leaders Shaped the Arctic Council," *Yearbook of Polar Law* 5 (2013): 18–22. The three indigenous organizations were the ICC, Nordic Sami Council, and the Soviet Association of Small Peoples of the North.

102. English, *Ice and Water*, 126–27.

CHAPTER 3: ARCTIC PLAYERS

1. See chapter 1 on the use of the terms "indigenous people" and "indigenous peoples."

2. See, for example, Jessica Green, *Rethinking Private Authority: Agents and Entrepreneurs in Global Environmental Governance* (Princeton, NJ: Princeton University Press, 2013).

3. Timothy Heleniak and Dimitry Bogoyavlensky, "Arctic Populations and Migration," in *Arctic Human Development Report: Regional Processes and Global Linkages* [AHDR II], ed. Joan Nymand Larsen and Gail Fondahl (Akureyri, Iceland: Norden, 2014), 53.

4. The full list can be found at: Об утверждении перечня коренных малочисленных народов Севера, Сибири и Дальнего Востока Российской Федерации (с изменениями на 26 декабря 2011 года): Правительство Российской Федерации Распоряжение от 17 апреля 2006 года N 536-р [On the Approval of the List of Indigenous Peoples of the North, Siberia, and the Far East of the Russian Federation (as amended on December 26, 2011): Government of the Russian Federation Order of April 17, 2006 No. 536-r], http://docs.cntd.ru/document/901976648 (in Russian). On the seven other groups, see commentary to article 1 of Russian Federation Federal Law on General Principles of Organization the Indigenous Small-Numbered Peoples' Communities of the North, Siberia, and the Far East of the Russian Federation, adopted by the State Duma on July 16, 2000, approved by the Federation Council on July 7, 2000, in Maksim Zadorin, Olga Klisheva, Ksenia Vezhlivtseva, and Daria Antufieva,

Russian Laws on Indigenous Issues: Guarantees, Communities, Territories of Traditional Land Use, Translated and Commented (Rovaniemi, Finland: University of Lapland, 2017).

5. Russia Federation Federal Law on the Guarantees of the Rights of the Indigenous Small-Numbered Peoples of the Russian Federation, adopted by the State Duma on April 16, 1999, approved by the Federation Council on April 22, 1999, article 1.

6. Mauro Mazzi, *Aurora borealis: Diritto polare e comparazione giuridica* [The Northern Lights: Polar law and legal comparison] (Bologna: Filo diritto editore, 2014), 400–401.

7. See "Treaty with Russia for the Purchase of Alaska," Library of Congress, accessed November 24, 2017, https://www.loc.gov/rr/program/bib/ourdocs/Alaska .html (for electronic versions of all the original documents pertaining to the Alaska purchase).

8. Michael Fakhri, "Gauging US and EU Seal Regimes," in *The European Union and the Arctic*, ed. Nengye Liu, Elizabeth A. Kirk, and Tore Henriksen (Leiden, Netherlands: Brill, 2017), 211.

9. Alistair Campbell and Kirk Cameron, "Constitutional Development and Natural Resources in the North," in *Governing the North American Arctic: Sovereignty, Security and Institutions*, ed. Dawn Alexandrea Berry, Nigel Bowles, and Halbert Jones (Basingstoke, UK: Palgrave Macmillan, 2016), 181–82.

10. "Maine and the Arctic," accessed April 10, 2017, http://www.maineandthearc tic.com.

11. See "The Arctic Council" section for an explanation of the Senior Arctic Officials' role.

12. "Quick Facts: Alaska," US Census Bureau, accessed March 1, 2018, https:// www.census.gov/quickfacts/AK.

13. Stephen Haycox, *Frigid Embrace: Politics, Economics, and Environment in Alaska* (Corvallis: Oregon State University Press, 2002), 8.

14. Campbell and Cameron, "Constitutional Development and Natural Resources in the North," 182.

15. Ibid.

16. Haycox, *Frigid Embrace*, 83 and 100.

17. Alaska Native Claims Settlement Act, 1971, 43 US Code § 1601 (ANCSA).

18. The thirteenth corporation received only a cash payment and no land rights.

19. William L. Iggiagruk Hensley, "Conclusion: Inuit Peoples and the Governance of the North American Arctic," in Berry, Bowles, and Jones, eds., *Governing the North American Arctic*, 262; and Campbell and Cameron, "Constitutional Development and Natural Resources in the North," 182–83.

20. Campbell and Cameron, "Constitutional Development and Natural Resources in the North," 183.

21. R. M. Huhndorf and S. M. Huhndorf, "Alaska Native Politics since the Alaska Native Claims Settlement Act," *South Atlantic Quarterly* 110, no. 2 (2011): 385, doi:http://doi.org/10.1215/00382876.1162507.

22. Haycox, *Frigid Embrace*; Fakhri, "Gauging US and EU Seal Regimes," 211.

23. Huhndorf and Huhndorf, "Alaska Native Politics since the Alaska Native Claims Settlement Act."

24. See Chanda L. Meek and Emily Russell, "The Challenges of American Federalism in a Rapidly Changing Arctic," in Berry, Bowles, and Jones, eds., *Governing the North American Arctic*, 165–79 (for an exploration of the overlapping and competing jurisdictions in Alaska).

25. United States, *National Strategy for the Arctic Region* (Washington, DC: The White House, 2013).

26. UN Convention on the Law of the Sea 1982, 1833 U.N.T.S. 397 (UNCLOS).

27. United States, *National Strategy*, 9–10. The US Navy also recognizes the UNCLOS's "provisions related to traditional ocean uses" as customary international law; see US Navy, *Arctic Roadmap 2014–2030* (Washington, DC, 2014), 13.

28. See Joël Plouffe, "U.S. Arctic Foreign Policy in the Era of President Trump: A Preliminary Assessment," Policy Paper, Canadian Global Affairs Institute, November 2017, http://www.cgai.ca/us_arctic_foreign_policy_in_the_era_of_president_trump_a_preliminary_assessment.

29. "Communication Regarding Intent to Withdraw from Paris Agreement," US Department of State, Media Note, August 4, 2017, https://www.state.gov/r/pa/prs/ps/2017/08/273050.htm.

30. Plouffe, "U.S. Arctic Foreign Policy in the Era of President Trump," 12.

31. Alaska Arctic Policy Commission, *Final Report* (2015), 24.

32. Lee Huskey, Ilmo Mäenpää, and Alexander Pelyasov, "Economic Systems," in AHDR II, 152.

33. Campbell and Cameron, "Constitutional Development and Natural Resources in the North," 185.

34. Ibid., 190.

35. Ibid., 191.

36. Tony Penikett, *Hunting the Northern Character* (Vancouver: University of British Columbia Press, 2017), 160 and 171–72.

37. Campbell and Cameron, "Constitutional Development and Natural Resources in the North," 195.

38. See Thierry Rodon, "Offshore Development and Inuit Rights in Inuit Nunangat," in *Governance of Arctic Offshore Oil and Gas*, ed. Cécile Pelaudeix and Ellen Margrethe Basse (Abingdon, UK: Routledge, 2017), 171, on the background to the land claims agreement.

39. Nunavut Land Claims Agreement Act, S.C. 1993, c. 29, articles 3 and 29.

40. Campbell and Cameron, "Constitutional Development and Natural Resources in the North," 185.

41. See Mazzi, *Aurora borealis*, 108–22 (on Nunavik).

42. See Ron Macnab, "'Use It or Lose It' in Arctic Canada: Action Agenda or Election Hype?" *Vermont Law Review* 34 (2009): 3. In fact, the origins of this phrase lie with Franklyn Griffiths; see John English, *Ice and Water: People, Politics and the Arctic Council* (Toronto: Allen Lane, 2013), 146.

43. See Shelagh D. Grant, "Arctic Governance and the Relevance of History," in Berry, Bowles, and Jones, eds., *Governing the North American Arctic*, 42; and Campbell and Cameron, "Constitutional Development and Natural Resources in the North," 187. Although formally granted the right to vote in 1950, most Inuit could not exercise it as they had no polling stations until 1962; First Nations were

universally granted the vote in 1960; see "Indigenous Suffrage," Historic Canada, accessed April 14, 2017, http://www.thecanadianencyclopedia.ca/en/article/indige nous-suffrage.

44. See Grant, "Arctic Governance and the Relevance of History."

45. P. Whitney Lackenbauer and Suzanne Lalonde, "Searching for Common Ground in Evolving Canadian and EU Arctic Strategies," in Liu, Kirk, and Henriksen, eds., *The European Union and the Arctic*, 147. Chapter 7 of this book will explore indigenous rights and human rights in more detail, and we will see that it is not as simple as Trudeau made it first appear.

46. Northwest Territories, Yukon, and Nunavut, *A Northern Vision: A Stronger North and a Better Canada*, Yellowknife, May 2007, http://www.anorthernvision .ca/documents/newvision_english.pdf.

47. Northwest Territories, Yukon, and Nunavut, *A Northern Vision: Building a Better North*, Yellowknife, August 2014, http://www.anorthernvision.ca/documents /NorthernVisionEnglish.pdf.

48. "*Plan nord*," Government of Quebec, accessed April 10, 2017, http://plannord .gouv.qc.ca/en.

49. See Erik Beukel, Frede P. Jensen, and Jens Elo Rytter, *Phasing Out the Colonial Status of Greenland, 1945–1954: A Historical Study* (Copenhagen: Museum Tusculanum Press, University of Copenhagen, 2010).

50. Act no. 473 of June 12, 2009, on Greenland Self-Government.

51. Mazzi, *Aurora borealis*, 300.

52. On Faroese arguments for self-determination, see Gudmundur Alfredsson, "The Faroese People as a Subject of Public International Law," *Faroese Law Review: Fólk of Fullveldi* 1, no. 1 (2001): 45.

53. Denmark Ministry of Foreign Affairs, *Denmark, Greenland, the Faroe Islands: Kingdom of Denmark Strategy for the Arctic 2011–2020* (Copenhagen, 2011) 11.

54. Faroe Islands Prime Minister's Office and Foreign Service, *The Faroe Islands— A Nation in the Arctic: Opportunities and Challenges* (Tórshavn, 2013); see also Alyson Bailes and Beinta í Jákupsstovu, "The Faroe Islands: Genesis of a Strategy," *Stjórnmál og Stjórnssysla* 9, no. 2 (2013).

55. Icelandic Ministry of Foreign Affairs, *Ísland á norðurslóðum* [Iceland in the Arctic] (Reykjavík, 2009), 8 (authors' own translation).

56. Ibid.; see also Rachael L. Johnstone, "Little Fish, Big Pond: Icelandic Interests and Influence in Arctic Governance," *Nordicum Mediterraneum* 11, no. 2 (2016), http:// nome.unak.is/wordpress/volume-11-no-2-2016/conference-proceeding-volume-11 -no-2-2016/little-fish-big-pond-icelandic-interests-influence-arctic-governance.

57. Heleniak and Bogoyavlensky, "Arctic Populations and Migration," 88.

58. Act no. 85 of June 17, 2005, relating to Legal Relations and Management of Land and Natural Resources in the County of Finnmark.

59. See the section on "The Barents Euro-Arctic Region (BEAR)."

60. Norwegian Ministry of Foreign Affairs, *The Norwegian Government's High North Strategy* (Oslo, 2006).

61. Ibid., 7.

62. Huskey, Mäenpää, and Pelyasov, "Economic Systems," 152.

63. Heleniak and Bogoyavlensky, "Arctic Populations and Migration," 88.

64. See, for example, Sverker Sörlin, "The Reluctant Arctic Citizen: Sweden and the North," in *Polar Geopolitics: Knowledges, Resources and Legal Regimes*, ed. Richard C. Powell and Klaus Dodds (Cheltenham, UK: Edward Elgar, 2014), 149–65.

65. Swedish Ministry of Foreign Affairs, *Sweden's Strategy for the Arctic Region* (Stockholm, 2011), 12–17.

66. Finland, Prime Minister's Office, *Finland's Strategy for the Arctic Region 2013*, Prime Minister's Office Publications 16/2013 (Helsinki, 2013), 7.

67. Heleniak and Bogoyavlensky, "Arctic Populations and Migration," 88.

68. *Finland's Strategy*, 44.

69. *Finland's Strategy*, 43. Graczyk contrasts Finland with Sweden's more closed approach to Arctic governance; see Piotr Graczyk, "The Arctic Council Inclusive of Non-Arctic Perspectives: Seeking a New Balance," in *The Arctic Council: Its Place in the Future of Arctic Governance*, ed. Thomas S. Axworthy, Timo Koivurova, and Waliul Hasanat (Toronto: Gordon Foundation, Monk School of Global Affairs and Arctic Centre, 2012), 275. See also *Finland's Strategy*, 46–47.

70. Markku Heikkilä and Marjo Laukkanen, *The Arctic Calls: Finland, the European Union and the Arctic Region* (Helsinki: Europe Information/Finnish Ministry for Foreign Affairs, 2013), 51.

71. Marlene Laruelle, *Russia's Arctic Strategies and the Future of the Far North* (Abingdon, UK: Routledge, 2013), xxi.

72. The Republic of Crimea and the Federal City of Sevastopol.

73. The Decree of the President of the Russian Federation on Land Territory in the Arctic Zone of the Russian Federation, no. 296, Signed May 2, 2014, by the President in Moscow (translated by Irina Zhilina).

74. Geir Hønneland, *Russia and the Arctic: Environment, Identity and Foreign Policy* (London: I. B. Taurus, 2016), 64.

75. Huskey, Mäenpää, and Pelyasov, "Economic Systems," 170.

76. Ibid., 173–76.

77. See "Arctic State Socioeconomic Circumpolar Database," accessed October 30, 2018, http://www.arcticstat.org.

78. Ibid., 54–55 and 64–65.

79. Laruelle, *Russia's Arctic Strategies and the Future of the Far North*, 47.

80. See, for example, Mazzi, *Aurora borealis*, 288–96 (on Inuit in Chukotka).

81. Russian Federation Federal Law on General Principles of Organization the Indigenous Small-Numbered Peoples' Communities; Russian Federation Federal Law on Territories of Traditional Land Use of the Indigenous Small-Numbered Peoples of the North, Siberia, and the Far East of the Russian Federation, adopted by the State Duma on April 3, 2001.

82. Russia Federation Federal Law on the Guarantees of the Rights of the Indigenous Small-Numbered Peoples, article 1(1).

83. Heleniak and Bogoyavlensky, "Arctic Populations and Migration," 88.

84. Laruelle, *Russia's Arctic Strategies and the Future of the Far North*, 37.

85. Russian Federation Federal Law on General Principles of Organization the Indigenous Small-Numbered Peoples' Communities, articles 8 and 20.

86. Anna Koch and Alexandra Tomaselli, "Indigenous Peoples' Rights and Their (New) Mobilizations in Russia," EDAP Paper 02/2015 (2015), 13–14, http://aei.pitt.edu/62427.

87. The full statement is reproduced in Jane George, "Arctic Council Officials Call for Reinstatement of Russian Indigenous Org," *Nunatsiaq Online*, November 15, 2012, http://www.nunatsiaqonline.ca/stories/article/65674arctic_council_calls_for _russian_indigenous_orgs_return.

88. Mazzi, *Aurora borealis*, 292–95.

89. Heleniak and Bogoyavlensky, "Arctic Populations and Migration," 88.

90. President of the Russian Federation, *The Fundamentals of State Policy of the Russian Federation in the Arctic in the Period till 2020 and Beyond*, September 18, 2008. Unofficial English Translation: https://icr.arcticportal.org/index.php?op tion=com_content&view=article&id=1791%3. See also K. Zaikov, A. Tamitskiy, and M. Zadorin, "Legal and Political Framework of the Federal and Regional Legislation on National Ethnic Policy in the Russian Arctic," *Polar Journal* 7, no. 1 (2017): 125.

91. Hønneland, *Russia and the Arctic*, 51–53 and 173.

92. Ibid., 171; see also Lackenbauer and Lalonde, "Searching for Common Ground in Evolving Canadian and EU Arctic Strategies," 151; and chapter 8 of this volume.

93. "Free Trade Agreement between Iceland and China," Iceland Ministry for Foreign Affairs, accessed April 10, 2017, http://www.mfa.is/foreign-policy/trade/free -trade-agreement-between-iceland-and-china; see also Matthew Willis and Duncan Depledge, "How We Learned to Stop Worrying about China's Arctic Ambitions," The Arctic Institute, September 22, 2014, http://www.thearcticinstitute.org/092214-chi na-arctic-ambitions-arctic-counci.

94. See, for example, Andreas Kuersten, "Russian Sanctions, China, and the Arctic," *Diplomat*, January 3, 2015, http://thediplomat.com/2015/01/russian-sanctions -china-and-the-arctic; Atle Staalesen, "Russians Choose Chinese Explorers for Arctic Oil," *Alaska Dispatch News*, April 28, 2016, https://www.adn.com/arctic/article /russians-choose-chinese-explorers-arctic-oil/2016/04/28; and "Russia's Yamal LNG Gets Round Sanctions with $12B Chinese Loan Deal," *Alaska Dispatch News*, May 4, 2016, http://www.adn.com/article/20160504/russias-yamal-lng-gets-round-sanc tions-12b-chinese-loan-deal.

95. The State Council Information Office of the People's Republic of China, *China's Arctic Policy* (English translation), January 2018, http://english.gov.cn/archive /white_paper/2018/01/26/content_281476026660336.htm.

96. Japan, Headquarters for Ocean Policy, *Japan's Arctic Policy* (Tokyo, 2015).

97. See, generally, P. Whitney Lackenbauer and James Manicom, "Asian States and the Arctic: National Perspectives on Regional Governance," in *Handbook of Politics in the Arctic*, ed. Leif Christian Jensen and Geir Hønneland (Cheltenham, UK: Edward Elgar, 2015), 517–32; Timo Koivurova, Tianbao Qin, Sébastien Duyck, and Tapio Nykänen, eds., *Arctic Law and Governance: The Role of China and Finland* (Oxford: Hart Publishing, 2017); and Linda Jakobson and Seong-Hyon Lee, "North East Asia Eyes the Arctic," in *The New Arctic Governance*, ed. Linda Jakobson and Neil Melvin (Oxford: Oxford University Press, 2016), 111–46.

98. If, as expected, the United Kingdom leaves, the EU will have only twenty-seven member states.

99. Treaty amending, with regard to Greenland, the Treaties establishing the European Communities, February 1, 2015, *Official Journal of the European Communities*, no. L 29/4.

100. See, for example, Piotr Kobza, "European Union–Greenland Relations after 2015: A Partnership Beyond Fisheries," *Journal of Military and Strategic Studies* 16, no. 4 (2016): 130.

101. Nengje Liu, Elizabeth A. Kirk, and Tore Henriksen, "Conclusion," in *The European Union and the Arctic*, 360.

102. See, for example, Njord Wegge, "The European Union's Arctic Policy," in Jensen and Hønneland, eds., *Handbook of Politics in the Arctic*, 533–49.

103. Adam Stępień and Timo Koivurova, "Formulating a Cross-Cutting Policy: Challenges and Opportunities for Effective EU Arctic Policy-Making," in Liu, Kirk, and Henriksen, eds., *The European Union and the Arctic*, 14.

104. EU Council, *Council Conclusions on Developing a European Union Policy towards the Arctic Region*, 3312th Foreign Affairs Council meeting, May 12, 2014.

105. See "The Arctic Council" section.

106. EU Directorate General for External Policies, Policy Department, *EU Competences Affecting the Arctic*, EP/EXPO/B/AFET/FWC/2009-01/LOT2/04 (Brussels, 2010), 8.

107. Ibid., 8–10.

108. EU Parliament, Resolution of 9th October 2008 on Arctic Governance, OJ C 316 E 41, December 11, 2008.

109. See box 6.2 in chapter 6 for a summary of the dispute.

110. EU Commission, *Joint Communication to the European Parliament and the Council: An Integrated European Union Policy for the Arctic* [JOIN (2016) 21 final], April 27, 2016.

111. Piotr Graczyk and Timo Koivurova, "The Arctic Council," in Jensen and Hønneland, eds., *Handbook of Politics in the Arctic*, 312.

112. See Klaus Dodds, "Anticipating the Arctic and the Arctic Council: Preemption, Precaution and Preparedness," in Axworthy, Koivurova, and Hasanat, eds., *The Arctic Council*, 1–28.

113. English, *Ice and Water*, 176, 262, and 270.

114. Arctic Council Rules of Procedure, as adopted by the Arctic Council at the First Arctic Council Ministerial Meeting, Iqaluit, Canada, September 17–18, 1998, and revised by the Arctic Council at the Eighth Arctic Council Ministerial Meeting, Kiruna, Sweden, May 15, 2013, Rule 19, https://oaarchive.arctic-council.org/handle/11374/940.

115. Ibid., Rule 7; the same applies to decisions of working groups, see Rule 8.

116. Michael Byers, *International Law in the Arctic* (Cambridge: Cambridge University Press, 2013), 229–30; Douglas C. Nord, *The Arctic Council: Governance within the Far North* (Abingdon, UK: Routledge, 2016), 38 and 70. Yet the EU was accepted as an observer ad hoc (and, in practice, is treated the same as all the standing observers) notwithstanding objections from at least one of the permanent participants. See also Erik J. Molenaar, "Current and Prospective Roles of the Arctic Council System within the Context of the Law of the Sea," in Axworthy, Koivurova, and Hasanat, eds., *The Arctic Council*, 164.

117. Arctic Council Rules of Procedure, Rule 36 and Annex 2.

118. Ibid., Annex 2.

119. Ibid., Rule 38.

120. Ibid., Rules 12, 19, and 38.

121. Arctic Council Observer Manual for Subsidiary Bodies, as adopted by the Arctic Council at the Eighth Arctic Council Ministerial Meeting, Kiruna, Sweden, May 15, 2013, and Addendum, approved by the Senior Arctic Officials at the Meeting of the Senior Arctic Officials, Anchorage, United States, October 20–22, 2015, and Portland, Maine, United States, October 4, 2016, para. 7.3, https://oaarchive.arctic-council.org/handle/11374/939.

122. Arctic Council Rules of Procedure, Rule 37 and Annex 2, Rule 5.

123. United Kingdom, House of Lords Select Committee on the Arctic, *Responding to a Changing Arctic*, HL Paper 118, London, The Stationery Office, Ltd., 2015 (London: HLAC, 2015), para. 141.

124. Ibid., para. 225, referencing Jeffrey Mazo.

125. Graczyk, "The Arctic Council Inclusive of Non-Arctic Perspectives," 278–79.

126. See, for example, Daniel M. Kliman, *Fateful Transitions: How Democracies Manage Rising Powers, from the Eve of World War I to China's Ascendance* (Philadelphia: University of Pennsylvania Press, 2014), 106.

127. Joseph Nye, "Work with China, Don't Contain It," *New York Times* Op-Ed., January 25, 2013, http://www.nytimes.com/2013/01/26/opinion/work-with-china-dont-contain-it.html.

128. United States, National Security Presidential Directive and Homeland Security Presidential Directive, January 9, 2009, para. III.C.2, https://fas.org/irp/offdocs/nspd/nspd-66.htm; compare *Finland's Strategy*, 44.

129. Agreement on Cooperation on Aeronautical and Maritime Search and Rescue in the Arctic 2011, accessed March 1, 2018, https://oaarchive.arctic-council.org/handle/11374/531; Agreement on Cooperation on Marine Oil Pollution Preparedness and Response in the Arctic 2013, accessed March 1, 2018, https://oaarchive.arctic-council.org/handle/11374/529; Agreement on Enhancing International Arctic Scientific Cooperation 2017, accessed November 24, 2017, https://www.state.gov/e/oes/rls/other/2017/270809.htm.

130. Graczyk, "The Arctic Council Inclusive of Non-Arctic Perspectives," 274.

131. See Molenaar, "Current and Prospective Roles of the Arctic Council System," 141–89.

132. Declaration on the Establishment of the Arctic Council, September 19, 1996 (Ottawa Declaration), para. 1a, accessed April 10, 2017, https://oaarchive.arctic-council.org/handle/11374/85.

133. See Molenaar, "Current and Prospective Roles of the Arctic Council System," 155.

134. But see Byers, *International Law in the Arctic*, 256–61.

135. Different conceptions of security are the topic of the next chapter.

136. See Nord, *The Arctic Council*, 72–74.

137. Evan T. Bloom, "United States Perspectives on the Arctic," in Berry, Bowles, and Jones, eds., *Governing the North American Arctic*, 236.

138. Martin Breum, "When the Arctic Council Speaks: How to Move the Council's Communication into the Future," in Axworthy, Koivurova, and Hasanat, *The Arctic Council*, 120.

139. See Molenaar, "Current and Prospective Roles of the Arctic Council System," 157, and below, on the role of the IMO.

140. Foreign Ministers of Canada, Denmark, Norway, Russia, and the United States, *The Ilulissat Declaration*, May 2008.

141. See chapter 8.

142. The Kirkenes Declaration from the Conference of Foreign Ministers on Cooperation in the Barents Euro-Arctic Region, January 11, 1993; see also Hønneland, chapter 5; and Alyson J. K. Bailes and Kristmundur Þ. Ólafsson, "The EU Crossing Arctic Frontiers: The Barents Euro-Arctic Council, Northern Dimension, and EU-West Nordic Relations," in Liu, Kirk, and Henriksen, *The European Union and the Arctic*, 14.

143. Geir Hønneland, "Cross Border Cooperation in the North: The Case of Northwest Russia," in *Russia and the North*, ed. Elana Wilson Rowe (Ottawa: University of Ottawa Press, 2009), 35–52.

144. See Bailes and Ólafsson, "The EU Crossing Arctic Frontiers," 47.

145. Michael Łuszczuk, "Evolution of Poland's Approach towards the Arctic: From International Scientific Cooperation to Science Diplomacy," in Jensen and Hønneland, eds., *Handbook of Politics in the Arctic*, 573.

146. Elana Wilson and Indra Øverland, "Indigenous Issues," in *International Cooperation and Arctic Governance: Regime Effectiveness and Northern Region Building*, ed. Olav Schram Stokke and Geir Hønneland (Abingdon, UK: Routledge, 2007), 36–37.

147. Geir Hønneland and Leif Christian Jensen, "Norway's Approach to the Arctic: Policies and Discourse," in Jensen and Hønneland, eds., *Handbook of Politics in the Arctic*, 467–68.

148. See Irina Zhilina, "The Security Aspects in the Arctic: The Potential Role of NATO," *Nordicum Mediterraneum* 8, no. 1 (2013), http://nome.unak.is/word press/08-1/c48-article/the-security-aspects-in-the-arctic-the-potential-role-of-nato.

149. See chapters 8 and 9.

150. Paris Agreement, December 12, 2015, U.N.T.S., C.N. 92.2016. TREATIES-XXVII.7.d.

151. "Save the Arctic," Greenpeace, accessed April 10, 2017, https://www.savethe arctic.org.

152. Alyson J. K. Bailes, "Options for Closer Cooperation in the High North: What Is Needed?" in *Security Prospects in the High North: Geostrategic Thaw or Freeze?*, ed. Sven G. Holtsmark and Brooke A. Smith-Windsor (Rome: NATO Defence College, 2009), 29.

153. "The Arctic," WWF Global, accessed April 10, 2017, http://wwf.panda.org /what_we_do/where_we_work/arctic.

154. See chapter 7 on indigenous and human rights and chapter 10 on environmental law in the Arctic.

155. See Jennifer Rhemann, "Looking Within and Outside the Arctic to Increase the Governance Capacity of the Arctic Council," in Axworthy, Koivurova, and Hasanat, eds., *The Arctic Council*, 29 (for more or research and science).

156. James N. Rosenau, *Turbulence in World Politics* (Princeton, NJ: Princeton University Press, 1990); see also James N. Rosenau and Mary H. Durfee, *Thinking Theory Thoroughly*, 2nd ed. (Boulder, CO: Westview, 2000), chapter 4.

CHAPTER 4: SECURITIES IN THE ARCTIC

1. See, for example, John Lewis Gaddis, *The Cold War: A New History* (New York: Penguin, 2005), especially at 266: "It began with a return of fear and ended in a triumph of hope, an unusual trajectory for great historical upheavals."

2. See Gerald Zojer and Kamrul Hossain, *Rethinking Multifaceted Human Security Threats in the Barents Region: A Multilevel Approach to Societal Security,* Juridica Lapponica 42 (Rovaniemi, Finland: Lapin yliopisto, 2017) (for a discussion of how human securities interact in a region of the Arctic).

3. Alyson Bailes, "Security in the Arctic: Definitions, Challenges and Solutions," in *The New Arctic Governance*, ed. Linda Jakobson and Neil Melvin (Oxford: Oxford University Press, 2016), 13–40, esp. 37.

4. US Department of Defense, *National Security Implications of Climate-Related Risks and a Changing Climate,* July 2015, http://archive.defense.gov/pubs/150724-congressional-report-on-national-implications-of-climate-change.pdf?source=govdelivery.

5. Bailes, "Security in the Arctic," 32–34.

6. Lára Jóhannsdóttir and David Cook, *An Insurance Perspective on Arctic Opportunities and Risks: Hydrocarbon Exploration and Shipping* (Reykjavík: Institute of International Affairs, University of Iceland, 2015), http://ams.hi.is/wp-content/uploads/2015/04/An_Insurance_Perspective_PDF.pdf.

7. Knut Espen Solberg, Robert Brown, Eirik Skogvoll, and Ove Tobias Gudmestad, "Risk Reduction as a Result of Implementation of the Functional Based IMO Polar Code in the Arctic Cruise Industry," in *The Inter-Connected Arctic*, ed. Kiirsi Latola and Hannele Savela (Berlin: Springer, 2017), 266.

8. Arja Rautio, Birger Poppel, and Kue Young, "Human Health and Well-Being," in *Arctic Human Development Report: Regional Processes and Global Linkages* [AHDR II], ed. Joan Nymand Larsen and Gail Fondahl (Akureyri, Iceland: Norden, 2014), 309; Rasmus Ole Rasmussen, Grete K. Hoverlsrud, and Shari Gearheard, "Community Viability and Adaptation," in AHDR II, 437; Joan Nymand Larsen and Gail Fondahl, "Major Findings and Emerging Trends in Arctic Human Development," in AHDR II, 489–90.

9. See, for example, the discussions on whaling controversies in chapter 5 and on the sale of seal products in chapter 6.

10. Heather N. Nicol and Lassi Heininen, "Human Security, the Arctic Council and Climate Change: Cooperation or Coexistence," *Polar Record* 50, no. 11 (January 2014): 80–85.

11. UN Trust Fund for Human Security, *Human Security in Theory and Practice* (New York: United Nations, 2009), 7.

12. Zojer and Hossain, *Rethinking Multifaceted Human Security Threats.* See also Gérard Duhaime and Andrée Caron, "Economic and Social Conditions of the Arctic Regions," in *The Economy of the North 2008*, ed. Solveig Glomsrød and Julie Aslaksen (Oslo: Statistics Norway, 2009).

13. Stephen Cornell and Joseph Kalt, *Alaska Native Self-Government and Service Delivery: What Works?* Harvard Project on American Indian Economic Development, Joint Occasional Papers on Native Affairs, No. 2003-01 (Tucson: University of Arizona; Cambridge, MA: Harvard University).

14. See W. N. Adger et al., "Human Security," in *Climate Change 2014: Impacts, Adaptation, and Vulnerability. Part A: Global and Sectoral Aspects. Contribution of Working Group II to the Fifth Assessment Report of the Intergovernmental Panel on Climate Change*, ed. C. B. Field et al. (Cambridge: Cambridge University Press, 2014), 755–91 (for an overview of the human security issues connected to climate change).

15. Wendy Eisner, "How Has Inupiaq Knowledge Helped Our Understanding of Environmental Change on the North Slope of Alaska?" Lecture at Michigan Technological University, October 23, 2015.

16. The enjoyment of culture is also a *human right* that is protected for all people but especially for those who belong to minorities. See chapter 7.

17. See Bruce Forbes, "Cultural Resilience of Social-Ecological Systems in the Nenets and Yamal-Nenets Autonomous Okrugs, Russia: A Focus on Reindeer Nomads of the Tundra," *Ecology and Society* 18, no. 4 (2013): 36 (for examples of high human agency in living in the Arctic in spite of some government policies).

18. This is especially true of the United States and Russia, but not so much for Iceland, which has no military and relies on NATO. Sweden, at least at this writing, has maintained neutrality for more than a century.

19. Iceland then and now has a coast guard. See "Iceland's Defense and NATO Operations in Iceland," March 8, 2017, http://www.act.nato.int/images/stories /events/2017/resconf/keflavik-1.pdf (for a summary of Iceland's Coast Guard and NATO's operations).

20. Trude Pettersen, "U.S. Military Returns to Iceland," *Barents Observer*, February 10, 2016, https://thebarentsobserver.com/en/security/2016/02/us-military-re turns-iceland.

21. Quoted in Charles J. V. Murphy, "The Polar Concept Is Revolutionizing American Strategy," *Life*, January 20, 1947, 61–62.

22. Thomas Nilsen, "Russia Plays Massive Nuclear War Games across the Arctic," *Independent Barents Observer*, October 26, 2017, https://thebarentsobserver.com /en/security/2017/10/russia-launched-massive-nuclear-missiles-drill-across-arctic.

23. Jim Garamone, "NATO Defense Ministers Approve New Alliance Commands," US Department of Defense, February 14, 2018, https://www.defense.gov/News/Arti cle/Article/1441942/nato-defense-ministers-approve-new-alliance-commands.

24. Founding Act on Mutual Relations, Cooperation, and Security between NATO and the Russian Federation, May 27, 1997, https://www.nato.int/nrc-website /media/59451/1997_nato_russia_founding_act.pdf.

25. NATO, "About NRC," accessed March 27, 2018, https://www.nato.int /nrc-website/en/about/index.html.

26. NATO, "Secretary General Discusses NATO-Russia Council," October 26, 2017, https://www.nato.int/cps/en/natohq/news_147972.htm.

27. See Michael Byers, "Canada—Russia's Toxic Waste Dump," *National Post*, May 18, 2016, http://nationalpost.com/opinion/canada-russias-toxic-waste-dump (on concerns about the danger and toxicity of some Russian rocket stages).

28. See Arctic Coast Guard Forum, accessed April 17, 2018, https://www.arctic coastguardforum.com/; see also Rebecca Pincus, "The Arctic Coast Guard Forum: A Welcome and Important Step," *Arctic Yearbook* (2015), https://www.arcticyear book.com/toc2015.

29. Alex Horton, "The Navy Is Resurrecting a Fleet to Protect the East Coast and North Atlantics from Russia," *Washington Post*, May 6, 2018. The Navy decided on this after a review of accidents in the Pacific. It may be an effort to cope with handling too many global missions with too few people.

30. The theory was originally proposed by A. F. K. Organski, *World Politics* (New York: Alfred A. Knopf, 1958).

31. Ian Clark, *Hegemony in International Society* (Oxford: Oxford University Press, 2011). See also Ian Clark, "China and the United States: A Succession of Hegemonies?" *International Affairs* 87, no. 1 (2011): 13–28; and Yongjin Zhang, "China and Liberal Hierarchies in Global International Society: Power and Negotiation of Normative Change," *International Affairs* 92, no. 4 (2016): 795–816.

32. The State Council Information Office of the People's Republic of China, *China's Arctic Policy* (English translation), January 2018, http://english.gov.cn/archive/white_paper/2018/01/26/content_281476026660336.htm.

33. US Department of Defense, *Report to Congress on Strategy to Protect United States National Security Interests in the Arctic Region*, December 2016, 3–4, https://www.sullivan.senate.gov/imo/media/doc/2016_ArcticStrategy-Unclass.pdf.

34. President of the Russian Federation, *The Fundamentals of State Policy of the Russian Federation in the Arctic in the Period till 2020 and Beyond*, September 18, 2008. Unofficial English translation: https://icr.arcticportal.org/index.php?option=com_content&view=article&id=1791%3; President of the Russian Federation, *The Development Strategy of the Arctic Zone of the Russian Federation and the National Security up to 2020*, February 12, 2013. Unofficial English translation: www.mid.ru/brp_4.nsf/0/76389FEC168189ED44257B2E0039B16D.

35. Lassi Heininen, Alexander Sergunin, and Gleb Yarovoy, *Strategies in the Arctic: Avoiding a New Cold War*. Research Report to the Valdai Discussion Club, 2014. http://vid-1.rian.ru/ig/valdai/arctic_eng.pdf.

36. One might compare the Russian situation to US bases along the East, West, and Gulf coasts; California alone has just over two dozen military bases; see Governor's Military Council, "California Military Bases," accessed April 17, 2018, http://militarycouncil.ca.gov/s_californiamilitarybases.php.

37. Marlene Laruelle, *Russia's Arctic Strategies and the Future of the Far North* (New York: M. E. Sharpe, 2014), 126.

38. Robert McNamara, secretary of defense under John F. Kennedy, asked that question. See Alain C. Enthoven and K. Wayne Smith, *How Much Is Enough? Shaping the Defense Program, 1961–1969* (Santa Monica, CA: Rand Publishing, 2006).

39. A "blue water" navy is one that can sail long distances from home.

40. Neil MacFarquhar, "A Powerful Russian Weapon: The Spread of False Stories," *New York Times*, August 28, 2016, https://www.nytimes.com/2016/08/29/world/europe/russia-sweden-disinformation.html. Russian disinformation has proven far more robust and widespread than originally thought.

41. Consolidated Versions of the Treaty on European Union and the Treaty on the Functioning of the European Union, 2010 O.J. (C83), 2012 O.J. (C326).

42. European Union External Action Service, Permanent Structured Cooperation (PESCO)—Fact Sheet, April 5, 2018, https://eeas.europa.eu/headquarters/headquarters-homepage/34226/permanent-structured-cooperation-pesco-factsheet_en.

43. NATO, "Secretary General Participates in Hybrid Center of Excellence Inauguration with Finnish Leaders and EU High Representative," October 2, 2017, https://www.nato.int/cps/en/natohq/news_147497.htm.

44. See chapters 8 and 9.

45. Marie-Danielle Smith, "Trudeau Government Announces 'Rational' Shift in Arctic Policy, Will Seek to Work with Russia," *National Post*, October 1, 2016, http://news.nationalpost.com/news/canada/canadian-politics/trudeau-government -announces-rational-shift-in-arctic-policy-will-seek-to-work-with-russia.

46. Ken Booth and Nicholas J. Wheeler, *The Security Dilemma: Fear, Cooperation, and Trust in World Politics* (London: Palgrave Macmillan, 2008), 4–5.

47. Conor Sweeny, "Medvedev Objects to 'Endless' NATO Expansion," *Reuters*, February 25, 2010, https://www.reuters.com/article/us-russia-medvedev-nato/med vedev-objects-to-endless-nato-expansion-idUSTRE61O2OQ20100225.

48. See Ole Wæver, "Peace and Security: Two Evolving Concepts and Their Changing Relationship," in *Globalization and Environmental Challenges: Reconceptualizing Security in the 21st Century*, ed. Hans Grunter Brauch et al. (Berlin: Springer-Link, 2008), 99–111.

49. Nerijus Adomaitis, "Hundreds of U.S. Marines in Norway Irks Russia," *Reuters*, January 16, 2017, http://www.reuters.com/article/us-norway-usa-military-idUSKB N1501CD.

50. Björn von Sydow, "Resilience: Planning for Sweden's 'Total Defence,'" *NATO Review Magazine*, April 4, 2018, https://www.nato.int/docu/review/2018 /Also-in-2018/resilience-planning-for-swedens-total-defence/EN/index.htm.

51. Mikhail Gorbachev, Speech in Murmansk, October 1, 1987, accessed April 17, 2018, https://www.barentsinfo.fi/docs/Gorbachev_speech.pdf.

52. See Håvard Hegre, "Democracy and Armed Conflict," *Journal of Peace Research* 51, no. 2 (2014): 159–72.

53. See, for example, John Mearsheimer, *The Tragedy of the Great Powers* (London: W. W. Norton & Co., 2014).

54. Kristofer Bergh and Ekaterina Klimenko, "Understanding National Approaches to Security in the Arctic," in Jakobson and Melvin, eds., *The New Arctic Governance*.

55. See Siemon T. Wezeman, *Military Capabilities in the Arctic: A New Cold War in the High North?* Stockholm International Peace Research Institute, October 2016, https://www.sipri.org/sites/default/files/Military-capabilities-in-the-Arctic.pdf (arguing that armaments in the Arctic were for defensive purposes).

56. Colin Grey, "The Arms Race Phenomenon," *World Politics* 24, no. 1 (1971): 39–79.

57. Frédéric Lasserre, Jérôme Le Roy, and Richard Garon, "Is There an Arms Race in the Arctic?" *Journal of Military and Strategic Studies* 14, nos. 3 and 4 (2012): 1–56, esp. 47.

58. Ibid., 48.

59. The estimated direct costs of US military activity in these areas through 2016 is $4.79 trillion USD, excluding the cost of lives lost or the expenses and losses of other states. See Neta Crawford, "US Budgetary Costs of Wars through 2016," Watson Center, Brown University, September 2017, http://watson.brown.edu/costsof war/files/cow/imce/papers/2016/Costs%20of%20War%20through%202016%20 FINAL%20final%20v2.pdf.

60. Samuel Osborne, "Sweden Brings Back Military Conscription in Face of Growing Russia Threat," *Independent*, March 2, 2017, https://www.independent.co.uk/news/world/europe/sweden-military-conscription-draft-russia-balkan-threat-men-women-a7607411.html.

61. Bailes, "Security in the Arctic," 18.

62. Ibid.

63. US Department of Defense, Office of Economic Adjustment, *Defense Spending by State, Fiscal Year 2015*, http://www.oea.gov/sites/default/files/resources/fy2015-statesonly-508-final-sm_0.pdf.

64. Carl Conetta and Charles Knight, "Post–Cold War US Military Expenditures in the Context of World Spending Trends," Project on Defense Alternatives, January 1997, http://www.comw.org/pda/bmemo10.htm#2, table 1 (illustrating before and after Cold War spending).

65. It is not even clear that there is a US-Chinese arms race, though the Chinese are surely spending heavily and are second only to the United States in total military expenditure.

66. See, for example, Jon Bowerman, "The Last Front of the Cold War," *Atlantic*, November 1993, https://www.theatlantic.com/past/politics/foreign/front.htm.

67. Andres Mäe, *Impact of Sanctions on the Russian Oil Sector*, Estonian Foreign Policy Institute, No. 29 (March 2016), http://www.evi.ee/wp-content/uploads/2016/02/EVI-mottepaber29_m%C3%A4rts16.pdf.

68. EEAS diplomat, personal communication to Durfee, March 2015.

69. Heininen, Sergunin, and Yarovoy, *Strategies in the Arctic*, 74.

70. US Department of Defense, *National Security Implications of Climate-Related Risks and Changing Climate* (Washington, DC: Department of Defense, 2015), 5.

CHAPTER 5: ARCTIC ECONOMIES AND RESOURCES

1. Lee Huskey, Ilmo Mäenpää, and Alexander Pelyasov, "Economic Systems," in *Arctic Human Development Report: Regional Processes and Global Linkages* [AHDR II], ed. Joan Nymand Larsen and Gail Fondahl (Akureyri, Iceland: Norden, 2014), 156.

2. Bruce Forbes and Gary Kofinas, "Resource Governance," in AHDR II, 271.

3. See, for example, Stephen Cornell and Joseph Kalt, *Alaska Native Self-Government and Service Delivery: What Works?* Joint Occasional Papers on Native Affairs, No. 2003-01 (Cambridge, MA: Harvard Project on American Indian Economic Development, 2003).

4. Huskey, Mäenpää, and Pelyasov, "Economic Systems," 163; see also Joan Nymand Larsen et al., "Tracking Change in Human Development in the Arctic," in *Arctic Social Indicators ASI II: Implementation* [ASI II], ed. Joan Nymand Larsen, Peter Schweitzer, and Andrey Petrov (Copenhagen: Norden, 2014), 26.

5. See Davin Holen et al., "Interdependency of Subsistence and Market Economies in the Arctic," in *The Economy of the North 2015*, ed. Solveig Glomsrød, Gérard Duhaime, and Iulie Aslaksen (Oslo: Statistics Norway, 2017).

6. Iulie Aslaksen et al., "Interdependency of Subsistence and Market Economies in the Arctic," in *The Economy of the North 2008*, ed. Solveig Glomsrød and Iulie Aslaksen (Oslo: Statistics Norway, 2009), 76.

7. Tony Penikett, *Hunting the Northern Character* (Vancouver: University of British Columbia Press, 2017), 111.

8. Ibid., 114.

9. Rasmus Ole Rasmussen, Johanna Roto, and Lawrence C. Hamilton, "West-Nordic Region," in ASI II, 171–72.

10. Frank Sejersen, *Rethinking Greenland and the Arctic in the Era of Climate Change* (London: Earthscan, 2015), 205–8.

11. Gail Fondahl, Susan Crate, and Viktoria V. Filippova, "Sakha Republic (Yakutia), Russian Federation," in ASI II, 76.

12. Huskey, Mäenpää, and Pelyasov, "Economic Systems," 156.

13. Ibid.

14. Iceland is an exception to the Arctic pattern, having a large tertiary sector: ibid., 165, table 4.2.

15. Timothy Heleniak and Dimitry Bogoyavlensky, "Arctic Populations and Migration," in AHDR II, 16, 71; Stephen Haycox, *Frigid Embrace: Politics, Economics, and Environment in Alaska* (Corvallis: Oregon State University Press, 2002), x.

16. See Joan Nymand Larsen and Gail Fondahl, "Major Findings and Emerging Trends in Arctic Human Development," in AHDR II, 486.

17. Huskey, Mäenpää, and Pelyasov, "Economic Systems," 156.

18. Ibid., 157.

19. Ibid., 151.

20. Ibid., 160.

21. Gérard Duhaime, "Economic Systems," in *Arctic Human Development Report* [AHDR], ed. Joan Nymand Larsen and Gail Fondahl (Akureyri, Iceland: Stefansson Arctic Institute, 2004), 71; see also Forbes and Kofinas, "Resource Governance," 271.

22. Huskey, Mäenpää, and Pelyasov, "Economic Systems," 157–58; and Larsen and Fondahl, "Major Findings," 480.

23. Sovereign rights are explained in depth in chapter 8.

24. Sometimes nuclear energy is considered renewable, but most nuclear power stations depend on the use of radioactive elements found in nature, which are in finite (albeit still very large) supply.

25. "Eight New Sites Inscribed on UNESCO's World Heritage List," UNESCO, July 9, 2017, http://whc.unesco.org/en/news/1689.

26. Gunnar S. Eskeland and Line Sunniva Flottorp, "Climate Change in the Arctic: A Discussion of the Impact on Economic Activity," in *The Economy of the North 2006*, ed. Solveig Glomsrød and Iulie Aslaksen (Oslo: Statistics Norway, 2006), 83.

27. David Michelsen, ed., *Greenland in Figures 2012* (Nuuk, Greenland: Statistics Greenland, 2012), 13, 21.

28. See, for example, Thierry Rodon, "Offshore Development and Inuit Rights in Inuit Nunangat," Cécile Pelaudeix, "Governance of Offshore Hydrocarbon Activities in the Arctic and Energy Policies," and Roman Sidortsov, "The Russian Offshore Oil and Gas Regime," in *Governance of Arctic Offshore Oil and Gas*, ed. Cécile Pelaudeix and Ellen Margrethe Basse (Abingdon, UK: Routledge, 2017).

29. Pelaudeix, "Governance of Offshore Hydrocarbon Activities," 109.

30. See Indra Øverland, "Norway: Public Debate and the Management of Petroleum Resources and Revenues," in *Public Brainpower: Civil Society and Natural Resource Management*, ed. Indra Øverland (New York: Springer, 2018).

31. Pelaudeix, "Governance of Offshore Hydrocarbon Activities," 117.

32. Ibid., 110 and 116.

33. Nina Poussenkova and Indra Øverland, "Russia: Public Debate and the Petroleum Sector," in *Public Brainpower*, 261.

34. Sidortsov, "The Russian Offshore," 127; and Roman Sidortsov, "At the Crossroads of Policy Ambitions and Political Reality: Reflections on the Prospects of LNG Development in Russia," *Oil, Gas and Energy Law Intelligence* 15, no. 4 (2017).

35. Alexander Sergunin, "Is Russian Going Hard or Soft in the Arctic?" *Into the Arctic: The Wilson Quarterly* (Summer/Fall 2017).

36. Sidortsov, "The Russian Offshore."

37. See, for example, Haycox, *Frigid Embrace*; Victoria Herrmann, *Arctic Melt: Turning Resource Extraction into Human Development* (Washington, DC: The Arctic Institute, 2015), 9.

38. Sidortsov, "The Russian Offshore," 129. See also Tina Hunter, "Russian Arctic Policy, Petroleum Resources Development and the EU," in *The European Union and the Arctic*, ed. Nengye Liu, Elizabeth A. Kirk, and Tore Henriksen (Leiden, Netherlands: Brill, 2017).

39. William L. Iggiagruk Hensley, "Conclusion: Inuit Peoples and the Governance of the North American Arctic," in *Governing the North American Arctic: Sovereignty, Security and Institutions*, ed. Dawn Alexandrea Berry, Nigel Bowles, and Halbert Jones (Basingstoke, UK: Palgrave Macmillan 2016), 265.

40. Chris D'Angelo, "Senate One Step Closer to Allowing Drilling in Fragile Arctic Wildlife Refuge," *Huffington Post*, November 15, 2017, http://www.huffingtonpost.co.uk/entry/murkowski-arctic-national-wildlife-refuge-bill_us_5a0c3a33e4b0b17ffce18061; Matt Lee-Ashley, "The Energy Case against Drilling in the Arctic National Wildlife Refuge," *Center for American Progress*, November 13, 2017, https://www.americanprogress.org/issues/green/news/2017/11/13/442603/energy-case-drilling-arctic-national-wildlife-refuge/.

41. Gérard Duhaime and Andrée Caron, "Economic and Social Conditions of the Arctic Regions," in *The Economy of the North 2008*.

42. Marlene Laruelle, *Russia's Arctic Strategies and the Future of the Far North* (Abingdon, UK: Routledge 2013), 81.

43. Laruelle, *Russia's Arctic Strategies*, 138 ($120/barrel); United Kingdom, House of Lords Select Committee on the Arctic, *Responding to a Changing Arctic*, HL Paper 118 (London: The Stationery Office Ltd., 2015), para. 74 ($110/barrel).

44. Bruce Forbes, "Indigenous-Industrial Relations in the Tundra Zone of Russia's Timan-Pechora and Western Siberian Basins," in AHDR II, 270.

45. "Fact Sheet: World Energy Outlook 2016," International Energy Agency, https://www.iea.org/media/publications/weo/WEO2016Factsheet.pdf; see also Pami Aalto and Iida Jaakkola, "Arctic Energy Policy," in *Handbook of Politics in the Arctic*, ed. Leif Christian Jensen and Geir Hønneland (Cheltenham, UK: Edward Elgar, 2015).

46. Duhaime and Caron, "Economic and Social Conditions."

47. Ibid., 13.

48. Ibid., 16.

49. Gérard Duhaime et al., "Social and Economic Inequalities in the Circumpolar Arctic," in *The Economy of the North 2015*, 22.

50. Duhaime and Caron, "Economic and Social Conditions," 16–17.

51. Ibid. (Duhaime and Caron use "Scandinavian" in a broad sense to include Finland and Iceland, which are not geographically Scandinavian.)

52. Ibid., 17–19.

53. Ibid., 15, figure 2.5.

54. Ibid., 21; see also Forbes, "Indigenous-Industrial Relations," 271.

55. Fondahl, Crate, and Filippova, "Sakha Republic," 71.

56. Duhaime and Caron, "Economic and Social Conditions," 20–21; Fondahl, Crate, and Filippova, "Sakha Republic," 61–63 and 68–72.

57. Duhaime and Caron, "Economic and Social Conditions," 20–21; Fondahl, Crate, and Filippova, "Sakha Republic," 80.

58. See, for example, Haycox, *Frigid Embrace*.

59. See, for example, Craig Proulx, "Aboriginal Hip Hoppers," in *Indigenous Cosmopolitans*, ed. Maximilian Christian Forte (New York: Peter Lang, 2010), 50–52.

60. See, for example, Rodon, "Offshore Development," and Katja Göcke, "Uranium Mining in Nunavut," *Yearbook of Polar Law* 5 (2013): 119.

61. See, for example, Peter P. Schweitzer et al., "Inuit Regions of Alaska," in ASI II, 213, and Birger Poppel, "The Inuit World," in ASI II, 264.

62. See chapter 9.

63. Irini Papanicolopulu, "On the Interaction between Law and Science: Considerations on the Ongoing Process of Regulating Underwater Acoustic Pollution," *Aegean Review of the Law of the Sea and Maritime Law* 1, no. 2 (2011): 247; Nicholas Cunningham, "Offshore Oil Drilling in the US Arctic, Part Three: Concerns and Recommendations," Arctic Institute, July 19, 2012, http://www.thearcticinstitute.org/offshore-oil-drilling-in-us-arctic-part3; and Jon M. Van Dyke, Emily A. Gardner, and Joseph R. Morgan, "Whales, Submarines, and Active Sonar," *Ocean Yearbook* 18 (2004): 330, 332, and 337–38.

64. Van Dyke, Gardner, and Morgan, "Whales, Submarines, and Active Sonar," 335–36 and 338.

65. *Clyde River (Hamlet) v. Petroleum Geo-Services Inc.* Supreme Court (Can.) 2017 SCC 40.

66. Rachael Lorna Johnstone, *Offshore Oil and Gas Development in the Arctic under International Law: Risk and Responsibility* (Leiden, Netherlands: Brill, 2015), 61–62.

67. For case studies, see Forbes, "Indigenous-Industrial Relations," 259–85.

68. Nils Aarsæther, Larissa Riabova, and Jørgen Ole Bærenholdt, "Community Viability," in AHDR, 142–43.

69. Cornell and Kalt, *Alaska Native Self-Government*.

70. For example, Alcoa will only invest in Greenland on condition it may bring its own labor; see Klaus Georg Hansen, "Alcoa Aluminium Coming to Greenland," *Journal of Nordregio: The Arctic Goes Urban* 2 (2011): 20–21; and see Penikett, "Hunting," 162 (for a similar story in Arctic Canada).

71. Victoria Sweet, "Rising Waters, Rising Threats: The Human Trafficking of Indigenous Women in the Circumpolar Region of the United States and Canada," *Yearbook of Polar Law* 6 (2014): 162.

72. See Nunavummi Nangminiqaqtunik Ikajuuti (NNI) Policy, April 20, 2006, http://nni.gov.nu.ca/sites/nni.gov.nu.ca/files/01nniPolicyEng.pdf.

73. "Save the Arctic," Greenpeace, accessed April 10, 2017, https://www.savethe arctic.org.

74. Much of the hostility toward Greenpeace stems from its campaigns against seal products in the 1980s.

75. For example, Clyde River Hamlet teamed up with Greenpeace in the aforementioned seismic testing case.

76. Poppel, "The Inuit World," 264.

77. Progressive Party, Draft Resolution for the 33rd party meeting of the Progressive Party, April 10–12, 2015, 3 (authors' own translation).

78. See, for example, Chris Mooney, "The Remote Alaskan Village That Needs to Be Relocated Due to Climate Change," *Washington Post*, February 24, 2015, http://www.washingtonpost.com/news/energy-environment/wp/2015/02/24/the-remote -alaskan-village-that-needs-to-be-relocated-due-to-climate-change.

79. The 2015 International Paris Agreement from 2015 is discussed in chapter 10.

80. Terry D. Prowse et al., "Implications of Climate Change for Economic Development in Northern Canada: Energy, Resource, and Transportation Sectors," *Journal of the Human Environment* 38, no. 5 (2009): 272.

81. Ibid., 272–73.

82. Ibid., 273–75.

83. Ibid., 278.

84. Ibid., 279; see also "SWIPA: Snow, Water, Ice and Permafrost in the Arctic, Arctic Monitoring and Assessment Program," accessed April 11, 2017, https://www .amap.no/swipa.

85. Prowse, "Implications," 272 and 275–77.

86. Arctic shipping is explored in depth in chapter 9.

87. Prowse, "Implications," 277–78.

CHAPTER 6: THE POLITICAL ECONOMY OF THE ARCTIC

1. Melvyn P. Leffler, "The Emergence of an American Grand Strategy, 1945–1952," in *Cambridge History of the World War*, ed. Melvyn Leffler and Arne Westad (New York: Cambridge University Press, 2010), 1:67–89. See also G. John Ikenberry, *Liberal Leviathan: The Origins, Crisis, and Transformation of the American World Order* (Princeton, NJ: Princeton University Press, 2011), chapter 5.

2. See Ikenberry, *Liberal Leviathan*, 364 (arguing that from the perspective of the United States in 2018, this fusion of material and ideational power is an astonishing moment of American leadership. It was a time when "national security and social security were linked").

3. General Agreement on Tariffs and Trade, 1947, 55 U.N.T.S. 194 (GATT 1947).

4. WTO Agreement: Marrakesh Agreement Establishing the World Trade Organization, 1994, 1867 U.N.T.S. 154.

5. North American Free Trade Agreement (US-Can.-Mex.) 1992, *International Legal Materials* 32 (1993): 289 (NAFTA).

6. Mark Nuttall, *The Arctic Is Changing*, accessed April 18, 2018, http://www .thearctic.is/articles/overviews/changing/enska/kafli_0300.htm.

7. Elvar Orri Hreinsson and Ingólfur Bender, *Icelandic Seafood Market Report: November 2015* (Reykjavík: Íslandsbanki, 2015), 6–8 and 14.

8. Ibid., 6.

9. *The State of World Fisheries and Aquaculture* (Rome: FAO, 2016), 11 (showing some decline in Iceland's fishing share between 2012 and 2014. Iceland nevertheless ranked among the top twenty producers of caught oceanic fish. The other Arctic states in the top twenty, which together account for 82 percent of global production, are the United States, Russia, Norway, Canada, and Denmark).

10. Lars Lindholt and Solveig Glomsrød, *The Role of the Arctic in Future Global Petroleum Supply*, Discussion Paper No. 645 (Oslo: Statistics Norway, 2011), https://www.ssb.no/a/publikasjoner/pdf/DP/dp645.pdf; see also Pami Aalto and Iida Jaakkola, "Arctic Energy Policy: Global, International, Transnational and Regional Levels," in *Handbook of Politics in the Arctic*, ed. Leif Christian Jensen and Geir Hønneland (Cheltenham, UK: Edward Elgar, 2015).

11. Conor Dillon, "For All but Shell, Alaska Was Just Too Risky," *Deutsche Welle*, November 1, 2013, http://www.dw.com/en/for-all-but-shell-alaska-was-just-too-risky/a-16516535.

12. Florian Stammler, *Reindeer Nomads Meet the Market: Culture, Property and Globalisation at the "End of the Land,"* Halle Studies in the Anthropology of Eurasia (Münster: LIT Verlag, 2009), 6:283.

13. Gerald Zojer and Kamrul Hossain, *Rethinking Multifaceted Human Security Threats in the Barents Region: A Multilevel Approach to Societal Security*, Juridica Lapponica 42 (Rovaniemi, Finland: Lapin yliopisto, 2017), 20. See also W. G. Rees, F. M. Stammler, F. S. Danks, and P. Vitebsky, "Vulnerability of European Reindeer Husbandry to Global Change," *Climatic Change* 87 (2008): 199.

14. World Bank, "Time Required to Start a Business (Days)," accessed April 18, 2018, http://data.worldbank.org/indicator/IC.REG.DURS. The global average in 2003 was 51.9 days; it was 20.9 days in 2016.

15. Government is essential to capitalism. Government creates systems so that contracts are enforceable, facilitates money, establishes education and labor rules, and makes some activities illegal that in a purely free market would be open—for example, minimum qualifications for claiming professional titles like doctor or lawyer. It allocates public spaces like the electromagnetic spectrum or, especially in the New World, "government" land.

16. Federal Trade Commission, "FTC Distributes 300,000 Postcards and Brochures to Educate Shoppers Seeking Authentic Alaska Native Art," July 22, 2003, https://www.ftc.gov/news-events/press-releases/2003/07/ftc-distributes-300000-postcards-and-brochures-educate-shoppers.

17. See Beth DeSombre, *Domestic Sources of International Environmental Policy: Industry, Environmentalists, and U.S. Power* (Cambridge, MA: MIT Press, 2000).

18. See William Cronen's "Pricing the Future," in *Nature's Metropolis: Chicago and the Great West* (New York: W. W. Norton, 1991).

19. See Naomi Klein, *This Changes Everything* (New York: Simon and Schuster, 2014) (for an extended discussion of neoliberalism as ideology and the core cause of climate change).

20. Kevin Banks, "Must Canada Change Its Labour and Employment Laws to Compete with the United States?" *Queen's Law Journal* 38, no. 2 (2013): 419.

21. Petra Pinzler, "How to Free Trade," *Foreign Affairs*, March 17, 2018, https://www.foreignaffairs.com/articles/united-states/2016-04-06/how-free-trade.

22. Miguel A. Centeno and Joseph N. Cohen, "The Arc of Neoliberalism," *Annual Review of Sociology* 38, no. 2 (2012): 317–40.

23. Andrew MacLeod, "BC Forest Policy Killing Jobs in Small Communities, Say Critics," *Tyee*, November 21, 2016, https://thetyee.ca/News/2016/11/21/BC-Forest-Policy-Killing-Jobs/.

24. F. Joseph Dresin, *The Role of State Capitalism in the Russian Economy*, The Wilson Centre, October 1, 2012, https://www.wilsoncenter.org/publication/the-role-state-corporations-the-russian-economy#sthash.iCDjaAbi.dpuf.

25. US State Department Office of Investment Affairs, "Russia Country Commercial Guide, Russia-7-State-Owned Enterprises," July 17, 2017, https://www.export.gov/article?id=Russia-State-Owned-Enterprises.

26. See Tax Policy Center, *Briefing Book*, accessed April 18, 2018, http://www.taxpolicycenter.org/briefing-book/how-do-us-taxes-compare-internationally (for a comparison of taxes as percent of GDP in different countries; most of the Nordics are in the 40 percent range, Canada and the United States are in the 22 to 28 percent range).

27. Torben M. Anderson et al., *The Nordic Model: Embracing Globalization and Sharing Risks*, Research Institute of the Finnish Economy (Helsinki: Taloustieto Oy, 2007).

28. David Reid, "Norway Taps Its Oil Fund for the First Time," CNBC, March 3, 2016, http://www.cnbc.com/2016/03/07/norway-taps-its-oil-fund-for-the-first-time.html.

29. Norges Bank Investment Management, "Norges Bank Recommends the Removal of Oil Stocks from the Benchmark Index of the Government Pension Fund Global (GPFG)," November 16, 2017, https://www.nbim.no/en/transparency/news-list/2017/norges-bank-recommends-the-removal-of-oil-stocks-from-the-benchmark-index-of-the-government-pension-fund-global-gpfg/. The Fund's ethics committee also recommends withdrawal from firms that build nuclear weapons or commit human rights abuses.

30. Norges Bank Investment Management, *Government Pension Fund Global Annual Report, 2017* (Oslo, 2018), 26.

31. Only permanent residents are eligible for these payments, based on residence for at least one year and intention to remain in Alaska.

32. Rasmus Gjedssø Bertelsen, Jens C. Justinussen, and Coco Smits, "Energy as a Developmental Strategy: Creating Knowledge-Based Energy Sectors in Iceland, the Faroe Islands, and Greenland," in *Handbook of the Politics of the Arctic*, ed. Leif Christian Jensen and Geir Hønneland (Cheltenham, UK: Edward Elgar, 2015), 6.

33. Ibid., 11–12.

34. Ibid., 33.

35. Nordic Marine Think Tank, *Synthesis Report Blue Growth in the NE Atlantic and Arctic*, Working Paper (Copenhagen: Norden, 2015), http://cdn.lms.fo/media/6466/synteserapport-sidste-version-tema-nord-format-fin.pdf; "Ministers Recognise the Potential of Blue Economy," *Ice Fish News*, July 20, 2015, http://icefishnews.com/ministers-recognise-the-potential-of-blue-economy.

36. See, for example, Aisling Murtagh and Patrick Collins, "Northern Peripheries and Creative Capital and Its Role in Contributing to Regional Development in Nordic Regions," *Arctic Yearbook*, 2017, https://www.arcticyearbook.com/toc2017.

37. "New Strong Force behind London Mining Greenland A/S," Government of Greenland (Naalakkersuisut), January 8, 2015, http://naalakkersuisut.gl/en/Naalak kersuisut/News/2015/01/080115-London-Mining.

38. See Rannsóknarnefnd Alþingis, *The Report of the Icelandic Parliament's Special Investigation Commission*, April 12, 2010, http://www.rannsoknarnefnd.is; and Ásgeir Jónsson and Hersir Siguregeirsson, *The Icelandic Financial Crisis: A Study into the World's Smallest Currency Area and Its Recovery from Total Banking Collapse* (Basingstoke, UK: Palgrave Macmillan, 2016). See also Hjalti Ómar Ágústsson and Rachael Lorna Johnstone, "Practising What They Preach: Did the IMF and Iceland Exercise Good Governance in Their Relations 2008–2011?" *Nordicum-Mediterraneum* 8, no. 1 (2013) (assessing the IMF bailout process).

39. Renminbi is the official name of the currency, but it is also correct to use yuan, which is a particular piece of Chinese currency.

40. Enda Curran, "China's Yuan Faces a Rocky Road to Becoming a Truly Global Currency," *Bloomberg*, September 14, 2016, https://www.bloomberg.com/news/arti cles/2016-09-14/china-s-redback-awaits-pride-of-place-with-dollar-rome-s-aureus.

41. See Marc Lanteigne, *China's Emerging Arctic Strategies: Economics and Institutions* (Reykjavík: Centre for Arctic Policy Studies, University of Iceland, 2014), http://ams.hi.is/wp-content/uploads/2014/11/ChinasEmergingArcticStrategiesPDF _FIX2.pdf (for an excellent summary of China's economic interests in the Arctic); see also Marc Lanteigne, "'Have You Entered the Storehouses of the Snow?' China as a Norm Entrepreneur in the Arctic," *Polar Record* 53, no. 2 (2017): 117–30.

42. Ellen Sheng, "The 5 Biggest Chinese Investments in the US in 2016," *Forbes*, December 21, 2016, http://www.forbes.com/sites/ellensheng/2016/12/21/5-biggest -chinese-investments-in-us-2016/#1bf994c777d3; and Gwladys Fouche, "Chinese Firm Unlikely to Develop $2 Billion Greenland Iron Ore Mine Soon: Minister," *Reuters*, January 26, 2016, http://www.reuters.com/article/us-greenland-mining-china -idUSKCN0V425D.

43. "China's Economic Outlook in Six Charts," International Monetary Fund, August 15, 2017, http://www.imf.org/en/News/Articles/2017/08/09/NA081517 -China-Economic-Outlook-in-Six-Charts; Tom Mitchell, "IMF Warns China over 'Dangerous' Level of Debt," *Financial Times*, August 15, 2017, https://www.ft.com /content/4ca05a5a-81a3-11e7-a4ce-15b2513cb3ff; "China Hit by First Moody's Downgrade since 1989 on Debt Risk," *Bloomberg News*, May 23, 2017, https:// www.bloomberg.com/news/articles/2017-05-24/china-downgraded-to-a1-by -moody-s-on-worsening-debt-outlook.

44. Vitor Gaspar and Laura Jaramillo, "Bringing Down High Debt," IMF Blog, April 18, 2018, https://blogs.imf.org/2018/04/18/bringing-down-high-debt/.

45. Jeffry Frieden and Lisa L. Martin, "International Political Economy: Global and Domestic Interaction," in *Political Science: The State of the Discipline*, ed. Ira Katznelson and Helen V. Milner (New York: W. W. Norton, 2003), 118–46.

46. Richard Portes, "The Economy According to Trump," *London Business School*, January 31, 2017, https://www.london.edu/faculty-and-research/lbsr/the-economy -according-to-trump#.WtF6pcj9mT8; and Eduardo Porter, "'How Long Can We Last?' Trump's Tariffs Hit Home in the US," *New York Times*, April 10, 2018, https:// www.nytimes.com/2018/04/10/business/economy/tariffs-steel.html.

47. Agreement on the European Economic Area (EEA Agreement), May 2, 1992, 1791–1818 U.N.T.S.; see also Kristine Offerdal, "The EU in the Arctic: In Pursuit of Legitimacy and Influence," *International Journal* 66, no. 4 (2011): 861–77.

48. See US Department of Commerce, "Russia Trade Agreements," August 11, 2017, https://www.export.gov/article?id=Russia-Trade-Agreements (for a summary).

49. Free Trade Agreement between Iceland and China, April 15, 2015, full text available from Iceland Ministry for Foreign Affairs, "Free Trade Agreement between Iceland and China," accessed April 18, 2018, https://www.government.is/topics/for eign-affairs/external-trade/free-trade-agreements/free-trade-agreement-between-ice land-and-china.

50. Karen Everett, "Trade and the Canadian North," *Polar Connection*, March 21, 2018, http://polarconnection.org/canadian-north-trade.

51. North American Agreement on Environmental Cooperation (US-Can.-Mex.) 1993, *International Legal Materials* 32 (1993): 1482.

52. Geoffrey Garver, "Forgotten Promises: Neglected Environmental Provisions of the NAFTA and the NAAEC," in *NAFTA and Sustainable Development: History, Experience, and Prospects for Reform*, ed. Hoi L. Kong and L. Kinvin Wroth (New York: Cambridge University Press, 2015), 15–36.

53. Betsy Baker, "Assessing Assessments of NAFTA's Marine Environment: The Commission for Environmental Cooperation Meets the World Ocean Assessment," in Kong and Wroth, eds., *NAFTA and Sustainable Development*, 191–203.

54. David Shepardson, "Auto Industry Tells Trump 'We're Winning with NAFTA,'" *Reuters*, October 24, 2017, https://www.reuters.com/article/us-trade-nafta-autos /auto-industry-tells-trump-were-winning-with-nafta-idUSKBN1CT1FJ.

55. David Lawder and Lesley Wroughton, "NAFTA Washington Talks Said to Leave Major Differences Untouched," *Reuters*, December 15, 2017, https://www .reuters.com/article/us-trade-nafta/nafta-washington-talks-said-to-leave-major-dif ferences-untouched-idUSKBN1E92NT.

56. Alexander Panetta, "Canada, U.S. Spar over Late-Stage Sticking Point in NAFTA: Sunset Clause," *Toronto Star*, April 25, 2018, https://www.thestar.com /news/canada/2018/04/25/canada-us-spar-over-late-stage-sticking-point-in-nafta -sunset-clause.html.

57. Ashely Joannu, "Northerners Keep an Eye on NAFTA," *Yukon News*, August 24, 2017, https://www.yukon-news.com/news/northerners-keep-an-eye-on-nafta.

58. Royal Greenland Company, "Royal Greenland Invests in Quin-Sea Fisheries of Canada," December 3, 2015, https://www.royalgreenland.com/royal-greenland /news-and-seafood-insight/royal-greenland-invests-in-quin-sea-fisheries-of-canada. See also the company's website: https://www.royalgreenland.com/royal-greenland.

59. *Nordic Countries in Global Value Chains* (Copenhagen: Statistics Denmark, 2017), 8.

60. See "Northern Food Retail Data Collection & Analysis by Enrg Research Group," Government of Canada, accessed May 2, 2018, http://www.nutritionnorth canada.gc.ca/eng/1424364469057/1424364505951.

61. Aude Feltz, "Towards Sustainable and Ethical Supply Chains," *OSCE Magazine*, accessed May 2, 2018, https://www.osce.org/magazine/302931.

62. See chapter 9.

63. "Russia's Yamal LNG Gets Round Sanctions with $12B Chinese Loan Deal," *Alaska Dispatch News*, May 18, 2016, http://www.adn.com/article/20160504/rus sias-yamal-lng-gets-round-sanctions-12b-chinese-loan-deal; Nadezhda Filimonova, "Gazprom and China's 'Breakthrough' in the Russian Arctic," *Diplomat*, August 8, 2017, https://thediplomat.com/2017/08/gazprom-and-chinas-breakthrough-in-the -russian-arctic.

64. Jerry Maxie and David Slayton, *Russia's Arctic Dreams Have Chinese Characteristics* (Seattle: National Bureau of Asian Research, 2016).

65. Comprehensive and Progressive Agreement for Trans-Pacific Partnership (CPTPP), March 8, 2018, full text available from Government of Canada, "Comprehensive and Progressive Agreement for Trans-Pacific Partnership (CPTPP)," accessed April 18, 2018, https://www.international.gc.ca/trade-commerce/trade-agreements -accords-commerciaux/agr-acc/cptpp-ptpgp/index.aspx?lang=eng&menu_id=95. This page also has links to reports on the anticipated benefits to the different provinces and territories of Canada.

66. Comprehensive Economic and Trade Agreement, October 30, 2016, entered into force provisionally September 21, 2017 (CETA), full text available from Government of Canada, "Text of the Comprehensive Economic and Trade Agreement," accessed April 18, 2018, http://www.international.gc.ca/trade-commerce/trade-agreements-ac cords-commerciaux/agr-acc/ceta-aecg/text-texte/toc-tdm.aspx?lang=eng.

67. Matthew P. Goodman, "From TPP to CPTPP," Center for Strategic and International Studies, March 8, 2018, https://www.csis.org/analysis/tpp-cptpp.

68. Government of Canada, Joint Interpretive Instrument on the Comprehensive Economic and Trade Agreement (CETA) between Canada and the European Union and its Member States, November 4, 2016, section 8. http://www.international.gc .ca/trade-commerce/trade-agreements-accords-commerciaux/agr-acc/ceta-aecg/jii -iic.aspx?lang=eng.

69. CETA, article 800.

70. "The Arbitration Game," *Economist*, October 11, 2014. See also Stephan W. Schill, "Reforming Investor-States Dispute Settlement: A (Comparative and International) Constitutional Law Framework," *Journal of International Economic Law* 20, no. 3 (2017): 649–72.

71. See "CETA Explained," European Commission, September 21, 2017, http:// ec.europa.eu/trade/policy/in-focus/ceta/ceta-explained/index_en.htm.

72. European Commission, *Handbook for Trade Sustainability Impact Assessment*, 2nd ed. (Luxembourg: European Union, 2016).

73. "Entrepreneurship and Small and Medium-Sized Enterprises (SMES)," *European Commission*, accessed May 2, 2018, https://ec.europa.eu/growth/smes_en.

74. "Small and Medium-Sized Enterprises Reaching New Markets," US Department of Commerce, May 2, 2017, https://www.commerce.gov/news/blog/2017/05 /small-and-medium-sized-enterprises-reaching-new-markets.

75. Joint Interpretive Instrument on the Comprehensive Economic and Trade Agreement (CETA) between Canada and the European Union and Its Member States, November 4, 2016, paragraphs 8 and 14, http://www.international.gc.ca/trade-com merce/trade-agreements-accords-commerciaux/agr-acc/ceta-aecg/jii-iic.aspx?lang=eng.

76. David Murphy, "Nunavut Will Benefit from CETA, Aglukkaq Says," *Nunatsiaq News*, October 25, 2013, http://www.nunatsiaqonline.ca/stories/article/65674nun avut_will_benefit_from_ceta_aglukkaq_says.

77. "IITIO, NAFTA, Indigenous Chapter-Round 6-Update," *International Inter-Tribal Trade and Investment Organization*, February 1, 2018, http://iitio.org/nafta -6-update.

CHAPTER 7: HUMAN RIGHTS AND THE RIGHTS OF INDIGENOUS PEOPLES IN THE ARCTIC

1. Indigenous and Tribal Peoples Convention 1989, International Labor Organisation Convention 169 [ILO C169], *International Legal Materials* 28 (1989): 1382.

2. Universal Declaration of Human Rights [UDHR], UN General Assembly Resolution 217 (A)(III), December 10, 1948; UN Declaration on the Rights of Indigenous Peoples [UNDRIP], UN General Assembly Resolution 61/295, September 13, 2007.

3. Philip Alston and Ryan Goodman, *International Human Rights* (Oxford: Oxford University Press, 2013), 139–45.

4. Ibid., 142.

5. International Covenant on Economic, Social and Cultural Rights [ICESCR] 1966, 993 U.N.T.S. 3; International Covenant on Civil and Political Rights [ICCPR] 1966, 999 U.N.T.S. 171.

6. There is one exception: the right to property, which is found in article 17 of the UDHR, is not replicated in either the ICCPR or the ICESCR. This is because by this time, the Cold War was at its height, and East and West could not agree on whether it should protect individual ownership, communal ownership, or both.

7. Mattias Åhrén, "The Provisions on Lands, Territories and Natural Resources in the UN Declaration on the Rights of Indigenous Peoples: An Introduction," in *Making the Declaration Work*, ed. Claire Charters and Rodolfo Stavenhagen (Copenhagen: International Work Group for Indigenous Affairs, 2009), 201–2; see also Isabelle Schulte-Tenckhoff, "Treaties, Peoplehood and Self-Determination: Understanding the Language of Indigenous Rights," in *Indigenous Rights in the Age of the UN Declaration*, ed. Elvira Pulitano (Cambridge: Cambridge University Press, 2012); and Paul Patton, "Justifications for Indigenous Rights," in *Handbook of Indigenous Peoples' Rights*, ed. Corinne Lennox and Damien Short (Abingdon, UK: Routledge, 2016).

8. ILO C169, article 3; UNDRIP, article 1.

9. On the use of the terms "indigenous people" and "indigenous peoples," see chapter 1.

10. See, for example, ICCPR, article 27.

11. UNDRIP, article 33.

12. ILO C169, article 1(1).

13. Ibid., article 1(2).

14. Henry Shue, *Basic Rights: Subsistence, Affluence and US Foreign Policy* (Princeton, NJ: Princeton University Press, 1980), 78.

15. Rachael Lorna Johnstone and Aðalheiður Ámundadóttir, "Human Rights in Crisis: Securing the International Covenant on Economic, Social and Cultural Rights

(ICESCR) in Economic Downturns," *International Journal of Human Rights and Constitutional Studies* 1 (2013): 6, 8.

16. *Clyde River (Hamlet) v. Petroleum Geo-Services Inc.* Supreme Court (Can.) 2017, SCC 40.

17. Optional Protocol to the Convention on the Rights of the Child on the Involvement of Children in Armed Conflict 2000, 2173 U.N.T.S. 222; Optional Protocol to the Convention on the Rights of the Child on the Sale of Children, Child Prostitution and Child Pornography 2000, 2171 U.N.T.S. 227.

18. Convention on the Rights of the Child 1989 [CRC], 1577 U.N.T.S. 3.

19. All the general comments and recommendations can be accessed at "Human Rights Treaty Bodies—General Comments," Office of the High Commissioner for Human Rights, accessed April 11, 2017, http://www.ohchr.org/EN/HRBodies/Pages/TBGeneralComments.aspx.

20. All the committees' work can be found on the treaty bodies' database, Office of the High Commissioner for Human Rights, accessed April 11, 2017, https://tbinternet.ohchr.org/_layouts/treatybodyexternal/TBSearch.aspx?Lang=en.

21. ICESCR, articles 2(1) and 3; and ICCPR, articles 2(1) and 3.

22. CRC, articles 17(d), 29(d), and 30.

23. Committee on the Elimination of Racial Discrimination, General Recommendation XXIII on the Rights of Indigenous Peoples, 1997, UN Doc. A/52/18, Annex V.

24. ILO C169, articles 13–15.

25. ILO Constitution 1919, as amended, article 24.

26. Report of the Committee set up to examine the representation alleging nonobservance by Denmark of the Indigenous and Tribal Peoples Convention, 1989 (No. 169), made under article 24 of the ILO Constitution by the National Confederation of Trade Unions of Greenland (Sulinermik Inuussutissarsiuteqartut Kattuffiat [SIK]) (*SIK v. Denmark*), GB.277/18/3; GB.280/18/5.

27. Ibid., para. 43.

28. Ibid., para. 29.

29. For a critical reading, see Irene Watson and Sharon Venne, "Talking Up Indigenous Peoples' Original Intent in a Space Dominated by State Interventions," in Pulitano, ed., *Indigenous Rights in the Age of the UN Declaration*.

30. Record of the 108th Plenary Meeting of the UN General Assembly, September 13, 2007, UN Doc. A/61/PV.108.

31. Australia, Minister for Families, Housing, Community Services and Indigenous Affairs, Statement on the United Nations Declaration on the Rights of Indigenous Peoples, April 3, 2009, http://www.un.org/esa/socdev/unpfii/documents/Australia_official_statement_endorsement_UNDRIP.pdf; Canada, Aboriginal Affairs and Northern Development Canada, Statement of Support on the United Nations Declaration on the Rights of Aboriginal Peoples, November 12, 2010, http://www.aadnc-aandc.gc.ca/eng/1309374239861/1309374546142; New Zealand, Statement, Ninth Session of the UN Permanent Forum on Indigenous Issues, Opening Ceremony, April 19, 2010, archived by Converge, http://www.converge.org.nz/pma/NZ%20UNDRIP%20statements.pdf; and US President, Announcement of U.S. Support for the Declaration on the Rights of Indigenous Peoples, archived by Advisory Council on Historic Preservation, http://www.achp.gov/docs/US%20Support%20for%20Declaration%2012-10.pdf.

32. Nigel Bankes and Timo Koivurova, "Legal Systems," in *Arctic Human Development Report: Regional Processes and Global Linkages* [AHDR II], ed. Joan Nymand Larsen and Gail Fondahl (Akureyri, Iceland: Norden, 2014), 233.

33. See, for example, Announcement of U.S. Support, 1, para. 2.

34. UN Permanent Forum on Indigenous Issues, "Study on National Constitutions and the United Nations Declaration on the Rights of Indigenous Peoples," February 20, 2013, UN Doc. E/C.19/2013/18; Siegfried Weissner, "The Cultural Rights of Indigenous Peoples: Achievements and Continuing Challenges," *European Journal of International Law* 22, no. 1 (2011): 121, at 130.

35. P. Whitney Lackenbauer and Suzanne Lalonde, "Searching for Common Ground in Evolving Canadian and EU Arctic Strategies," in *The European Union and the Arctic*, ed. Nengye Liu, Elizabeth A. Kirk, and Tore Henriksen (Leiden, Netherlands: Brill, 2017), 147.

36. Truth and Reconciliation Commission of Canada, *Final Report*, 2015, http://www.trc.ca/websites/trcinstitution/index.php?p=890.

37. Justin Trudeau, Prime Minister of Canada, "Statement by Prime Minister on Release of the Final Report of the Truth and Reconciliation Commission," December 15, 2015, http://www.pm.gc.ca/eng/news/2015/12/15/statement-prime-minis ter-release-final-report-truth-and-reconciliation-commission; see also Lackenbauer and Lalonde, "Searching for Common Ground in Evolving Canadian and EU Arctic Strategies," 147–48.

38. "Minister Bennett Clarifies Canada's Position on Implementing UNDRIP and FPIC," *Northern Public Affairs*, May 4, 2016, http://www.northernpublicaffairs.ca /index/minister-bennett-clarifies-canadas-position-on-implementing-undrip-and-fpic.

39. See, for example, International Law Association, Committee on the Rights of Indigenous Peoples, "Rights of Indigenous Peoples: Interim Report," in Report of the Seventy-Fourth Conference, The Hague, Part 12, April 2010; James Anaya (UN Special Rapporteur) and Siegfried Weissner, "The UN Declaration on the Rights of Indigenous Peoples: Towards RE-empowerment," *Jurist Forum*, October 3, 2007, http://www.jurist.org/forum/2007/10/un-declaration-on-rights-of-indigenous.php.

40. Concluding Observations of the Committee on the Elimination of Racial Discrimination: US, March 5, 2008, UN Doc. CERD/C/USA/CO/6, para. 29.

41. Concluding Observations of the Committee on the Elimination of Racial Discrimination: Canada, March 7–8, 2012, UN Doc. CERD/C/CAN/CO/19–20, para. 19.

42. Bankes and Koivurova, "Legal Systems," 234.

43. Convention for the Protection of Human Rights and Fundamental Freedoms 1950 [ECHR], ETS 005.

44. See, for example, *Hingitaq 53 v. Denmark*, 2006, European Court of Human Rights, First Section, Application No. 18584/04; see also Nigel Bankes, "The Protection of the Rights of Indigenous Peoples to Territory through the Property Rights Provisions of the International Regional Human Rights Instruments," *Yearbook of Polar Law* 3 (2011): 57, 95–100; and *G and E v. Norway* 1993, European Commission of Human Rights, Applications Nos. 9278/81 and 9415/82, Decision on Admissibility, "The Law," para. 2.

45. American Convention on Human Rights 1969 [ACHR], 1144 U.N.T.S. 123.

46. American Declaration of the Rights and Duties of Man 1948 [ADRDM] OAS Resolution XXX.

292 ★ Notes to Chapter 7

47. The Inter-American Commission has further powers, such as making reports on member countries and conducting inquiries.

48. American Declaration on the Rights of Indigenous Peoples 2016 [ADRIP] OAS Resolution AG/RES.2888 (XLVI-O/16) 167.

49. For example, the ADRIP explicitly prohibits genocide in "any form" and respects the rights of peoples in voluntary isolation to remain so: ibid., articles XI and XXVI.

50. ADRIP, notes 1 and 2.

51. International Law Commission, Articles on Responsibility of States for Internationally Wrongful Acts 2001 [ILC Articles on State Responsibility], in Report of the International Law Commission on the Work of Its Fifty-Third Session, UN GAOR, UN Doc. A/56/10 (2001), articles 4 and 8.

52. See, generally, Riccardo Pisillo-Mazzeschi, *Responsabilité de l'état pour violations des obligations positives relatives aux droits de l'homme* [State Responsibility for Violations of Positive Obligations of Human Rights], Collected Courses of the Hague Academy of International Law 2008, Vol. 333 (Leiden, Netherlands: Martinus Nijhoff, 2009).

53. See International Law Association, Study Group on Due Diligence, First Report, March 2014, and Second Report, April 2016 (on due diligence in international law).

54. Asbjørn Eide, *Report on the Right to Adequate Food as a Human Right*, UN Doc. E/CN.4/Sub.2/1987/23 (1987), paras. 34–36, 112–15, and 167–81.

55. For examples, see Rachael Lorna Johnstone, "Feminist Influences on the United Nations Human Rights Treaty Bodies," *Human Rights Quarterly* 28 (2006): 148; and Rachael Lorna Johnstone, "State Responsibility: A Concerto for Court, Council and Committee," *Denver Journal of International Law and Policy* 37, no. 1 (2008): 63, 93–108.

56. Pisillo-Mazzeschi, *Responsabilité de l'état*, 414–20.

57. Rome Statute of the International Criminal Court 1998, 2187 U.N.T.S. 3, articles 1 and 6–8.

58. Guiding Principles on Business and Human Rights: Implementing the United Nations "Protect, Respect and Remedy" Framework, March 21, 2011, UN Doc. A/HRC/17/31.

59. Ibid., principle 13(b).

60. Working Group on Indigenous Populations, Eleventh Session, 20 July 1993 (working on the draft UNDRIP), as reported in *Indigenous Peoples, the United Nations, and Human Rights*, ed. Sarah Pritchard (Sydney: Zed Books, 1998), 46.

61. Report of the Special Rapporteur on the Rights of Indigenous Peoples, James Anaya: Addendum: The Situation of Indigenous Peoples in the United States of America, 2012, UN Doc. A/HRC/21/47/Add.1, paras. 59 and 62.

62. Alistair Campbell and Kirk Cameron, "Constitutional Development and Natural Resources in the North," in *Governing the North American Arctic: Sovereignty, Security and Institutions*, ed. Dawn Alexandrea Berry, Nigel Bowles, and Halbert Jones (Basingstoke, UK: Palgrave Macmillan, 2016), 184.

63. Inuvialuit Final Agreement 1984, enacted by the Western Arctic (Inuvialuit) Claims Settlement Act, S.C. 1984, c. 24.

64. Nunavut Land Claims Agreement Act, S.C. 1993, c. 29; Nunavut Act, S.C. 1993, c. 28.

65. Madeleine Redfern, Mayor of Iqaluit, "Inuit Governance in Nunavut," Keynote Presentation at the 9th Polar Law Symposium, Akureyri, October 5, 2016.

66. Act No. 85 of June 17, 2005, relating to Legal Relations and Management of Land and Natural Resources in the County of Finnmark.

67. K. Zaikov, A. Tamitskiy, and M. Zadorin, "Legal and Political Framework of the Federal and Regional Legislation on National Ethnic Policy in the Russian Arctic," *Polar Journal* 7, no. 1 (2017): 125–47, at 127.

68. Elana Wilson Rowe, "Introduction: Policy Aims and Political Realities in the Russian North," in *Russia and the North*, ed. Elana Wilson Rowe (Ottawa: University of Ottawa Press, 2009), 4.

69. Russia Federation Federal Law on the Guarantees of the Rights of the Indigenous Small-Numbered Peoples of the Russian Federation, adopted by the State Duma on April 16, 1999, approved by the Federation Council on April 22, 1999; Russian Federation Federal Law on General Principles of Organization the Indigenous Small-Numbered Peoples' Communities of the North, Siberia and the Far East of the Russian Federation, adopted by the State Duma on July 16, 2000, approved by the Federation Council on July 7, 2000, in Maksim Zadorin, Olga Klisheva, Ksenia Vezhlivtseva, and Daria Antufieva, *Russian Laws on Indigenous Issues: Guarantees, Communities, Territories of Traditional Land Use, Translated and Commented* (Rovaniemi, Finland: University of Lapland, 2017); Russian Federation Federal Law on Territories of Traditional Land Use of the Indigenous Small-Numbered Peoples of the North, Siberia and the Far East of the Russian Federation, adopted by the State Duma on April 3, 2001, in Zadorin et al., *Russian Laws on Indigenous Issues.*

70. Campbell and Cameron, "Constitutional Development and Natural Resources in the North," 187.

71. See Human Rights Watch, https://www.hrw.org/news/2008/02/20/putins-crack down-ngos.

72. Atle Staalesen, "Nordic Countries Close Offices in Russia," *Barents Observer*, March 13, 2015, http://barentsobserver.com/en/politics/2015/03/nordic-countries -close-offices-russia-13-03.

73. ILO C169, articles 13(2) and 14(1).

74. Ibid., article 14(1).

75. Ibid., article 13(1); see also articles 13–19, on indigenous rights to land and resources.

76. UNDRIP, articles 25–26.

77. ICCPR, article 27.

78. *Kitok v. Sweden*, 1988, Human Rights Committee Communication No. 197/1985, July 27, 1988, UN Doc. CCPR/C/33/D/197/1985; *Länsman, Ilmari et al. v. Finland*, 1994, Human Rights Committee, Communication No. 511/1992, November 8, 1994, UN Doc. CCPR/C/52/D/511/1992; *Länsman, Jouni E. et al. v. Finland*, 1996, Human Rights Committee, Communication No. 671/1995, October 30, 1996, UN Doc. CCPR/C/58/D/671/1995; *Länsman, Jouni et al. v. Finland*, 2005, Human Rights Committee, Communication No. 1023/2001, March 17, 2005, UN Doc. CCPR/C/83/D/1023/2001; *Mahuika et al. v. New Zealand*, 2000, Human Rights Committee Communication No. 547/1999, November 15, 2000, UN Doc. CCPR/C/70/D/547/1933.

79. *Ominayak and the Lubicon Lake Band v. Canada*, 1990, Human Rights Committee, Communication No. 167/1984, May 10, 1990, UN Doc. CCPR/C/38/D/167/1984.

80. ECHR, article 8; Protocol to the Convention for the Protection of Human Rights and Fundamental Freedoms 1952, ETS 009, article 1; ADRDM, article XXIII; and ACHR, article 21.

81. *Mayagna (Sumo) Awas Tingni Community v. Nicaragua* (Judgment) 2001, Inter-American Court of Human Rights, Petition 11,577, para. 148; see also *Maya Indigenous Community of the Toledo District v. Belize* (Merits) 2004, Inter-American Court of Human Rights, Petition 12.053, para. 115 (recognizing the right of the indigenous people concerned to their ancestral land and states' positive obligations to protect it).

82. UNDRIP, article 10; ILO C169, article 16.

83. *Sawhoyamaxa Indigenous Community of the Enxet People v. Paraguay* (Merits, Reparations and Costs) 2006, Inter-American Court of Human Rights, Petition 0322/2001, para. 212.

84. Ibid., para. 132.

85. *Xákmok Kásek Indigenous Community v. Paraguay* (Merits, Reparations and Costs) 2010, Inter-American Court of Human Rights, Petition 12420, para. 291.

86. *Saramaka People v. Suriname* (Preliminary Objections, Merits, Reparation and Costs) 2007, Inter-American Court of Human Rights, Petition 12338, para. 121.

87. *McDowell v. State* 1989, 785 P.2d 1 (1989).

88. The Situation of Indigenous Peoples in the United States of America, para. 60. See also *Alaska Subsistence: A National Park Service Management History*, archived by Internet Archive, accessed April 11, 2017, https://archive.org/details/alaskasubsis tenc00norr (for more on the history and regulation of Alaskan subsistence).

89. ILO C169, article 8; UNDRIP, article 11.

90. UNDRIP, article 8.

91. ICESCR, article 15; see also Committee on Economic, Social and Cultural Rights, General Comment No. 21, "The Right of Everyone to Take Part in Cultural Life (art. 15, para. 1[a] of the International Covenant on Economic, Social and Cultural Rights)," November 20, 2009, UN Doc. E/C.12/GC/21.

92. *Sarayaku, Kichwa Indigenous People of v. Ecuador* (Merits and Reparations) 2012, Inter-American Court of Human Rights, Petition 12465, para. 164 (holding that the principle of consultation with indigenous communities is a "general principle" of international law and hence binding on all states, irrespective of their treaty ratifications or endorsement of the UNDRIP).

93. UNDRIP, article 32(2); a similar provision appears in the ADRIP, article XXIX(4).

94. James Anaya, Report of the Special Rapporteur on the Rights of Indigenous Peoples, James Anaya: Extractive Industries and Indigenous Peoples, 2013, UN Doc. A/HRC/24/41, paras. 26–36; and James Anaya, Report of the Special Rapporteur on the Rights of Indigenous Peoples: The Situation of Indigenous Peoples in Canada, 2014 UN Doc. A/HRC/27/52/Add.2, para. 98.

95. Robert Hagen, "Explanation of Vote by Robert Hagen, US Adviser, on the Declaration on the Rights of Indigenous Peoples, to the UN General Assembly," US Mission to the UN, New York, September 13, 2007.

96. J. Wilson-Raybould, Canada, House of Commons Debates, 42nd Parl., 1st Sess., Vol. 148, No. 37, April 12, 2016, at 2010; Tim Fontaine, "Canada Officially Adopts UN Declaration on Rights of Indigenous Peoples," CBC News, May 10, 2016, http://www.cbc.ca/news/indigenous/canada-adopting-implementing-un-rights-dec laration-1.3575272.

97. Thierry Rodon, "Offshore Development and Inuit Rights in Inuit Nunangat," in *Governance of Arctic Offshore Oil and Gas*, ed. Cécile Pelaudeix and Ellen Margrethe Basse (Abingdon, UK: Routledge, 2017), 171.

98. See, for example, International Law Association, "Rights of Indigenous Peoples" Committee Report, in International Law Association, Report of the Seventy-Fifth Conference, Sofia, paras. 508–9; and Rachael Lorna Johnstone, Arctic Oil and Gas Research Centre, Ilismatusarfik, Greenland, Briefing Note 11: Free Prior and Informed Consent within the UN Human Rights Treaty System, November 14, 2017, http://uk.uni.gl/research/arctic-oil-and-gas-research-centre/briefing-notes.aspx.

99. See, for example, Concluding Observations of the Committee on the Elimination of Racial Discrimination: United States, para. 29; Concluding Observations of the Committee on the Elimination of Racial Discrimination: Canada, para. 20; Concluding Observations of the Committee on the Elimination of Racial Discrimination: Russian Federation, February 26–27, 2013, UN Doc. CERD/C/RUS/CO/20-22, para. 20(d); Concluding Observations of the Committee on the Elimination of Racial Discrimination: Sweden, August 29, 2013, UN Doc. CERD/C/SWE/CO/19-21, para. 17; Concluding Observations of the Committee on Economic, Social and Cultural Rights: Russian Federation, May 20, 2011, UN Doc. E/C.12/RUS/CO/5, para. 7(b). See also Concluding Observations of the Committee on Economic, Social and Cultural Rights: Ecuador, November 30, 2012, UN Doc. E/C.12/ECU/CO/3, para. 9; and Concluding Observations of the Committee on Economic, Social and Cultural Rights: Colombia, May 20, 2010, UN Doc. E/C.12/COL/CO/5, para. 9.

100. *Poma Poma v. Peru*, 2009, Human Rights Committee, Communication No. 1457/2006, UN Doc. CCPR/C/95/D/1457/2006, para. 7.6.

101. Ibid.

102. Ibid., para. 7.7.

103. Ibid., para. 7.5; see also Mattias Åhrén, "International Human Rights Law Relevant to Natural Resource Extraction in Indigenous Territories: An Overview," *Nordic Environmental Law Journal* 1 (2014): 21, 36.

104. *Saramaka*, paras. 129 and 134; *Centre for Minority Rights Development (Kenya) and Minority Rights Group International on Behalf of Endorois Welfare Council v. Kenya* 2009, African Commission on Human and Peoples Rights, Communication 276/2003, AHRLR 75, para. 226. See also *Endorois*, paras. 257–66 (referencing *Saramaka*) and para. 232 (citing article 28 of the UNDRIP, which requires redress for damage to or loss of lands and resources in the absence of free, prior, and informed consent).

105. ILO C169, article 15(2).

106. See, for example, *Saramaka*, paras. 129 and 140; *Endorois*, paras. 294–96; and Concluding Observations of the Committee on the Elimination of Racial Discrimination: Ecuador, March 20, 2003, UN Doc. CERD/C/62/CO/2, para. 16.

107. Convention on Access to Information, Public Participation in Decision-Making and Access to Justice in Environmental Matters 1998, *International Legal*

Materials 38 (1999): 517 (Aarhus Convention), articles 2(4) and (5), 4 and 6. See also Alexander Langshaw, "Giving Substance to Form: Moving Towards an Integrated Governance Model of Transboundary Environmental Impact Assessment," *Nordic Journal of International Law* 81 (2012): 21, 33.

108. Aarhus Convention, article 3(9).

109. UN Treaty Series, Ch. XXVII, 13, Convention on Access to Information, Public Participation in Decision-Making and Access to Justice in Environmental Matters 1998. Status as at April 11, 2017, https://treaties.un.org/Pages/ViewDetails.aspx?src=TREATY&mtdsg_no=XXVII-13&chapter=27&lang=en.

110. European Union, Council Directive 2003/35/EC of May 27, 2003, providing for public participation in respect to the drawing up of certain plans and programs relating to the environment and amending with regard to public participation and access to justice Council Directive 85/337/EEC and 96/61/EC [2003] OJ L156/17.

111. "UNECE Welcomes the Russian Federation's Intention to Ratify the Aarhus and Espoo Environmental Conventions," UN Economic Commission for Europe (UNECE), Press Release, June 23, 2011, http://www.unece.org/press/pr2011/11env_p26e.html.

112. *Öneryildiz v. Turkey* 2004, European Court of Human Rights, Application 48389/99, ECHR 2004: 657, para. 108; *Guerra v. Italy* 1998, European Court of Human Rights, Application 14967/89, ECHR 1998: 7, para. 53.

113. *Claude Reyes, et al. v. Chile* (Merits, Reparations and Costs) 2006, Inter-American Court of Human Rights, Petition 12108, paras. 76–77.

114. Ibid.

115. See, generally, ICESCR, articles 6, 11–13; ILO C169, articles 20–22, 25–29; and UNDRIP, articles 14, 17, 21, and 24. See also Arja Rautio, Birger Poppel, and Kue Young, "Human Health and Well-Being," in AHDR II; and Diane Hirshberg and Andrey N. Petrov, "Education and Human Capital," in AHDR II.

116. Committee on Economic, Social and Cultural Rights, General Comment No. 12: The Right to Adequate Food, 1999, reprinted in Compilation of General Comments and General Recommendations Adopted by Human Rights Treaty Bodies, Vol. I (May 27, 2008), UN Doc. HRI/GEN/1/Rev.9, Vol. I, 55, para. 8.

CHAPTER 8: LAW OF THE SEA IN THE ARCTIC

1. Convention on the Territorial Sea and the Contiguous Zone 1958, 516 U.N.T.S. 205; Convention on the High Seas 1958, 450 U.N.T.S. 11; Convention on Fishing and Conservation of the Living Resources of the High Seas 1959, 559 U.N.T.S. 285; Convention on the Continental Shelf 1958, 499 U.N.T.S. 311.

2. Donald R. Rothwell and Tim Stephens, *The International Law of the Sea*, 2nd ed. (Oxford: Hart Publishing, 2010), 9–10.

3. UN Convention on the Law of the Sea 1982 [UNCLOS], 1833 U.N.T.S. 397.

4. Agreement for the Implementation of the Provisions of the United Nations Convention on the Law of the Sea of 10 December 1982 relating to the Conservation and Management of Straddling Fish Stocks and Highly Migratory Fish Stocks 1995 [Fish Stocks Agreement], 2167 U.N.T.S. 3.

5. Development of an Internationally Legally Binding Instrument under the United Nations Convention on the Law of the Sea on the Conservation and Sustainable Use

of Marine Biological Diversity of Areas beyond National Jurisdiction, UN General Assembly Resolution 69/292, July 6, 2015.

6. See David L. Larson, "The Reagan Rejection of the U.N. Convention," *Ocean Development and International Law* 14, no. 4 (1995): 337.

7. President Ronald Reagan, Statement on United States Ocean Policy, March 10, 1983, accessed January 10, 2018, https://www.reaganlibrary.gov/sites/default/files/archives/speeches/1983/31083c.htm.

8. Foreign Ministers of Canada, Denmark, Norway, Russia, and the United States of America, The Ilulissat Declaration, May 28, 2008.

9. There are some exceptions when straight baselines are drawn: if the area was not previously considered internal waters, ships from other states enjoy a right of "innocent passage," and if there are straits through the closed area, ships enjoy the right of "transit passage." This is discussed in more depth in chapter 9.

10. UNCLOS, article 5.

11. Alex G. Oude Elferink and Donald R. Rothwell, "Challenges for Polar Maritime Delimitation and Jurisdiction: The Current Regime and Its Prospects," in *The Law of the Sea and Polar Maritime Delimitation and Jurisdiction*, ed. Alex G. Oude Elferink, and Donald R. Rothwell (Leiden, Netherlands: Martinus Nijhoff, 2001), 339–41.

12. UNCLOS, article 7; see also UNCLOS, article 10.

13. Tullio Scovazzi, "The Baseline of the Territorial Sea: The Practice of Arctic States," in Oude Elferink and Rothwell, eds., *The Law of the Sea and Polar Maritime Delimitation*, 69. The United States does not generally employ straight baselines. Designation of baselines is a federal, not an Alaskan, matter. See Erik Molenaar et al., *Legal Aspects of Arctic Shipping* (Brussels: DG Maritime Affairs & Fisheries, 2010), paras. 700 and 702.

14. Scovazzi, "The Baseline," 79 and 81.

15. UNCLOS, article 3.

16. Order no. 191 of 27 May 1963 on the Delimitation of the Territorial Sea of Greenland, s1(2).

17. Submerged Lands Act 1953, 43 U.S.C. §§1301(a) (2), 1311(a) (2012).

18. UNCLOS, articles 17–26.

19. Ibid., article 19.

20. Ibid., article 20. Ships in international straits do not have to sail on the surface or display their flags, even if they are in territorial waters. The rules regarding straits are explained in some detail in the following chapter.

21. Ibid., article 33; freedom of navigation (and its limits) are discussed in chapter 9.

22. Rothwell and Stephens, *The International Law of the Sea*, 82.

23. UNCLOS, article 57.

24. Ibid., article 121(3).

25. See Rothwell and Stephens, *The International Law of the Sea*, 89 (giving examples from the Antarctic).

26. *The South China Sea Arbitration (The Republic of Philippines v. The People's Republic of China)* (Judgment), PCA Case No. 2013-19, 2016, paras. 401, 466, and 578.

27. Ibid., paras. 483 and 622.

28. Ibid., para. 541.

29. UNCLOS, article 56.
30. Ibid., article 60.
31. Ibid., article 246.
32. Rothwell and Stephens, *The International Law of the Sea*, 320.
33. UNCLOS, article 61.
34. Ibid., article 62.
35. Ibid., article 297(3). Most of the UNCLOS is subject to compulsory dispute settlement, which means that states parties have to allow the International Court of Justice, ITLOS, or an arbitral tribunal to resolve their disputes; see UNCLOS, part XV; see also Rothwell and Stephens, *The International Law of the Sea*, 92.
36. UNCLOS, article 65.
37. Ibid., article 63.
38. Ibid., articles 63–64.
39. Fish Stocks Agreement.
40. U.N.T.S., chapter XXI, 2, Agreement for the Implementation of the Provisions of the United Nations Convention on the Law of the Sea of 10 December 1982 relating to the Conservation and Management of Straddling Fish Stocks and Highly Migratory Fish Stocks. Status as at April 12, 2017, accessed February 9, 2018, https://treaties.un.org/pages/ViewDetails.aspx?src=TREATY&mtdsg_no=XXI-7&chapter=21&clang=_en.
41. UNCLOS, 76(1).
42. Ron Macnab, "Nationalizing the Arctic Maritime Commons: UNCLOS Article 76 and the Polar Sea," *Yearbook of Polar Law* 2 (2010): 171, 181.
43. Macnab, "Nationalizing the Arctic Maritime Commons," 173.
44. UNCLOS, article 76(4)(b).
45. Ibid., 76(4)(a)(ii).
46. Alex G. Oude Elferink, "The Outer Continental Shelf in the Arctic: The Application of Article 76 of the LOS Convention in a Regional Context," in Oude Elferink and Rothwell, eds., *The Law of the Sea and Polar Maritime Delimitation and Jurisdiction*, 141.
47. Mostly muds with some sand and gravel.
48. Rothwell and Stephens, *The International Law of the Sea*, 115.
49. UNCLOS, article 76(5).
50. Ibid., article 76(5).
51. Ibid., article 76(6); see also Oude Elferink, "The Outer Continental Shelf," 141.
52. Oceanic ridges are geologically part of the deep ocean floor and are beyond the continental margin (the area landward of the foot of the slope and the continental rise). For a fuller explanation of ocean ridges, submarine ridges, and submarine elevations, see "Law of the Sea: Article 76," NIWA, accessed April 12, 2017, http://www.gns.cri.nz/static/unclos/ridges.html; see also Michael Byers, *International Law in the Arctic* (Cambridge: Cambridge University Press, 2013), 97–99.
53. Submarine ridges are natural prolongations of the land territory but not part of the continental margin. See Rothwell and Stephens, *The International Law of the Sea*, 115; and Byers, *International Law in the Arctic*, 99–104.
54. Submarine elevations are "natural components of the continental margin, such as its plateaux, rises, caps, banks and spurs": UNCLOS, article 76(6).

55. For a comparison of the two submissions, see "Arctic Maps," IBRU Centre for Borders Research, Durham University, accessed January 10, 2018, https://www.dur .ac.uk/ibru/resources/arctic.

56. Oude Elferink, "The Outer Continental Shelf," 142.

57. *Bay of Bengal Case (Bangladesh v. Myanmar)* (Judgment) 2012, International Tribunal for the Law of the Sea, Case No. 16, paras. 408–9; see also Ted L. McDorman, "The International Legal Regime of the Continental Shelf with Special Reference to the Polar Regions," in *Polar Law Textbook II*, ed. Natalia Loukacheva (Copenhagen: Nordic Council of Ministers, 2013), 82–83.

58. Oude Elferink, "The Outer Continental Shelf," 143–44.

59. UNCLOS, article 77.

60. States may have a duty of conservation of living things (but not minerals) on the seabed under the Convention on Biological Diversity 1992, 1760 U.N.T.S. 79; see also chapter 10.

61. UNCLOS, article 79.

62. Macnab, "Nationalizing the Arctic Maritime Commons," 187.

63. UNCLOS, article 87.

64. Ibid., articles 116–20. On the tragedy of the commons, see Garrett Hardin, "The Tragedy of the Commons," *Science* 162, no. 3859 (1968): 1243.

65. Fish Stocks Agreement, article 8(3).

66. See Tore Henriksen, Geir Hønneland, and Are Sydnes, *Law and Politics in Ocean Governance: The UN Fish Stocks Agreement and Regional Fisheries Management Regimes* (Leiden, Netherlands: Martinus Nijhoff Publishers, 2006), 68 (noting that the North Atlantic Fisheries Organization expelled Romania and Bulgaria on these grounds).

67. "Canada; Denmark; Norway; Russia; United States: Fishing Declaration Covering Central Arctic," US Library of Congress, Global Legal Monitor, July 21, 2015, http://www.loc.gov/law/foreign-news/article/canada-denmark-norway-russia-united -states-fishing-declaration-covering-central-arctic.

68. Agreement to Prevent Unregulated High Seas Fisheries in the Central Arctic Ocean, available at Commission of the European Union, Proposal for a Council Decision on the Signing on Behalf of the European Union, of the Agreement to Prevent Unregulated High Seas Fisheries in the Central Arctic Ocean, Annex, COM (2018) 454 final, June 12, 2018, articles 3–5.

69. Ibid., article 4(4).

70. The European Union has exclusive competence to negotiate fisheries for all its members, including Denmark and Sweden.

71. UNCLOS, article 136.

72. Ibid., article 148.

73. Ibid., article 144.

74. Ibid., article 151.

75. Agreement Relating to the Implementation of Part XI of UNCLOS 1994, 1836 U.N.T.S. 42; see also Rothwell and Stephens, *The International Law of the Sea*, 141–42.

76. Oude Elferink and Rothwell, "Challenges," 352.

77. Oval Schram Stokke, "Institutional Complexity in Arctic Governance: Curse or Blessing?" in *Handbook of Politics in the Arctic*, ed. Leif Christian Jensen and Geir Hønneland (Cheltenham, UK: Edward Elgar, 2015), 344.

78. Robin Churchill, "Arctic Maritime Claims," in Oude Elferink and Rothwell, eds., *The Law of the Sea and Polar Maritime Delimitation and Jurisdiction*, 121–23; Oude Elferink, "The Outer Continental Shelf," 197.

79. UNCLOS, article 15.

80. Ibid., article 74 (EEZ) and article 83 (continental shelf).

81. Peter Ørebech, "The Negotiation Principle, Pretention Lines and the Demise of the Sector Line as a Principle of Law in the Arctic: The 2010 Norway-Russia Delimitation Line," *Yearbook of Polar Law* 4 (2012): 505.

82. Oude Elferink and Rothwell, "Challenges," 345.

83. UNCLOS, Annex II, article 2.

84. Ibid., Annex II, article 9.

85. Yoshifumi Tanaka, "Reflections on Arctic Maritime Delimitations: A Comparative Analysis between the Case Law and State Practice," *Nordic Journal of International Law* 80 (2011): 459, 467.

86. See *Question of the Delimitation of the Continental Shelf between Nicaragua and Colombia beyond 200 Nautical Miles from the Nicaraguan Coast (Nicaragua v. Colombia)* (Preliminary Objections) March 17, 2016, para. 114.

87. Treaty between the Kingdom of Norway and the Russian Federation concerning Maritime Delimitation and Cooperation in the Barents Sea and the Arctic Ocean 2010: English translation available, accessed April 12, 2017, http://www.regjeringen .no/upload/SMK/Vedlegg/2010/avtale_engelsk.pdf. See, generally, Geir Hønneland, *Russia and the Arctic: Environment, Identity and Foreign Policy* (London: I. B. Taurus, 2016), chapter 3. On the reports of illegal fishing, see Geir Hønneland, "Cross Border Cooperation in the North: The Case of Northwest Russia," in *Russia and the North*, ed. Elana Wilson Rowe (Ottawa: University of Ottawa Press, 2009), 38–42.

88. Agreement between the Government of the Kingdom of Norway and the Government of the Union of Soviet Socialist Republics on Co-operation in the Fishing Industry 1975, 983 U.N.T.S. 8.

89. Agreement between the United States of America and the Union of Soviet Socialist Republics on the Maritime Boundary, *International Legal Materials* 29 (1990): 941.

90. Byers, *International Law and the Arctic*, 34–46.

91. Great Britain/Russia: Limits of Their Respective Possessions on the North-West Coast of America and the Navigation of the Pacific Ocean, 1825, 75 *Consolidated Treaty Series* 95.

92. US Department of State, "Notice of Limits of 1 March 1977," *International Legal Materials* 6 (1977): 418–21; see also Tanaka, "Reflections," 465–66.

93. Byers, *International Law and the Arctic*, 60–62.

94. Tanaka, "Reflections," 466.

95. Evan T. Bloom, "United States Perspectives on the Arctic," in *Governing the North American Arctic: Sovereignty, Security and Institutions*, ed. Dawn Alexandrea Berry, Nigel Bowles, and Halbert Jones (Basingstoke, UK: Palgrave Macmillan, 2016), 236–37.

96. Ted McDorman, *Salt Water Neighbors: International Ocean Law Relations between the United States and Canada* (New York: Oxford University Press, 2009), 188.

97. Alan H. Kessel, "Canadian Arctic Sovereignty: Myths and Realities," in Berry, Bowles, and Jones, eds., *Governing the North American Arctic*, 243.

98. Treaty Concerning the Archipelago of Spitsbergen, 1920, *League of Nations Treaty Series* 2 (1920): 7.

99. Erik Molenaar, "Fisheries Regulation in the Maritime Zones of Svalbard," *International Journal of Marine and Coastal Law* 27 (2012): 3, 17–21; see also Peter Ørebech, "The Geographic Scope of the Svalbard Treaty and Norwegian Sovereignty: Historic—or Evolutionary—Interpretation?" *Croatian Yearbook of European Law and Policy* 13 (2017): 53–86.

100. Irina Kim, "Legal Aspects of Liability for Environmental Damage Caused by Offshore Petroleum Operations in Greenland," in *Responsibilities and Liabilities for Commercial Activity in the Arctic: The Example of Greenland*, ed. Vibe Ulfbeck, Anders Møllmann, and Bent Ole Mortensen (Abingdon, UK: Routledge, 2016).

101. Maria Gallucci, "New Russia Sanctions: Latest EU Moves on Russian Oil Sector Would Hinder Drilling in Arctic Ocean and Shale Fields," *International Business Times*, July 29, 2014, http://www.ibtimes.com/new-russia-sanctions-latest-eu-moves-russian-oil-sector-would-hinder-drilling-arctic-1642528.

102. Andreas Kuersten, "Russian Sanctions, China, and the Arctic," *Diplomat*, January 3, 2015, http://thediplomat.com/2015/01/russian-sanctions-china-and-the-arctic; see also Atle Staalesen, "Russians Choose Chinese Explorers for Arctic Oil," *Alaska Dispatch News*, July 8, 2016, http://www.adn.com/article/20160428/russians-choose-chinese-explorers-arctic-oil; and "Russia's Yamal LNG Gets Round Sanctions with $12B Chinese Loan Deal," *Alaska Dispatch News*, May 17, 2016, http://www.adn.com/article/20160504/russias-yamal-lng-gets-round-sanctions-12b-chinese-loan-deal.

103. See chapter 3; see also Rachael L. Johnstone, "Little Fish, Big Pond: Icelandic Interests and Influence in Arctic Governance," *Nordicum-Mediterraneum* 11, no. 2 (2016), http://nome.unak.is/wordpress/volume-11-no-2-2016/conference-proceeding-volume-11-no-2-2016/little-fish-big-pond-icelandic-interests-influence-arctic-governance.

104. See Johnstone, "Little Fish."

105. *Request for an Advisory Opinion Submitted by the Sub-Regional Fisheries Commission (SRFC)* (Advisory Opinion) 2015, International Tribunal for the Law of the Sea, Case No. 21.

106. Hønneland, *Russia and the Arctic*, 47 and 171.

107. UNCLOS, part XV. However, some of the provisions of the UNCLOS are exempted from compulsory dispute settlement; see articles 297–98.

108. Treaty between the Kingdom of Norway and the Russian Federation.

CHAPTER 9: ARCTIC SHIPPING AND NAVIGATION

1. See "Arctic Bridge," accessed April 13, 2017, http://arcticbridge.com (for a simple map of the NSR and NWP); see also "Maps," Arctic Portal, accessed April 13, 2017, http://arcticportal.org (for a more complex interactive map).

2. See "The Water Area of the NSR," NSR Authority, accessed April 13, 2017, http://www.nsra.ru/en/ofitsialnaya_informatsiya/granici_smp.html (for a map of the NSR area). Previously, the NSR was defined as reaching up to the ice sheet (wherever that happens to be at any given time), potentially into the high seas, but this recently changed: see Erik Franckx, "The 'New' Arctic Passages and the 'Old' Law of the Sea," in *Jurisdiction over Ships: Post-UNCLOS Developments in the Law of the Sea*, ed. Henrik Ringbom (Leiden, Netherlands: Brill, 2015), 211–12.

3. Hugo Grotius, *The Freedom of the Seas or the Right Which Belongs to the Dutch to Take Part in the East Indian Trade* (Oxford: Oxford University Press, 1633; translation 1916).

4. UN Convention on the Law of the Sea 1982 [UNCLOS], 1833 U.N.T.S. 397, Part XII.

5. UNCLOS, article 234.

6. "Arctic Ship Traffic Data," Protection of the Marine Environment Working Group (PAME), accessed January 12, 2018, https://pame.is/index.php/projects/arctic-marine-shipping/astd.

7. PAME, *Arctic Marine Shipping Assessment* (Akureyri, Iceland: Arctic Council, 2009), 71–73.

8. Gail Fondahl and Joan Nymand Larsen, "Introduction," in *Arctic Human Development Report: Regional Processes and Global Linkages* [AHDR II], ed. Joan Nymand Larsen and Gail Fondahl (Akureyri, Iceland: Norden, 2014), 34.

9. PAME, *Arctic Marine Shipping Assessment*, 45.

10. Stephen Haycox, *Frigid Embrace: Politics, Economics, and Environment in Alaska* (Corvallis: Oregon State University Press, 2002), 42.

11. Erik Molenaar et al., *Legal Aspects of Arctic Shipping* (Brussels: DG Maritime Affairs and Fisheries, 2010), para. 665.

12. Marlene Laruelle, *Russia's Arctic Strategies and the Future of the Far North* (Abingdon, UK: Routledge, 2013), 182; see also Arild Moe, "The Northern Sea Route: Smooth Sailing Ahead?" in *Arctic: Commerce, Governance and Policy*, ed. Uttam Kumar Sinha and Jo Inge Bekkevold (Abingdon, UK: Routledge, 2015), 19; Molenaar et al., *Legal Aspects*, para. 582.

13. President of the Russian Federation, "The Fundamentals of State Policy of the Russian Federation in the Arctic in the Period till 2020 and Beyond" (Moscow: 2008); English translation accessed February 11, 2018, http://www.arctis-search.com/Russian+Federation+Policy+for+the+Arctic+to+2020.

14. "Yamal LNG," accessed February 11, 2018, http://yamallng.ru/en/.

15. Moe, "The Northern Sea Route," 25–26; see also Nadezhda Filimonova and Svetlana Krivokhizh, "China's Stakes in the Russian Arctic," *Diplomat*, January 18, 2018, https://thediplomat.com/2018/01/chinas-stakes-in-the-russian-arctic.

16. Trudi Pettersen, "Medvedev Orders Plan to Increase NSR Capacity," *Barents Observer*, June 10, 2015, http://barentsobserver.com/en/arctic/2015/06/medvedev-orders-plan-increase-northern-sea-route-capacity-10-06.

17. Quoted in Gleb Bryanski, "Russia's Putin Says Arctic Trade Route to Rival Suez," *Reuters*, September 22, 2011, https://www.reuters.com/article/us-russia-arctic-idUSTRE78L5TC20110922.

18. "Transit Statistics," NSR Authority Information Office, accessed April 13, 2017, http://www.arctic-lio.com/nsr_transits.

19. Malte Humpert, "Arctic Shipping: An Analysis of the 2013 NSR Season," *Arctic Yearbook*, 2014.

20. Ibid.

21. "Transit Statistics." See also "NSR Traffic Plummets," *Hellenic Shipping News*, December 19, 2014, http://www.hellenicshippingnews.com/northern-sea-route-traf fic-plummets.

22. "Transit Statistics." See also Malte Humpert, "Arctic Shipping on the NSR in Deep Freeze?" *High North News*, June 1, 2016, http://www.highnorthnews.com /arctic-shipping-on-the-northern-sea-route-in-deep-freeze.

23. "Transit Statistics."

24. "Transits in 2015," Vessel 3, *Winter Bay*, in "Transit Statistics."

25. See also Moe, "The Northern Sea Route," 21–22.

26. "Transit Statistics," Canal de Panamá [Panama Canal], accessed April 13, 2017, https://www.pancanal.com/eng/op/transit-stats.

27. "Navigation Statistics," Suez Canal, accessed April 13, 2017, https://www.suez canal.gov.eg/English/Navigation/Pages/NavigationStatistics.aspx.

28. Atle Staalesen, "Russia's Rosatom to Be in Charge of NSR," *Eye on the Arctic*, December 8, 2017, http://www.rcinet.ca/eye-on-the-arctic/2017/12/08/russias-rosa tom-to-be-in-charge-of-northern-sea-route.

29. Moe, "The Northern Sea Route," 26.

30. Ibid., 21 and 27; and Franckx, "The 'New' Arctic Passages," 202 and 205.

31. Michael Byers, "Arctic Cruises: Fun for Tourists, Bad for the Environment," *Globe and Mail*, April 18, 2016, http://www.theglobeandmail.com/opinion/arctic -cruises-great-for-tourists-bad-for-the-environment/article29648307.

32. Erik Bjerregaard, general manager of Hotel Arctic, Ilulissat, quoted in Kevin McGwin, "See Greenland before Mass Tourism Ruins It," *Arctic Journal*, October 17, 2016, http://arcticjournal.com/business/2628/see-greenland-mass-tourism-ruins-it.

33. See International Association of Antarctic Tour Operators, accessed April 13, 2017, http://iaato.org/home.

34. Association of Arctic Expedition Cruise Operators, accessed April 13, 2017, http://www.aeco.no.

35. "Our Members," Association of Arctic Expedition Cruise Operators, accessed April 13, 2017, https://www.aeco.no/members.

36. See chapter 2 on types of sea ice.

37. PAME, *Arctic Marine Shipping Assessment*, 24–43; see also "Arctic Climate Impact Assessment," accessed April 13, 2017, http://www.acia.uaf.edu (for more detailed studies); and "Scientific Data for Research," National Snow and Ice Data Center, accessed April 13, 2017, http://nsidc.org (for the latest figures).

38. Humpert, "Arctic Shipping," 9.

39. Hjalti Þór Hreinsson, "Arctic Shipping and China: Governance Structure and Future Developments" (master's thesis, University of Akureyri, 2014), 30–31.

40. See Charles Emmerson and Glada Lahn, *Arctic Opening: Opportunity and Risk in the High North* (London: Lloyd's, 2012).

41. "Interview: Secretary-General of the International Maritime Organization [IMO]," Arctic Council, August 24, 2015, http://www.arctic-council.org/index.php /en/our-work2/8-news-and-events/279-interview-with-secretary-general-of-the-in ternational-maritime-organization-imo; see also Karl Magnus Eger, "Shipping and

Arctic Infrastructure," in *Shipping in Arctic Waters: A Comparison of the Northeast, Northwest and Trans Polar Passages*, ed. Willy Østreng et al. (New York: Springer 2013), 202 (noting that GPS coverage is inadequate at high latitudes).

42. "Interview: Secretary-General of the IMO."

43. See, for example, Malte Humpert, "The Future of Arctic Shipping: A New Silk Road for China?" *Arctic Institute*, November 13, 2013, http://www.thearcticinstitute.org/the-future-of-arctic-shipping-new-silk, 4; and Malte Humpert, "China Sends More Than a Dozen Vessels through the Arctic Ocean," *High North News*, December 6, 2017, http://www.highnorthnews.com/china-sends-more-than-a-dozen-vessels-through-the-arctic-ocean.

44. Laruelle, *Russia's Arctic Strategies*, 177; see Molenaar et al., *Legal Aspects*, chapters 8.2–8.3.

45. See Nengye Liu, "China's Role in the Changing Governance of Arctic Shipping," *Yearbook of Polar Law* 6 (2014): 545, 553 (on the importance of freedom of navigation in Chinese international policy and their concerns regarding environmental regulations).

46. Japan, *Japan's Arctic Policy* (Tokyo: Headquarters for Ocean Policy, 2015).

47. Ibid.

48. See section below, "Arctic Controversies."

49. UNCLOS, article 21.

50. Ibid., article 234.

51. UNCLOS, article 236; see also Henrik Ringbom, "The European Union and Arctic Shipping," in *The European Union and the Arctic*, eds. Nengye Liu, Elizabeth A. Kirk, and Tore Henriksen (Leiden, Netherlands: Brill, 2017), 253–55.

52. Hugo Caminos and Vincent P. Cogliati-Bantz, *The Legal Regime of Straits* (Cambridge: Cambridge University Press, 2014), 416.

53. UNCLOS, articles 7 and 10.

54. See Suzanne Lalonde and Frédéric Lasserre, "The Position of the United States on the NWP: Is the Fear of Creating a Precedent Warranted?" *Ocean Development and International Law* 44, no. 1 (2013): 28, 29, and 40, for maps of the Canadian and Russian Arctic baselines.

55. Donat Pharand, *Canada's Arctic Waters in International Law* (Cambridge: Cambridge University Press, 1988), 162.

56. UNCLOS, article 7.

57. Caminos and Cogliati-Bantz, *The Legal Regime*, 67–70.

58. See Donat Pharand, "The Arctic Waters and the NWP: A Final Revisit," *Ocean Development and International Law* 38, no. 1–2 (2007): 3, 11–13; and Caminos and Cogliati-Bantz, *The Legal Regime*, 67–70. The straight baselines are probably justified under customary law and the UNCLOS but not the claims of historic waters; hence the waters inside are internal waters, but other states may still have rights of innocent or transit passage within them: see Pharand, "The Arctic Waters," 28.

59. Pharand, "The Arctic Waters," 29.

60. UNCLOS, articles 37 and 38.

61. Ibid., article 36.

62. Ibid., articles 18–19, 38, and 45.

63. In theory, it could also join the high seas if the nearest coastal state has not declared an EEZ. It can also be wider than 24 nm if the EEZ channel running down

the middle is not "of similar convenience"—for example, owing to rocks, sandbanks, strong currents, and the like.

64. Federal Act on the Internal Maritime Waters, Territorial Sea and Contiguous Zone of the Russian Federation, adopted by the State Duma on July 16, 1998, approved by the Federation Council on July 17, 1998, article 14. See also "The Water Area of the NSR."

65. See Lalonde and Lasserre, "The Position of the United States," 29 (for a map of the Canadian Arctic baselines and Northwest Passage).

66. UNCLOS, article 37; *Corfu Channel Case (United Kingdom v. Albania)* (Merits) 1949 International Court of Justice, *ICJ Reports* 1949: 4, 28–29.

67. *Corfu Channel.*

68. Caminos and Cogliati-Bantz, *The Legal Regime,* 127–28; Convention on the Territorial Sea and the Contiguous Zone, 1958, 206 U.N.T.S. 1964, article 16(4).

69. Ibid., 129.

70. Michael Byers, *International Law in the Arctic* (Cambridge: Cambridge University Press, 2013), 134.

71. Canadian Statement on Canadian Sovereignty over the Arctic Region, *International Legal Materials* 24 (1985): 1723; see also Byers, *International Law in the Arctic,* 134 (arguing that the critical date for the NWP might be 1969, based on the first dispute regarding the passage of the American vessel *SS Manhattan*; on the *Manhattan* voyage, see below).

72. Caminos and Cogliati-Bantz, *The Legal Regime,* 129.

73. Donald R. Rothwell and Tim Stephens, *The International Law of the Sea,* 2nd ed. (Oxford: Hart Publishing, 2010), 14.

74. UNCLOS, preambular para. 1; see also *The South China Sea Arbitration (The Republic of Philippines v. The People's Republic of China)* (Judgment), PCA Case No. 2013-19, 2016, paras. 245–46, 261–62.

75. Caminos and Cogliati-Bantz, *The Legal Regime,* 130; and Pharand, "The Arctic Waters," 36 (pointing out that the more common view among states is that actual use is necessary).

76. Michael Byers and Suzanne Lalonde, "Who Controls the Northwest Passage?" *Vanderbilt Journal of Transnational Law* 42 (2009): 1133, 1162; Tullio Scovazzi, "The Baseline of the Territorial Sea: The Practice of Arctic States," in *The Law of the Sea and Polar Maritime Delimitation and Jurisdiction,* ed. Alex G. Oude Elferink and Donald R. Rothwell (Leiden, Netherlands: Martinus Nijhoff, 2001), 79–80.

77. EU Council, *Council Conclusions on Arctic Issues,* 2985th Foreign Affairs Council meeting, December 8, 2009, para. 16 (reiterating "the rights and obligations for flag, port and coastal states . . . in relation to freedom of navigation, the right of innocent passage and transit passage"). However, in the 2014 *Council Conclusions,* the council refers only to "freedom of navigation and the right of innocent passage," but not transit passage; see EU Council, *Council Conclusions on Developing a European Union Policy Towards the Arctic Region,* 3312th Foreign Affairs Council meeting, May 12, 2014, para. 10. See also Molenaar et al., *Legal Aspects,* para. 36 (casting doubt on Canada's assertions of historic waters).

78. Caminos and Cogliati-Bantz, *The Legal Regime,* 138–39.

79. John D. Negroponte, "Who Will Protect Freedom of the Seas?" Department of State bulletin, October 1986, 42.

80. National Security Presidential Directive and Homeland Security Presidential Directive, January 9, 2009, para. III.B.5.

81. United States, *National Strategy for the Arctic Region* (Washington, DC: The White House, 2013), 6.

82. Lalonde and Lasserre, "The Position of the United States," especially 30–31.

83. Foreign Ministers of Canada, Denmark, Norway, Russia, and the United States of America, *The Ilulissat Declaration*, May 28, 2008.

84. See Rothwell and Stephens, *The International Law of the Sea*, 253 (on the number of voyages in the twentieth and twenty-first centuries); see also Caminos and Cogliati-Bantz, *The Legal Regime*, 140–41.

85. PAME, *Arctic Marine Shipping Assessment*, 37.

86. Since Canada was then a British colony, this does not constitute "international" navigation; see Pharand, "The Arctic Waters," 9.

87. Ibid., 42.

88. PAME, *Arctic Marine Shipping Assessment*, 39; Byers and Lalonde, "Who Controls the Northwest Passage?" 1148.

89. Byers and Lalonde, "Who Controls the Northwest Passage?" at note 89; Byers, *International Law in the Arctic*, 135.

90. Byers and Lalonde, "Who Controls the Northwest Passage?" 1156–59. "Without prejudice" means that they reach a working understanding, but the agreement and their actions are not to be considered as giving up or modifying in any way their legal claims.

91. Canadian statement on Canadian sovereignty.

92. Arctic Waters Pollution Prevention Act, R.S.C., 1975, c. A-12.

93. Byers and Lalonde, "Who Controls the Northwest Passage?" 1150.

94. Ted McDorman, "The New Definition of 'Canada Lands' and the Determination of the Outer Limits of the Continental Shelf," *Journal of Maritime Law and Commerce* 14 (1983): 215.

95. Tony Penikett, *Hunting the Northern Character* (Vancouver: University of British Columbia Press, 2017), 197.

96. Byers, *International Law in the Arctic*, 168.

97. The picture changes if evidence comes to light that Canada was in fact aware of American submarines in the NWP, as this would constitute acquiescence: see Byers, ibid. Given the Soviet response to the American icebreakers, it is unlikely that the Soviets were aware of individual NATO submarine voyages, even if they may have suspected that NATO submarines were in the straits from time to time.

98. Wendy Stueck, "Ship Crosses NWP, Sails into History," *Globe and Mail*, September 25, 2013, http://www.theglobeandmail.com/news/british-columbia/bulk-car rier-becomes-first-to-successfully-traverse-northwest-passage/article14516278.

99. Ibid.

100. Pharand, "The Arctic Waters," 31–33, table 1.

101. "Malacca Strait Traffic Hits an All Time High in 2014, VLCCs and Dry Bulk Lead Growth," *Seatrade Maritime News*, February 27, 2015, http://www .seatrade-maritime.com/news/asia/malacca-strait-traffic-hits-an-all-time-high-in -2014-vlccs-and-dry-bulk-lead-growth.html.

102. PAME, *Arctic Marine Shipping Assessment*, 43.

103. Eric Franckx, "The Legal Regime of Navigation in the Russian Arctic," *Journal of Transnational Law and Policy* 18, no. 2 (2009): 327, 328–29.

104. Mikhail Gorbachev, Speech in Murmansk, October 1, 1987, accessed April 17, 2018, https://www.barentsinfo.fi/docs/Gorbachev_speech.pdf.

105. Franckx, "The Legal Regime," 329.

106. Ibid., and PAME, *Arctic Marine Shipping Assessment*, 44.

107. Franckx, "The Legal Regime," 329.

108. Caminos and Cogliati-Bantz, *The Legal Regime*, 147.

109. See Erik Franckx, "Non-Soviet Shipping in the Northeast Passage, and the Legal Status of Proliv Vil'kitskogo," *Polar Record* 24 (1988): 269–76.

110. Under the UNCLOS agreed fifteen years later, warships do enjoy a right of innocent passage in the territorial sea.

111. Byers, *International Law in the Arctic*, 145; see also Caminos and Cogliati-Bantz, *The Legal Regime*, 145–46.

112. Byers, *International Law in the Arctic*, 146; Said Mamoudi, "International Navigation in the Arctic Waters," in *Ocean Law and Policy: Twenty Years of Development under the UNCLOS Regime*, ed. Carlos Espósito et al. (Leiden, Netherlands: Brill, 2014), 458.

113. Erik Franckx, "De reis van het Greenpeace schip, de MV *Solo*, naar Novaia Zemlia en het internationaal recht: enkele bemerkingen" [The voyage of the Greenpeace ship, MV *Solo*, to Novaya Zemlya and international law: Some remarks], in *Liber Amicorum Paul De Vriede* [Book in honor of Paul de Vriede], ed. C. Eliaerts, M. Flamée, and P. Colle (Diegem, Belgium: Kluwer Rechtswetenschappen België, 1994), 803–36; see also Franckx, "The 'New' Arctic Passages," 214.

114. Franckx, "The 'New' Arctic Passages," 208.

115. Ibid.

116. Ibid., 207–8.

117. See Alex G. Oude Elferink, "The *Arctic Sunrise* Incident: A Multi-Faceted Law of the Sea Case with a Human Rights Dimension," *International Journal of Marine and Coastal Law* 29 (2014): 244.

118. Pharand, "The Arctic Waters, 44.

119. Agreement between the Government of Canada and the Government of the United States of America on Arctic Cooperation 1988, 1852 U.N.T.S. 59.

120. Byers, *International Law in the Arctic*, 140–41.

121. James Kraska, "Canadian Arctic Shipping Regulations and the Law of the Sea," in *Governing the North American Arctic: Sovereignty, Security and Institutions*, ed. Dawn Alexandrea Berry, Nigel Bowles, and Halbert Jones (Basingstoke, UK: Palgrave Macmillan, 2016), 62–64.

122. Franckx, "The 'New' Arctic Passages," 196 and 213; Andrei Zagorski, "Russia's Arctic Governance Policies," in *The New Arctic Governance*, ed. Linda Jakobson and Neil Melvin (Oxford: Oxford University Press, 2016), 91.

123. Caminos and Cogliati-Bantz, *The Legal Regime*, 415.

124. Marc Lanteigne, "China and the NWP: A Widening Scope," *Arctic Journal*, April 20, 2016, http://arcticjournal.com/opinion/2292/widening-scope.

125. Maritime Safety Administration of the People's Republic of China, *Guidance on Arctic Navigation in the Northeast Route*, September 18, 2014; see also Nengye Liu and Kamrul Hossain, "China and Arctic Shipping," in *Arctic Law and Governance: The Role of China and Finland*, ed. Timo Koivurova, Tianbao Qin, Sébastien Duyck, and Tapio Nykänen (Oxford: Hart Publishing, 2017), 244.

126. Lalonde and Lasserre, "The Position of the United States," 42–43 and 45.

127. UNCLOS, part XII.

128. Conservation of Arctic Flora and Fauna (CAFF), *State of the Arctic: Marine Biodiversity Report* (Akureyri, Iceland: Arctic Council, 2017), 18.

129. See, for example, Lisa Johnson, "Tofino Boat Rescue Triggered by Single Flare That Almost Wasn't Seen," CBC News, October 27, 2015, http://www.cbc.ca/news/canada/british-columbia/tofino-boat-rescue-story-1.3290892; Bethany Lindsay and Joanne Lee-Young, "Five British Citizens Dead, One Person Missing after Whale Watching Vessel Capsizes near Tofino," *Vancouver Sun*, October 27, 2015, http://www.vancouversun.com/news/least+five+people+dead+after+whale+watching+vessel+capsizes+near+tofino/11467007/story.html; Dirk Meissner, "'It Happened Super Quick': Giant Wave Knocked over Leviathan II," CTV News, November 24, 2015, http://www.ctvnews.ca/canada/it-happened-super-quick-giant-wave-knocked-over-leviathan-ii-1.2671934.

130. Jane George, "Stranded Passengers Find Warmth in Kugluktuk," *Nunatsiaq Online*, August 30, 2010, http://www.nunatsiaqonline.ca/stories/article/3008109_Stranded-passengers_crew_find_warm_welcome_in_Kugluktuk.

131. See PAME, *Arctic Marine Shipping Assessment*, 80, on contagious diseases.

132. Eger, "Shipping and Arctic Infrastructure," especially at 40 (for an explanation of kinds of pollution by vessel type).

133. Rothwell and Stephens, *The International Law of the Sea*, 338–39 (with reference to a 1990 study that found ship-sourced pollution to constitute 12 percent of ocean pollution but with grounds to believe that the share has since fallen, owing to stricter regulation of ships. Most ocean pollution originates on land or in rivers and is washed into the oceans [44 percent], or it comes from airborne pollution that is absorbed into the ocean [33 percent]).

134. *Hagsmunir Íslands á norðurslóðum: tækifæri og áskóranir* [Iceland's interests in the Arctic: Opportunities and challenges] (Reykjavík: Office of the Prime Minister of Iceland, 2016), https://www.forsaetisraduneyti.is/media/Skyrslur/HAGsmunamat_Skyrsla-LR-.pdf, 39.

135. Eger, "Shipping and Arctic Infrastructure," 172.

136. Rothwell and Stephens, *The International Law of the Sea*, 229.

137. PAME, *Arctic Marine Shipping Assessment*, 141–45.

138. See chapter 10 on the Black Carbon Framework, according to which Arctic states and observers at the Arctic Council log their black carbon and methane emissions with a view to reduction.

139. PAME, *Arctic Marine Shipping Assessment*, 138–41.

140. Ibid., 146–50.

141. Ibid., 145–46; see also Elena McCarthy, "International Regulation of Transboundary Pollutants: The Emerging Challenge of Ocean Noise," *Ocean and Coastal Law Journal* 6 (2001): 257.

142. PAME, *Arctic Marine Shipping Assessment*, 146.

143. Ibid., 150.

144. Eger, "Shipping and Arctic Infrastructure," chapter 4.4 (on the effects of an oil spill in Arctic waters).

145. PAME, *Arctic Marine Shipping Assessment*, 88–89.

146. International Code for Ships Operating in Polar Waters [Polar Code], IMO, Doc. No. MEPC 68/21/Add.1.

147. UNCLOS, article 211(1).

148. Ibid., article 211(4).

149. Ibid., article 211(5).

150. Ibid., article 211(3).

151. Ibid., article 218.

152. See PAME, *Arctic Marine Shipping Assessment*, 50–69; and Molenaar et al., *Legal Aspects*, chapter 3 (but note that both were published before the Polar Code was concluded).

153. Revised guidelines for the identification and designation of Particularly Sensitive Sea Areas (PSSAs), IMO Resolution A.982(24), December 1, 2005. See also Suzanne Lalonde, "Marine Protected Areas in the Arctic," in *The Law of the Sea and the Polar Regions: Interactions between Global and Regional Regimes*, ed. Erik J. Molenaar, Alex G. Oude Elferink, and Donald R. Rothwell (Leiden, Netherlands: Martinus Nijhoff, 2013), 91; Andrea Scassola, "An International Polar Code of Navigation: Consequences and Opportunities for the Arctic," *Yearbook of Polar Law 5* (2013): 271, 294–95.

154. International Convention for the Prevention of Pollution from Ships & Protocols (MARPOL), 1973, 1978, and 1997, 1340 U.N.T.S. 61; see Scassola, "An International Polar Code," 293–94.

155. See, generally, Lalonde, "Marine Protected Areas."

156. Agreement on Cooperation on Aeronautical and Maritime Search and Rescue in the Arctic 2011, accessed March 1, 2018, https://oaarchive.arctic-council.org/handle/11374/531.

157. See Convention on International Civil Aviation (Chicago Convention) 1944, 15 U.N.T.S. 295; and International Convention on Maritime Search and Rescue 1979, 1405 U.N.T.S. 23489; see also Byers, *International Law in the Arctic*, 274–79.

158. Agreement on Cooperation on Marine Oil Pollution Preparedness and Response in the Arctic 2013 [MOPPR], accessed March 1, 2018, https://oaarchive.arctic-council.org/handle/11374/529.

159. MOPPR appendix IV, "Operational Guidelines" (as revised, January 28, 2014), http://www.arctic-council.org/eppr/wp-content/uploads/2014/03/NCR-5979727 -v1-OPERATIONAL_GUIDELINES_ENGLISH_FINAL_WITH_UPDATE_PROCE DURES_NO_PHONE_NR.pdf.

160. Framework Plan for Cooperation on Prevention of Oil Pollution from Petroleum and Maritime Activities in the Marine Areas of the Arctic 2015, accessed February 11, 2018, http://arctic-council.org/eppr/wp-content/uploads/2015/04/ACMMCA 09_Iqaluit_2015_SAO_Report_Annex_3_TFOPP_Framework_Plan.pdf.

161. Polar Code.

162. *Guidelines for Ships Operating in Polar Waters* (London: IMO, 2010).

163. International Convention for the Safety of Life at Sea (SOLAS) 1974, 1184 U.N.T.S. 278.

164. Knut Espen Solberg, Robert Brown, Eirik Skogvoll, and Ove Tobias Gudmestad, "Risk Reduction as a Result of Implementation of the Functional Based IMO Polar Code in the Arctic Cruise Industry," in *The Inter-Connected Arctic*, ed. Kiirsi Latola and Hannele Savela (New York: Springer, 2017), 257–68.

165. Parts IA and IIA are binding; parts IB and IIB are recommendatory. See full text for details, accessed February 11, 2018, http://www.imo.org/en/Media Centre/HotTopics/polar/Documents/POLAR%20CODE%20TEXT%20AS%20 ADOPTED.pdf.

166. Liu, "China's Role," 556–57 (explaining that the Chinese taxation system makes it very expensive to register a foreign-built ship as "Chinese," as to do so would subject it to heavy customs and VAT duties. On the other hand, if a ship owner registers a Chinese-built ship to another state, it qualifies as an "export" for which the owner can claim a tax rebate).

167. Rothwell and Stephens, *The International Law of the Sea*, 366. But see *Request for an Advisory Opinion Submitted by the Sub-Regional Fisheries Commission (SRFC)* (Advisory Opinion), April 2, 2015, International Tribunal for the Law of the Sea, Case No. 21 (indicating that this is now a distinct possibility).

168. Molenaar et al., *Legal Aspects*, para. 883.

169. See ibid., chapter 4.3, for details.

170. Northern Canada Vessel Traffic Services Zone Regulations, SOR/2010-127 (amending the Canada Shipping Act, 2001), section 2.

171. Ibid., sections 6–8.

172. Kraska, "Canadian Arctic Shipping," 60–61.

173. "Safe and Responsible Marine Practices in the Arctic," Arctic Waterways Safety Commission, accessed April 13, 2017, http://www.arcticwaterways.org.

174. Laruelle, *Russia's Arctic Strategies*, 172.

175. In the Antarctic, the International Association of Antarctic Tour Operators has adopted the practice of sending cruise ships in pairs—sufficiently close in case a rescue is needed but sufficiently distant that they are not in sight of one another.

176. PAME, *Arctic Marine Shipping Assessment*, 27; for full data on all 220 transits from 1853 to 2014, see R. K. Headland, "Transits of the NWP to End of the 2014 Navigation Season," Scott Polar Research Institute, accessed April 13, 2017, http://www.americanpolar.org/wp-content/uploads/2014/10/NWP-2014-X-5-lay out-for-PDF.pdf.

177. Laruelle, *Russia's Arctic Strategies*, 169.

CHAPTER 10: ENVIRONMENTAL PROTECTION IN THE ARCTIC

1. The origins of this principle go back to a 1941 case of a Canadian factory sending air pollution across the US border: *Trail Smelter Arbitration (United States v. Canada)* 1941, Ad Hoc International Arbitral Tribunal, *UN Reports of International Arbitral Awards* 4 (1941): 1905; see also *Corfu Channel Case (United Kingdom v. Albania)* (Merits) 1949 International Court of Justice, *ICJ Reports* 1949: 4.

2. Stephen Haycox, *Frigid Embrace: Politics, Economics, and Environment in Alaska* (Corvallis: Oregon State University Press, 2002), 139.

3. "Toxic Release Inventory (TRI) Program," US Environmental Protection Agency (EPA), accessed January 22, 2018, https://www.epa.gov/toxics-release-inventory-tri-program.

4. Mauro Mazzi, *Aurora borealis: Diritto polare e comparazione giuridica* [The Northern Lights: Polar law and legal comparison] (Bologna: Filo diritto editore, 2014), 49.

5. Tom Barry, Hólmgrímur Helgason, and Soffía Guðmundsdóttir, "Arctic Protected Areas in 2017: Status and Trends," *Biodiversity* 18, no. 4 (2017): 4, doi:1 0.1080/14888386.2017.1390496. Since publication of the aforementioned article, Kujataa and Aasivissuit–Nipisat (both in Greenland) have been given World Heritage status by UNESCO. See UNESCO, "Kujataa Greenland: Norse and Inuit Farming at the Edge of the Ice Cap," accessed September 3, 2018, https://whc.unesco.org/en/list/1536; and UNESCO, "Aasivissuit–Nipisat: Inuit Hunting Ground between Ice and Sea," accessed September 3, 2018, https://whc.unesco.org/en/list/1557.

6. This is usually expressed in Latin as *sic utere tuo ut alienum non laedas*, sometimes abbreviated to *sic utere tuo.*

7. Patricia Birnie, Alan Boyle, and Catherine Redgwell, *International Law and the Environment*, 3rd ed. (Oxford: Oxford University Press, 2009), 137; *Case Concerning Pulp Mills on the River Uruguay (Argentina v. Uruguay)* 2010, International Court of Justice, *ICJ Reports* 2010: 14, para. 101; see also ibid., para. 265 ("deleterious effects or caused harm"). See also Convention on Environmental Impact Assessment in a Transboundary Context 1991, *International Legal Materials* 30 (1991): 800 (Espoo Convention); Stockholm Declaration on the Human Environment 1972, *International Legal Materials* 11 (1972): 1416, principles 21 and 22; and Rio Declaration on Environment and Development 1992, *International Legal Materials* 31 (1992): 876, principles 2 and 13.

8. *Legality of the Threat or Use of Nuclear Weapons* (Advisory Opinion) 1996, International Court of Justice, *ICJ Reports* 1996: 254, para. 29.

9. National Environmental Policy Act, 1969 (NEPA), 42 U.S.C. §§ 4321–27 (2000).

10. Roman Sidortsov, "At the Crossroads of Policy Ambitions and Political Reality: Reflections on the Prospects of LNG Development in Russia," *Oil, Gas and Energy Law Intelligence* 15, no. 4 (2017): 1, 15–16.

11. Convention on Access to Information, Public Participation in Decision-Making and Access to Justice in Environmental Matters 1998, *International Legal Materials* 38 (1999): 517 (Aarhus Convention); see also chapter 7.

12. *Pulp Mills*, para. 204.

13. *Certain Activities Carried Out by Nicaragua in the Border Area (Costa Rica v. Nicaragua)* and *Construction of a Road in Costa Rica along the San Juan River (Nicaragua v. Costa Rica)* 2015, International Court of Justice, *ICJ Reports* 2015: 665, para. 153.

14. UN Convention on the Law of the Sea [UNCLOS] 1982, 1833 U.N.T.S. 397, articles 205 and 206.

15. Espoo Convention; see also Rachael Lorna Johnstone, "Evaluating Espoo: What Protection Does the Espoo Convention Offer the Arctic Marine Environment?" *Yearbook of Polar Law* 5 (2013): 337.

16. "Points of Contact regarding Notification," UNECE, accessed April 14, 2017, http://www.unece.org/env/eia/points_of_contact.html.

17. Wiek Schrage, "The Convention on Environmental Impact Assessment in a Transboundary Context," in *Theory and Practice of Transboundary Environmental Impact Assessment*, ed. Kees Bastmeijer and Timo Koivurova (Leiden, Netherlands: Martinus Nijhoff, 2008), 44.

18. Timo Koivurova, "Transboundary Environmental Assessment in the Arctic," *Impact Assessment and Project Appraisal* 26, no. 4 (2008): 265, 268.

19. "Guidelines for Environmental Impact Assessment (EIA) in the Arctic" (Finnish Ministry for the Environment, 1997).

20. Robin Warner, "Environmental Assessments in the Marine Areas of the Polar Regions," in *The Law of the Sea and the Polar Regions: Interactions between Global and Regional Regimes*, ed. Erik J. Molenaar, Alex G. Oude Elferink, and Donald R. Rothwell (Leiden, Netherlands: Martinus Nijhoff, 2013), 156, 165–67, and 169; see also Timo Koivurova, *Environmental Impact Assessment in the Arctic: A Study of International Legal Norms* (Farnham, UK: Ashgate, 2002); "Arctic EIA Project," Sustainable Development Working Group, last modified September 20, 2017, http://www.sdwg.org/arctic-eia/.

21. Protection of the Marine Environment Working Group, "Arctic Offshore Oil and Gas Guidelines," 3rd ed. (Akureyri, Iceland: Arctic Council, 2009).

22. Ibid., 4.

23. For example, NEPA, §1351(h).

24. See, for example, Alexander Langshaw, "Giving Substance to Form: Moving towards an Integrated Governance Model of Transboundary Environmental Impact Assessment," *Nordic Journal of International Law* 81 (2012): 21, 29.

25. See Rachael Lorna Johnstone, *Offshore Oil and Gas Development in the Arctic under International Law: Risk and Responsibility* (Leiden, Netherlands: Brill, 2015), chapter 10 (on the consequences of wrongful acts in international law).

26. *Responsibilities and Obligations of States Sponsoring Persons and Entities with Respect to Activities in the Area* (Advisory Opinion) 2011, International Tribunal for the Law of the Sea: Seabed Disputes Chamber Case No. 17, accessed April 13, 2017, http://www.itlos.org/index.php?id=109, para. 145.

27. Ibid., para. 131; but see *Southern Bluefin Tuna* cases (*New Zealand v. Japan; Australia v. Japan*) (Order for Provisional Measures) 1999, International Tribunal for the Law of the Sea, Cases Nos. 3 and 4, *International Legal Materials* 38 (1999): 1624, paras. 79–80 (referring to "prudence and caution" to justify provisional measures).

28. Rio Declaration, principle 15.

29. If the scientific evidence *conclusively* points to a risk of transboundary harm, then the no-harm principle applies: the state must conduct a transboundary EIA and take its findings into account, and the state must not permit an activity that it knows is likely to significantly damage its neighbor.

30. Malgosia Fitzmaurice, *Contemporary Issues in International Environmental Law* (Cheltenham, UK: Edward Elgar, 2009), 29–30.

31. Agreement on Cooperation on Marine Oil Pollution Preparedness and Response in the Arctic 2013, accessed March 1, 2018, https://oaarchive.arctic-council.org/handle/11374/529.

32. For example, the Marine Mammal Protection Act, 1972, 16 U.S.C. § 31; see also, for example, "EPA Administrator Scott Pruitt Suspends Withdrawal of Proposed Determination in Bristol Bay Watershed, Will Solicit Additional Comments,"

EPA News Release, January 26, 2018, https://www.epa.gov/newsreleases/epa-ad ministrator-scott-pruitt-suspends-withdrawal-proposed-determination-bristol-bay.

33. Convention on Biological Diversity (CBD) 1992, 1760 U.N.T.S. 79.

34. Ulrich Beyerlin and Thilo Marauhn, *International Environmental Law* (Oxford: Hart Publishing, 2011), 179 and 193.

35. CBD, article 8(j).

36. Nagoya Protocol on Access to Genetic Resources and the Fair and Equitable Sharing of Benefits Arising from Their Utilization to the 1992 Convention on Biological Diversity 2010, UNTS, UNEP/CBD/COP/DEC/X/1.

37. Convention on Biological Diversity, Conference of the Parties 7, Akwé: Kon Voluntary Guidelines for the Conduct of Cultural, Environmental and Social Impact Assessment Regarding Developments Proposed to Take Place on, or Which Are Likely to Impact on, Sacred Sites and on Lands and Waters Traditionally Occupied or Used by Indigenous and Local Communities, CBD, COP 7, Decision VII/16 F (2004), http://www.cbd.int/doc/publications/akwe-brochure-en.pdf.

38. Convention on Biological Diversity, Conference of the Parties 8, Voluntary Guidelines on Biodiversity–Inclusive Impact Assessment, CBD, COP 8, Decision VIII/28 (2006), http://www.cbd.int/doc/publications/imp-bio-eia-and-sea.pdf.

39. Conservation of Arctic Flora and Fauna Working Group (CAFF), *Arctic Biodiversity Assessment* (Akureyri, Iceland: Arctic Council, 2014).

40. Secretariat of the Convention on Biological Diversity and CAFF, Resolution on Cooperation between the Secretariats of the Convention on Biological Diversity and the Conservation of Arctic Flora and Fauna Working Group, March 21, 2009, https://www.cbd.int/doc/agreements/agmt-caff-2009-04-14-moc-web-en.pdf.

41. See "International Partners," CAFF, accessed April 14, 2017, http://www.caff .is/international-partnerships (for the full and current list of CAFF Resolutions of Cooperation and other international partnerships).

42. Convention on Wetlands of International Importance Especially as Waterfowl Habitat 1971, 996 U.N.T.S. 245.

43. "Arctic Migratory Birds Initiative," CAFF, accessed April 14, 2017, http://www .caff.is/arctic-migratory-birds-initiative-ambi.

44. Convention Concerning the Protection of the World Cultural and Natural Heritage 1972, 1037 U.N.T.S. 151.

45. Marine Mammal Protection Act.

46. Executive Order 13158, May 26, 2000, "Marine Protected Areas," *Federal Register* 65, no. 105 (2000): 34909.

47. Mark Dowie, *Conservation Refugees: The Hundred-Year Conflict between Global Conservation and Native Peoples* (Cambridge, MA: MIT Press, 2009), xvii–xviii.

48. Report of the World Commission on Environment and Development, "Our Common Future," August 1987, UN Doc. UN General Assembly Resolution 42/187 (Brundtland Report), second preambular paragraph.

49. John English, "The Emergence of an Arctic Council," in *Governing the North American Arctic: Sovereignty, Security and Institutions*, ed. Dawn Alexandrea Berry, Nigel Bowles, and Halbert Jones (Basingstoke, UK: Palgrave Macmillan, 2016), 221.

50. See, for example, "The SDGs in the Arctic: Local and Global Perspectives," SAO Meeting, March 22, 2018, Levi, Finland, https://oaarchive.arctic-council.org /handle/11374/2149.

51. "Sustainable Development Goals in the Arctic: Local and Global Perspectives," International High-Level Conference, December 1, 2017, Copenhagen, http://um.dk /en/foreign-policy/the-arctic/the-sdgs-in-the-arctic/program/.

52. "Rovaniemi Arctic Spirit Conference," November 14–16, 2017, accessed February 12, 2018, http://www.rovaniemiarcticspirit.fi/EN.

53. See "Arctic Climate Impact Assessment," accessed April 14, 2017, http://www .acia.uaf.edu; see also chapter 2.

54. Arctic Circle Forum, "Scotland and the New North," Edinburgh, November 20, 2017, available at "Videos from the Arctic Circle Forum in Edinburgh: Scotland and the New North," accessed January 22, 2018, http://www.arcticcircle.org /forums/scotland/videos.

55. United Nations Framework Convention on Climate Change 1992, 1771 U.N.T.S. 107.

56. Kyoto Protocol to the United Nations Framework Convention on Climate Change 1997, 2303 U.N.T.S. 162.

57. Timo Koivurova, *Introduction to International Environmental Law* (Abingdon, UK: Routledge, 2014), 166; and Beyerlin and Marauhn, *International Environmental Law*, 159–64.

58. Koivurova, *Introduction to International Environmental Law*, 166–67; Beyerlin and Marauhn, *International Environmental Law*, 168–71.

59. Jorge E. Viñuales, "The Paris Climate Agreement: An Initial Examination, Part I," *European Journal of International Law: Talk!*, February 7, 2016, https://www .ejiltalk.org/the-paris-climate-agreement-an-initial-examination-part-i-of-ii.

60. Prime Minister Trudeau was "green" both in the sense of being environmentally aware and in the sense of being new to the job, having taken office just twenty-six days before.

61. United Nations Treaty Series, chapter XXVII, 7.d, Paris Agreement 2015. Status as of April 14, 2017, https://treaties.un.org/Pages/ViewDetails.aspx?src= TREATY&mtdsg_no=XXVII-7-d&chapter=27&clang=_en.

62. Coral Davenport, "Top Trump Advisers Are Split on Paris Agreement on Climate Change," *New York Times*, March 2, 2017, https://www.nytimes.com/2017/03/02 /us/politics/climate-change-trump.html?_r=0.

63. Fiona Harvey and Jonathan Watts, "US Groups Honouring Paris Climate Pledges Despite Trump," *Guardian*, November 11, 2017, https://www.theguardian.com/envi ronment/2017/nov/11/us-groups-honouring-paris-climate-pledges-despite-trump.

64. Paris Agreement, December 12, 2015, U.N.T.S., C.N. 92.2016. TREATIES-XX-VII.7.d.

65. Ibid., article 2(1)(a).

66. Ibid., article 4(2).

67. Cécile Pelaudeix, "Towards an Integrated and Participatory Governance of the Arctic Marine Areas," in *Governance of Arctic Offshore Oil and Gas*, ed. Cécile Pelaudeix and Ellen Margrethe Basse (Abingdon, UK: Routledge, 2017), 287.

68. Jorge E. Viñuales, "The Paris Climate Agreement: An Initial Examination, Part II," *European Journal of International Law: Talk!*, February 8, 2016, https://www.ejiltalk.org/the-paris-climate-agreement-an-initial-examination-part-ii-of-iii.
69. Paris Agreement, articles 4(3), 4(11), and 28.
70. Ibid., article 4(4).
71. Ibid., article 5.
72. Ibid., article 7 and preamble.
73. Ibid., article 7(5).
74. Ibid., article 8; Viñuales, "The Paris Climate Agreement . . . Part II."
75. Paris Agreement, article 15.
76. Convention on Long-Range Transboundary Air Pollution 1979, 1302 U.N.T.S. 127.
77. UNCLOS, article 192.
78. Ibid., article 193.
79. Statute of the International Court of Justice 1945, *United States Treaty Series* 1945: 993, article 36.
80. "Jurisdiction," International Court of Justice, accessed February 21, 2018, http://www.icj-cij.org/en/jurisdiction.
81. See, for example, Agreement on Cooperation on Marine Oil Pollution.
82. *Case Concerning Pulp Mills on the River Uruguay (Argentina v. Uruguay)* (Provisional Measures) 2006, International Court of Justice, *ICJ Reports* 2006: 113; *Case Concerning Pulp Mills on the River Uruguay (Argentina v. Uruguay)* (Provisional Measures) 2007, International Court of Justice, *ICJ Reports* 2007: 3.
83. *Pulp Mills* (Provisional Measures) 2006, paras. 73–74. See also *Mox Plant Case (Ireland v. United Kingdom)* (Order for Provisional Measures) 2001, International Tribunal for the Law of the Sea, Case No. 10, accessed April 14, 2017, http://www.itlos.org/fileadmin/itlos/documents/cases/case_no_10/Order.03.12.01.E.pdf (separate opinion of Judge Wolfrum) (on the exceptional nature of provisional measures); but see *Southern Bluefin Tuna* cases (where provisional measures were awarded).
84. *Pulp Mills* (Provisional Measures) 2007, paras. 39, 42, and 50.
85. See generally, Rachael Lorna Johnstone, "Environmental Governance through the Arctic Council: The Arctic Council as Initiator of Norms of International Environmental Law," Working Paper No. 1, Polar Cooperation and Research Centre, Kobe University, Japan, 2016.

CHAPTER 11: THE FUTURE OF ARCTIC GOVERNANCE

1. Reuven Glick and Alan M. Taylor, "Collateral Damage: Trade Disruption and the Economic Impact of War," *Review of Economics and Statistics* 92, no. 1 (2010): 102–27. The evidence is less clear if the tension is purely political.
2. Thomas S. Axworthy and Ryan Dean, "Cooperation and Geopolitics in the North Changing the Arctic Paradigm from Cold War to Cooperation: How Canada's Indigenous Leaders Shaped the Arctic Council," *Yearbook of Polar Law* 5 (2013): 7.
3. IGOs can accede to treaties in their own right and even join other IGOs. For example, the EU is a member of the World Trade Organization and various fisheries management organizations as well as a party to the Paris Agreement on climate

change. By contrast, forums such as the Arctic Council cannot enter treaties, they cannot hold property, and they cannot bring actions before courts.

4. See box 10.3 in chapter 10.

5. See chapter 3.

6. See chapter 3.

7. Inuit Circumpolar Council, *An Inuit Vision for the Future of the Pikialasorsuag*, November 23, 2017, http://www.inuitcircumpolar.com/uploads/3/0/5/4/30542564/pikialasorsuaq_release__nov_23.pdf.

8. Sebastian Schmidt, "Foreign Military Presence and the Changing Practice of Sovereignty: A Pragmatist Explanation of Norm Change," *American Political Science Review* 108, no. 4 (2014): 817–29.

9. See box 1.2 in chapter 1.

10. See chapter 10; see also Beth DeSombre, *The Global Environment and World Politics: International Relations in the 21st Century*, 2nd ed. (London: Continuum, 2007) (for an extended discussion on the "internationalization" of domestic rules).

11. Camila Domonoske, "Norwegian Pension Fund Divests from Companies behind DAPL," *NPR*, March 17, 2017, http://www.npr.org/sections/thetwo-way/2017/03/17/520545209/norwegian-pension-fund-divests-from-companies-behind-dapl.

12. See box 10.2 in chapter 10.

13. Arctic Council, *Arctic Resilience Action Framework: Cooperating for a More Resilient and Prosperous Arctic Region*, May 2017, https://oaarchive.arctic-council.org/handle/11374/2019.

14. Ibid., 2, box 1.

15. Ibid., 6–7.

Index

Note: Page numbers followed by "b," "m," "p," or "t" indicate, respectively, boxes, maps, photographs, and tables.

About the Authors

MARY H. DURFEE is professor emerita of government at Michigan Technological University, United States. She is coauthor with James N. Rosenau of *Thinking Theory Thoroughly* and has published in *Millennium, Publius,* and the *Journal of Planning History.* She has been an Annenberg Scholar and twice a Fulbright Scholar. She has attended Strategy Week at the US National Defense University and was appointed to the US EPA Science Advisory Board's Homeland Security Advisory Committee. She is on the editorial board of *PS,* a journal of the American Political Science Association, and is a past chair of the International Law Section of the International Studies Association. Professor Durfee holds a doctorate in government from Cornell University, an MA in government from Cornell, and a BA in history and in Central and East European studies from the University of Colorado at Boulder.

RACHAEL LORNA JOHNSTONE is a professor of law at the University of Akureyri, Iceland, and at Ilisimatusarfik (University of Greenland). She is also co-director of the Arctic Oil and Gas Research Centre at Ilisimatusarfik. Professor Johnstone specializes in Polar law: the governance of the Arctic and the Antarctic under international and domestic law. She is the author of *Offshore Oil and Gas Development in the Arctic under International Law: Risk and Responsibility* (2015) and has published widely on the rights of indigenous people, international human rights law, governance of extractive industries in the Arctic, international environmental law, due diligence, state responsibility, and Arctic strategies. Professor Johnstone holds a doctorate in juridical science (SJD) from the University of Toronto, an MA in Polar law from the University of Akureyri, an LLM magna cum laude in legal theory from the European Academy of Legal Theory, and an LLB (Hons) from the University of Glasgow.